Export-Oriented Development
Strategies

Westview Special Studies

The concept of Westview Special Studies is a response to the continuing crisis in academic and informational publishing. Library budgets are being diverted from the purchase of books and used for data banks, computers, micromedia, and other methods of information retrieval. Interlibrary loan structures further reduce the edition sizes required to satisfy the needs of the scholarly community. Economic pressures on university presses and the few private scholarly publishing companies have greatly limited the capacity of the industry to properly serve the academic and research communities. As a result, many manuscripts dealing with important subjects, often representing the highest level of scholarship, are no longer economically viable publishing projects--or, if accepted for publication, are typically subject to lead times ranging from one to three years.

Westview Special Studies are our practical solution to the problem. As always, the selection criteria include the importance of the subject, the work's contribution to scholarship, its insight, originality of thought, and excellence of exposition. We accept manuscripts in camera-ready form, typed, set, or word processed according to specifications laid out in our comprehensive manual, which contains straightforward instructions and sample pages. The responsibility for editing and proofreading lies with the author or sponsoring institution, but our editorial staff is always available to answer questions and provide guidance.

The result is a book printed on acid-free paper and bound in sturdy, library-quality soft covers. We manufacture these books ourselves using equipment that does not require a lengthy make-ready process and that allows us to publish first editions of 300 to 1000 copies and to reprint even smaller quantities as needed. Thus, we can produce Special Studies quickly and can keep even very specialized books in print as long as there is a demand for them.

About the Book and Editors

The success of industrializing countries that have
export-oriented development strategies has prompted many
Third World countries to question and revise their own
development plans. The authors--focusing on financial and
trade policies, employment and income distribution, and
sources of economic growth--relate the experiences of and
the lessons learned by five industrializing countries that
have strongly encouraged exports. The performances of
Chile, Hong Kong, South Korea, Taiwan, and Singapore are
examined individually and comparatively in order to find
their common traits and to assess their economic success
in relation to that of other semi-industrialized nations.

Vittorio Corbo is an economic adviser at the World Bank
and a professor of economics at the Pontificia Universidad
Católica de Chile (on leave). *Anne O. Krueger* is a vice president of the Economics and Research Staff at the World
Bank. *Fernando Ossa* is professor of economics and former
director of the Economic Institute at the Pontificia Universidad Católica de Chile.

Export-Oriented Development Strategies
The Success of Five
Newly Industrializing Countries

edited by
Vittorio Corbo, Anne O. Krueger,
and Fernando Ossa

Routledge
Taylor & Francis Group

LONDON AND NEW YORK

First published 1985 by Westview Press

Published 2018 by Routledge
52 Vanderbilt Avenue, New York, NY 10017
2 Park Square, Milton Park, Abingdon, Oxon OX14 4RN

Routledge is an imprint of the Taylor & Francis Group, an informa business

Library of Congress Cataloging-in-Publication Data
Main entry under title:
Export-oriented development strategies
  (westview special studies in social, political, and economic development)
  Includes bibliographical references.
  1. Foreign trade promotion--case studies--Addresses, essays, lectures.
2. states, Small--Economic conditions--Case studies--Addresses, essays,
lectures.   3. East Asia--Economic conditions--Case studies--Addresses,
essays, lectures.   I. Corbo, Vittorio.   II. Krueger, Anne o.   III. ossa,
Fernando Jose, 1941–   ·   IV. series.
HF1417.S.E94   1984   382'.6   84–19582
ISBN 0-8133-7016-7

ISBN 13: 978-0-367-00815-4 (hbk)
ISBN 13: 978-0-367-15802-6 (pbk)

Contents

Tables

Figures

Preface

This book originated with a conference that we held at Pontificia Universidad Católica de Chile in late 1981. When we organized the conference, our focus was to provide policymakers and entrepreneurs with a summary of the experiences and lessons of countries that have pursued policies geared to export-led growth. After the conference we decided that the papers would be useful to a much wider audience and should be prepared for publication. The revised papers are contained in this volume.

We are grateful to the Pontificia Universidad Católica de Chile, and specifically the Dean of the Faculty of Economics and Administrative Sciences, Juan Ignacio Varas, for their support of the conference. We are also very appreciative of the patience the authors showed in answering our many queries. Whitney Watriss provided valuable editorial assistance, and special thanks go to Thelma Rapatan for typing the numerous drafts of the papers.

The affiliations of the contributors are as follows:

Vittorio Corbo
  The World Bank
  Washington, D.C., U.S.A., and
  Pontificia Universidad Católica de Chile,
  Santiago, Chile (on leave).

Hernán Cortés Douglas
  The World Bank
  Washington, D.C., U.S.A.

Pang Eng Fong
  Institute of Economics
  Singapore

Maxwell J. Fry
  University of California at Irvine
  Irvine, California, U.S.A.

Anne O. Krueger
  The World Bank
  Washington, D.C., U.S.A.

Kwang Suk Kim
  Kyongkee University
  Seoul, Republic of Korea

Linda Lim
  Institute of Economics
  Singapore

Jaime de Melo
  The World Bank
  Washington, D.C., U.S.A.

Fernando Ossa
  Pontificia Universidad Católica de Chile
  Santiago, Chile

Gustav Ranis
  Yale University
  New Haven, Connecticut, U.S.A.

Yun Wing Sung
  Chinese University of Hong Kong
  Hong Kong

S. C. Tsiang
  Cornell University
  Ithaca, New York, U.S.A., and
  Chung-Hua Institution for Economic Research
  Taiwan, China

1
Introduction

In the last few years, a large number of developing countries, as well as some of newly industrialized ones, have been struggling to adjust to the sharp drop in their growth rates. In some cases, they have also had to contend with high inflation. A subset of these countries, because they combined inadequate macro policies and easy external financing, have run unsustainable large current account deficits for a number of years and have accumulated substantial external debt. For these countries, the drop in growth rate has resulted from the forced reduction in their current account deficits.

To resume growth, developing countries that have experienced a sharp decline in growth, and that at the same time have been faced with pressure to provide employment to a growing labor force and to improve the standard of living, have been trying to adjust their economies. In the highly indebted ones, the sharp drop in net capital inflows has necessitated a drastic reduction in their current account deficit through emergency programs. In the short run, most of the adjustment has taken the form of large cutbacks in absorption and some switching policies involving currency devaluations and/or import controls. Some countries have also tried to manage the crisis of this period by implementing discriminatory import restrictions, but the result has been to impair efficient resource allocation. In other cases, the cut in absorption has produced a sharp decline in investment. Consequently, not only has current output suffered, but the efficiency of investment may have been reduced at the same time. Ultimately, the prospects for growth have worsened.

The medium-term solution to the current crisis requires that these countries move from crisis management to recovery, that is, to a situation of a sustainable macroeconomic balance compatible with the

growth of output to its potential. In light of the
need to lower the current account deficits, this
solution will require better use of resources or a
change in the structure of production, with a greater
share of tradables in total output. It is also quite
clear by now that, for most developing countries, the
sustainable level of the current account deficit is
much smaller today than it was in the late seventies
and early eighties. Thus, a large part of the
investment effort will have to be financed from
domestic savings.

The problems that developing and newly industrialized countries are facing today are similar to
some of the ones faced by the Republic of Korea (South
Korea), Taiwan, Singapore, and Hong Kong in the fifties
and early sixties. Thus, a thorough examination of the
latters' successful adjustment is useful not only to
people interested in these economies, but also to
policy-makers in general.

The papers in this book explore that process.
They were originally presented at a conference on the
"Experiences and Lessons of Small Open Economies"
organized by the Instituto de Economía of the
Pontificia Universidad Católica de Chile, which took
place in November 1981 in Santiago, Chile. The papers
have been revised extensively for this publication. In
chapter 2, Professors Vittorio Corbo and Fernando Ossa
review the main issues concerning small open economies
from the point of view of both theory and the empirical
evidence. In chapter 3, Professor S. C. Tsiang examines the contribution of foreign trade and investment
to the dramatic turnaround in the economy of Taiwan.
He also elaborates on the role of financial liberalization and the dramatic increase in the rate of
national saving.

Chapter 4 by Professor Kwang Suk Kim examines the
lessons that can be drawn from South Korea's experience
with industrialization. It highlights the role of the
two key instruments—adjustment of the exchange rate
and access to imports at international prices—in
effecting the growth of exports. Professor Kim also
emphasizes that although the government of South Korea
has intervened extensively in the economy, the net
effect of its intervention has been an incentive system
that does not discriminate against exports. In chapter
5, Professors Peng Eng Fong and Linda Lim evaluate
Singapore's economic development over the last thirty
years. They find that in Singapore's case, the policy
of free trade and the growth of foreign investment were
important factors in its successful economic performance. However, the stable economic and political
environment and the quality of the labor force were
also important contributors.

Dr. Yun Wing Sung examines the experience of Hong Kong in chapter 6. He first addresses the determinants of commodity trade and tourism and then highlights the main economic problems that policy-makers will need to address in the 1980s. In chapter 7, Professor Hernán Cortés Douglas examines the recent experience of Chile with opening up and liberalizing trade. Professor Cortes evaluates the effects of trade liberalization on industrial output and employment. His conclusion is that trade liberalization had a positive effect on both output and employment. He argues that the increase in unemployment was caused mostly by a decrease in the size of the public sector and by an increase in labor force participation. One puzzle in the Chilean case was the high real interest rate during the period of the substantial liberalization of capital inflows, achieved by early 1979.

In chapter 8, Professor Anne O. Krueger studies the experience and lessons of Asia's super exporters. Starting with a comparative evaluation of their economic performance, she then looks at the role of exports. She ends with the policy lessons that can be derived from the economic performance of these countries. Chapter 9 by Professor Jaime de Melo analyzes the sources of growth and structural change in South Korea and Taiwan. Professor de Melo uses both supply-side and demand decomposition measures. His conclusion is that the growth in total factor productivity in South Korea and Taiwan were substantially above that achieved by countries with comparable income per capita. Thus, overall efficiency rather than factor input growth was the major contributor to output growth.

In chapter 10, Professor Gustav Ranis presents a comparative study of employment, income distribution, and growth in the East Asian countries. He concludes that the East Asian experience shows clearly that more expansion can be achieved via--rather than in spite of--a more equitable, employment-intensive growth path. In the final chapter, Professor Maxwell Fry analyzes the interaction among financial structure, monetary policy, and economic growth in the East Asian countries. He notes that contrary to most developing countries, those in East Asia did not use monetary expansion to finance government deficits. Moreover, lending rates above equilibrium levels encouraged capital accumulation. Finally, all four countries followed consistent monetary and exchange rate policies, avoiding undue appreciation of the real exchange rate.

Evaluation of the experiences presented in this book reveal a set of basic conditions for sustained export-led growth. Among them are:

(1) The economic authorities should provide a stable macroeconomic framework.

(2) The level of the <u>real</u> exchange rate has to be appropriate and stable over time. An appropriate real exchange rate is one that, given the expansion in expenditures, generates a commensurate trade balance that is sustainable in the medium term.

(3) Exporters should operate under a regime very close to free trade. For this purpose, traded raw materials have to be priced close to world prices, while nontradable services have to be supplied at prices and terms not too different from those facing main competitors.

(4) Financial markets should guarantee that the export-oriented sector will receive timely financing at domestically competitive rates.

(5) Any discrimination against savings should be lifted.

2
Small Open Economies: The Main Issues

Vittorio Corbo
Fernando Ossa

SIZE OF THE ECONOMY AND INTEGRATION IN THE WORLD ECONOMY

The Concept of a Small Country in International Trade

From an economic standpoint, different indicators can be used to measure country size. For the most part, however, population or national income is used as the yardstick of relative economic size.[1] In the theory of international trade, the concept of a "small" country is used in a specific sense. The theoretical models concerned with a country's economic relations with the rest of the world offer two definitions. The simpler one classifies a country as small when it is confronted with given prices for internationally tradable goods and assets. By definition, the economic policies of a small country do not have repercussions on the rest of the world either through income or through prices. The theoretical model of a small open economy makes no reference to other characteristics such as geographical area, size of the population, and national income, although the price-taker status of the country may coincide with the more usual determinants of smallness such as national income.[2]

The second alternative assumes interdependence between the country and the rest of the world (in the model, a second country).[3] In this case, the prices of tradable goods and assets are determined jointly. Moreover, the policies applied by either party affect the other and cause it to undertake new actions. Obviously, this assumption leads to a much more complex model of a country's economic relations with the rest of the world. The popularity of the small open economy model is understandable, since, by contrast, it allows

a great deal of simplification by eliminating interdependence.

The development of a large part of international
economic theory on the basis of the small-economy
assumption is very useful for countries similar to the
theoretical abstractions described above, although the
significant differences from highly simplified models
must always be borne in mind.

Degree of Openness

A country's degree of economic openness is the
extent to which its economy is integrated with the rest
of the world. This integration depends, in the first
place, on the degree of international mobility of its
goods, services, and factors of production. Mobility,
in turn, is determined by the difference between the
prices that would prevail in a situation of autarky and
world prices, and by the natural and artificial
barriers to mobility among countries.

To take the case of a small economy's degree of
openness to trade, imagine a typical, small developing
economy in a situation of autarky. In this closed
economy, the prices of the staple goods, which might be
exportable if the economy were open for external trade,
would be much lower than world prices. On the other
hand, because of the absence of economies of scale, it
seems likely that in an autarkic regime, the prices of
importable goods would be very high in comparison with
world prices. In other words, comparative advantages
would appear to be very marked. In such circumstances,
an economy would have much to gain from promoting trade
with the rest of the world.[4] Obviously these
potential gains may be frustrated by artificial
barriers if the latter are sufficiently high.[5]

The classical assumption in international trade
models is that the factors of production are totally
immobile between countries, but perfectly mobile between sectors within a country. Given this postulate,
if there are no international barriers, that is, there
is free trade, trade will itself equalize the prices of
goods between countries. However, if there were no
natural or artificial barriers to the international
mobility of the factors of production, they would be
prone to emigrate, with changes ensuing to their stocks
in the different countries. Thus, the mobility of
factors to some extent acts as a substitute for the
mobility of goods. Insofar as there are barriers to
trade in goods, but not to the international mobility
of factors, international equilibrium will be produced
through factor migration. In a world in which there
are many barriers to the mobility of unskilled labor,

capital is the factor that will tend to migrate from one country to another.[6]   The greater the inter-country differentials between the rates of return on capital, the greater will be the potential mobility of this factor.   However, the potential mobility may be frustrated by sufficiently high barriers.[7]

In practice, the degree of a country's openness to trade is measured by the ratio between aggregate exports and imports and gross domestic product (GDP). Similarly, a country's financial openness can be measured by the ratio between international assets and the total assets traded in the country.

The Opening-Up Process: Commercial and Financial Openness

If a country decides to achieve a higher degree of integration with the world economy, the opening-up process may involve elimination of artificial barriers to the flow of goods, capital, or both.   The adjustment of the economy will differ according to the means chosen.   If a small country opens up its current account but not its capital account, trade will be very brisk, but the domestic rate of interest will differ from the world rate (Ossa 1983).   Alternatively, if barriers to the mobility of capital are removed in an economy where this factor is scarce, but barriers against imports are maintained, capital will flow in and will give rise to export flows to finance the servicing of the debt incurred.   The rest of the world will obtain part of its imports through exports and the remainder from the proceeds of the capital invested. However, only the rate of interest will be equalized, since in the real world the assumptions whereby the mobility of capital takes the place of the mobility of goods in equalizing their prices are not fulfilled (Mundell 1957).

The main issues in the opening-up of a country relate to sequence and the dynamics of financial and trade liberalization, for example, the pace of liber-alization and the evolution of the tariff structure and rate of exchange.   The models constructed to date are very simple and do not allow for particular forms of opening-up and their complex implications.

Tradable and Nontradable Goods and Assets

Another important issue relating to the integra-tion of an economy with the rest of the world is the degree of substitution among goods and financial assets.   In this connection, it is necessary to charac-

terize substitution. It can be used to mean, in one
sense, the substitution between internationally
tradable goods and assets and those that are not
internationally tradable within the pertinent price
range. For example, the price of a good that is not
internationally traded but is a perfect substitute for
a tradable good will behave in the same way as if the
good were physically tradable. To be more precise,
nontradable goods and financial assets are those whose
domestic prices cannot be directly deduced from world
prices, nor from the structure of the barriers to and
incentives for international mobility.

Another dimension of substitution is the degree to
which it exists between domestic and foreign goods and
financial assets. In the theoretical model of a small
open economy mentioned above, it is assumed that goods
and financial assets originating in a small country are
perfect substitutes for those of the rest of the
world. But if the financial assets issued in the small
country do not have this characteristic, the country
will not be "small" with respect to rates of interest,
in that it is not confronted with given prices for the
financial assets it issues. Those goods and financial
assets that are not considered perfect substitutes (and
so are perceived as different goods or assets) will not
be integrated in the same market. This differentiation
does not prevent the integration of the national with
the world economy through international transactions
and through substitution between tradable and nontradable items.[8] It is possible, however, to imagine
cases in which differentiation by geographic origin
implies less integration of an economy with the rest of
the world. For example, if for want of information,
foreign goods are thought to be of inferior quality,
pertinent internal and external price differentials may
not be sufficiently high to surmount existing trade
barriers. This lack of significant price differentials
would signify a larger nontradable sector and, as a
consequence, a lesser degree of integration with the
world economy.

The development of the monetary approach to
balance of payments has brought into currency the
concept of substitution in relation to the opening-up
of an economy. An extreme version of this approach is
what Whitman (1975) has called "global monetarism."
The global monetarists postulate that in a world
without either artificial (tariff) or natural (cost of
transport) barriers, the law of one price prevails.
That is, economies are perfectly integrated as a result
of a high degree of substitution that would exist.
Substitution between tradable and physically
nontradable goods would indeed ensure that the domestic
prices of the latter behaved as if the goods were

internationally mobile. Furthermore, within tradables, domestically produced goods would be perfect substitutes for foreign goods. In these circumstances, a devaluation cannot produce a change in relative prices, which means that the "elasticities approach" to devaluation can be dismissed. At the same time, the rate of inflation would have to be the same in countries linked by fixed rates of exchange.

Empirical studies of the law of one price clearly show that it is not totally operative (Katseli-Papaefstratiou 1979; Kravis and Lipsey 1978). Neither is it operative, as has also been found, with respect to only internationally tradable goods (Corbo 1985; Richardson 1978; Aukurst 1977). The literature shows that it is important to separate tradable goods into those that are homogeneous (traded in auction markets) and those that are differentiated. In the case of the former, generally speaking the law of one price holds (Isard 1977; Gensberg 1978). In the case of differentiated tradables, by contrast, prices are determined by international prices for competitive goods and by factors connected with internal costs and demand. Thus, for differentiated tradables, the law of one price is rejected (Lindbeck 1979; Corbo 1985). Consequently, the impact of a devaluation in terms of the relative prices between tradables and nontradables cannot be analyzed using the law of one price alone. For this purpose, a more complete model is required.

REAL ASPECTS OF OPENNESS

Openness and Growth in Output

It is difficult from the methodological standpoint to study the relation between openness to trade with the outside world and the growth rate of an economy. It is very difficult to devise an experiment in which it is possible to isolate the effects of, ceteris paribus, the other variables that affect growth, such as the structure of the national product, capital accumulation, and the structure of the labor force. Isolating these variables requires the specification and estimation of a complete model that relates growth to its sources, with exports just one of several explanatory variables. In such a model it would be possible to test the hypothesis that exports make a positive contribution to growth.

The simpler models, which fall short of this general equilibrium approach, point instead to a positive association between the degree of openness to trade and the growth rate. Thus, Michaely (1977),

sample of 41 developing countries, correlated
age annual rate of change in the ratio between
and gross national product (GNP) with the
...₋₋ᴧᵧᵉ annual rate of change in per capita GNP. The
results show a Spearman rank correlation coefficient of
0.38, which, for his sample size, is statistically
significant at the 1 percent level. Next the sample
was divided into two, with one segment comprised of
developing countries with a per capita income of more
than U.S. $300 in 1972 (countries with some sort of
industrial base), and the other of countries with a per
capita income below U.S. $300. The respective
correlations were 0.52 and -0.4, both significant at
the 1 percent level. Balassa (1978), employing a
variant of the methodology used by Michaely and
alternative measurements as well, studied the
association between exports and the growth rate for a
sample of 11 more homogeneous and semi-industrialized
countries: the Republic of Korea, Singapore, Taiwan,
Israel, Yugoslavia, Argentina, Brazil, Colombia,
Mexico, Chile, and India. Balassa confirmed the
results obtained by Michaely. However, he also found a
high correlation (0.70) between the ratio of exports to
GNP and the growth rate of GNP, whereas Michaely found
that that correlation was not significant.
    One of the difficulties of the methodologies used
by Michaely and Balassa is, as noted, that they omit
other important variables that affect the growth rate
of GNP. Because of this omission, their results may be
distorted by biases stemming from specification
errors. In particular, countries that do not
discriminate against exports and whose export growth
rate is consequently high usually have larger capital
inflows. Thus, the increase in the GNP growth rate
might be attributable not only to the growth of exports, but also to the flow of capital from abroad.
Last, the growth rate also depends on the growth of the
factors of production and changes in the efficiency
with which they are used.
    Michalopoulos and Jai (1973) have attempted to
correct for these flaws by including, in addition to
growth in exports, domestic savings, external savings,
and growth of employment as variables in a multiple
regression. Using data from 39 developing countries
for 1966, they found that, when exports were excluded,
the remaining variables accounted for 53 percent of the
variation in the GNP growth rate. When exports were
added as an explanatory variable, that figure rose to
71 percent. In a similar exercise by Balassa (1978),
the corresponding percentages were 58 and 77,
respectively. Furthermore, both studies obtained the
same value for the export growth rate coefficient:
0.04. That is, an increase of 10 percentage points in

the growth rate of exports was associated with a 0.4 percentage point increase in the growth rate of GNP. Krueger (1978), in a cross-section of countries, obtained a higher coefficient for the growth rate of exports--0.10--using a regression in which dummy variables were used to identify the countries' external trade regimes as well.

Sufficient cumulative evidence exists to suggest that countries more open to world trade have higher GNP growth rates. However, it is important to note that this conclusion means only that there is a positive association between the degree of openness and GNP growth. The direction of that association is still open to question.

Openness and Employment

The traditional theory of international trade formulated by Heckscher-Ohlin-Samuelson (the HOS theory) provides a link between the external sector and employment. It establishes that in the case of two factors of production, labor and capital, and given certain crucial assumptions (expounded later), a country will export a basket of goods that is either capital-intensive or labor-intensive according to its more abundant factor endowment with respect to the rest of the world, and will import a basket of goods that is labor-intensive or capital-intensive depending on which factor is in relatively short supply. The HOS theory has been developed further by Krueger (1977) and Jones (1977) for a multilateral trade situation. According to their extensions, the relative shortage of the factors of production in a specific country will depend on the countries with which it trades. In the case of Chile, for example, in accordance with its endowment of resources in relation to developed countries, it would be expected that the industries that potentially would export to developed countries would be those making more intensive use of Chile's relatively more abundant factor, labor. In the case of Chile's trade with countries at a lower level of development, exactly the opposite would be expected, that is, the potential export industries would be capital-intensive. The converse would be expected for industries producing import-competing goods (Corbo and Meller 1979, 1981).

The HOS theory can easily be extended to cover three factors of production (labor, physical capital, and human capital) on the assumption that physical and human capital are complementary and that labor is a substitute for both. Accordingly, human capital could be added to physical capital in the preceding discussion.

The impact of openness to trade on manpower requirements depends on the direction of the trade through its effect on the composition of the basket of exportable goods. According to the HOS theory, labor requirements will be greater when expansion takes place in exports to the more developed countries than when it occurs in exports to the less developed countries.

When a comparison is drawn between the effects of an import-substitution strategy and a strategy of external openness on employment, the following propositions can be tested:

- The labor (physical and human capital) requirements of industries exporting to more developed countries are greater (smaller) than those of industries competing with imports of goods from more developed countries.
- The labor (physical and human capital) requirements of industries exporting to less developed countries are smaller (greater) than those of industries substituting imports of goods from developing countries.

A brief list from a series of arguments, both theoretical and empirical, that question a priori the validity of these propositions, follows (Corbo 1979).

1. The validity of the assumptions of the HOS theory had been criticized. The assumptions are: the existence of identical production functions for various countries, perfect competition, the possibility of reversals in factor intensities, technical progress and/or technological backwardness that may modify the comparative advantages based on relative endowments of the factors of production, the necessary presence of an additional productive resource (a natural resource or an imported input), and changes in the patterns of demand that may affect comparative advantage based on the factor intensity of production.

2. Critics have pointed to the existence of tariff and/or export quota barriers in developed countries that affect the exports of the developing countries, in particular, labor-intensive goods, and thus give origin to a trade structure different from the one determined by comparative advantage.

3. The large-scale activity of transnational corporations in nontraditional export sectors and their use of highly capital-intensive technologies, which are independent of local factor endowment, cast doubt on the prospect that an export promotion strategy oriented toward developed countries will create relatively more sources of employment.

4. A similar argument would also be valid for large-scale enterprises. Since exports usually call

for sizable volumes of production, apparently only large enterprises are capable of supplying the external market. Since they tend to use labor-saving technology, the relative labor requirements of an export promotion strategy compared with those of an import-substitution strategy in relation to the group of developed countries are not clear a priori.

5. The standards of quality required for exported products lead to the use of more (physical and human) capital-intensive techniques.

Given the above arguments, empirical studies to elucidate and validate the theoretical propositions described above are required. Fortunately, Krueger, et al. (1981) provide the requisite empirical evidence, which is analyzed in Krueger (1983). It was found for a group of developing countries that, in general, exports of manufactures create more employment for the same amount of value added than does the production of import-competing manufactures. These results are generally reinforced when, in addition to the direct effects, the indirect effects on industries producing nontradable goods are taken into account. Moreover, the results are more pronounced when the direction of trade is accounted for.

MONETARY AND FISCAL POLICY IN AN OPEN ECONOMY

The traditional model for the study of monetary and fiscal policy in an open economy is that of Fleming (1961) and Mundell (1968). The starting point in this model is a situation of underemployment. The model assumes the existence of two goods, one external, one produced domestically. For the external good, the law of one price is postulated, while for the domestic good, a fixed price for levels of output lower than that corresponding to full employment is postulated. In this model, which assumes perfect mobility of capital, arbitrage of the interest rate ensures that with a fixed exchange rate the money supply is endogenous. As such, monetary expansion causes a momentary fall in the rate of interest, which in turn, given perfect mobility of capital, causes an outflow of capital. To maintain the fixed rate of exchange, the central bank sells dollars, as a result of which the supply of money declines and the rate of interest returns to its equilibrium level (given by the international rate), as does the level of output. As long as the situation of underemployment persists, fiscal policy is very effective in increasing the level of output.

Exactly the opposite result occurs when the exchange rate is flexible. Then monetary policy is effective, and fiscal policy is not. This result obtains because, with an expansionary fiscal policy, the initial stimulus to output is neutralized by a revaluation of the domestic currency and a consequent decline in net exports. The effect of monetary policy is enhanced, however, by a devaluation of the currency and a gain in competitiveness. This conclusion, however, is crucially dependent on the assumption that devaluation does not affect the price of the domestic good.[9]

In this same model but with a fixed exchange rate, if there is no arbitrage of the interest rate and if the aggregate supply of the domestic good is characterized by price elasticity, then in the short run both monetary and fiscal policy have real effects on output (Turnovsky 1977, 204; Frenkel, et al. 1980). (For critiques of this model, see Goldstein 1980, and Corbo 1983.)

A modification of Mundell's model that has an explicit assets market may lead to monetary policy producing real effects. If there is no arbitrage in the interest rates because domestic financial instruments are not perfect substitutes for international financial instruments, then monetary policy is, in fact, effective and will be more so, the lower the degree of substitution between domestic and international assets (Dornbusch 1980; Corbo 1983). In this same model, fiscal policy is less effective than where there is arbitrage of the interest rate.

On the other hand, the monetary model, in contrast to the foregoing neo-Keynesian model, assumes full employment and the law of one price (Mundell 1968; Johnson 1977; Kreinin and Officer 1978). In this model, in the case of a small economy, devaluation affects only prices proportionally. Expansionary fiscal policy, by contrast, reduces private expenditures by the same amount and thus has no effects. Monetary policy has real effects in this model when the assumptions of full employment and commodity arbitrage are relaxed. Aghevli and Rodriguez (1979) constructed a monetary model for Japan in which an expansion in internal credit is not completely offset by losses of reserves, since it also affects domestic prices and output. Goldstein (1980), Dornbusch (1979), and Obstfeldt (1982) review the evidence relating to, in economies with fixed exchange rates, the offset to an increase in domestic credit via a loss of reserves. They conclude that the evidence is inconclusive: some countries have achieved a slight offset and others have not.

In contrast, in Salter, Swan, and Dornbusch's so-called Australian model, which incorporates two goods, tradable and nontradable, and flexibility of prices for nontradables, flexibility of wages, the law of one price for tradables, and no capital mobility, the economy is always in a situation of full employment (Dornbusch 1975). Given a fixed exchange rate, monetary and fiscal policy are ineffective. Monetary expansion causes a deficit on the current account and a loss of reserves until there is a return to the same equilibrium as before with the same absolute prices. Nor will macroeconomic policies have any effect on real variables under a flexible exchange rate. Similarly, a devaluation, a special form of monetary policy, produces only transient effects. Over the long term, all it does is bring about a rise in prices, with no change in the relative prices of tradable and nontradable goods and assets.

In the Australian model, with downward price rigidity in nontradables or downward nominal wage rigidity, and starting from full employment, a contraction in aggregate demand (caused either by deteriorating terms of trade or by decreasing government expenditures) will cause unemployment as long as downward rigidity is maintained. In this case, devaluation improves the relative price of tradables, bringing the economy back to full employment (Dornbusch 1975).

In the same type of model, under full indexation for wages and thus with real wage rigidity, a contraction in aggregate demand causes unemployment. Here devaluation is completely ineffective as a means of securing the requisite change in relative prices (Jones and Corden 1976).

Lately Dornbusch (1980) has used a model that incorporates rational expectations to analyze the effects of fiscal and monetary policy. His model is an extension of Taylor (1980) to an open economy. It assumes staggered wage contracts and no capital mobility. Working with this model and assuming underemployment and prices determined by a markup on wages, Dornbusch found that monetary and exchange rate policies that accommodate price shocks tend to stabilize output at the cost of persistent price and wage disequilibria. An exchange rate policy that attempts to maintain purchasing power parity implies that the evolution of prices is accommodated through devaluation. Such a policy keeps the real exchange rate relatively constant and thus reduces this source of variation in employment. But anticipation of this type of policy promotes price instability.

THE EXCHANGE RATE REGIME IN
A SMALL DEVELOPING ECONOMY

The discussion on various exchange rate policy alternatives for a small developing country assumes that it has already decided to have its own currency.[10] This point of departure is realistic, as noted by Friedman (1974), who contends that in most small developing countries the absence of the necessary political conditions rules out the alternative of their not having a currency of their own. In his view, the first best situation for most developing countries would be not to have a central bank of their own but instead to unify their currency with that of a large stable country with which they maintain close economic relations. An example is Panama and the United States, whose relationship is analogous to that of the different regions within a country in which a single currency is in circulation. This conclusion is based on the assumption that the monetary authority of the large country will follow more stable monetary policies than those that would be applied by the central bank of the small developing country. Friedman urges that this alternative be clearly distinguished from the situation in which the small country produces its own money and fixes the exchange rate with respect to a large country's currency. In this latter situation there is a possibility that the small country may not resist the temptation to resort to an inflationary tax through increases in domestic credit, a condition under which a fixed exchange rate cannot be sustained. Even when the small country produces its own money through its central bank, however, the fixing of the parity may be reflected in stricter monetary discipline. This situation will arise if, once a fixed exchange rate regime has been adopted, the political cost implied by devaluation makes it imperative to control the expansion of domestic credit. This brake on the expansion of domestic credit is not present under a free exchange rate system, as concern about the exhaustion of international reserves in those systems is nonexistent. With a flexible exchange rate, an overexpansion of domestic credit will raise the internal rate of inflation above the world rate, which may also have political costs.

Whether the monetary discipline of the fixed exchange rate has or has not been operative is in practice an empirical problem. As Goldstein (1980) points out, the existing empirical evidence for various countries does not yield a definitive conclusion on this point.

Given that a country has its own fiduciary money, a decision has to be taken whether any sort of measure is to be adopted to fix its price in relation to a foreign currency. That is, a choice has to be made between the alternatives of a fixed exchange rate or some degree of exchange rate flexibility, which may go as far as a totally free (flexible) rate of exchange.

The controversy over fixed versus flexible exchange rates has gone on for many years, giving rise to
a copious literature that discusses in detail such aspects of the problem as the above-mentioned "monetary
discipline," the effects of speculation on the stability of the exchange rate, the effectiveness of macroeconomic policies under different exchange regimes, the
role of capital mobility, etc. These discussions were
given fresh impetus by the novel approach devised by
Mundell (1961) in his theory of optimum currency
areas. Mundell placed the accent on the absence of any
reason why an optimum exchange system must be the same
for all nations, a view that gave rise to a literature
centering on different country characteristics that
might have a bearing on the choice of exchange regime
(good summaries exist of this extensive literature,
such as Ishiyama 1975 and Tower and Willet 1976). Here
the focus is on a few considerations relevant to the
choice of exchange regime, with specific emphasis on
the types of disturbances with which economies may have
to cope.
Discussions on the effects of disturbances under
different exchange rate regimes have generally been
based on the assumption that the countries under consideration have only limited access to the world
capital market. Many of the discussions have not been
conclusive owing to a failure to include an objective
function in the analysis. Fischer (1976) is an
exception, since he includes an objective function in
his work. It consists of minimizing the variation in
domestic consumption. In this context, Fischer shows
that when disturbances are real, the variation in
consumption is less under a fixed exchange rate regime
than under a flexible one. On the other hand, when the
shocks are of a monetary nature, the variation in
consumption is minimized by a flexible exchange rate.
This result means that the optimum exchange rate policy
is to depart from parity only in the face of monetary
disturbances. Frenkel (1980), however, has pointed out
that the problem is the nonexistence of information
with which to distinguish what type of shocks are
occurring, since only their combined effect is known.
This lack of knowledge prevents the application of the
optimum policy. In view of this situation, Frenkel
proposes minimizing the losses in consumption resulting
from the lack of information by using a system midway
between the fixed and flexible exchange rate regimes.
All the foregoing discussion has assumed that
there is no mobility of international capital. That
assumption is not pertinent for countries that have
opted to open up not only the current account but also
the capital account. Dornbusch (1976) has shown that
when capital is mobile, under a flexible exchange rate

monetary shocks are transmissible among countries. This situation is true for changes in both the level of external prices and the domestic money supply. A short-term lack of homogeneity in the system occurs, based on the assumption that speculators are not guided by rational expectations. This want of homogeneity signifies that monetary shocks upset the real equilibrium of the system even if the exchange rate is flexible.[11]

In many small developing economies, the concentration of production on a few goods increases the probability of real shocks occurring. This outcome tends to strengthen the case in favor of a fixed exchange rate. To this conclusion must be added the possibility that a flexible exchange rate may not be capable of warding off the impact of monetary shocks on real equilibrium. Probably, too, a fixed exchange rate may yield stricter monetary discipline. Moreover, the macroeconomic literature in recent years has brought into prominence the difficulty in attaining macroeconomic objectives through discretionary monetary policies. As devaluations and revaluations are a form of monetary policy, discretionary variations in parity will face difficulties of the same type. To all these issues must be added the possibility that many small developing countries may not have reached the stage of financial development necessary for a free exchange rate system to operate.

The foregoing considerations suggest that in many developing countries it may be desirable to opt for a fixed exchange rate, although the theory of optimum monetary areas points out that in order to make that decision with respect to a given country, a detailed study of its specific characteristics must be made.

If a small developing country opts for a fixed parity, it has to face the problem of deciding what will be the currency or currencies in relation to which it establishes the value of its own money. In an idealized world without international movement of capital, with perfect commodity arbitrage, without transport costs, etc., fixing the exchange rate in relation to any currency is equivalent to maintaining a fixed exchange rate with the whole world, even if the rest are floating currencies.[12] But as these conditions do not exist in practice, establishing the exchange rate in relation to a given country implies a variable rate of exchange vis-a'-vis the rest of the world, if there are variations in the exchange rates between the chosen currency and the others.

The concept of an "effective exchange rate" has evolved within this context. The effective exchange rate is a weighted average of a set of exchange rates, all of which are measured in relation to a base

period.[13]   In a world in which the industrialized
countries have floating exchange rates and in which the
law of one price is not operative, some countries have
attempted to stabilize their effective exchange rate by
adjusting their parity in accordance with a formula
that in one way or another weights the various currencies, or by fixing their parity in relation to a
basket of currencies whose exchange rates are
variable.[14]   But implementing a system of this type
is not easy because of the problems involved in
choosing the appropriate weights.   Moreover, there is
still a good deal of analysis to be undertaken at the
theoretical level with respect to this topic that may
be highly relevant for some small developing countries.
     Last, reference should be made to exchange rate
policy for a small economy with serious internal monetary disequilibria that dominate real disturbances.   In
this case, there is a good deal of agreement that a
policy aimed at adjusting the nominal exchange rate in
accordance with the rule of maintaining the purchasing
power parity of the domestic currency is generally more
efficient than fixed exchange rate policy.   When real
shocks are dominant, however (changes in trade policy,
in transfers of capital, in technology, etc.), the real
exchange rate must be adjusted.   In this connection,
maintaining purchasing power parity would make it
impossible to achieve the requisite adjustment
(Samuelson 1964; Thygesen 1979; Gensberg 1978).

NOTES

     1.   There is a considerable dearth of literature
dealing specifically with this subject.   See Robinson
(1960), Lloyd (1968), and Chenery and Syrquin (1975).
     2.   Some countries do not fit the classifications
easily.   Prachowny (1975), for example, cites the case
of the Soviet Union, which, although a very large
country by any standard of measurement in terms of
population, national income, geographic area, etc., in
its commercial transactions with the West comes close
to being a price-taker in the context of the
theoretical model of a small economy.   There are also
instances of countries that are small from the
standpoint of national income and that are confronted
with given prices for importable goods, but that can
influence the price of one or more of their exportable
goods when their supply of these goods meets a
significant part of world demand.   A case in point is
the petroleum-exporting countries.

3. Theoretical models do not generally involve more than a two-country world.

4. For a review of the main propositions relating to the gains derived from openness, see Bhagwati (1968).

5. If a country wants to promote an activity for noneconomic reasons, then the appropriate instrument is not a tariff but a direct subsidy to production (Bhagwati 1971).

6. For empirical evidence of this tendency, see Harberger (1978).

7. It should be noted that "international mobility of capital" does not necessarily imply international migration of capital goods or human capital. It may take the form of changes in inter-country indebtedness, which makes it possible to finance imports of consumer goods and thus to release domestic resources for use in capital formation.

8. On the concept of substitution in relation to economic integration, see Scitowsky (1969), Allen (1976), Kenen (1976), and Allen and Kenen (1980). It should be noted that in some parts of this literature it is not clear whether the concept of integration is being applied in the sense of integration of an economy with the rest of the world or in the sense of specific goods or financial assets being traded in one and the same market as perfect substitutes.

9. For a critique of these results for a flexible exchange rate, see Goldstein (1980, 41), among others.

10. Reference is made only to cases in which fiduciary money exists. If in the various countries commodity monies exist, parity is established by the commodity content of the different currencies.

11. See Goldstein (1980) for a summary of the experience with flexible exchange rates of recent years and a discussion of whether this regime is capable of insulating economies against external shocks. See also Mussa (1979).

12. Flanders and Helpman (1978) analyze exchange rate policy options for a small country in a model in which these idealized conditions are fulfilled. They conclude that if a small country in which there is downward price and wage rigidity in its own economy and which desires to minimize unemployment decides to fix its parity, it must do so in relation to a large country in which price levels are rising.

13. For a detailed discussion on this point, see Black (1976) and Artus and Rhomberg (1973).

14. A particular case is the fixing of parity in relation to the International Monetary Fund's Special Drawing Rights.

REFERENCES

Aghevli, B., and C. Rodriguez. 1979. "Trade, Prices and Output in Japan: A Simple Monetary Model." IMF Staff Papers (March).

Allen, P. R. 1976. Organization and Administration of a Monetary Union. Princeton Studies in International Finance, No. 38. Princeton, N.J.: Princeton University Press.

Allen, P. R., and P. B. Kenen. 1980. Asset Markets, Exchange Rates and Economic Integration. Cambridge: Cambridge University Press.

Artus, J., and R. Rhomberg. 1973. "A Multilateral Exchange Rate Model." IMF Staff Papers (November).

Aukurst, O. 1977. "Inflation in the Open Economy: A Norwegian Model." In Worldwide Inflation-Theory and Recent Experience, edited by L. Krause and W. S. Salant. Washington, D.C.: The Brookings Institution.

Balassa, B. 1978. "Exports and Economic Growth: Further Evidence." Journal of Development Economics (June).

Bhagwati, J. 1968. The Theory and Practice of Commercial Policy: Departures from Unified Exchange Rates. Princeton Special Papers in International Economics, No. 8. Princeton, N.J.: Princeton University Press.

——————. 1971. "The Generalized Theory of Distortions and Welfare." In Trade, Balance of Payments and Growth, edited by J. Bhagwati, et al. Amsterdam: North-Holland Publishing Co.

Black, S. W. 1976. Exchange Policies for Less Developed Countries in a World of Floating Rates. Essays in International Finance, No. 119. Princeton, N.J.: Princeton University Press, December.

Chenery, H. B., and M. Syrquin. 1975. Patterns of Development 1950-1970. London: Oxford University Press.

Corbo, V. 1979. "Comercio Exterior y Empleo: Algunas Experiencias de Paises en Desarrollo." [External Trade and Employment: The Experience of Some Developing Countries]. Cuadernos de Economía (47).

——————. 1983. "Un Modelo de Corto Plazo para Economía Pequeña y Abierta" [A Short-Term Model of a Small Open Economy]. Photocopy. Cuadernos de Economía (60)(August).

——————. 1985. "International Prices, Wages and Inflation in an Open Economy: A Chilean Model." Review of Economics and Statistics (forthcoming).

Corbo, V., and P. Meller. 1979. "Estrategías de Comercio Exterior y Su Impacto sobre el Empleo: Chile en la Decada del 60" [Foreign Trade Strategies and Their Impact on Employment: Chile in the 1960s]. Estudios de Economía [Economic Studies] 13 (First Semester).
——————. 1981. "Alternative Trade Strategies and Employment Implications." In Trade and Employment in Developing Countries: Vol. 1: Individual Studies, edited by Anne O. Krueger, et al. Chicago: University of Chicago Press.
Dornbusch, R. 1975. "Real and Monetary Aspects of the Effects of Exchange Rate Changes." In National Monetary Policies and the International Financial System, edited by R. Z. Aliber. Chicago: University of Chicago Press.
——————. 1976. "The Theory of Flexible Exchange Regimes and Macroeconomic Policies." Scandinavian Journal of Economics (May).
——————. 1979. "Exchange Rate Policy and Macroeconomic Stability." In The Crawling Peg: Future Prospects and Past Performance, edited by J. Williamson. London: Macmillan.
——————. 1980. Open Economy Macroeconomics. New York: Basic Books.
Fischer, Stanley. 1976. "Stability and Exchange Rate Systems in a Monetarist Model of the Balance of Payments," 59-73. In The Political Economy of Monetary Reform, edited by R. Z. Aliber. New York: Macmillan.
Flanders, M. J., and E. Helpman. 1978. "On Exchange Rate Policies for a Small Country." The Economic Journal (March).
Fleming, M. 1961. "Domestic Financial Policies under Fixed and under Floating Exchange Rates." IMF Staff Papers (November).
Frenkel, Jacob A. 1980. "Macroeconomic Policy in an Open Economy." Estudios Monetarios [Monetary Studies]. Santiago: Banco Central de Chile.
Frenkel, Jacob A., et al. 1980. "A Synthesis of the Monetary and Keynesian Approaches to Short Run Balance-of-Payments Theory." Economic Journal (September).
Friedman, Milton. 1974. "Monetary Policy in Developing Countries." In Nations and Households in Economic Growth, edited by Paul A. David and Melvin W. Reder. New York: Academic Press.
Gensberg, H. 1978. "Purchasing Power Parity under Fixed and Flexible Exchange Rates." Journal of International Economics (May).
Goldstein, M. 1980. Have Flexible Exchange Rates Handicapped Macroeconomic Policy? Special Papers

in International Economics, No. 14. Princeton, N.J.: Princeton University Press, June.

Harberger, Arnold C. 1978. "Perspectives of Capital and Technology in Less Developed Countries." Photocopy. Chicago: University of Chicago.

Isard, P. 1977. "How Far Can We Push the Law of One Price?" American Economic Review (December).

Ishiyama, Yoshihide. 1975. "The Theory of Optimum Currency Areas: A Survey." IMF Staff Papers (July).

Johnson, H. G. 1977. "The Monetary Approach to the Balance of Payments: A Non-Technical Guide." Journal of International Economics (August).

Jones, R. 1977. Two-Ness in Trade Theory: Costs and Benefits. Princeton Special Papers in International Economics, No. 12. Princeton, N.J.: Princeton University Press.

Jones, R., and W. Corden. 1976. "Devaluation, Non-Flexible Prices, and the Trade Balance for a Small Country." Canadian Journal of Economics (February).

Katseli-Papaefstratiou, L. 1979. The Reemergence of the Purchasing Power Parity Doctrine in the 1970s. Princeton Special Papers in International Economics, No. 13. Princeton, N.J.: Princeton University Press.

Kenen, P. B. 1976. Capital Mobility and Financial Integration: A Survey. Princeton Studies in International Finance, No. 39. Princeton, N.J.: Princeton University Press.

Kravis, I. B., and R. B. Lipsey. 1978. "Price Behaviour in the Light of Balance of Payments Theories." Journal of International Economics (May).

Kreinin, M. E., and L. H. Officer. 1978. The Monetary Approach to the Balance of Payments: A Survey. Princeton Studies in International Finance, No. 43. Princeton, N.J.: Princeton University Press.

Krueger, A. O. 1977. Growth, Factor Market Distortions and Patterns of Trade among Many Countries. Princeton Studies in International Finance, No. 40. Princeton, N.J.: Princeton University Press.

——————. 1978. Foreign Trade Regimes and Economic Development: Liberalization Attempts and Consequences. Cambridge, Mass.: Ballinger Press for the National Bureau of Economic Research.

——————. 1983. Trade and Employment in Developing Countries: Vol. 3: Synthesis and Conclusion. Chicago: University of Chicago Press.

Krueger, A. O., et al. 1981. Trade and Employment in Developing Countries: Vol. 1: Individual Studies. Chicago: University of Chicago Press.

Lindbeck, A. 1979. "Imported and Structural Inflation and Aggregate Demand: The Scandinavian Model Reconstructed." In <u>Inflation and Employment in Open Economies</u>, edited by A. Lindbeck. Amsterdam: North-Holland Publishing Co.

Lloyd, Peter J. 1968. <u>International Trade Problems of Small Nations</u>. Durham, N.C.: Duke University Press.

Michaely, M. 1977. "Exports and Growth: An Empirical Investigation." <u>Journal of Development Economics</u> (March).

Michalopoulos, C., and K. Jai. 1973. "Growth of Exports and Income in the Developing World: A Neoclassical View." USAID. Discussion Paper No. 28. Washington, D.C.

Mundell, R. A. 1957. "International Trade and Factor Mobility." <u>The American Economic Review</u> (June).

──────────. 1961. "A Theory of Optimum Currency Areas." <u>American Economic Review</u> (September).

──────────. 1968. <u>International Economics</u>. New York: Macmillan.

Mussa, M. 1979. "Macroeconomic Interdependence and the Exchange Rate Regime." In <u>International Economic Policy</u>, edited by R. Dornbush and J. Frenkel. Baltimore: John Hopkins University Press.

Obstfeldt, M. 1982. "Can We Sterilize: Theory and Evidence." <u>American Economic Review</u> (May).

Ossa, F. 1983. <u>Teoría Real de la Economía Internacional</u> [Real Theory of the International Economy]. Santiago: Ediciones Universidad Católica de Chile.

Prachowny, Martin F. J. 1975. <u>Small Open Economies</u>. New York: Lexington Books.

Richardson, J. D. 1978. "Some Empirical Evidence on Commodity Arbitrage and the Law of One Price." <u>Journal of International Economics</u> (May).

Robinson, E. A. G. 1960. <u>Economic Consequences of the Size of Nations</u>. London: Macmillan.

Samuelson, P. 1964. "Theoretical Notes on Trade Problems." <u>Review of Economics and Statistics</u> (May).

Scitowsky, T. 1969. <u>Money and the Balance of Payments</u>. New Haven: Yale University Press.

Taylor, J. 1980. "Aggregate Dynamics and Staggered Contracts." <u>Journal of Political Economy</u> (February).

Thygesen, N. 1979. "Inflation and Exchange Rates: Evidence and Policy Guidelines for the European Community." <u>Journal of International Economics</u> (May).

Tower, Edward, and Thomas D. Willet. 1976. <u>The Theory of Optimum Currency Areas and Exchange Rate Flexibility</u>. Special Papers in International Economics, No. 11. Princeton, N.J.: Princeton University Press, May.

Turnovsky, S. J. 1977. Macroeconomic Analysis and
    Stabilization Policy. Cambridge: Cambridge Uni-
    versity Press.
Whitman, M. 1975. "Global Monetarism and the Monetary
    Approach to the Balance of Payments." Brookings
    Papers on Economic Activity, No. 3. Washington,
    D.C.: Brookings Institution.

3
Foreign Trade and Investment as Boosters for Take-off: The Experience of Taiwan

S. C. Tsiang

INTRODUCTION

The process through which a poor underdeveloped country at a low level of per capita income gradually breaks loose from stagnation and achieves continuous, self-sustained growth in the living standard of its people has been described most picturesquely by Rostow (1961) as economic take-off. This term very aptly conveys the idea that what used to be a strenuous, often futile, and self-defeating struggle for growth might, after a developing country attains a certain stage of preparation, become a facile and self-perpetuating upward climb. The recent experience of Taiwan provides a good illustration of just this kind of transformation.

The mechanism of growth in the real per capita income of a country is essentially the gradual increase in per capita productive capacity. Assuming that the natural resources of the country are more or less fixed, the ways to increase real per capita productive capacity are principally: (1) to increase the productive capital per capita, and (2) to increase productivity by improved techniques and other means. The introduction of improved techniques is, however, often connected with the increase in capital per capita, as those techniques are often incorporated in, or have to be applied together with, new capital equipment. Consequently, the increase in productive capital per capita is commonly regarded as the most essential condition for real economic growth.

The increase in productive capital must be financed out of savings, which in the first stage of development may be borrowed or received as grants and aid from abroad. However, for a country to achieve continuous, self-sustained growth, the finances for raising productive capital must come from domestic savings. As Lewis (1955) once remarked, "the central problem in the theory of economic growth is to understand the process by which a community is converted from being a 5 percent to 12 percent saver (investor)--with all the changes in attitudes, in institutions and in techniques which accompany this conversion." (Ibid., 225-26)

The figure of 12 percent for the ratio of savings to national income as a sort of rough dividing line between pretake-off and posttake-off economies was not pulled out of thin air. The implicit assumptions are probably that population can be expected to grow at roughly 3 percent, and that the appropriate capital/output ratio is roughly in the range of 3-4 in most cases. Thus, with a domestic savings ratio of 12 percent or more, the economy should be able to increase its capital/labor ratio continuously with its own domestic savings.

By definition, an underdeveloped country has a low per capita income, so low that it is not far above the subsistence level. With such a low level of real per capita income, it is extremely hard for a country to save any significant percentage of its national income. Even the hypothetical 5 percent mentioned by Lewis might be optimistic. At the same time, because of modern, improved medical services, the population often keeps increasing, and at a rate that is sufficient to offset any increase in capital the country might manage to finance with domestic savings and foreign assistance. The result is stagnation of real per capita income (or the standard of living) at a low level. Such stagnation at a poverty level is sometimes called the poverty trap. For a poor underdeveloped country to attempt to break loose from this trap mostly on its own is a process frequently compared to lifting oneself up by the bootstraps.

Against this background, Taiwan, a small island of 13,900 square miles without many natural resources and with a very high population density, managed to achieve a fivefold increase in real per capita income from 1952 to 1980, and this even though the population more than doubled (from 8.14 million in 1952 to 17.4 million in 1980). Indeed, Taiwan has successfully launched itself into continuous, self-sustained economic growth. Its success is worth studying, as it can convey some very useful lessons for other developing countries still struggling to break out of the poverty trap.

THE THEORETICAL FRAMEWORK OF THE ANALYSIS

How an underdeveloped country may launch itself onto a path of continuous, self-sustained growth can be shown by means of Figure 3.1, which was actually developed in a previous article (Tsiang 1964).[1] Growth in the real per capita income of a country, given its natural resources, depends essentially on its productive capital per capita. Thus capital per units of labor, $r = K/L$, will be measured along the horizontal axis as the all-important explanatory variable, while the real per capita income, $\bar{Y}$, of the country will first be drawn as a function of r (taking as given the natural resources and state of technology). Assuming the usual well-behaved production function of positive but diminishing marginal productivity of capital per unit of labor, this curve will rise with a diminishing upward slope. The savings per unit of labor, $\bar{S}$, may be drawn as a curve some distance below the curve for per capita output, as savings are generally a fractional function of income. The stylized assumption of Solow (1958) that savings are a constant proportion of the national income is not used, as it obviously does not apply in the case of developing countries. Instead, a more realistic assumption is that when per capita income is very low, savings will presumably be negative, but once they approach the subsistence level, they will rise gradually to a positive level and then rise perhaps even faster than per capita income, thus becoming an increasing proportion of the latter. That is, the supply of per capita savings, i.e., the $\bar{S}$ curve, will take the shape shown in Figure 3.1.

The next step is to draw a curve whose vertical coordinate measures the capital required per capita to supply the increase in the working population with the same amount of per capita capital as has already been attained, i.e., $K/L \cdot \dot{L}/L = r\ell$, where $\ell = \dot{L}/L$, the rate of growth of the population. This quantity obviously rises with increases in r, but it also varies with ℓ. Here it is assumed, in accordance with neo-Malthusian population theory, that population growth is a function of real per capita income such that below the subsistence level of per capita income, ℓ will be negative, and that it will increase with real per capita income (mainly because of the falling off of the death rate) until it reaches a certain maximum. After that, ℓ will gradually decline because higher real per capita income brings awareness of family planning to an increasing proportion of the population. Thus the curve representing $r\ell$ will first dip to the negative side because ℓ will be negative, given a very low level of real per capita income and hence a very low level of r, and then will rise rather rapidly as r increases because ℓ will also rise toward its maximum. After ℓ reaches its maximum, the rising slope of the $r\ell$ curve will gradually decline as ℓ declines. The $r\ell$ curve therefore will be somewhat S-shaped, as is shown in Figure 3.1.

FIGURE 3.1
The determinants of economic growth

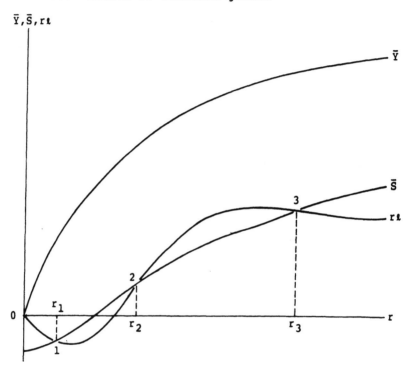

Note: $\bar{Y}$ = Real per capita income

$\bar{S}$ = Savings per unit of labor

r = Capital per unit of labor

ℓ = $\dot{L}/L$, the rate of growth of the population

It is very likely that the $\bar{S}$ and $r\ell$ curves will intersect at several points as shown in Figure 3.1, creating stable as well as unstable equilibrium points for economic growth. For instance, points of intersection such as 1 and 3 are unstable equilibria, whereas 2 is stable. As an excess of $\bar{S}$ over $r\ell$ (i.e., the $\bar{S}$ curve lies above the $r\ell$ curve) implies that r, or the capital per unit of labor, will increase (that is, $\dot{r} > 0$), whereas an excess of $r\ell$ over $\bar{S}$ (i.e., the $r\ell$ curve lies above the S curve) implies that r will decrease (i.e., $\dot{r} <$ 0).[2] A slight deviation of r from either r_1 or r_3, corresponding to the intersection point 1 or 3, respectively, in either direction would bring about movement of r (i.e., $\dot{r}$), as measured by the vertical distance between the $\bar{S}$ and $r\ell$ curves, carrying it further and further away from r_1 or r_3, as the case may be. On the other hand, any deviation of r from r_2 corresponding to intersection point 2 in either direction would bring about changes in r (as measured by the vertical distance between the $\bar{S}$ and $r\ell$ curves) that would return it to r_2. An underdeveloped economy may, before achieving take-off, be characterized as bogged down at such a low-income stable equilibrium point as 2, where the corresponding capital/labor ratio, r_2, yields a real per capita income very close to the bare subsistence level (i.e., a real per capita income that corresponds to the point of intersection of the $r\ell$ curve with the horizontal axis). The fundamental problem in economic development is how to raise the capital/labor ratio from such a low and stubbornly stable level as r_2, in the face of forces that tend always to be pushing it back to where it starts, and to get it beyond a level such as r_3, from which it will be able to take off into self-sustained growth--until perhaps some possible high level equilibrium point is again reached (not shown in the figure).

Thus it has been suggested that the hurdle for take-off might be cleared if it were possible to push the current capital/labor ratio, r, beyond the hump of the $r\ell$ curve between intersections 2 and 3. This could be done by injecting a giant additional dose of capital either from outside or from domestic sources, created by forcing the domestic population to make a greater effort to save. This approach has been tried in some totalitarian countries (for example, the Big Push Theory or the Great Leap Forward).[3] This scenario is certainly possible theoretically, provided the push is carried through to a genuine take-off point like r_3, that is, provided the domestic economy is inherently ready for take-off under its own steam after the exogenous push lets up. If the push stops short of reaching a take-off point such as r_3, the economy will retrogress toward a low-income stable equilibrium point such as r_2 and bog down there again.

External assistance, such as foreign economic aid and capital imports, can be powerful boosters in the domestic preparation for take-off and can shorten the process, even if they are not massive enough by themselves to propel a country into a successful take-off, as might be observed in the case of Taiwan.

An underdeveloped country may choose to undertake its own domestic measures to prepare for take-off: (1) lowering the rℓ curve by reducing the net reproduction rate of the population at each level of per capita income (hence at each level of r); (2) raising the $\bar{S}$ curve by increasing the willingness of the population to save at each level of per capita income and hence at each level of r; and (3) introducing improved technology that increases real per capita productivity at each level of the capital/labor ratio to overcome the possible adverse effect of increasing population pressure on fixed natural resources. This latter measure would have the effect of shifting the $\bar{Y}$ and, hence, the $\bar{S}$ curves upward and to the left relative to the rℓ curve.[4] When the $\bar{S}$ curve is shifted sufficiently upward and/or leftward relative to the rℓ curve, the two points of intersection 2 and 3 will converge such that the $\bar{S}$ and rℓ curves would become tangent to each other at one single point, which is where the intersections 2 and 3 would merge. In Figure 3.2, the new saving function is $\bar{S}'$ and 2 and 3 converge at the point 2',3'.

Once that condition is reached, the economy will easily take off into continuous, self-sustained growth. The reason is that the point of tangency (2 and 3) is stable in the leftward (backward) direction but unstable in the rightward (forward) direction. A slight deviation of r to the left would set up changes in r, moving it back to the point of tangency, whereas a deviation to the right would bring about changes in r that would move it further and further to the right (the direction of positive increase). Thus the excess of per capita savings over the capital investment (also per capita) needed to maintain the existing capital/labor ratio in the face of population growth may be regarded as the basic condition for take-off. It signifies that the supply of domestic savings should be more than sufficient to maintain a constant capital/labor ratio in spite of a continuous population increase and thus should be capable of increasing that ratio steadily. This situation would in turn yield a steady increase in per capita output, provided the constant adverse effect exerted upon it by the increasing pressure of the population on land resources is largely offset by technical progress, which may be

FIGURE 3.2
Growth and technical progress

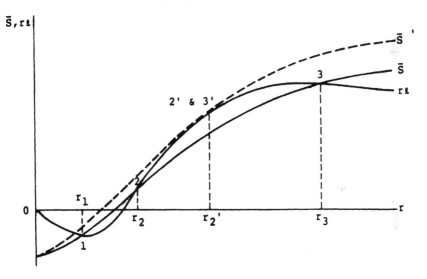

Note: $\bar{S}$ = Savings per unit of labor

  r = Capital per unit of labor

  ℓ = $\dot{L}/L$, the rate of growth of the population

regarded as the supplementary condition for take-off (see the Appendix).

The condition that $\bar{S} > r\ell$, or $S/L > (K/L)\ell$, can be transformed into more familiar form by multiplying both sides by the inverse of average per capita income (output), i.e., L/Y, which always has a positive magnitude. That process yields the alternative formulation of the basic condition for take-off:

$$S/Y > (K/Y)\ell ,$$

which signifies that the average propensity to save should be greater than the average capital/output ratio times the rate of population growth.

TRADE LIBERALIZATION AND PREPARING FOR TAKE-OFF

Wise economic policy for promoting development should include the following measures: (1) campaigns to reduce the birth rate; (2) campaigns to raise the population's propensity to save; (3) monetary and taxation policies that give plenty of incentives to save as well as to invest in productive enterprises; (4) the introduction of improved technology in all fields of production; (5) and the allocation of the resources of the country in optimum ways that achieve the highest possible real per capita income, given natural resources, capital, and the state of technology.

The question is how foreign trade fits into the picture. Its role is very significant: taking full advantage of the opportunity to trade has the same effect on real per capita income as does an enormous improvement in production technology. Full utilization of the opportunity to trade enables a country to specialize in those industries in which it has the highest comparative advantages and to exchange those products on the world market for others in which it has comparative disadvantages. As a result, the country can enjoy, if it chooses to, more of both its own products and the imports than if it tried to produce them all at home without trading. Conversely, if a country that originally had the opportunity to trade should decide to stop trading with other parts of the world, or should put up barriers for the sake of developing those industries in which the country actually has comparative disadvantages, it will only set back its own progress toward take-off as if there had been a catastrophic decline in its aggregate productive capacity. This approach causes the $\bar{S}$ curve to shift downward and to the right more than the $r\ell$ curve and thus increases the hump to be crossed on the way to take-off.

Unfortunately, during the early postwar years, most underdeveloped countries were influenced by the misguided thinking prevalent in those days that the surest way to speed industrial development at home was to provide a safe, sheltered market for import-substituting industries. In addition, it was seen as astute policy to keep domestic currency overvalued in the face of inflation at home, because it was believed that devaluation would greatly worsen the terms of trade and exacerbate domestic inflation by imparting a strong cost-push to the price level.

Taiwan at first followed that development strategy; it let the currency become grossly overvalued in the face of domestic inflation, but kept the balance of payments in equilibrium by strict quantitative controls and a high tariff wall. As a consequence, its only exports were a few traditional ones--sugar, rice, and pineapples, plus a few other minor items--and they went chiefly to markets established through prewar trade relationships, for example, Japan. New markets for export industries and for exports simply could not be developed. Industrialization therefore had to be limited to the development of firms producing cheap consumer products for the domestic market, sheltered by quantitative restrictions and high tariffs. Given that Taiwan is so small--roughly the size of the Netherlands--and given the very low per capita income of domestic consumers in the early fifties, it was impossible to develop industries for import substitution on the scale necessary for efficient operation with modern techniques.

Keeping the domestic currency grossly overvalued through quantitative restrictions on imports was equal to Taiwan's denying itself the tremendous benefits of specialization based on comparative advantage, and the chance to pursue industries of economical scale based on broad foreign markets for exportable goods.

When the late Professor T. C. Liu of Cornell University and this author were asked by the government of Taiwan to advise on economic policy, they seized the opportunity to advocate a policy of devaluation coupled with trade liberalization. That is, they encouraged the government to devalue the exchange rate of the domestic currency to a realistic level that would ensure the balance of trade equilibrium without the need for stringent quantitative restrictions and high protective tariffs. Initially, a well-informed cabinet minister actually admonished the two economists, stating that the demand for Taiwan's chief exports was highly inelastic with respect to the exchange rate, given that Taiwan's two primary exports at that time were sugar and rice, together accounting for nearly 80 percent of the value of exports in the early fifties. Exports of sugar were fixed by the international sugar agreement that annually allotted world market shares for each participating sugar-producing country. Rice exports went exclusively to Japan, and their quantity and price (in terms of the U.S. dollar) were fixed each year by direct negotiations between the two governments. Thus, these two major items literally did face zero demand elasticity with respect to the exchange rate. Thus Taiwan seemed to the minister to be the typical case of a developing country producing only a few traditional export products confronted by an extremely inelastic world demand. Devaluation would only worsen the terms of trade, drive up the domestic prices of imported goods, and add fuel to domestic inflation.

The two economists persisted in arguing that even if the elasticity of the major traditional exports was low, there must be hundreds of new products that could be produced with cheap labor and readily sold in countries with a relative scarcity of labor and hence high wage costs. A precondition, however, was that the relative abundance and cheapness of labor in Taiwan not be artificially smothered by the overvaluation of the currency (Tsiang 1980, 322). To rebut the view that devaluation would spur domestic inflation, they pointed out that it was incorrect to think that the domestic market prices of imported goods would be determined by the strength of effective domestic demand and the quantities actually allowed. With devaluation and trade liberalization, assuming that the foreign demand for all Taiwan's potential exports in the aggregate was not inelastic, the proceeds from exports would increase, and hence the quantities of imports permitted would also increase. On the other hand, if imports were allowed to expand pari passu with exports after devaluation and liberalization, such that trade would continue to balance, there would be no expansion in aggregate effective demand in monetary terms attributable to devaluation. Thus there was no reason the prices of imported goods should rise, as long as devaluation was coupled with trade liberalization.

Indeed, so long as the implicit tariff on imports implied by the initial quantitative restrictions cum tariffs was higher than the so-called optimum tariff rate, there would no doubt be an increase in real income as a result of an efficient reallocation of resources. Thus, provided that no monetary expansion was inadvertently permitted during the process of resource reallocation, the general price level was more likely to fall than to rise, as claimed by the cost-push theorists (Tsiang 1980, 322-23).

Fortunately, this argument slowly and gradually won the approval of the government. In April 1958, a minister whom the two economists had convinced became the chairman of the Foreign Exchange and Trade Control Commission. At that time, a policy of devaluation coupled with trade liberalization was finally adopted for gradual implementation, and that very month the basic exchange rate was devalued from new Taiwan yuan (NT $) $15.55 to NT $24.58 buying and NT $24.78 selling. Even more significant, henceforth exporters (except those of sugar, rice, and salt) would be awarded exchange surrender certificates representing the full amount of the export proceeds they had surrendered to the Bank of Taiwan. They could sell those certificates on the market to importers, who would have to present them in the amount of the foreign exchanges they wished to purchase from the Bank of Taiwan for their imports. At the same time, to make the market demand for exchange certificates reflect the market demand for imports correctly, the quota restrictions on all types of permissible imports were boldly removed, although luxury goods still could not be imported. In general, the existing high tariffs on imports were still maintained, but the 20 percent defense surcharge that used to be assessed on the basis of the value of imports was henceforth assessed on the basis of the duty payable. Thus the market-determined price of the certificates would constitute a flexible margin to be added to the fixed basic rate and would enable the resulting effective rate to approach the equilibrium exchange rate under the existing tariff system and to adjust automatically in accordance with changes in supply and demand.

The same effective rate thus obtained was gradually made applicable to all imports and exports and to most remittances and transfers. At last the complicated multiple exchange rate system was unified. In August 1959, to comply with the regulations of the IMF, the Bank of Taiwan discontinued the practice of separating the effective exchange rate into the two components of basic rate and the price of exchange certificates. Henceforth, the exchange rate of the new Taiwan yuan was to be NT $38.08 to U.S. $1 buying, and NT $38.38 selling. This rate was allowed to creep up to NT $40.00 to U.S. $1 in 1960, where it was pegged until February 1973 (Tsiang 1980, 329-31).

The effect this policy of devaluation had on the foreign trade of Taiwan, coupled with the liberalization, was truly remarkable, as can be seen from Table 3.1. The devaluations and tax rebates on exports initiated in 1955 were very effective in reviving exports from their low point in 1954, despite the predictions of the elasticity pessimists. But it was only in the 1960s, after the exchange rate was linked with the liberalized demand for imports, that the expansion of

TABLE 3.1
Merchandise trade

	Exports (U.S. $ Millions)	Average Annual Rate of Growth (%)	Quantum Index[a]	Imports (U.S. $ Millions)	Average Annual Rate of Growth (%)	Quantum Index[a]	Trade Balance (U.S. $ Millions)
1950	93.1		n.a.	123.9		n.a.	-30.8
51	93.1		n.a.	142.5		n.a.	-49.4
52	119.5		3.0	208.3		5.3	-88.8
53	128.6		4.5	192.9		6.6	-62.3
54	95.9		3.1	204.9		6.9	-109.0
55	127.1	5.8	3.9	184.7	8.7	6.4	-57.6
56	124.1		3.8	222.1		6.2	-98.0
57	148.3		4.4	244.7		4.2	-96.4
58	155.8		5.4	273.5		5.5	-117.7
59	156.9		5.0	263.9		6.0	-107.0
1960	164.0		5.0	286.5		6.0	-122.5
61	195.2		5.1	330.3		6.7	-135.1
62	218.2		5.8	328.0		7.8	-109.8
63	333.7		7.2	373.3		9.4	-39.6
64	434.5		9.4	395.4		12.2	39.1
65	450.8	24.5	10.8	517.2	16.9	17.3	-66.4
66	542.7		12.9	545.6		18.3	-2.9
67	653.7		15.0	728.1		23.6	-74.4
68	816.3		18.4	888.8		26.6	-72.5
69	1,081.4		23.5	1,093.0		35.7	-11.6
1970	1,468.6		31.0	1,363.4		44.0	105.2
71	2,047.2		42.1	1,754.6		50.1	292.6
72	2,979.3		56.5	2,331.9		60.9	647.4
73	4,476.0		69.5	3,741.8		70.7	766.0
74	5,592.0		66.5	6,422.4		88.0	-811.9
75	5,304.1	29.6	66.5	5,558.6	30.4	78.4	-254.5
76	7,809.6		100.0	7,125.0		100.0	699.9
77	9,517.2		107.8	8,316.9		103.7	1,214.7
78	12,602.0		133.9	10,367.4		116.5	2,234.6
79	15,828.9		142.6	14,421.3		126.9	1,407.6
1980	19,575.0		157.7	19,428.0		138.2	147.0

Source: Central Bank of China (various issues).

a These quantum indexes are taken from Council for Economic Planning and Development (various issues [1980, 1981]). These indexes must be used with caution, as many new commodities have entered trade during this period, and the composition of both exports and imports has changed dramatically.

Note: n.a. = Not available.

exports really took off. By 1970, the value of Taiwan's exports had already increased to U.S. $1,469 million. Compared with the low of U.S. $96 million in 1954, exports expanded 15.3 times in 16 years. The average annual rate of increase during the sixties was 23.6 percent. The rapid expansion continued in the seventies, so that by 1980, the dollar value of Taiwan's exports reached U.S. $19,575 million, more than 200 times that of 1954. The average annual rate of increase during the seventies was 29.6 percent.

STRUCTURAL CHANGE AND THE EXPANSION OF EXPORTS

Implicit in the rapid expansion of exports under the policy of trade liberalization and a realistic exchange rate was that the economy would have to be restructured to concentrate on industries in which Taiwan could use its resource endowment to greatest advantage and to avoid industries in which it was handicapped by limited resources. The restructuring showed up in changes in the structure of exports as well as of industries.

With regard to the structure of exports, in 1952 agricultural products and processed agricultural products together constituted 91.9 percent of the total value of exports. By 1970 the combined share of these two groups had dropped to 21.4 percent and by 1980 was a mere 9.2 percent. Conversely, the share of industrial products in exports rose sharply from just 8.1 percent in 1952 to 78.6 percent in 1970 and 90.8 percent in 1980 (Table 3.2).

This shift says that for Taiwan, a small congested island with only one-third of its land arable and an overall population density in excess of that of the Netherlands, agricultural products such as rice and sugar are certainly not areas of comparative advantage. Rather, its comparative advantage lies with those industries requiring relatively large amounts of labor and little land space and large amounts of capital. In line with this conclusion, textile products, clothing, shoes, umbrellas, toys, and other products of light industries seemed best suited to conditions in the early stages. Moreover, the agricultural products being exported also changed in character. Instead of products that required relatively more land to produce such as rice and sugar, the new agricultural exports tended to be very labor-intensive but relatively land-economical, such as mushrooms, which can be grown in stacked layers all year around; asparagus; and, in later years, eels for Japan and edible snails for France, although these items involve stretching the term agricultural products.

40

Table 3.2
Relative shares of agricultural and industrial
products in total exports
(percent)

	Agricultural Products[a]	Industrial Products
1952	91.9	8.1
1955	89.6	10.4
1960	67.7	32.3
1965	54.0	46.0
1970	21.4	78.6
1975	16.4	83.6
1980	9.2	90.8

Source: Council for Economic Planning and
Development (various issues).

[a] Includes processed agricultural products.

The apparent ease with which Taiwan expanded its
exports after devaluation and liberalization (their
dollar value increased 204 times in 26 years) is a
sound refutation of the arguments of the elasticity
pessimists that prevailed in the early postwar years.
On the other hand, the experience of Taiwan does not
really endorse a new assumption that many international
trade theorists have espoused recently--that a "small"
country faces an infinitely elastic world market demand
for its tradable goods.
The experience of Taiwan indicates that neither
the old pessimism about elasticity, nor the new assumption of an infinitely elastic demand for tradable
goods, represents the reality confronting a small country such as Taiwan. Although Taiwan's total exports
expanded by leaps and bounds after devaluation and
liberalization, eventually many goods were subjected
to quantitative restraints imposed by other countries
when imports from Taiwan increased to a level that
threatened their domestic producers (sometimes these
restraints went by the euphemism of "voluntary"). The
curve of the foreign demand for each export product
would suddenly turn from a fairly horizontal and elastic one into a downward, vertical one of zero elasticity. Taiwan then could only try to discover new export markets for the product, eventually to run into
similar quantitative restraints when the inroads into
the new markets became too great. It also sought new

products for export. This process is well-illustrated by the evolution of both its agricultural and manufactured exports. As mentioned, the increasing population density of Taiwan very quickly made the production of rice for export unprofitable. Instead, Taiwan developed the mushroom. This new crop became a major export item worth more than U.S. $100 million a year. It was not long, however, before the United States imposed what was called a voluntary restraint on Taiwan's exports of mushrooms. Taiwan then had to find a new customer--the European Common Market--and to develop a new export crop, asparagus. The same story, however, was repeated with asparagus. Very soon the United States and the European Common Market both imposed quantitative restraints on asparagus exported from Taiwan, just as they had with the mushrooms. Therefore Taiwan has had constantly to develop new export products and to discover new markets, such as eels and onions for Japan and edible snails for France.

A similar process pertained to the expansion of manufactured exports. For instance, textile products, shoes, umbrellas, black-and-white and colored television sets, mechanical and electronic toys, and the like were subjected to restraints both in the United States and Western European countries. Only by constant development of new export products and the discovery of new markets was Taiwan able to expand total exports at such a remarkable rate.

Thus, the world demand that a small, but not so small as to be literally atomistic, developing country confronted in terms of exportable products is neither as inelastic as the early elasticity pessimists assumed, nor as infinitely elastic as modern international trade theorists assume. The aggregate demand curve a small developing country faces is likely to be highly elastic within a certain range (i.e., to have a nearly horizontal stretch) that will terminate abruptly in a vertical bend downward. However, if the country's entrepreneurs are sufficiently ingenious and resourceful, they will soon discover new products for export or new markets for their old products, with their own stretches of nearly horizontal demand curves that will, however, some day end again in a vertical bend downward. And so on. Thus, the curve for the aggregate world demand for exportables might be seen as a sort of step function. When the country's entrepreneurs are resourceful enough, the horizontal steps may be spaced very closely in the vertical dimension but stretched out rather widely in the horizontal dimension, and the resulting aggregate demand curve may approach a highly elastic, smooth curve. If the entrepreneurs are not very resourceful, the steps will be rather steep and far apart vertically. The resulting aggregate demand curve will be equivalent to a relatively inelastic curve. It is very fortunate for Taiwan that it was endowed with an ample supply of capable entrepreneurs. But it should be emphasized that the realistic exchange rate afforded a proper incentive by assuring the exporters the full market equilibrium value of the export proceeds they earned. Further, Taiwan's enlightened attitude toward foreign direct investment as well as foreign participation in domestic industries was also a great help, for foreign investors often bring new ideas about products and have connections to untapped markets.

The profound changes in the composition of exports and the rapid increase in the relative importance of production for export naturally brought about corresponding changes in the structure of Taiwan's economy. In 1951, the share of agricultural output in Taiwan's gross domestic product (GDP) was 32.5 percent, while that of industrial output (including mining, manufacturing, utilities, and construction) was only 32.9 percent. By 1970, the share of agricultural output had declined to 15.5 percent, while that of industrial output had climbed to 41.3 percent. This trend continued in the seventies, so that by 1980 the share of agricultural products was down to only 7.7 percent, while that of industrial products was 52.2 percent (Table 3.3).

This shift in the weight in GDP away from agriculture and toward industrial production was of immense importance to the steady increase in real per capita income and the standard of living. Given Taiwan's size and population density, agriculture is inevitably subject to the relentless law of diminishing returns. The only way to circumvent this situation on a large scale was to shift labor away from agriculture into industrial production. This reallocation of productive resources and the ability to concentrate on those industries in which Taiwan had true comparative advantage were the basic reasons Taiwan was able not only to support a much larger population (it grew from 8.13 million in 1952 to 17.81 million in 1980), but to provide them with a real per capita income five times higher (Table 3.4). This resource reallocation and concentration were only possible because of the devaluation and liberalization of trade, which launched Taiwan onto the course of export-oriented development.

THE IMPORTANCE OF PROMOTING THE PROPENSITY TO SAVE

With the increase in real per capita income brought about by foreign trade and specialization in industries with comparative advantage, the domestic population must be induced to save larger and larger amounts in order to achieve take-off, since the basic precondition for take-off into continuous self-sustained growth is per capita domestic savings that are more than sufficient to finance the per capita investment required just to maintain the existing capital/labor ratio in the face of domestic population growth, that is, $\bar{S} > r\ell$. An alternative formulation is S/Y > (K/Y) . ℓ-- the average propensity to save must be greater than the average capital/labor ratio times the rate of domestic population growth.

Unfortunately, the academic monetary theory prevailing in the fifties and sixties suggests a totally misguided monetary policy that would discourage rather than promote saving by the public. Given the influence of Keynesian economics, most developing countries adopted a monetary policy of keeping the structure of nominal interest rates in their domestic banking system at the low conventional levels of developed countries with much more abundant capital and more stable prices. The reason, erroneous as it turned out, was that this policy was needed to stimulate real investment as well as to prevent cost-push inflation. Actually, this type of government-enforced, low-interest rate policy in the face of inflationary conditions and a great scarcity of domestic capital both fuels domestic inflation by creating an enormous excess demand for bank credit, and slows real domestic capital formation by discouraging the inflow of genuine savings of

TABLE 3.3
Relative shares of agricultural and
industrial products in GDP
(percent)

	Agricultural	Industrial[a]	Service
1951	35.5	23.9	43.6
1955	29.2	26.4	44.4
1960	28.7	29.6	41.7
1965	23.7	33.9	42.4
1970	15.5	41.3	43.2
1975	12.8	45.9	41.3
1980	7.7	52.2	40.1

Source: Directorate-General of Budget, Accounting, and Statistics (various issues).

[a] Includes processed agricultural goods.

44

TABLE 3.4
National income at market prices
(constant 1976 prices)

| | Aggregate National Income | | Per Capita Income | |
	Amount (NT $ millions)	Index (1976=100)	Amount (NT $)	Index (1976=100)
1952	87,308	13.5	10,222	25.9
1955	112,760	17.5	11,895	30.1
1960	151,718	23.5	13,601	34.5
1965	240,229	37.3	18,582	47.1
1970	387,166	60.1	26,582	67.4
1975	558,598	86.7	34,910	88.5
1980	879,139	136.4	49,832	126.3
1981	918,899	142.6	51,161	129.6

Source: Council for Economic Planning and Development (various issues).

the public into organized financial intermediaries,
instead diverting them to the hoarding of precious metals and foreign exchanges or to direct personal investment in real estate or other nonproductive areas.
    Taiwan was probably the first among the developing
countries to abandon, as early as 1950, the traditional
policy of low interest rates by raising the interest
rate on savings deposits to approximately the prevailing rate of price inflation, which was, at the
beginning of that year, well above 100 percent.   In
March, the Bank of Taiwan introduced a special system
of savings deposits called the Preferential Interest
Rate Deposits (PIR);   they offered a hitherto unheard-
of nominal rate of interest of 7 percent a month that,
when compounded monthly as stipulated, came to a remarkable 125 percent a year.
    The impact of this high interest policy was very
rapid and successful.   Total time and savings deposits
quickly rose from a meager NT $6 million, or barely 1.7
percent of the contemporary money supply (currency plus
demand deposits), at the end of March 1950 to NT $28
million at the end of June, or approximately 7.0 percent of the money supply.   Even more remarkable is that
price inflation came rapidly to a halt.   Whereas its
average monthly rate during the first three months of
1950 was as high as 10.3 percent a month, it dropped
dramatically to only 0.4 percent a month in the second
quarter.   Indeed, starting in May 1950, prices actually
declined a little.   This surprisingly quick result hap-

pened before the propitious turn of fortune in favor of
Taiwan--the resumption of U.S. aid soon after the out-
break of the Korean War on June 27, 1950.

Partly encouraged by the immediate success and
partly fearing that the 125 percent a year interest
rate would be intolerable with stable prices, in July
the government cut the interest rate payable on one-
month deposits sharply to 3.5 percent a month, a 50
percent reduction, and again in October to only 3.0
percent. The public, taken aback by this abrupt reversal of policy, reacted by stopping the flow of new savings into the banking system and even started to with-
draw their deposits. By the end of December 1950,
total savings and time deposits had fallen to only NT
$26 million, or 4.5 percent of the current money sup-
ply. Moreover, in August, prices resumed their rapid
rise, until by February 1951 they were 65 percent higher than in July 1950, when the first cut in interest
rates was announced.

Alarmed by the prospect of renewed rampant inflation, on March 26, 1951, the monetary authorities
raised the rate on one-month deposits from 3 percent to
4.2 percent (equivalent to an annual rate of 64 percent). Apparently, this action appeased the public
sufficiently, and the flow of savings into the banking
system resumed at a spectacular pace--one year later,
by the end of March 1952, total savings and time deposits had already reached NT $271 million, or 31.2 per-
cent of the contemporary money supply, and six months
later had risen further to NT $541 million, or 56.4
percent of the contemporary money supply. Prices were
once more completely stabilized. (See Table 3.5.)

Thenceforth, the monetary authorities gingerly
lowered the interest rate step by step whenever they
felt that price stability warranted it. Because the
money market was not free at that time, however, these
successive downward adjustments were guided only by the
subjective feelings of the monetary authorities with
regard to the public's expectations about price inflation. Not infrequently they overestimated the public's
confidence in price stability and willingness to supply
savings to the banking system. They would then make
overly precipitous cuts in interest rates, sending
prices on an upward climb again. However, when interest rates were raised again in time, prices would once
more stabilize, and the upward trend in the savings and
time deposits in the banking system would resume
(Tsiang 1979, 593-97).

Thus the fact that adequate interest rates on time
and savings deposits are a necessary inducement to attract voluntary public savings into the banking system
and also constitute a significant anti-inflationary instrument was demonstrated repeatedly and convincingly

46

TABLE 3.5
Money supply; savings, time, and
Preferential Interest Rate (PIR) deposits;
interest rates; and wholesale prices, 1950-54

End of Period	Money Supply	Savings, Time & PIR Deposits[a] (NT $ Millions)	Col. 2 as % of Col. 1	Monthly Interest Rate on One-Month PIR Deposits	Monthly Rate of Price Inflation during the Quarter (%)
	(1)	(2)	(3)	(4)	(5)
1950					
Mar.	348	6	1.7	7.00 (effective)	10.3
June	401	28	7.0	7.00 (from Mar. 25)	0.4
Sept.	595	36	6.1	3.50 (from July 1)	6.0
Dec.	584	26	4.5	3.00 (from Oct. 1)	5.4
1951					
Mar.	732	30	4.1	4.20 (from Mar 26)	4.8
June	942	59	6.3	4.20	3.9
Sept.	687	164	23.9	4.20	1.8
Dec.	940	163	17.3	4.20	3.9
1952					
Mar.	867	271	31.2	4.20	2.6
June	942	494	52.4	3.80 (from Apr. 29) 3.30 (from June 2)	-1.0
Sept.	959	541	56.4	3.00 (from July 7) 2.40 (from Sept. 8)	-0.4
Dec.	1,336	467	34.9	2.00 (from Nov. 30)	0
1953					
Mar.	1,074	499	46.5	2.00	1.5
June	1,198	640	53.4	2.00	1.4
Sept.	1,292	671	51.9	1.50 (from July 16)	1.6
Dec.	1,683	599	35.6	1.20 (from Oct. 10)	0.5
1954					
Mar.	1,622	667	41.1	1.20	0
June	1,809	747	41.3	1.20	-1.4
Sept.	1,923	782	40.6	1.00 (from July 1)	-0.6
Dec.	2,128	765	35.9	1.00	1.3
1955					
Mar.	2,300	816	35.5	1.00	2.7

Source: The Central Bank of China, (various issues); and Taiwan Provincial Government (various issues).

[a] The PIR deposit scheme was phased out in March 1955. At that time, PIR deposits were merged into ordinary savings deposits, and the name was abolished.

by the experience of Taiwan. This situation conclu-
sively gave the lie to the allegation of the cost-push
inflation theorists that raising the officially controlled low interest rates would surely bring about a
spurt in domestic inflation.

The relative stability of prices and the fairly
attractive interest rates for savings deposits revived
and stimulated the traditional thrifty habits of the
Chinese people and restored the capacity of the banking
system to collect their savings. Other tax measures
were also adopted to encourage savings and investment,
for example, exempting from personal income tax the
interest income from savings and time deposits with
maturity terms of two years or more and exempting from
corporate income tax those profits plowed back into
investment. These inducements led rapidly to an en-
larged inflow of voluntary savings that provided the
much-needed noninflationary financing for domestic
investment, stimulated by the concurrent devaluation
and trade liberalization that themselves opened up vast
investment opportunities in the new export industries. Since 1960, the investment made possible by
these noninflationary sources of finance has brought
about a rapid growth in productivity per worker and
hence a rapid growth in real per capita income. The
surge in real income in turn made savings relatively
easy because of the natural tendency for consumption to
lag behind rising income.

Thus, Taiwan was rapidly converted from a country
with a very low propensity to save into a country with
a remarkably high propensity. In 1952, the percentage
of national income saved in Taiwan had been only 5.2
percent. By 1963, that percentage had already risen to
13.4 percent, surpassing the corresponding percentages
of both the United Kingdom (9.8 percent) and the United
States (9.1 percent) in the same year. In 1971, the
percentage of national income saved began to surpass
even that of Japan, which used to have the highest level in the world. In 1978, the percentage saved climbed
to the extraordinarily high level of 35.2 percent
compared with 20 percent in Japan, 8.3 percent in the
United Kingdom and 6.5 percent in the United States in
the same year (Table 3.6).

It was this ability to generate sufficient domestic savings that made possible Taiwan's economic
take-off. If that term is understood as the transformation process that turns a struggling developing country which barely managed to prevent the standard of
living of its increasing population from slipping backward, into one that now finds it easy to maintain rapid
self-sustained growth in real per capita income with or
without foreign assistance, then Taiwan has been emi-
nently successful.

48

TABLE 3.6
Net domestic savings as a percentage
of gross national product

	Taiwan	Japan	U.K.	U.S.
1952	5.2	24.1	6.4	10.4
55	4.9	20.4	9.8	12.2
1960	7.6	27.7	10.9	8.6
61	8.0	29.9	11.0	8.4
62	7.6	28.4	9.4	9.0
63	13.4	26.6	9.8	9.1
64	16.3	25.2	11.2	9.8
65	16.5	23.3	12.4	11.5
66	19.0	24.7	11.5	10.3
67	20.1	27.5	10.4	9.7
68	19.8	29.4	11.2	9.8
69	22.1	29.8	13.8	9.8
1970	23.8	30.5	13.6	7.6
71	27.6	27.4	11.3	7.6
72	31.6	26.8	9.8	8.2
73	35.0	28.4	9.5	9.5
74	31.5	25.1	5.7	6.7
75	25.3	21.4	5.3	3.8
76	32.2	20.9	7.1	4.9
77	32.3	20.3	8.4	5.7
78	35.2	20.0	8.3	6.5
79	34.9	19.9	8.3	6.4
1980	32.9	19.7	7.7	4.3

Sources: For Taiwan, Council for Economic Planning
and Development (various issues [1981]); for other
countries, United Nations (1982).

ESTIMATING THE APPROXIMATE YEAR
OF ECONOMIC TAKE-OFF

As quoted above, Lewis (1955) once gave a 12 percent or higher propensity to save as a sort of criterion for success in economic development. Here the
basic condition for take-off presented above--that per
capita savings be more than sufficient to maintain the
capital/labor ratio, or rather its transformation,

$S/Y > (K/Y)(\dot{L}/L)$,

is applied to the case of Taiwan. The purpose is to
see how Taiwan gradually achieved the condition of
take-off and when that was accomplished (Table 3.7).
It may be seen from Table 3.7 that before the devalua-

TABLE 3.7
Estimation of the approximate year of
economic take-off

	K/Y	$\dot{L}/L$	(K/Y)($\dot{L}/L$)	S/Y	S/Y-(K/Y)($\dot{L}/L$)
1952	6.0	3.3	19.8	5.2	-14.6
55	4.8	3.8	18.2	4.9	-13.3
1960	3.7	3.5	13.0	7.6	-5.4
61	3.6	3.3	11.9	8.0	-3.9
62	3.4	3.3	11.2	7.6	-3.6
63	3.2	3.2	10.2	13.4	3.2
64	2.9	3.1	9.0	16.3	7.3
65	2.7	3.0	8.1	16.5	8.4
66	2.6	2.9	7.5	19.0	11.5
67	2.5	2.3	5.8	20.1	14.3
68	2.4	2.7	6.5	19.8	13.3
69	2.3	2.5	5.8	22.1	16.3
1970	2.2	2.4	5.3	23.8	18.5
72	2.0	2.0	4.0	31.6	27.6
74	2.1	1.8	3.8	31.5	27.7
76	2.2	2.2	4.8	32.2	27.4
78	2.0	1.9	3.8	35.2	31.4

Sources: Council for Economic Planning and
Development (various issues [1981]).

Note: The ratio (K/Y) was estimated by
Professor R. I. Wu and this author.

tion and trade liberalization policy was carried out in
the late fifties, the condition for take-off was far
from being satisfied. However, when the trade liberalization and consequent export expansion was in full
gear, and the sensible interest rate policy had restored the traditional thriftiness of the Chinese
people, the propensity to save went up by leaps and
bounds. Then the insufficiency of domestic savings
relative to fulfillment of the basic condition for
take-off was quickly made good.

In 1963 the domestic propensity to save began to
exceed the requirement for investments to maintain a
constant capital/labor ratio in the face of population
growth. It is true that the excess for that year was
at first quite minor, i.e., only 3 percentage points
approximately. However, as might be expected on the
basis of theoretical reasoning (Tsiang 1964), the ex-

cess grew progressively thereafter--to 7.3 percentage points in 1964, 8.4 in 1965, 11.5 in 1966, and so on. In the 1970s, the propensity to save continued to rise rapidly, reaching well above 20 percent and eventually attaining the high level of 35 percent. The excess of S/Y over $(K/Y)(\dot{L}/L)$ continued to widen. This condition implies that Taiwan is now fully capable of achieving a continuous and fairly satisfactory rate of growth in real per capita income even without inflows of foreign capital.

Before the presumed take-off year of 1963, Taiwan had to rely very heavily on foreign aid and capital inflows for its capital formation: they constituted no less than 30-50 percent of the sources of funds for gross capital formation until 1962 (Table 3.8). These funds greatly reduced the burden on domestic savings to carry Taiwan's capital/labor ratio forward over the hump to a take-off point, for example, intersection point 3 in Figure 3.1. Consequently, they considerably shortened the preparation for take-off, which otherwise would no doubt have taken much longer.

Beginning in 1963, there was a sharp decline in foreign capital inflows and transfers, as U.S. aid to Taiwan was rapidly closed down in anticipation of the termination date set for 1965. However, fortunately, Taiwan's economy took off under its own steam in 1963, and thereafter domestic savings not only successfully filled the gap left by foreign aid, but sustained domestic capital formation at an increasing rate. Since

TABLE 3.8
Sources of funds for gross domestic
capital formation

	Gross Domestic Capital Formation	Gross Domestic Savings	Foreign Capital Inflow
1952-55	100.0	59.3	40.7
1956-60	100.0	60.0	40.0
1961-65	100.0	85.1	14.9
1966-70	100.0	95.0	5.0
1971-75	100.0	97.4	2.6
1976-80	100.0	106.0	-6.0

Source: Council for Economic Planning and Development (various issues [1981]).

1975, it seems that Taiwan might even become a capital-exporting country, as can be observed from Table 3.8.

INCOME DISTRIBUTION AND ECONOMIC GROWTH

There is one incidental beneficial effect of Taiwan's development strategy. Despite the very rapid rate of industrial growth, the distribution of income in Taiwan, instead of becoming more unequal as such authorities as Kuznets and others say is inevitable, actually improved in equity, at least until 1978 (Table 3.9). This fact attracted the attention of Chenery, et al. (1974), who conducted a comprehensive study comparing the experiences of 66 countries. In view of the fact that many eminent development economists, e.g., Kuznets, Paukert, and Adelman and Morris, actually believed that there might be an inevitable trade-off between growth and equity (Kuznets 1955, 1963; Paukert 1955; Adelman and Morris 1973), the concurrent rapid growth and improvement in income distribution in Taiwan has called forth explanations (e.g., Ranis, Fei, and Kuo 1979; and Kuo, Ranis, and Fei 1981).

With the benefit of hindsight, an explanation is not difficult to find. In fact, the twin pillars of Taiwan's development strategy could have been expected to contribute to the improvement of income distribution

TABLE 3.9
Changes in income distribution--percentage shares in the aggregate income, by quintiles of families

Quintiles	1964	1970	1974	1978	1979
1st Quintile (the Poorest)	7.7	8.4	8.8	8.9	8.6
2nd Quintile	12.6	13.3	13.5	13.7	13.7
3rd Quintile	16.6	17.1	17.0	17.5	17.5
4th Quintile	22.0	22.5	22.1	22.7	22.7
5th Quintile (the Richest)	41.1	38.7	38.6	37.2	27.5
Income Share of the Richest Quintile/ Poorest Quintile	5.3	4.6	4.4	4.2	4.4

Source: Directorate-General of Budget, Accounting, and Statistics (1977).

in favor of labor for two reasons. First, trade liberalization and export promotion, after the exchange rate had been properly adjusted, induced, as was seen, a vast shift in labor from land-intensive agriculture, which inevitably suffered from diminishing returns because of limited land, toward labor-intensive industries in which Taiwan obviously had superior comparative advantages, i.e., the new export industries. Inherent in this major shift from agriculture with low marginal productivity to the rapidly expanding new export industries was a big net increase in the marginal productivity of labor and, hence, of the real wage rate.

Second, the abandonment of the policy of artificial, government-enforced low interest rates enabled Taiwan to avoid the selection of excessively capital-intensive and labor-saving methods of production and the industries based on those methods of production. Many other developing countries were frequently tempted to pursue those industries by the seeming but false cheapness of capital, reinforced by considerations of national prestige. The erroneous, yet highly popular, low interest policy tended to reduce greatly the number of workers that could be absorbed into productive employment with a given amount of investable funds. It left a large portion of the labor force in traditional low productivity areas. In addition, as was pointed out, the low interest policy reduced the inflow of savings into financial institutions and thus reduced the supply of noninflationary investable funds. By avoiding those common mistakes, Taiwan was able rapidly to provide new and increasing employment opportunities in the expanding export industries. The result was outstandingly fast growth in the real income of the working class.

CONCLUDING REMARKS

If any lesson is to be drawn from the remarkable experience of Taiwan--rapid economic growth accompanied by greater equity in income distribution--it is the merit of rejecting the fashionable postwar development theories that suggested clever gimmicks in terms of controls and regulations as ways to speed up economic development. The postwar period is now of sufficient length that it is possible to compare the results of the following two opposite types of development strategies: (1) the traditional highly popular policy of using quantitative restrictions and a tariff wall to shelter the domestic market for import-substituting industries, and of keeping interest rates low by strict regulation of banks and other financial intermediaries;

and (2) trade liberalization and export promotion at an equilibrium exchange rate, plus a market-determined interest rate to ensure the maximization of voluntary savings and the efficient allocation of capital funds. Taiwan's success seems to speak clearly which choice was wiser.

APPENDIX

The mathematical model given in (Tsiang 1964), upon which Figure 3.1 on the theory of economic take-off presented in the introduction is based, is a simple, one-commodity model with an aggregate production function of the Cobb-Douglas type, such as

$$Y = AK^{\alpha(t)} L^{\beta(t)} N^{\gamma(t)} \exp \left(\int_{o}^{t} g(\tau) d\tau \right), \tag{1}$$

where K = Total capital
   L = Labor
   N = Natural resources; and
   A = A constant.

The parameters α, β, and γ are supposed to be variable over time according to the biased nature of technical progress, but are always subject to the restriction that

$$\alpha(t) + \beta(t) + \gamma(t) = 1. \tag{2}$$

Assuming that N, the amount of natural resources, cannot be increased (is an inaugmentable constant), the rate of growth of output in general, or real GDP, is

$$y = \dot{Y}/Y = \alpha k + \beta \ell + g^*, \tag{3}$$

where $k = \dot{K}/K,$

   $\ell = \dot{L}/L,$ and

   $g^* = g + \dot{\alpha} \ln K + \dot{\beta} \ln L + \dot{\gamma} \ln N. \tag{4}$

Therefore, g^* is the net effect on the rate of growth of output attributable to technical progress that might be biased toward different factors of production at different times. When technical progress is strictly neutral, g^* is identical with g, which then represents the rate of neutral technical progress (in the Hicksian sense).

The rate of growth of the population, hence the labor supply, is assumed to be a function of the current real wage rate, so that

$$L_t = L_0 \exp\left(\int_0^t \ell(Y_L) d\tau\right), \tag{5}$$

where Y_L, the marginal productivity of labor, is equal to

$$\beta(Y/L) \text{ or } \beta\bar{Y},$$

with $\bar{Y}$ being defined as Y/L.

If $\bar{y}$ is substituted for the rate of growth of $\bar{Y}$, then

$$\bar{y} = (1/\bar{Y}) \quad d\bar{Y}/dt = \alpha\hat{r} + g^* - \gamma\ell, \tag{6}$$

where $\hat{r}$ is the rate of growth of $r = K/L$.

Assuming that domestic savings always result in an equal increase in domestic capital and that for the time being, no investment is financed by foreign capital inflows or aid, then

$$\bar{S} = \dot{K}/L$$

and

$$\hat{r} = (1/r)(dr/dt) = (1/r)[\dot{K}/L-(K/L)\dot{L}/L] = (1/r)(\bar{S}-r\ell).$$

Thus it may be concluded that, provided the two conditions

(i) $\bar{S} - r\ell > 0$

and

(ii) $g^* - \gamma\ell > 0$

are satisfied, then real per capita income of the economy will be capable of continuous self-sustained growth. These two conditions are what has been called here the basic and the supplementary conditions for take-off, respectively.

NOTES

1. A condensed version of the model is presented in the appendix.

2. $\dot{r} = dr/dt = d(K/L)/dt = \dot{K}/L - K/L\ \dot{L}/L =$
$\bar{S} - r\ell$, when $\bar{S} = \dot{K}/L$.

3. Since $(\bar{S} - r\ell)$ in the figure measures only the domestic supply of savings available for increasing the capital equipment per unit of labor, the $\dot{r}$ defined in the figure represents only the domestically financed increases in r. If foreign capital inflows and foreign aid are available, in addition to domestic savings, to finance domestic investment, they contribute an exogenous push that would propel the capital/labor ratio of the country forward independently of domestic savings.

4. This result has been demonstrated in Tsiang (1964, 627-37).

REFERENCES

Adelman, Irma, and Cynthia Taft Morris. 1973. Economic Growth and Social Equity in Developing Countries. Stanford, Calif.: Stanford University Press.

Central Bank of China. Various issues. Taiwan Financial Statistics Monthly. Taipei.

Chenery, H., M. S. Ahluwalia, C. L. G. Bell, J. H. Duloy, and R. Jolly. 1974. Redistribution with Growth. London: Oxford University Press.

Council for Economic Planning and Development. Various issues. Taiwan Statistical Data Book. Taipei.

Directorate-General of Budget, Accounting, and Statistics. Various issues. National Income of the Republic of China. Taipei.

——————. 1977. Report on the Survey of Personal Income Distribution in Taiwan Area, Republic of China. Executive Yuan. Taipei.

Kuo, Shirley W. Y., Gustav Ranis, and John C. H. Fei. 1981. The Taiwan Success Story: Rapid Growth with Improved Distribution in the Republic of China, 1952-1979. (Boulder, Colo.: Westview Press.

Kuznets, Simon. 1955. "Economic Growth and Income Inequality." American Economic Review 45(March): 1-28.

——————. 1963. "Quantitative Aspects of the Economic Growth of Nations: VIII, Distribution of Income by Size." Economic Development and Cultural Change 11:1-80.

56

Lewis, W. A. 1955. The Theory of Economic Growth. Homewood, Ill.: Irwin.

Paukert, Felix. 1955. "Income Distribution at Different Levels of Development: A Survey of Evidence." International Labour Review 108(August and September):97-124.

Ranis, G., J. C. H. Fei, and S. W. Y. Kuo. 1979. Growth with Equity, The Taiwan Case. London: Oxford University Press.

Rostow, W. W. 1961. The Stages of Economic Growth: A Non-Communist Manifesto. London: Cambridge University Press.

Solow, R. M. 1958. "A Contribution to the Theory of Economic Growth." Quarterly Journal of Economics 62(November):65-94.

Taiwan Provincial Government. Bureau of Accounting and Statistics. Various issues. Taiwan Commodity Prices Statistics Monthly. Taipei.

Tsiang, S. C. 1964. "A Model of Economic Growth in Rostovian Stages." Econometrica 32(October):619-48.

——————. 1979. "Fashions and Misconceptions in Monetary Theory and Their Influences on Financial and Banking Policies." Zeitschrift fur die gesamte Staatswissenschaft 135(December):584-604.

——————. 1980. "Exchange Rate, Interest Rate, and Economic Development, The Experience of Taiwan." In Quantitative Economics and Development, 309-46, edited by L. Klein, M. Nerlove, and S.C. Tsiang. New York: Academic Press.

United Nations. 1982. Yearbook of National Accounts Statistics. New York.

4
Lessons from South Korea's Experience with Industrialization

Kwang Suk Kim

INTRODUCTION

It is widely known that the Republic of Korea (South Korea) achieved rapid industrialization and growth from the early sixties until the late seventies. Gross national product (GNP) grew by an average annual rate of approximately 10 percent from 1962 to 1978, while per capita GNP roughly tripled from U.S. $239 to U.S. $776 in constant 1975 prices. This growth in GNP was led by the manufacturing sector, which rose at an average annual rate of 19 percent during 1962-1978. The share of the manufacturing sector in GNP almost doubled, from 14 percent to 27 percent, during the same period, while the share of the agriculture-forestry-fishery sector declined from 37 percent to 22 percent.

Prior to the early sixties economic development had been quite slow, even stagnant, because of serious economic disruptions caused by noneconomic factors. For approximately 35 years, until the conclusion of World War II, the Korean people lived under Japanese rule. Liberation was accompanied by the unexpected partition of the country into South Korea and the Democratic People's Republic of Korea (North Korea), which led to the enormously destructive Korean War. By the end of this war, nearly half the existing industrial facilities in South Korea lay in ruin.

Without the massive inflow of foreign assistance after the war, particularly from the United States, the South Korean economy would have collapsed completely. Even with that assistance, economic performance during the postwar reconstruction period was quite frustrating for both government policy-makers and the public. Although significant progress was made in stabilizing prices by the end of the 1950s, the growth in production was slow.

The already precarious political and economic situation in South Korea was further strained by two political uprisings, a student revolution and a military coup, which took place in 1960 and 1961, respectively.

In 1963 South Korea reached a turning point in its economic development, and from that year until the late seventies it sustained a high rate of growth in GNP. It is generally believed that, in the South Korean context, the sudden increase in the growth of output was attributable to the change in the development strategy adopted in the early sixties. Although there were certainly other economic and noneconomic factors that cannot be easily quantified, the shift from an inward-looking import substitution strategy to an export-oriented development strategy is considered an important factor in the acceleration of output growth.

After nearly two decades of rapid growth, in 1979 the South Korean economy began to slow. In 1980 the GNP growth rate declined to an unprecedented negative 6 percent. While GNP grew by about 7 percent the following year, this increase was not enough to compensate for the previous year's decline in real per capita income. Today the economy is still experiencing slow growth in output, along with relatively high inflation and large deficits in the balance of payments. It is indisputable that something went wrong in South Korea after 1978.

This paper reviews the South Korean experience in industrialization from the early sixties on to determine what South Korea and other developing countries might learn of use in formulating future policy. The shift in industrialization strategy in the early sixties that led to the rapid expansion in exports and industrial growth is discussed first. South Korea's economic performance during the period of rapid growth is then addressed by contrasting it with the performance of the economy in an earlier period. The following section discusses the recent economic difficulties and their causes. In the last section, the lessons to be learned from South Korea's successful industrialization experience and its recent economic difficulties are considered, along with the prospects for the economy.

CHANGES IN INDUSTRIALIZATION STRATEGY

The development of industrial policy in the post-Korean War period (1953-1981) may be divided into three phases that correspond with the evolution of South Korea's industrial incentive system. The first phase lasted from the end of the Korean War to 1960 and was characterized by easy import substitution. The second phase encompassed the years 1961-1965 and was marked by the transition to an export-oriented industrialization strategy. The third phase began in 1966 and lasted until 1978 and is the period during which the export-oriented strategy became institutionalized and rapid economic growth was achieved.

During the first phase, South Korea developed some simple manufacturing. However, growth in this period was limited by the small size of the domestic market and the reduction in aid flows. In the early sixties, the strategy of industrialization shifted from import substitution to export promotion during the first half of the 1960s. This transition occurred for several reasons. First, by around 1960 South Korea had virtually exhausted the possibility of rapid growth through easy import substitution of nondurable consumer goods and the intermediate products used in their manufacture. A growth strategy based on import substitution of machinery, consumer durables, and their intermediate products was found to be inappropriate because of the smallness of the domestic market and the large capital requirements of such ventures. Second, South Korea's natural resource endowment is so poor that a development strategy based on the utilization of domestic resources was inconceivable. Third, policymakers had to find a source of foreign exchange in order to meet the balance of payment difficulties that were arising as U.S. assistance programs were phased out. Fourth, the availability of a well-motivated, low-wage labor force with a high level of education provided the country with a comparative advantage in exports of labor-intensive goods. Last, the political leadership was determined to attain a high rate of growth (Kim 1975).

In the fifties, the government had provided direct subsidies to promote exports of selected primary products. These export promotion measures were generally short-lived and were in many cases offset by other economic policies inconsistent with the measures. Then in 1964, in the transition to an export-oriented strategy, the government devalued the won, a policy that marked an important turning point. It also adopted a full-scale export-import link system,[1] and undertook a series of policy reforms in order to establish a system of incentives consistent with the export-oriented industrialization strategy.

The May 1964 devaluation was quite drastic--the official exchange rate went from 130 won to 256 won per U.S. dollar. This devaluation, although proportionally large, only restored the real exchange rate to the 1961 level. Because the government coupled the devaluation with fiscal and monetary restraint, however, the exchange rate was successfully unified. Beginning in March 1965, the won was allowed to float. Unlike its response before, this time the government made serious efforts to increase tax revenues through administrative improvements and a tax reform in 1965. Further, in September 1965, the interest rates on bank savings deposits and loans were raised sharply to increase domestic savings and discourage the use of loans for unproductive purposes.

During the transitional period from 1961 to 1965, the export incentive system was expanded greatly. Preferential export credits became an important incentive, since the interest rate reform of 1965 substantially widened the interest rate differential between export credits and ordinary bank loans. Among the other export incentives that were provided during this period were (1) tariff exemptions on imports of raw materials for use in the production of exports (drawback system); (2) indirect domestic tax exemptions on intermediate inputs used for production and sales of exports; (3) direct tax reductions on income earned from exports and other foreign exchange earning activities (abolished in 1973); (4) wastage allowances for raw materials imported for the production of exports; (5) a system of linking import business to export performance; (6) tariff and indirect domestic tax exemptions for domestic suppliers of intermediate goods used in the production of exports; and (7) accelerated depreciation allowances for the fixed assets of major export industries.

These measures were designed mainly to assure that South Korean exporters, who must sell their products at world market prices, purchase intermediate goods for export production at world market prices. In other words, the major incentives served mainly to offset the disincentive effect on exports that the trade regime would otherwise have had. The incentives applied to all exporters on a nondiscriminatory basis.

In addition to these measures, an export targeting system was set up in 1962 to promote the export drive further. In addition, the government-supported Korea Trade Promotion Corporation (KOTRA) was created in the early sixties to promote overseas marketing of Korean traders. The establishment by private traders of overseas marketing branches has since been encouraged by providing tax concessions and preferential credit.[2]

Some adjustments were made to the export incentive system after 1965 to accommodate the changing economic conditions; these adjustments did not, however, significantly change the system. The government gradually relaxed the quantitative restrictions on imports and reduced tariffs through several reforms after 1965. What was particularly important was that the government

was able roughly to maintain the real exchange rate at
the same level as in 1965, even during the period 1966-
1978, through periodic adjustments of the rate and/or
adjustment of the subsidies included in the overall incentive schemes for exports.

Table 4.1 shows the trends in the nominal exchange
rates and the effective exchange rates as adjusted by
the purchasing power parity (PPP) for exports and
imports between 1958 and 1979. The effective exchange
rate for exports takes into account exchange rate
premiums resulting from multiple exchange rates (1958-
1961 and 1963-1964), direct cash subsidies (1961-1964),
direct tax reductions (through 1973), and preferential
export credits, all per dollar of exports. It excludes
those indirect tax and tariff exemptions that did not
directly affect the profit margins of exporters. The
effective exchange rate for imports takes into account
actual tariffs and tariff-equivalent barriers per
dollar of imports, but it excludes the effect of
quantitative restrictions on imports. The nominal
effective exchange rates for exports and imports have
both been adjusted for changes in domestic and world
prices in order to obtain the PPP-adjusted effective
exchange rates.

The production patterns of industries that the
government has promoted have changed over time, reflecting the changing domestic and external conditions
facing the economy. South Korea concentrated on
expanding the production and export of labor-intensive,
light industry sectors for a decade up to the early
seventies. At that time, emphasis was placed on heavy
and chemical industries for both import substitution
and export purposes.[3] Because of the economic difficulties arising from the second oil shock, as well as
the domestic political instability during 1979-1980,
the effects of which were significantly aggravated by
overinvestment in some capital-intensive heavy industries, government policy seems to have shifted once
again to a strategy based primarily on export-oriented
industrialization.

EXPORT-ORIENTED INDUSTRIALIZATION
AND GROWTH, 1962-1978

The shift in industrialization strategy from import substitution to export promotion is evidenced by
the growth in South Korean exports. Commodity exports,
which averaged only about U.S. $25 million annually in
the postwar fifties, increased very rapidly in the
1960s and 1970s, particularly after 1962. The expansion of exports in current prices during 1963-1978 was,
on the average, 40 percent a year; in nominal value

TABLE 4.1
Nominal and purchasing power parity (PPP)-
adjusted effective exchange rates, 1958-1979
(won per U.S. dollar)

Year	Nominal Exchange Rate			Wholesale Price Index (1965=100)		PPP-Adjusted Exchange Rate		
	Official Rate	Effective Rate[a] Exports	Imports	South Korea	Major Trade Partners[b]	Official Rate	Effective Rate Exports	Imports
1958	50.0	115.2	64.4	39.9	96.8	121.4	279.6	156.6
1959	50.0	136.0	82.8	40.8	97.5	119.5	324.9	197.9
1960	62.5	147.6	100.2	45.2	98.0	135.6	320.1	217.4
1961	127.5	150.6	147.0	51.2	98.4	244.9	289.3	282.2
1962	130.0	141.7	146.4	56.0	97.7.	226.7	247.1	255.5
1963	130.0	177.5	148.1	67.5	98.4	189.5	258.8	215.9
1964	214.3	263.7	247.0	90.9	98.6	232.5	286.1	268.0
1965	265.4	275.3	293.1	100.0	100.0	265.4	275.3	293.1
1966	271.3	283.8	296.4	108.8	102.8	256.4	268.2	280.4
1967	270.7	290.7	296.2	115.8	103.9	242.8	260.8	265.4
1968	276.6	294.8	302.5	125.2	105.5	233.2	248.5	255.0
1969	288.2	306.6	312.7	133.7	108.7	234.3	249.3	254.5
1970	310.7	331.5	336.4	145.9	112.7	239.9	255.9	260.0
1971	347.7	370.5	369.5	158.5	115.5	253.5	270.1	269.7
1972	391.8	404.3	415.2	180.7	126.8	275.0	283.1	290.2
1973	398.3	407.0	417.7	193.3	155.6	320.6	327.6	332.5
1974	407.0	415.6	425.5	274.7	188.4	279.2	285.1	288.1
1975	485.0	497.9	509.9	347.4	197.0	275.0	282.3	286.6
1976	485.0	493.7	516.6	389.2	207.8	258.9	263.6	275.8
1977	485.0	493.8	520.7	424.3	226.4	258.8	263.5	277.8
1978	485.0	494.5	527.9	474.0	258.9	264.9	270.1	288.3
1979	485.0	496.5	521.0	562.8	285.7	246.2	252.0	264.5

Source: See Westphal and Kim (1977, 1-13) for the period 1958-1975; and
Nam (1981) and Suh (1981) for the later period.

[a] The effective exchange rate for exports includes exchange
premiums resulting from multiple exchange rates, direct cash
subsidies, direct tax reductions, and interest rate subsidies
per dollar of exports, but excludes indirect tax and tariff
exemptions. The effective rate for imports includes actual
tariffs and tariff-equivalent barriers per dollar of imports but
excludes the quantitative restrictions on imports.
[b] An average of the wholesale price indexes of the United States
and Japan (Japanese prices converted into U.S. dollars), weighted
by South Korea's annual trade volume with the respective
countries.

they rose from some U.S. $55 million, or 2 percent of
GNP, in 1962 to about U.S. $12.7 billion, or 28 percent
of GNP, by 1978. During the same period, the real
value of South Korean exports, discounted to account
for the rise in export prices, increased at an average
annual rate of over 30 percent (see Table 4.2).[4]

As shown in Table 4.3, the rapid growth in exports
was accompanied by a substantial change in their composition. In the fifties and early sixties, the greater
part of South Korean exports involved primary products
such as tungsten, iron ore, fish, raw silk, agar-agar,
rice, and coal, while manufactured exports constituted
only a small fraction of the total. By 1978, manufactured goods such as clothing, electrical machinery,
textile yarns and fabrics, transport equipment, iron
and steel products, footwear, and rubber tires and
tubes, which together accounted for some 27 percent of
the nation's exports in 1962, comprised about 90
percent of the total.

Accompanying the structural change in export commodities was a significant diversification in export
markets. As shown in Table 4.4, about 65 percent of
the exports in 1962 were destined to the United States
and Japan. In 1970, the proportion of exports going to
these two countries was as high as 75 percent. By
1978, however, their share declined to about 53
percent, as sales to Europe, the Middle East, and other
areas outside Asia expanded. In particular, exports to
Middle Eastern countries, which had accounted for a
mere 1 percent of total exports in 1970, increased
sharply after the first oil crisis, reaching 11 percent
by 1978. On the other hand, exports to Asian countries
other than Japan declined substantially in relative
terms between 1962 and 1978. The diversification in
export markets can also be measured by the number of
countries to which South Korea exported: to as many as
167 in 1970, as compared with only 33 in 1962.

It is noteworthy that the diversification in
export commodities and markets was largely a consequence of South Korea's own efforts to penetrate lucrative foreign markets. The level of foreign direct
investment and joint venture investment in South Korea
has always been relatively low in comparison with
annual gross investment and annual gross inflow of
foreign capital. Thus, foreign investors have not
played a major role in opening new markets for South
Korean exporters. Rather, it has been the resident
branches of foreign trading companies, particularly the
Japanese "general trading companies," that have played
a significant role in exploring new export markets for
South Korean firms. These companies can more easily
gain access to foreign markets because of their extensive overseas contacts.

TABLE 4.2
Annual growth rate of GNP by industrial origin, 1954-1980[a]
(percent)

| Year | Primary | Industry | | Services | GNP | Commodity Exports |
		Total	Manuf.			
Average 1954- 1962	2.6	11.1	11.5	3.8	3.7	(4.2)
Average 1963- 1970	4.9	19.6	19.2	9.9	9.5	(37.8)
1971	3.6	14.1	18.8	12.6	9.4	(28.3)
1972	1.8	11.0	14.0	6.3	5.8	(43.2)
1973	6.9	28.8	29.2	12.7	14.9	(52.5)
1974	6.7	13.4	15.8	5.7	8.0	(6.6)
1975	5.6	13.0	12.6	6.0	7.1	(20.2)
1976	10.2	20.9	22.6	10.7	15.1	(39.5)
1977	2.6	16.0	14.4	9.7	10.3	(18.1)
1978	-3.5	21.4	20.7	11.0	11.6	(15.1)
1979	6.2	8.7	9.8	6.0	6.4	(-1.8)
1980	-20.7	-0.8	-1.1	-4.2	-6.2	(12.5)
Average 1971- 1978	4.2	17.2	18.4	9.3	10.2	(27.1)
Average 1963- 1978	4.5	18.4	18.8	9.6	9.9	(32.3)
Average 1963- 1980	3.0	16.7	17.1	8.4	8.7	(29.0)

Source: Bank of Korea (1978, 1982); and Bank of Korea (Economic Statistics Yearbook 1980).

[a] Based on 1975 constant price data.

Note: See Table 4.6 for the composition of the primary, industry, and service sectors.

TABLE 4.3
Exports by commodity group and major commodities
(percent of total exports)

SITC Group and Commodities	1954	1962	1978	1980
(0) Food and Live Animals	12.1	39.8	7.3	6.5
Fish and Fish Preparations	2.9	14.8	5.0	3.5
Rice	0.0	16.2	0.2	0.0
Dried Laver (Seaweed)	0.0	1.3	0.0	0.0
(1) Beverages and Tobacco	0.1	0.2	0.9	0.8
(2) Crude Materials except Fuel	82.4	35.4	2.6	1.9
Raw Silk	15.8	7.3	0.5	0.1
Iron, Tungsten Ores and Concentrates	39.5	13.1	0.2	0.1
Agar-Agar	5.7	2.4	0.0	0.1
(3)-(4) Mineral Fuels; Animal and Vegetable Oils and Fats	0.1	5.1	0.4	0.3
(5) Chemicals	0.0	1.8	2.7	4.3
Chemical Elements and Compounds	0.0	0.0	0.8	1.2
Fertilizers, Manufactured	0.0	0.0	1.3	2.0
(6) Manufactured Goods Classified Chiefly by Materials	4.6	11.3	29.8	35.7
Plywood	0.0	4.2	2.7	1.7
Rubber tires and tubes	0.0	0.0	1.6	2.7
Textile Yarns	0.0	0.0	3.8	3.6
Textile Fabrics	0.0	3.3	8.3	9.1
Iron and Steel Products	0.0	0.0	4.5	9.5
(7) Machinery and Transport Equipment	0.3	2.6	20.4	19.8
Electrical Machinery	0.0	n.a.	9.8	10.7
Transport Equipment	0.0	n.a.	8.8	6.6
(8) Miscellaneous Manufactures	0.2	3.6	35.7	30.2
Clothing	0.0	n.a.	20.3	17.0
Footwear	0.0	n.a.	5.4	5.0
Wigs and False Beards	0.0	n.a.	0.5	0.3
(9) Unclassifiable	0.2	0.2	0.2	0.5
Total Exports	100.0	100.0	100.0	100.0
U.S. $ millions	24	55	12,711	17,505

Source: Bank of Korea (Economic Statistics Yearbook, various years); and Bank of Korea (1981).

Note: n.a. = Not available.

TABLE 4.4
Exports by destination
(percent of total exports)

	1954	1962	1970	1978	1980
United States	56.3	21.9	47.3	31.9	26.3
Japan	32.9	42.9	28.1	20.7	17.4
Other Asia	9.6	22.3	8.8	9.1	14.8
Europe	1.1	11.5	9.1	18.3	17.8
Middle East	0.0	0.0	1.0	11.4	14.6
Rest of the					
World	0.1	1.4	5.7	8.6	9.1
Total	100.0	100.0	100.0	100.0	100.0
U.S. $ Mil.	24	55	835	12,711	17,505
Total Number of					
Countries to					
Which South					
Korea Exported	5	33	126	167	163

Source: Bank of Korea (Economic Statistics Yearbook, various years); and Bank of Korea (1981).

During the period of rapid export expansion from 1962 to 1978, the growth rate of commodity imports also accelerated substantially, particularly after 1965. The nominal value of merchandise imports, which was U.S. $389 million in 1962, increased to U.S. $14.5 billion by 1978 (see Table 4.5), an average annual growth rate of about 25 percent. Even when the rising prices of imports are discounted, the volume of imports still registered a 19 percent annual increase. Thus, the ratio of imports to GNP rose from a little over 15 percent to 32 percent during the same period. This significant development can be explained by the following factors. First, the rapid expansion of exports during this period not only increased the amount of financial resources available for imports, but also necessitated a corresponding increase in imports for export production. Second, while the share of imports financed by U.S. foreign assistance rapidly declined, stopping altogether by 1972, other sources of foreign exchange, particularly foreign loans, replaced that aid. Finally, the rapid export-oriented industrialization and growth created an ever-increasing demand for imports, while import liberalization and the improved foreign exchange position made possible the expansion of imports.

TABLE 4.5
Balance of payments: receipts/payments ratio in the current account
(U.S. $ million and percent)

	Trade Balance			Goods and Services Balance		
	Exports	Imports	Exports/Imports	Exports	Imports	Exports/Imports
1954	17	129	13.2	45	132	34.1
1962	55	389	14.1	163	453	36.0
1965	175	420	41.7	290	488	59.4
1970	882	1,804	48.9	1,379	2,181	63.2
1971	1,132	2,190	51.7	1,620	2,639	61.4
1972	1,676	2,250	74.5	2,227	2,768	80.5
1973	3,271	3,837	85.2	4,121	4,620	89.2
1974	4,515	6,452	70.0	5,353	7,598	70.5
1975	5,003	6,674	75.0	5,884	7,997	73.6
1976	7,815	8,405	93.0	9,458	10,120	93.5
1977	10,047	10,523	95.5	13,074	13,284	98.4
1978	12,711	14,491	87.7	17,161	18,717	91.7
1979	14,705	19,100	77.0	19,531	24,121	81.0
1980	17,212	21,972	78.3	22,497	28,638	78.6

Source: Bank of Korea (Economic Statistics Yearbook, various years); and Bank of Korea (1981).

Although commodity imports increased rapidly from 1962 to 1978, they grew less rapidly than exports. As a result, the trade balance improved significantly during the period, despite the adverse impact of the international oil crisis during 1974-1975. As shown in Table 4.5, the ratio of commodity exports to commodity imports, which was 14 percent in 1962, rose almost steadily to about 96 percent by 1977. The exceptional period corresponds to the first oil shock, 1974-1975. Then, in 1978, this ratio declined to 88 percent because of a greater increase in imports than exports that year. In the later half of the seventies, earnings from construction contracts in Middle Eastern countries began to contribute to the improvement in South Korea's balance of payments and trade balance. Reflecting this betterment in the trade balance, South Korea's overall balance of payments steadily improved during the period 1962 to 1978.

As a result of the expansion in exports, real growth in GNP accelerated significantly during the 1962 to 1978 period. It was led by the industrial sector, particularly the manufacturing industries. As shown in Table 4.2, the rate of growth of value added in manufacturing, which had averaged about 12 percent a year during 1954-1962, rose to 19 percent during 1963-1978, while the annual rate of growth of GNP increased from about 4 percent to 10 percent during the two periods. Thus, the share of manufacturing in GNP almost doubled from 14 percent in 1962 to 27 percent by 1978, as shown in Table 4.6. The social overhead and service sectors as a share of GNP remained, however, almost unchanged, at around 40 percent, during the same period.

The above figures indicate that the rapid industrialization and growth in South Korea from 1962 to 1978 depended largely on the expansion of exports. This trend does not imply, however, that import substitution was neglected. It was promoted, but on a very selective basis, until the early seventies; then, beginning in the mid-seventies it was pushed on an expanded scale in connection with the development of heavy and chemical industries.

Finally, with regard to the effects of export-oriented industrialization on income distribution, it should be noted that the distribution of income in South Korea was already fairly equitable even before the takeoff in the mid-1960s. However, it did improve during 1965-1970. Then, between 1970 and 1976, it deteriorated.[5] The relatively equitable income distribution during the earlier years of economic growth can largely be attributed to three historical or initial conditions: (1) the homogeneity of the South Korean population; (2) the land reform movement of the late forties; and (3) the educational background of the

TABLE 4.6
Share of GNP by industrial origin, 1953-1980
(share in percent based on current price data)

	1953	1962	1978	1980
Primary, Total	47.8	38.6	23.3	17.7
Agriculture, Forestry, and Fisheries	46.7	36.6	21.9	16.3
Mining and Quarrying	1.1	2.0	1.4	1.4
Industry, Total	11.5	18.8	36.6	40.4
Manufacturing	8.9	14.3	27.0	28.8
Construction	2.2	3.2	8.3	9.4
Utilities	0.4	1.3	1.3	2.2
Services, Total	39.5	41.7	40.6	45.0
Transportation, Storage, and Communications	1.6	4.8	6.1	6.3
Wholesale and Retail Trade	15.0	14.9	17.1	18.0
Banking, Insurance, and Real Estate	0.9	1.9	3.9	4.8
Ownership of Dwellings	12.6	5.2	2.5	3.0
Public Administration and Defense	5.8	7.4	4.3	4.9
Other Services	3.6	7.5	6.7	8.0
Rest of the World	1.2	0.9	-0.5	-3.1
Gross National Product	100.0	100.0	100.0	100.0
Memo Item: Social Overhead (Utilities plus Transportation)	2.0	6.1	7.4	8.5

Source: Bank of Korea (1978, 1982).

population (Kim and Roemer 1979, 163-94). Export-oriented industrialization was very important with respect to income distribution in the sense that it led to the rapid growth in urban employment and the rise in real wages. The change in the terms of trade between the agriculture and the urban sectors also helped improve income distribution.

In later years, a number of factors seem to have contributed to the deterioration in income distribution: (1) an increasing concentration in business; (2) widening wage differentials between workers according to educational level; (3) the government agricultural subsidy program, which benefited large producers more than small-scale farmers; and (4) the relative decline in the percentage of farm households, whose incomes tended to be more equitably distributed than those of urban households (Choo 1980; Kim 1980, 174-77).

RECENT ECONOMIC DIFFICULTIES AND THEIR CAUSES

After having achieved success through export-oriented industrialization for nearly two decades, South Korea encountered severe economic difficulties in the 1979-1981 period. Economic activity actually began to slow in early 1979. Commodity exports, which previously had been the fastest growing area in the economy, decelerated, while the costs of imports increased in the wake of the sharp rise in the world price of crude oil. The volume of exports in 1979, discounted for the increase in export prices, actually declined by a small margin for the first time since the early sixties. The growth rate of GNP also slowed substantially, from about 12 percent in the previous year to 6.4 percent.

The situation was further aggravated in 1980. Although exports of commodities increased by nearly 10 percent in real terms after the devaluation of the Korean won in January 1980, real GNP declined sharply by 6 percent in 1979-1980, the largest negative figure since the end of the Korean War. This decline in economic activity led to a rise in the unemployment rate from 3.8 percent in 1979 to nearly 5 percent in 1980. In addition, price inflation, when measured in terms of the national wholesale price index, accelerated from an average annual rate of 10 percent during 1976-1978 to approximately 39 percent during 1979-1980 (Table 4.7).

What were the causes of this sudden economic recession and inflationary explosion? It may be argued that external factors were the major cause: the external conditions facing South Korea became quite unfavorable during 1979-1980 because of the second oil

TABLE 4.7
Annual changes in the wholesale price index,
import price index, money supply, and real GNP
(percent)

Period	Wholesale Price Index All Commodities	Food	Nonfood	Import Price Index[a]	Money Supply	GNP (1975 Prices)
1955-1957	24.0	35.3	19.8	n.a.	24.2	3.0
1957-1960	1.9	-4.9	4.7	-5.8	16.1	3.4
1960-1964	19.1	26.1	15.0	1.4	21.1	6.6
1964-1973	8.7	9.9	8.4	3.6	35.0	9.7
1973-1976	26.3	28.9	25.0	16.2	28.3	10.0
1976-1978	10.3	19.9	6.1	3.9	32.6	10.9
1978-1980	38.9	27.7	44.4	26.9	16.3	-6.2
1955-1962	10.5	11.3	10.1	-3.7[b]	22.7	3.4
1962-1980	15.8	17.8	14.8	7.9	28.9	8.7

Source: Bank of Korea (Economic Statistics Yearbook, various
years); and Bank of Korea (1982).

[a] Based on the wholesale price index for imported goods for 1957-
1962 and the import unit value index for the later periods.
[b] Average annual rate of increase for 1957-1962.

Note: n.a. = Not available.

crisis and the subsequent recession in the western industrialized countries. In view of the uninterrupted rapid growth observed in other Asian countries, however, it must be accepted that domestic factors were also responsible.[6] The most important ones are summarized below.

First, the political upheaval after the assassination of President Park Chung Hee further dampened domestic economic activities, which had already begun to slow because of the unfavorable external factors. The implication is that the rate of economic growth, particularly of the nonagricultural sectors, would not have declined so sharply had there not been such political uncertainty and social confusion during the period October 1979 to about mid-1980.

Second, agricultural output, particularly rice, declined sharply in 1980 (by 24 percent) because of an unusually cool summer that year.

Third, South Korea had been relying on a strategy of growth maximization through industrialization for nearly two decades. Even during the first oil shock of 1974-1975, it did not pursue a serious retrenchment policy. Instead, it surmounted the economic difficulties arising from the quadrupling of the world oil price by simply increasing foreign borrowing and allowing the rate of domestic inflation to rise. Thus the country was able to attain a relatively high rate of growth during this period, whereas many foreign countries, particularly industrialized ones, registered sharp reductions in their economic growth rates.

As the world economy began its rapid recovery from the recession of 1974-1975, South Korea was able to accelerate its GNP growth by following an expansionist policy. However, domestic inflationary pressure continued to build in the course of this rapid growth. When the higher world oil price began to affect the economy in early 1979, South Korea had no choice but to initiate a strong economic stabilization program, in view of the rapid increases in both domestic prices and the balance of payments deficits. The sudden shift in policy from growth maximization to economic stabilization did not immediately reduce the rate of inflation, but rather resulted in the disruption of many ambitious investment activities and a reduction in the overall economic growth rate.

Fourth, the government's overambitious promotion of heavy and chemical industries since the mid-seventies resulted in resource misallocation. These industries were promoted with two main objectives in mind: (1) diversification of South Korea's exports into capital-intensive products, and (2) the development of the country's defense industries. The first objective was justified in view of the growing protectionism in advanced industrialized countries against labor-intensive goods and the rapidly increasing wage/-rental ratio in South Korea.[7] The announced government policy was intended to promote selected skill- and labor-intensive heavy and chemical industries in which South Korea might develop a comparative advantage. However, in effect it encouraged business investment in primarily capital-intensive industries because of the factor price distortion and its promotion efforts. In any case, increased investment in heavy and chemical industries resulted in a sharp decline in the capital utilization in those industries, while investment in light industries was neglected in relative terms. When the economy began to slow in 1979, the overinvestment in capital-intensive industries became an additional heavy burden, as those industries could not operate without government assistance.

Finally, the government did not make the necessary policy adjustments in 1979 because political considerations were the overwhelming concern of policy-makers that year. Devaluation of the won was called for in early 1979 to maintain the international competitiveness of South Korea's industries. Devaluation was needed because the rate of inflation had been much higher than that of South Korea's major trading partners since 1974 (when the last devaluation was made). Nevertheless, the government delayed acting until early 1980, a delay that was at least partly responsible for the slowdown in the volume of South Korean exports and the sharp increase in the balance of payment deficits during 1979 and the first half of 1980.

PROSPECTS AND LESSONS

The economic situation in South Korea has been improving gradually since the fourth quarter of 1980, with the restoration of domestic political stability and improvement in external conditions. The difficulties that South Korea encountered during the 1979-1981 period had been largely overcome by the middle of 1984. The government's continuous effort to stabilize prices since early 1979 had brought that stability by early 1983. The rate of inflation, measured in terms of the national wholesale price index, which had been as high as 39 percent in 1980, declined to 0.2 percent by 1983. On the other hand, real GNP, which had fallen sharply in 1980, grew by around 6 percent in both 1981 and 1982, and by a high 9 percent in 1983. Because commodity exports increased continuously, surpassing the expansion in imports, South Korea's trade deficits declined gradually from U.S. $4.4 billion in both 1979 and 1980 to U.S. $1.7 billion in 1983. The current balance of goods and services also improved, dropping from the highest deficit of U.S. $5.3 billion in 1980 to U.S. $1.6 billion in 1983. Although the current account balance is expected to improve further in 1984, a major policy objective of the government is to reduce still further the balance of payments deficit through a restrictive policy of demand management. It seems that the large amount of outstanding foreign debt, which exceeded U.S. $40 billion by the end of 1983, is an effective constraint on South Korean policy-makers, who tend to prefer a more ambitious growth strategy for the country.

The Fifth Five-Year Economic and Social Development Plan of South Korea was implemented beginning in 1982. It forecasts that the nation's real GNP will increase by an average annual rate of 7.6 percent during the 1982-1986 period, while the inflation rate will level off at about 10 percent. This growth rate is much lower than that achieved during the sixties and seventies because the policy emphasizes stability during the Fifth Plan period. The Plan target also reflects a conservative view of the world economy, including the uncertain prospects for world trade and oil markets. Even if the possibility of another oil shock in the next five years is excluded, it is expected that attainment of the growth target of the Fifth Plan will largely depend on the performances of the economies of advanced industrial countries, the major markets for South Korean exports. In addition, South Korea will have to take or continue some specific policy options if it is to sustain reasonably high growth in the future. They are listed below.

First, priority is being given to reducing the balance of payments deficits on the current account, which have caused a substantial increase in outstanding foreign debt in recent years (1979-1981). Accordingly, the export-oriented industrialization policy should be intensified, but not by increasing government assistance as in the past, rather by enhancing industrial productivity through increased competition in domestic markets.

Second, because the labor force is projected to grow at an average annual rate of nearly 3 percent during the 1980s, skilled labor-intensive industries should be promoted, while investment in primarily capital-intensive industries should be discouraged. This policy means that the heavy and chemical industries to be promoted should be selected carefully in light of South Korea's factor endowment, so that mistakes are not repeated.

Third, the attainment of price stability is as crucial as that of economic growth in the future, although the rate of inflation has declined substantially since 1980. South Korea has experienced chronic inflation since the mid-forties. Now the country has reached a stage where high economic growth cannot be achieved without price stability. Future growth will depend on improving the competitiveness of domestic industries in international markets and on increases in voluntary domestic savings, both of which cannot be accomplished without price stability. As such, it has been and must continue to be a priority.

Fourth, in view of the increasing public demand for improvement in social welfare, some retreat from the past policy of growth maximization will be required in order to allocate more resources to social welfare. To attain high growth and at the same time enlarge the government's role in the area of welfare, it will be desirable to reduce substantially the government's direct intervention in the industrial sector.

Fifth, it will be important to appraise carefully all future investment in energy and natural resource-intensive industries, not only because the smooth supply of such resources is uncertain in the future, but also because the country is not expected to have a comparative advantage in those industries.

A question must be asked in conclusion: what can be learned from South Korea's experience of successful industrialization in the sixties and seventies and from its recent economic difficulties? Many developing countries may wonder whether their exports will increase as did South Korea's, if they adopt a similar system of export incentives.

The answer to this question is mixed. Although such a system is important in the sense that it provides a general guideline for export promotion, continuous growth in exports requires a steady expansion of domestic production that is internationally competitive. The expansion of efficient domestic industries in turn requires both ambitious entrepreneurs and a reasonably well-educated labor force that is willing to work hard if proper incentives are given. Close collaboration between the government and the private sector is also essential, particularly in the early stage of export-oriented industrialization.

Additional lessons are as follows.

First, high economic growth cannot be sustained for long periods if price stability is not achieved (or if the rate of inflation is not reduced substantially). After nearly two decades of successful export-oriented industrialization, it became increasingly difficult for South Korea to maintain its industrial competitiveness because of accelerated inflation. In addition, the chronic inflation led to structural distortions in the economy that further impeded growth.

Second, direct government intervention in business decision-making is not always effective, since it often, as an economy becomes more complex, gives rise to economic inefficiency through resource misallocation. A good example is the failure of certain heavy and chemical industries in South Korea, despite their strong promotion by the government. Thus, it is important to reduce the role of government in the allocation of investable resources as an economy becomes more developed.

Third, the prices of the primary factors of production (capital and labor) should reflect their relative scarcity in the economy. The August 3rd Measure of 1972, a turning point in South Korea's interest rate policy, gave the wrong signals to the business sector, effectively encouraging investment in capital-intensive industries.

Fourth, as an economy becomes more open, it cannot afford to maintain an overvalued exchange rate for any length of time. An example of what can happen when this rule is not followed occurred in 1979, the year in which South Korean exports declined for the first time since the early sixties.

Finally, economic growth and stability cannot be attained without political stability. This fact became quite clear in South Korea during the 1979-1980 period.

NOTES

1. This export-import link system was adopted in 1963 to limit the volume of imports not directly linked to foreign aid relative to export earnings. This system created a market premium on foreign exchange earned through exports that could be used to import necessary commodities.

2. As a result of this measure, nearly 450 trading firms (out of a total of about 3,000) maintained one or more foreign branches in 1977, while 12 large firms had more than 10 overseas branches.

3. "Heavy and chemical industries" include those such as chemical and petroleum products, rubber products (tires and tubes), nonmetallic mineral products, basic metals, primary metal products, machinery, and transport equipment.

4. The direct import content of the exports was negligible until 1963, but then increased rapidly to about 48 percent by 1969. Thereafter, the import content gradually declined, reaching about 26 percent

in 1978. The annual growth rate of net exports was thus not much different from that of gross exports for 1962-1978. See Economic Planning Board (1982, 219-27).

5. The Gini coefficient for all households in South Korea, which had been at 0.34 in 1965, declined slightly to 0.33 in 1970 but increased to 0.38 by 1976. Between 1965 and 1970, the Gini coefficient for urban households declined significantly from 0.42 to 0.35, while remaining unchanged at 0.29 for farm households. See Choo (1980).

6. The GNP growth rates in 1980 in selected Asian countries were as follows: 4.2 percent in Japan, 6.7 percent in Taiwan, 10.2 percent in Singapore, 6.3 percent in Thailand, and 4.7 percent in the Philippines. See International Monetary Fund (1981); and Republic of China (1981).

7. The wage/rental ratio had gradually been increasing even before the August 3rd Measure of 1972, which drastically reduced interest rates on bank deposits and loans. After 1972, the wage/rental ratio increased very sharply compared with the level in the latter half of the 1960s because the real interest rate on bank loans declined to a negative level, while the rapid increase in demand for experienced workers pushed real wages up. For data on the wage/rental ratio for 1955-1975, see Kim and Roemer (1979, 73).

REFERENCES

Bank of Korea. Various years. Economic Statistics Yearbook. Seoul: Bank of Korea.
──────────. 1978. National Income in Korea. Seoul: Bank of Korea.
──────────. 1981. Monthly Economic Statistics. Seoul: Bank of Korea, July.
──────────. 1982. Monthly Economic Statistics. Seoul: Bank of Korea, January.
Choo, Hakchung. 1980. "Economic Growth and Income Distribution." In Human Resources and Social Development in Korea, edited by Chong Kee Park. Seoul: Korea Development Institute Press.
Economic Planning Board. 1982. Major Statistics of Korean Economy. Seoul: Ministry of Planning.
International Monetary Fund. 1981. International Financial Statistics. Washington, D.C.: International Monetary Fund, July.
Kim, Kwang Suk. 1975. "Outward-Looking Industrialization Strategy: The Case of Korea." In Trade and

Development in Korea, edited by Wontack Hong and
Anne O. Krueger. Seoul: Korea Development Insti-
tute Press.
——————. 1980. The Pattern and Sources of Korea's
Industrialization. Seoul: Korea Development Insti-
tute Press, 1980. In Korean.
Kim, Kwang Suk, and Michael Roemer. 1979. Growth and
Structural Transformation, The Republic of Korea,
1945-1975. Cambridge, Mass.: Harvard University,
Council on East Asian Studies.
Nam, Chong Hyon. 1981. Industrial Incentive Policy
and the Structure of Protection by Industry in
Korea. Seoul: Korea Development Institute, 1981.
In Korean.
Republic of China. Council for Economic Planning and
Development. 1981. Industry of Free China. Tai-
pei, July.
Suh, Suk Tai. 1981. "The Effect of Export Incentives
on Korean Export Growth." Korea Development Insti-
tute Working Paper 8107. Korea Development Insti-
tute, Seoul.
Westphal, Larry E., and Kwang Suk Kim. 1977. Indus-
trial Policy and Development in Korea. World Bank
Staff Working Paper No. 263. Washington, D.C.:
World Bank.

5
Rapid Growth and Relative Price Stability in a Small Open Economy: The Experience of Singapore

Pang Eng Fong
Linda Lim

INTRODUCTION

Almost thirty years ago, when Great Britain granted its crown colony of Singapore self-government, virtually everybody, including the leaders of the political party voted into power, regarded the island's new political status as temporary. Historically, Singapore had served as the port and administrative headquarters for British Malaya, and the political assumption in both Singapore and Malaya (which had gained independence in 1957) was that the island could not survive independently and would eventually have to merge with its traditional hinterland. In 1963, after protracted negotiations with Malaya over the terms of the merger, Singapore finally joined it and two British territories, Sabah and Sarawak, to form the Federation of Malaysia.

The experiment failed--Singapore's leaders could not resolve their differences with the federal government.[1] In August 1965, less than two years after the union, Singapore separated from Malaysia and became an independent republic. Since then, it has made remarkable economic progress and proved that it is not too small to thrive as an independent city-state. Rapid growth averaging over 9 percent since independence has transformed its economy, once centered around entrepôt and military services, into a diversified one based on manufacturing for world markets and traded services. Today, Singapore enjoys full employment, a high rate of savings, a healthy and growing surplus in its balance of payments, a strong currency, and an inflation rate far below that of most countries.

This paper analyzes the internal and external factors that have contributed to Singapore's impressive economic performance. It highlights the role of the government and the liberal economic policies in accelerating noninflationary growth. It also discusses whether there are lessons to be learned from Singapore's experience as a small, open, and vulnerable economy.

ECONOMIC DEVELOPMENT BEFORE 1960

When Stamford Raffles founded Singapore as a trading post in 1819 in an era of competitive colonialism, he envisaged the island as a bastion of free trade in a region dominated by protected Dutch ports. He believed that as a free port Singapore's excellent location and deep harbor would make it the commercial emporium of the eastern seas. He was right, as his laissez-faire policies quickly transformed the island into the region's premier entrepôt.[2]

Throughout the nineteenth and twentieth centuries, Singapore's free port status and dedication to uninhibited free enterprise were maintained by successive colonial administrations. Colonial governors kept taxes low and allowed Asian and European traders, merchants, and bankers freedom to pursue profits. As a result, Singapore prospered as a competitive and efficient economic center linking its resource-rich hinterland to the world. Trade and supporting banking, insurance, and shipping services provided Singapore's urbanized, ethnically mixed immigrant population with a standard of living much higher than that enjoyed in its mainland agrarian areas.

But Singapore's high level of dependence on trade created a lopsided economy. During the colonial period, the island developed no large-scale manufacturing activities oriented to world markets, while the domestic market was too small to foster efficient domestic manufacturing. As far back as 1933, the colonial government had decided against tariff protection as a way to encourage export-oriented local manufacturing.[3] The only positive step it took to attract investment was the establishment of the Singapore Industrial Promotion Board in 1957. Operating with a revolving fund of only Singapore (S) $1 million, the Board promoted new industrial undertakings. However, it was hampered by a lack of funds and personnel and achieved little. Consequently, before 1960 Singapore had only a small manufacturing sector that produced mostly simple consumer goods for the domestic market.

DEVELOPMENT FROM 1960 TO 1980

On achieving self-government in 1959, the island's colonial legacy was mixed. On the one hand, laissez-faire colonialism had made Singapore an efficient en-

trepôt and exposed its people to foreign goods and
ideas. It had also given the island an English-
speaking civil administration that provided law and
order but did not closely regulate private business.
On the other hand, laissez-faire colonialism had neglected the social needs of an increasingly settled
population. It had not tackled the stagnating, uni-
dimensional economy, rapid population growth, high and
rising unemployment, and poor housing conditions.

When the People's Action Party (PAP) under the
leadership of Lee Kuan Yew was voted into power in
1959, it quickly embarked on a program of mass public
housing and a vigorous campaign on family planning. It
also expanded expenditures on education and instituted
industrial development policies to diversify the trade-
and service-oriented economy. These policies had barely gotten off the ground when Singapore separated from
the Federation of Malaysia in 1965. Tangible economic
achievements during the period 1960 to 1965 were
modest, partly because of a confrontation with Indonesia, which halted official Singapore-Indonesia trade,
and partly because of continuing political uncertainty
and labor unrest. Singapore's economic vulnerability
as a city-state with no natural resources was increased
by the phased withdrawal in 1968 of British military
forces, whose spending had generated a quarter of the
island's gross domestic product (GDP).

Fortunately, government policies and world economic conditions intervened to produce one of the most
spectacularly successful economic performances of any
country. Spurred by a boom in world trade, increased
demand for its services and goods arising from the war
in Vietnam, oil exploration in the region, and a strong
takeoff into manufacturing for exports led by multinational corporations—all occurring simultaneously in
the second half of the 1960s—gross national product
(GNP) averaged an annual rate of growth of 9.9 percent
from 1960-1969, while real GDP grew at 8.7 percent a
year (Table 5.1).

In the 1970s, the rapid rate of growth accelerated, with an annual average rate of increase in GNP
of 14.8 percent, or 9.4 percent of real GDP, despite
the slowdown in the world economy, the fourfold
increase in oil prices in 1973, the world recession in
1974 and 1975, and protectionist restrictions in the
leading industrialized countries against Singapore's
manufactured exports.

On the demand side, economic growth has derived
mainly from the export of goods and services, which
accounted for 62 percent of overall growth between 1965
and 1969 and 63 percent in the 1970s. Domestic exports
were concentrated in labor-intensive manufactures and

82

TABLE 5.1
Singapore: Basic economic data and performance indicators[a]

	1960[b]	1970[b]	1980	1981	1982	1983[c]
Land Area (sq km)	581.5	586.4	617.8	617.9	618.1	618.1
Population at Mid-Year (mil.)	1.65	2.07	2.41	2.44	2.47	2.5
Annual Change (%)	2.4	1.5	1.2	1.2	1.2	1.2
Labor Force (mil.)	0.48	0.69	1.1	1.15	1.17	1.21
Employed (mil.)	0.45	0.64	1.07	1.11	1.14	1.17
Unemployment Rate (%)	4.9[d]	6.0	3.0	2.9	2.6	3.2
Gross National Product (GNP) at Current Market Prices						
S $ mil.	2,189.0	5,861.1	23,312.9	27,372.1	31,046.5	34,485.9
Annual Change (%)	9.9	14.8	14.4	17.8	12.1	11.1
Per Capita GNP (S $)	1,329.6	2,825.3	9,657.8	11,202.9	12,560.3	13,783.3
Indigenous GNP (S $ mil.)	n.a.	4,989.9	17,921.7	22,531.6	24,972.2	27,600.2
Per Capita Indigenous GNP S $	n.a.	2,405.4	7,424.4	9,221.8	10,102.8	11,031.3
Annual Change (%)	n.a.	11.5	15.8	18.7	9.6	9.2
Real per Capita Indigenous GNP, Annual Change (%)	n.a.	5.9	7.3	10.5	5.7	8.0
Gross Domestic Product (GDP) at 1968 Factor Costs, Annual Change (%)	8.7	9.4	10.2	9.9	6.3	7.9
Inflation: Annual Change (%)						
Consumer Price Index	1.2	5.6	8.5	8.2	3.9	1.2
GDP Deflator	1.0	5.3	7.4	6.4	4.4	1.4

Gross Domestic Fixed Capital
Formation (GDFCF) at 1968
Prices:

Annual Change (%)	21.7	11.3	20.1	15.8	23.3	7.7
As % of GDP	9.4	32.2	41.0	43.8	47.7	48.2
Gross National Savings						
As % of GNP	n.a.	19.3	32.8	35.9	37.5	40.1
As % of GDFCF	n.a.	59.8	79.9	81.9	78.7	83.3
Index of Industrial Production (1978=100)	n.a.	43.0	129.2	141.8	134.0	136.8
Money Supply (M1)(S $ mil.)	n.a.	1,574.3	6,134.7	7,242.1	8,156.8	8,607.7
Total Trade						
S $ mil.	7,554.8	12,289.6	92,797.1	102,538.8	104,717.4	105,659.1
Annual Change (%)	4.2	20.2	34.0	10.5	2.1	0.9
Balance of Payments						
Current Account Balance (S $ mil.)	-244.7	-1,750.8	-3,349.3	-2,920.5	-2,781.8	-2,019.9
Overall Balance (S $ mil.)	140.1	564.8	1,433.8	1,938.4	2,517.5	2,237.7
Official Foreign Reserves						
Total at End of Year (S $ mil.)	n.a.	3,097.9	13,757.7	15,491.1	17,917.9	19,755.3
Ratio to Merchandise Imports (mos.)	n.a.	4.9	3.2	3.2	3.6	4.0

Source: Singapore, Ministry of Trade and Industry (1983 and 1984); and Singapore, Department of Statistics (1981b, 1983).

a S $1 = U.S. $.33 in 1960 and 1970; and U.S. $0.50 in 1980-1983, approximately.
b Annual changes refer to averages for the decades 1960-1969 and 1970-1979, respectively.
c Preliminary.
d 1957 figures is from Census of Population, 1957.

Note: n.a. = Not available.

traded services, mainly transport and communications, and in financial and business services. Capital investment contributed an average of 18 percent to growth in the 1960s, as the physical infrastructure for industrialization was being built up. This contribution declined to 11 percent in the 1970s, a trend that reflected a drop in private sector investment from 1975 to 1977. Much of this investment was financed by foreign capital, but the proportion of domestic investment financed by gross national savings rose from an average of 56 percent in the 1960s to 65 percent in the 1970s and 71 percent in 1980. Savings rose from an average of 11 percent of GNP in the 1960s to 25 percent in the 1970s and 28 percent in 1980 (Singapore, Ministry of Trade and Industry, 1980, 61).

On the supply side, growth has been the result of increased factor inputs and gains in productivity. The expansion of the labor force has been responsible for 43 percent of Singapore's output growth since 1960, with the other 57 percent attributable to capital deepening, economies of scale, technical changes, qualitative improvements in the labor force, and other factors. From 1966 to 1974, the main sources of output growth were gains in productivity and capital accumulation, whereas from 1975 the contribution of these factors declined, while that of labor force expansion increased, accounting for 71 percent of the output growth in 1979 (Fong, 1981a). Labor productivity, measured by real value-added per worker, averaged 7.9 percent growth annually between 1966 and 1970 and 5 percent between 1970 and 1973, when the manufacturing sector was expanding. It then slackened to an annual growth rate of 3.2 percent from 1974 to 1979, caused by the recession and subsequent recovery and expansion of labor-intensive industries. Since then, labor shortages and a government policy of high wages raised productivity growth from 2.6 percent in 1979 to 5 percent in 1980 and 1981 (Singapore, Ministry of Trade and Industry, 1980, 1981, 1982 second quarter).

Economic growth was achieved with relative price stability in the 1960s, when the GDP deflator and consumer price index registered average annual increases of around 1 percent. In the 1970s, world inflation and the oil crisis added to the pressures on domestic demand in this extremely open economy, causing the consumer price index to rise by 5.6 percent a year and the GDP deflator by 4.9 percent a year (Table 5.1). However, domestic inflation rates were lower after 1975 than in the early 1970s.

With economic growth came structural change: a diversification from trade and services into manufacturing in the 1960s, and a further diversification into transport and communications, and financial and business services, in the 1970s (Table 5.2), a shift that cushioned the economy from the deceleration in the trade and manufacturing sectors in the mid-1970s.

Since 1960, trade has been the largest sector of the economy in terms of output (although it dropped from 31 percent of GDP in 1960 to 24 percent in 1980), and the second largest in terms of employment (although dropping from 28 percent of all employment in 1957 to 21 percent in 1980). In 1960, other services (then including the British military) ranked second in terms of output and first in terms of employment (in 1957), but they fell to fifth and fourth places, respectively, by 1980. In 1960, manufacturing ranked fourth in terms of contribution to output (13 percent), but by 1970 accounted for 20 percent and by 1980 for 24 percent, second only to trade. It also went from the third largest employer in the economy in 1957 and 1970 (14 percent and 22 percent of total employment, respectively) to the largest employer by 1980, accounting for 30 percent of the total.

Within the manufacturing sector itself, there has been a change in the composition of industrial production (Table 5.3). While in 1960 nearly 90 percent of all manufacturing was for the domestic market, and food and printing were the largest industries, by 1970 60 percent of the manufacturing output was exported, and petroleum, transport equipment, and electrical machinery were the dominant industries. By 1980, when nearly two-thirds of all manufacturing output was exported and manufactures accounted for 90 percent of total domestic exports (Table 5.4), these three industries together accounted for 65 percent of all manufacturing value added.

Despite the increasing contribution of manufacturing to domestic output and especially to employment, Singapore remains a largely trade- as well as services-oriented economy. In 1980, the transport and communications sector reached 18 percent of GDP and 11 percent of employment, while the financial and business services sector more than doubled its contribution to GDP, going from 7 percent in 1960 to 17 percent in 1980, when it also accounted for 7 percent of total employment. These two sectors were the fastest and third fastest growing ones in the economy in the 1970s, with manufacturing in second place.

Throughout the 1960s and 1970s, Singapore's overall balance of payments was in surplus: the figure for 1980 was S $1,435.8 million, ten times the level in 1960. During this period, the current account deficit widened, a reflection of the country's dependence on imports for all its consumption and industrial requirements, and the effect of oil and other commodity price increases. Larger imports of intermediate and capital

TABLE 5.2
Economic structure: Gross domestic product (at 1968 market prices) and employment by industrial sector (percentages)

	GDP			Employment		
	1960	1970	1980	1957	1970	1980
Agriculture and Fishing	3.8	2.3	1.2	6.9	3.5	1.6
Quarrying	0.3	0.4	0.4	0.3	0.3	0.1
Manufacturing	12.8	20.5	24.1	14.3	22.0	30.1
Utilities	2.3	2.6	2.9	0.9	1.2	0.8
Construction	3.5	6.3	4.8	5.2	6.6	6.7
Trade	31.2	28.1	24.4	27.8	23.4	21.3
Transport and Communications	13.3	11.3	17.8	10.7	12.1	11.1
Financial and Business Services	7.1	13.9	16.6	4.3	4.0	7.4
Other Services	17.7	13.6	11.1	29.1	26.8	10.9
Total	100.0	100.0	100.0	100.0	100.0	100.0
GDP at 1968 Prices (S $ mil.)	2,304.5	5,579.3	13,349.9			
Total Employment (persons)				471,918	650,892	1,077,090

Source: Singapore, Department of Statistics (1973, 1975, 1981a, 1981b).

TABLE 5.3
Singapore: Percentage distribution of
manufacturing value added by industry

	1960	1970	1980
Food	31	12	5
Printing	17	a	4[b]
Metals	8	7	2
Wood	7	6	2
Transport Equipment	6	15	14
Electrical and Electronics	6	12	30
Petroleum	a	19	21
Chemicals	a	a	5
Other	25	29	17
Total	100	100	100

Source: Singapore, Ministry of Trade and
Industry (1980, 64; 1981, 83).

[a] Included in "Other" category.
[b] Includes paper products.

goods were also needed for the accelerated industrialization program--they accounted for over 84 percent of
total retained imports in the 1970s, compared with 66
percent in the 1960s.

The current account deficits were covered by increased net service earnings from the expansion of
transport and tourism, which averaged S $2,844 million
annually in the 1970s, compared with S $580 million
annually in the 1960s, and by net inflows of foreign
capital from long-term foreign investments and Singapore's growth as a financial center. Net capital inflows in the 1970s totaled S $14.3 billion, compared
with nearly S $1 billion in the 1960s (Singapore, Min-
istry of Trade and Industry, 1980, 63). Because of the
healthy balance of payments surplus and accumulation of
foreign reserves, the Singapore dollar appreciated
throughout the 1970s against most major currencies.

Employment performance was also good, both because
of the rapid, labor-intensive economic growth and because of a decline in population growth, which dropped
from 4.4 percent in 1957 to 2.4 percent a year in the
1960s, 1.5 percent a year in the 1970s, and 1.2 percent
in 1980. Thus, total population grew by less than half
between 1960 and 1980. Of that increase, 11 percent
was foreigners. From a state of high unemployment in
the late 1950s, Singapore reached full employment in
the early 1970s. During the 1974-1975 recession, unem-

TABLE 5.4
Summary statistics on trade and manufacturing

	1960[a]	1970[a]	1980
Index of Industrial Production (1978=100)	n.a.	43.0	128.8
Annual Change (%)	n.a.	12.1	11.9
Manufacturing Output as a % of GDP at 1968 Prices	12.8	20.5	24.1
Manufacturing Employment as a % of Total Employment	14.3[b]	22.0	30.1
Manufactured Direct Exports as a % of Manufacturing Output	11.9	59.5	65.6
Manufactured Direct Exports as a % of Domestic Exports	75.5	83.1	90.3
Trade/GDP	3.45	2.10	4.18
Annual Change in Total Trade (%)	4.2	20.2	34.0
Annual Change in Domestic Exports (%)	25.5	26.9	41.8
Balance of Payments Current Account Balance (S $ mil.)	-244.7	-1,750.8	-3,378.2
Overall Balance (S $ mil.)	140.1	564.8	1,435.8

Source: Singapore, Ministry of Trade and Industry (1983 and 1984); and Singapore, Department of Statistics (1981b and 1983).

[a] Annual changes refer to averages for the decades 1960-1969 and 1970-1979, respectively.
[b] The 1957 figure is from Census of Population, 1957.

ployment rose marginally, then fell again with the economic recovery. Since the late 1970s, the labor market has tightened, despite the second world recession in the early 1980s.

Given the high rates of growth in output and employment, relative price stability, and slow population growth, living standards improved greatly in the last two decades. Per capita GNP was seven times greater in 1980 than in 1960. Per capita indigenous GNP tripled between 1970 and 1980, registering an average annual rate of growth of 5.9 percent in real terms during the 1970s (Table 5.1). Unlike many other fast-expanding

developing countries, the rapid growth in Singapore has
not been accompanied by widening income disparities.
In fact, the distribution of income improved slightly
between the mid-1960s and the mid-1970s: according to
several studies, the Gini coefficient, a commonly used
measure of income equality, has fallen slightly since
1966 (Fong 1975; Rao and Ramakrishnan 1977; Singapore,
Department of Statistics 1979).

ECONOMIC LIBERALISM

     In general, the Singapore government has sub-
scribed to a philosophy of economic liberalism, with
some state controls, especially in the service sector. Given the openness of the economy, market forces,
especially world market forces, are the dominant influence on resource allocation, especially in the large
external sector. Since Singapore is a free port, there
are few import tariffs, which are mostly to raise revenue and to curb consumption of certain luxury items,
such as alcohol, tobacco, and motor vehicles. Protective tariffs on local industry have been gradually
removed, although they still apply--at a low level--to
a few items, such as chocolates and garments. There
are domestic price controls on only a few items,
including sugar and cement.
     In the manufacturing sector, apart from minor
health, safety, and pollution regulations, and regulations on the employment of labor and industrial relations, there are virtually no controls on private enterprise and investment. There are no antimonopoly
laws, no approval or licensing processes for foreign or
local private investment, no technology transfer controls or required registration of contracts or licenses, no import controls establishing required levels
of domestic value added, no controls on transfer
pricing, and no limitations on profit remittances,
technology payments, or repatriation of capital
overseas. Nevertheless, the government does influence
the allocation of resources through various investment
incentive schemes that involve tax exemptions, write-
offs, and other subsidies and allowances for desired
investment. Some industries also benefit from the
external protection offered to manufactured exports by
the Generalised System of Preferences (GSP) and the
Multi-Fibre Arrangement (MFA).
     Since the late 1960s, the financial sector has
been increasingly liberalized to make Singapore an
international financial center (Fong and Fang 1981; Lee
1981). The Asian Dollar Market was set up in Singapore
in 1968, and since then numerous incentives have been
offered to stimulate offshore banking and to attract

international banks. Various taxes and duties on
financial transactions and income have been abolished
or reduced, banks have been free to set their own
interest rates since 1975, and there have been no
foreign exchange controls since 1978.

Other traded services are more heavily regulated
than manufacturing and banking (for details, see Seow
1981). In general, while there is a free flow of services, investment in services, especially retail and
shipping ones, is subject to some restrictions. It is
difficult to assess whether these restrictions--for
example, those imposed by local professional associa-
tions--are necessary for reasons of safety, quality
control, security, and other noneconomic considerations, or are intended to protect local service
enterprises. In any case, recent government policy has
decreed progressive liberalization of traded services,
particularly business, professional, and engineering
ones; and foreign lawyers, bankers, doctors, archi-
tects, engineers, and other professionals are to be
allowed to practice in Singapore more easily than in
the past.

International labor flows are subject to more
regulation on a cyclical and sectoral basis, but these,
too, are being liberalized, especially at the skilled
and professional levels (Fong and Lim 1982). Thus market forces, aided by selective government investment
incentives and a few controls, have been largely responsible for allocating resources in an economy
characterized by free trade and capital flows.

THE ROLE OF THE STATE

Despite the relative lack of controls, the dominance of market forces, and the freedom of private
enterprise, Singapore's domestic economy is far from
laissez-faire. Rather, it is characterized by a
heavily interventionist government.

The government is the major actor in the institutional environment surrounding the Singapore economy.
The ruling party, in power since 1959, wields complete
political control through its exclusive representation
in parliament, and its de facto control of the government bureaucracy, the labor movement (through the
National Trades Union Congress), and local community
organizations (through the People's Association).[4]
Development strategy is decided by the government and
implemented in limited consultation with worker, employer, and other citizen groups. Within the government itself, policy measures are typically initiated by
the top political leaders and the bureaucracy rather
than by parliament.

The state's role in the economy extends beyond the passive provision of tax and other incentives to private investment. Government statutory boards, state enterprises, and joint ventures provide all the social and economic infrastructure and basic needs of the majority of the population. They also engage directly in productive activities, often in competition with the private sector. The Public Utilities Board (PUB), Telecommunications Authority of Singapore (TAS), Port of Singapore Authority (PSA), and Jurong Town Corporation (JTC) are state monopolies providing utilities, communications services, port services, and industrial estates, respectively. The Housing and Development Board (HDB) builds and manages industrial estates and apartment blocks where two-thirds of the population now live. The Urban Redevelopment Authority (URA) engages in urban renewal and property development on a commercial basis. The Economic Development Board (EDB) promotes local and foreign investments and approves industrial and training incentives for firms. The Singapore Tourist Promotion Board (STPB) promotes tourism and develops tourist facilities and services.

In the social services arena, the Ministry of Health provides public health care and medical services. The Ministry of Education is in charge of all education for the population, from the primary to the tertiary levels. The Vocational and Industrial Training Board (VITB) offers vocational and industrial training. The Ministry of Environment provides sanitation services, along with parks and recreational services. The state has a monopoly over radio and television through the Singapore Broadcasting Corporation (SBC).

There is a state airline, Singapore Airlines (SIA); a state trading company (INTRACO); a state industrial research institute, the Singapore Institute of Standards and Industrial Research (SISIR); a state shipping company, Neptune Orient Lines (NOL); two state/joint venture shipyards, Keppel and Sembawang; and various other wholly and partially state-owned productive and profit-making enterprises.

In the financial sector, the government's direct participation is extensive. The Central Provident Fund (CPF) and Post Office Savings Bank (POSB) hold a majority of the national savings. The CPF has more than two-thirds of the government's securities, while the POSB is active in taking deposits and making loans, particularly housing loans and big loans to state enterprises. The newly incorporated Government of Singapore Investment Corporation (GOSIC) will manage foreign reserves, a function previously performed by the Monetary Authority of Singapore (MAS), and will make foreign investments. The Development Bank of

Singapore (DBS) is a publicly quoted company with a majority government share; it operates as a commercial bank and invests in many private enterprises.

Thus, unlike governments in predominantly laissez-faire economies, the Singapore government does more than merely provide infrastructure and social services. On its own or in partnership with private enterprises or shareholders, it also finances and engages in direct production. Many state and quasi-state institutions, including those providing infrastructure and social services, are profit-making enterprises, a pattern that reflects a government philosophy opposed to subsidies and in favor of profit-making.

Because of its heavy direct and indirect involvement in the economy, the state can exercise considerable leverage on the domestic macroeconomy, beyond the use of conventional public revenue and expenditure instruments. More than half of domestic income passes through government hands in one way or another—through the 50 percent share of earned income that goes to the CPF in compulsory employer and employee contributions; the 2 percent payroll tax and 4 percent Skills Development Fund (SDF) levy on wages; the personal and corporate income taxes; the indirect taxes; and the tariffs charged and income earned by the various statutory boards and state enterprises. The public sector is also the largest employer in the economy, accounting for 20 percent of total employment. It regulates wages through the National Wages Council (NWC) and influences the construction sector through its own property development activities and control over construction by the private sector. It also regulates, through the MAS, the financial markets and the domestic money supply.

Despite these powers, the government has rarely chosen to regulate the macroeconomy in the typical Keynesian countercyclical manner. Exceptions have been pump priming through government investment during the economic downturns that followed the two world recessions in the mid-1970s and early 1980s, and the maintenance of lower-than-world inflation rates throughout the 1970s by regulating wages and siphoning off increasing proportions of purchasing power through CPF contributions.

Government intervention in the economy is particularly visible in the area of labor. Political moves by the ruling PAP succeeded in depoliticizing a radical labor movement by the mid-1960s, and today 90 percent of total union membership (which includes about a quarter of the labor force) is affiliated with the PAP-supported National Trades Union Congress (NTUC), which is headed by a government minister. Labor discipline has been ensured by administrative regulations governing the registration and deregistration of unions, compulsory arbitration procedures to limit strikes, and two pieces of labor legislation enacted in 1968. The Employment Act standardized the terms and conditions of employment and defined the minimum and maximum limits of fringe benefits. The Industrial Relations Amendment Act excluded certain issues, for example, dismissal and retrenchment, from collective bargaining and defined the framework and procedures for labor negotiations and conflict resolution.[5]

The industrial relations system is one of tripartism based on mutual tolerance rather than active cooperation or confrontation among workers, employers, and government. Since 1968, the man-days lost through strikes and other labor actions have been negligible, and since 1978 there have been no strikes. Labor peace more than infrastructural developments and tax incentives was the major factor attracting foreign investment into labor-intensive, export-oriented manufacturing in the late 1960s and 1970s.

The government also plays a major role in wage determination. In 1972 the tripartite National Wages Council (NWC) was established to formulate annual wage guidelines for the economy. Annual wage increases were modest, less than 10 percent a year in nominal terms, until it was realized that this cap was distorting the allocation of resources in the direction of excessive labor use. To "restore wages to market levels" and restructure the full employment economy toward less labor use, the NWC in 1979 introduced a three-year corrective high-wage policy. This policy increased labor costs by an average of 20 percent a year in the first two years and 18 percent in the third year, after which the policy was abandoned.

The government also influences the allocation of labor resources through its heavy investment in manpower training programs to benefit private industry. Together with subsidized infrastructure and selective tax incentives, subsidized manpower training is designed to channel more resources toward the manufacturing sector, which the government intends to upgrade into high-technology industries through the 1980s. Manpower planning, which encompasses the use of financial incentives and state determination of enrollment levels in tertiary institutions, strongly influences the educational and occupational choices of those leaving school.

THE CONTRIBUTION OF FOREIGN MANUFACTURING ENTERPRISES

Foreign enterprises have played a major role in the Singapore economy since colonial days. Originally concentrated in the trade and service sectors, foreign

enterprises have since 1960 greatly increased their
role in manufacturing. Singapore's industrialization
program, indeed its whole development strategy, relies
heavily on foreign investment, technology, and expertise. Foreign enterprises are welcomed and encouraged
with a host of investment incentives, and there are
liberal policies regarding the employment of expatriate
personnel and professionals.
   Although the contribution of foreign capital to
capital formation fell from 70 percent in the early
1960s to about 30 percent in the late 1970s, the inflow
of foreign capital increased in absolute terms from S
$1.1 billion in 1970 to S $3.4 billion in 1980 (Singapore, Ministry of Trade and Industry 1980, 1981). In
the manufacturing sector, the share of foreign investment in gross fixed assets rose from 45 percent in 1966
to 81 percent in 1979. In 1979, two-thirds of gross
capital formation in manufacturing were in enterprises
with some foreign capital, of which four-fifths were in
wholly or majority foreign-owned enterprises (accounting for 54 percent of total gross capital formation in
manufacturing) (Fong 1981b, Appendix Tables 1 and
11). In that same year, 87.2 percent of net investment
commitments in manufacturing was from foreign countries
(Singapore, Economic Development Board 1981).
   As shown in Table 5.5, in 1981 investment in the
manufacturing sector in terms of gross fixed assets is

TABLE 5.5
Singapore: Investments by industry group
(percent)

	Gross Fixed Assets		Net Invest. Commitments
	1970	1981	1983
Petroleum	55.8	40.3	19.8
Metals & Eng.	5.3	12.5	16.1
Transport Equip.	5.1	4.9	5.1
Elec. & Electronics	8.2	17.3	21.5
Chemicals	6.1	5.1	9.0
Others	19.5	19.9	28.4
Total	100.0	100.0	100.0
S $ Mil.	995	8,650	1,794.6[a]

Source: Singapore, Economic Development Board
(1984); and Singapore, Ministry of Trade and
Industry (1981, 84).

[a] Includes S $519.1 million in local investments.

concentrated in the petroleum industry, followed by electrical and electronics, metals and engineering, chemicals, and transport equipment, respectively. The above industries, excluding chemicals, together accounted for nearly three-quarters of all foreign manufacturing assets in Singapore in 1981. In terms of net investment commitments in 1983, the three leading industries--respectively, electrical and electronics, petroleum, and metals and engineering--together accounted for about three-fifths of the S $1,794 million committed.

Table 5.6 shows the distribution of foreign investment in manufacturing by region. In terms of gross fixed assets in 1981, Europe was the leader, followed by North America and Asia. The large share of the European countries reflects their disproportionate share in the petroleum industry (Royal Dutch Shell, British Petroleum, and so on). In terms of net investment commitments, the Europeans lag behind other Asian investors (including Japan, Hong Kong, and Taiwan), which in turn lag behind North American investors. In 1981, the latter accounted for over half the total foreign investment.

Table 5.7 shows the relative contributions of foreign and local enterprises in the manufacturing sector in 1982. Wholly foreign and majority foreign (minority local) joint venture enterprises together accounted for only 25 percent of the firms in this

TABLE 5.6
Singapore: Manufacturing investments by region (percent)

	Gross Fixed Assets		Net Investment Commitments	
	1971	1981	1972	1981
North America	32.1	31.1	12.7	34.9
Europe	40.7	38.8	11.1	13.5
Asia	27.2	30.1	56.6	21.1
Total For.			80.4	68.5
Total Local			19.6	31.5
Total For. and Local	100.0	100.0	100.0	100.0
S $ Mil.	1,575	8,650	195	1,938

Source: Singapore, Economic Development Board (Annual Reports 1979-82).

TABLE 5.7
Principal statistics on manufacturing by capital structure, 1982[a]

	Total	Wholly Local	Majority Local[b]	Minority Local[c]	Wholly Foreign
Establishments					
Number	3,586	2,289	385	323	589
%	100.0	63.8	10.7	9.0	16.4
Workers					
Number	275,450	84,505	38,457	38,015	114,473
%	100.0	30.7	14.0	13.8	41.6
Output					
S$ mil.	36,467.4	6,314.9	3,267.0	6,915.0	19,970.5
%	100.0	17.3	9.0	19.0	54.8
Value Added					
S$ mil.	9,355.9	1,984.6	1,142.9	1,112.9	5,115.5
%	100.0	21.2	12.2	11.9	54.7
Direct Exports					
S$ mil.	21,858.7	2,022.0	1,561.7	4,096.8	14,178.3
%	100.0	9.3	7.1	18.7	64.9
Capital Expenditures					
S$ mil.	2,222.7	528.0	281.7	202.3	1,210.7
%	100.0	23.0	12.0	9.0	54.0

Source: Singapore, Department of Statistics (1983, 4).

a Manufacturing exclusive of rubber processing and granite quarrying.
b More than half local.
c Less than half local.

sector, but for 55 percent of the employment, 74 percent of the output, 67 percent of the value added, 84 percent of the exports, and 63 percent of the capital expenditures. They are thus larger and more heavily export-oriented than the wholly local and minority foreign joint venture firms.

Despite their dominance in the industrial sector and strong representation in other sectors of the economy, foreign-owned enterprises do not have a strong say in economic policy-making. As with other economic actors in the system--local enterprises and workers--they respond to government policy initiatives. Both local and foreign employers' associations--such as the Singapore National Employer's Federation (SNEF), Singapore International Chamber of Commerce (SICC), Singapore Chinese Chamber of Commerce (SCCC), Singapore Manufacturers' Association (SMA), American Business Council (ABC), and other nationality groupings--are only indirectly involved in the formulation of economic policy. Employers' associations are, however, represented in various tripartite bodies, including the NWC, EDB, JTC, and NPC.

FACTORS CONTRIBUTING TO RAPID ECONOMIC GROWTH

Favorable external developments have contributed to Singapore's rapid economic growth since independence. These developments include the boom in regional oil exploration and the spread of multinational corporations in the late 1960s, the steady expansion in world output and trade in the late 1960s and early 1970s, and the rapid growth in trade and investment in the Asia-Pacific region in the latter 1970s. But these favorable external conditions would have been insufficient had domestic conditions and policies not been conducive to growth.

To begin with, Singapore's historical role as a colonial entrepôt importing raw materials and foreign manufactured goods and exporting the products of the hinterland required ancillary shipping, insurance, banking, and communications facilities and services. This infrastructure enhanced Singapore's attractiveness as an offshore manufacturing and servicing location for multinational companies.

Second, people in Singapore, mostly the descendants of highly motivated immigrants, were of necessity outward-looking and responsive to changes in the region and the world. They had no history of xenophobia and were receptive to foreign ideas, enterprises, and personnel.

Third, as a city-state, Singapore did not have a backward rural sector to act as a drag on development. The social and cultural problems of developing a modern industrial work force were also minimized.

Fourth, Singapore's small size and compactness made it easy for a strong government to bring about political order and labor discipline. It also reduced the problems of executing government policies relating to economic and social development, such as family planning, public housing, transportation, community services, general education, and industrial training.

These initial advantages of an established infrastructure, an open-minded population, small size, and urbanism would have been dissipated had Singapore's first representative government abandoned the free enterprise policies nurtured during the colonial period. But the PAP government, on assuming power in 1959, did not live up to its leftist image. It did not, for example, nationalize the few industries in Singapore. Instead, it took steps to reassure the private sector of its commitment to the free enterprise system and introduced various policies to improve the investment climate. It also strengthened the capacity of public sector institutions to implement development policies and vigorously developed new social infrastructure.

Since 1959, the range of investment incentives themselves has been expanded and modified in response to changing market conditions. In the 1960s, the incentives were designed to encourage labor-intensive firms. Since the late 1970s, they have favored skill-intensive and high-technology activities.

Important though they are, the tax incentives have not been the decisive factor that attracts investors to Singapore. Equally important have been the industrial peace and wage stability that the government achieved by various legal and political moves to ensure cooperative labor unions and to influence wages directly.

Perhaps the most important internal factor contributing to rapid growth has been an extraordinary blend of governmental leadership and economic liberalism. Since independence, Singapore's political leaders have realized that the island economy can thrive only if it remains open to foreign enterprise, technology, and expertise. This belief means minimum state intervention in private sector decisions on production and technology, and maximum state effort to improve conditions for private sector efficiency.

Unlike in many other countries, foreign investors in Singapore are not subject to a plethora of regulations. However, they are not free to pursue actions contrary to the national interests of Singapore. From the beginning, the government has made clear to investors that it is the sovereign authority and that foreigners must not involve themselves in domestic politics. It earns the respect of both local and foreign firms by dealing with them in a businesslike manner, avoiding arbitrary, capricious policy changes that upset firms and undermine their efficiency.

Various reforms that resulted in a high degree of institutional efficiency reinforced Singapore's reputation for fair and rational dealings with the private sector. In 1959, the government centralized decision-making by abolishing the two-tier system of administration consisting of a rural board and a city council, a move that greatly facilitated policy coordination. To ensure the smooth execution of development policy, it set up various statutory boards to undertake the specific tasks of investment promotion, housing development, industrial estate development, industrial financing, and so on. These state agencies operate efficiently, often profitably, and with a complete absence of corruption.

The government also implemented measures to mobilize domestic savings for infrastructure development and social programs while practicing fiscal conservatism. Tight controls on public spending on nondevelopment items produced budget surpluses, while a system of compulsory contributions by workers and employers to the Central Provident Fund (CPF), a workers' retirement scheme introduced in 1955, increased domestic savings. Consequently, the government did not have to depend on deficit financing or foreign aid for its public sector development programs. Public sector surpluses and a high rate of forced savings also had a deflationary effect on the economy.

Another internal policy that contributed to Singapore's rapid industrial growth after 1966 was the dismantling of tariff protection, following the adoption of an export-oriented industrialization strategy. Quota restrictions were removed and import tariffs cut to foster an efficient manufacturing sector. Unlike many other developing countries, Singapore experienced only a brief and mild phase of import substitution. Powerful interest groups dependent on tariff protection had not developed before the switch to an export-led strategy,[6] and the inefficiencies associated with protection were also not yet deeply embedded in the industrial structure. The government therefore encountered few political or economic problems when it began to reduce tariffs after 1966, a process that continues to this day.

FACTORS CONTRIBUTING TO RELATIVE PRICE STABILITY

In the 1960s, relative price stability accompanied rapid economic growth in the Singapore economy. The consumer price index (CPI) rose by an average of only 1.2 percent a year, even after growth accelerated in the late 1960s. By the early 1970s, however, there were strong domestic inflationary pressures in the full employment economy. These pressures, together with the sharp rise in world commodity prices, especially of rice and oil, resulted in double-digit inflation in 1972 and 1973. After 1973, the inflation rate dropped sharply through the recession of 1974 and 1975 and was actually negative in 1977. Over the entire period 1970-1979, consumer prices rose only 5.9 percent a year. In 1980, reflecting the large jump in the price of oil of the previous year and the increase in property and food prices, consumer prices rose by 8.5 percent. Since 1981, inflation has moderated greatly, reaching a low of 1 percent in 1983.

Several factors contributed to the fairly low rates of inflation in the 1960s and 1970s. An important one in keeping prices down was the appreciation of the Singapore dollar since the early 1970s.[7] This policy has kept imports cheap, especially foodstuffs, which form half the weight of the basket of goods included in the CPI.

A second factor has been the restrictive monetary and fiscal policies enacted during the inflationary period in the early 1970s. A third reason is that domestic purchasing power was siphoned off through forced savings and public sector surpluses.[8] Forced savings are achieved through the institutional mechanism of the CPF, which requires employers and employees to contribute a specified proportion of employee salaries to the publicly administered fund. These compulsory contributions have increased steadily from an employee share of 6 percent of the wages received in 1966 to 25 percent in 1984. Together with the employers' contribution of 25 percent, the CPF now siphons off half the total earned income in the economy. Almost all the CPF funds are invested in local government securities, making the fund the largest holder of government-registered stocks and thus the largest source of borrowed funds for the government.

The steady rise in the contribution rates to the CPF since 1968 has had three major direct effects on the level of domestic prices. First, it has reduced disposable income and hence demand. Second, it has raised the discounted present value of wealth, a factor that has raised demand. Third, the rise in the employers' rate of contribution has increased labor and production costs. The effects of the increases in the CPF rate on wealth and production are probably small compared with the income and demand effects (Fong 1983; Kapur 1983). Siphoning off disposable income through increased CPF rates therefore reduces the price-increasing effects of wage increases in a rapidly growing economy.

The CPF also affects living costs through its link to the cost of public housing. The HDB finances its housing construction program with loans from the Development Fund, which obtains its funds from the Consolidated Loan Fund, which in turn gets most of its funds from the proceeds of the sales of government stocks to the CPF. The low rate of interest paid on CPF deposits enables a low rate of interest to be paid on government bonds and thus a low rate of interest to be charged on loans to the HDB. As a result, the HDB can finance its housing program at a low cost, to the benefit of buyers and tenants in HDB apartments. Thus the financing of HDB housing indirectly through the mechanism of the CPF restrains the rise in a major component of the cost of living in an urban economy.

In addition to the CPF, the state-run Post Office Savings Bank (POSB) also siphons off domestic purchasing power. It offers interest payments (6.5 percent in 1984) and instant withdrawal on savings accounts from which public utility and other bills from state enterprises can be paid automatically.

Until very recently, CPF and POSB funds have been used exclusively in the public sector, a practice that permits the noninflationary financing of government development projects. There is now some input into the private sector, as workers are allowed to use their CPF savings to buy privately built houses and apartments.

Public sector surpluses also arise from the efficient and profit-making operations of the state enterprises. These entities not only monopolize the provision of utilities, telecommunications, port and airport services, industrial estates, and so on, but they are also involved in a broad range of market-oriented production and service activities, from banking and shipping to manufacturing and property development. The products and services of these state enterprises are priced above cost. Partial subsidies are provided only for education, health care, and some low-income public housing.

Were it not for the budget surpluses, Singapore's record on inflation would probably not be as impressive. Without the surpluses, budget deficits would have had to be financed by borrowing. Because Singapore has a Currency Board System, the government cannot monetize the deficit by selling bonds to the central bank. It has three options, all with inflationary consequences. First, it could draw down foreign reserves to finance the deficit. If reserves fell to a low level, then under a fixed exchange rate regime it must devalue the Singapore dollar, raising the prices of imports and possibly triggering destabilizing expectations of further devaluations. Second, it could borrow from international agencies and international financial markets at prevailing market rates and possibly run into a problem with debt servicing, should exports shrink. Third, it could borrow from the domestic market, crowding out private sector borrowing if it were to offer higher than market interest rates. All three methods of deficit financing would likely weaken business confidence and reduce capital inflows.

EXCHANGE RATE MANAGEMENT AND INFLATION

Until June 1973, Singapore operated under a fixed exchange rate system. Since then, the MAS has used an exchange rate policy rather than monetary/interest rate targets as its main policy instruments (Hewson 1981; Teh 1983). The government chose an exchange rate policy rather than monetary or interest rate targets because of the importance of tradable goods to Singapore's economy and the relative ease of controlling the exchange rate as compared to the supply of money.

Given perfect capital mobility, an exchange rate target implies that the money supply is endogenous and will be determined by money market equilibrium, that is, by the demand for money. The choice of an exchange rate policy together with withdrawal of funds through the CPF from the monetary system requires a mechanism whereby the MAS can put the money back into the system. The MAS does so by intervening in the foreign exchange market by selling Singapore dollars and buying foreign exchange. In this way, it injects needed liquidity into the system and builds up Singapore's foreign reserves, in the process moderating the appreciation of the Singapore dollar. The gradual appreciation of the Singapore dollar since 1973 has reduced the impact of foreign inflation on domestic prices.

DEVELOPMENT POLICIES AND PROSPECTS

For the past quarter century, the performance of the Singapore economy with respect to growth, price stability, employment, and improvement in real living standards has been one of the best in the world. This economic success has been the result of both favorable market forces and government development strategy.

Toward the end of the 1970s, changes in domestic and international market forces necessitated changes in the government's development policy. In particular, Singapore has gradually been losing its comparative

advantage in the export of labor-intensive manu-
factures--a key sector of the economy in the 1960s and
1970s--because of domestic labor shortages, rising
wages, an appreciating exchange rate, increased supply-
side competition from other newly industrialized and
developing countries, and the demand-side constraints
of slow growth and protectionism in the export markets
of developed countries.

For the 1980s, the government has set a growth
target of 8 percent to 10 percent a year in order to
reach Japan's present per capita GNP by 1990. This
target will require annual increases in productivity of
6 percent to 8 percent, or double the average rates
achieved during the 1970s. Manufacturing is to remain
the prime mover of the economy, increasing its share of
GDP from 23 percent in 1980 to 31 percent in 1990.
Trade, tourism, transport, and communications, along
with "brain services," are also projected to grow
rapidly (for details, see Tong 1981).

The development strategy for the 1980s is to restructure the economy, especially the manufacturing
sector, from its present low-wage, labor-intensive
base, into higher productivity, higher technology, more
capital-intensive, and up-market activities. The recently abandoned three-year high-wage policy was a
first step in this direction, aimed at stimulating the
phasing out or upgrading of labor-intensive activities. More generous tax and other incentives are being
offered for high-value, high-productivity manufacturing
investment. And the government has embarked on an
ambitious and expensive manpower training program
through its various tertiary and technical training
institutes, with the purpose of providing Singapore
with, among other things, the highest ratio of engineers to total population in the world.

Foreign capital, enterprise, technology, and
expertise will be even more vigorously encouraged than
previously, given the lack of an indigenous capacity
and comparative advantage in high-technology activities. More foreign skilled and professional personnel
will be encouraged not only to work, but also to settle
permanently, in Singapore, and more foreign students
will be admitted into Singapore's educational and
training institutes in order to make up for the shortfall between the number of Singapore citizens leaving
school and the numbers needed for the planned manpower
training programs. In the interim, foreign unskilled
labor will also be freely admitted into the country on
short-term contracts, in order to ameliorate the labor
shortage, especially in the construction sector.

Economic liberalization in the form of the removal
of protection for goods and services will accelerate.
In particular, the partial protection from foreign com-

petition that local skilled and unskilled labor enjoys will be progressively removed. It is also likely that many of the various remaining controls on foreign participation in traded and untraded services will be reduced or removed, a move that will make these sectors as open as manufacturing.

At the same time, the government is undertaking a major campaign to increase productivity and has set up a tripartite National Productivity Council for this purpose. A keystone of the campaign is to emulate aspects of the Japanese model of development, especially the Japanese industrial relations and management system. This campaign will involve a radical restructuring of the present division of labor between the private and public sectors, with a shift in the direction of increased privatization of social benefits. To date, much of Singapore's economic and social success, and the profitability of private businesses, have been based on the state's responsibility for the welfare of workers. The government provides subsidized housing, health, education, and recreational services for the mass of the population and manages the bulk of savings for retirement through the CPF and POSB. It also decides the annual wage increments and sets minimum fringe benefits. This role of government has won it the support and dependence of the population and has also minimized company responsibility for worker welfare.

The shift from state welfare to company welfare is motivated by two factors. First, the government is increasingly unwilling or unable to provide subsidized social services to match the ever-increasing demands and expectations of the population, given rising costs and its own philosophical opposition to subsidies and preference for market-based pricing. Second, the government believes that worker dependence on the state has inhibited the development of close worker-company ties and so has adversely affected productivity. It hopes by the shift to company welfarism to curb labor mobility and encourage the emergence of a more direct relationship between labor remuneration (wages and benefits), productivity, and company profitability. The government is not, however, proposing that part of employer contributions to the CPF be channeled instead to company-based employee benefit and pension programs, that the ceilings on bonuses related to company profitability be lifted, that companies take on a bigger role in providing worker welfare benefits, and that national industry unions be broken up into company-based house unions.

The prospects for the government's desired growth and productivity targets depend on both external and internal factors. Externally, the success of industrial upgrading depends heavily on world conditions relative to demand and supply, particularly with respect to competition from other newly industrialized countries embarked on the same path of development, to the growth of the world economy and of access to the markets of developed countries, and to the availability in Singapore of the high quality, technically skilled manpower so essential to high-technology manufacturing but in short supply throughout the world.

Internally, the success of the privatization strategy depends on the extent to which it is accepted by both companies and workers--neither of whom will be happy if they stand to lose anything from the change. For example, companies may not be willing to bear the additional expense of responsibility for workers' welfare, while workers may be reluctant to surrender the security and relative equity of state-provided social benefits.

Privatization does not necessarily mean that the government will not interfere. Rather, the government will retain its overall control to approve company policies, for example, through its leadership of the National Productivity Council, and will retain social and political control over the population despite their decreasing dependence on the state.

LESSONS FROM SINGAPORE'S DEVELOPMENT EXPERIENCE

Many of the features of Singapore's development are unique to the country itself--for example, the advantages it had at independence of an excellent location, a high level of urbanism, a developed infrastructure, a high level of income, and an enterprising and energetic immigrant population. Fortuitous external circumstances--such as the boom in regional oil exploration, the boom in world trade, and the spread of offshore sourcing by multinationals--also coincided with its timely entry as a relative newcomer among developing countries in labor-intensive export manufacturing in the late 1960s.

Nonetheless, these advantages and fortuitous market opportunities would have come to little without an explicit and appropriate government development strategy. The Singapore government enhanced its early opportunities by investing early and heavily in the development of infrastructure, mass education, and birth control. It established political stability and labor peace. It offered fiscal incentives to attract foreign investors looking for offshore manufacturing bases.

Despite its originally socialist philosophy, the PAP maintained an open economy based on free trade and

private enterprise, welcoming foreign capital, technology, enterprises, and expertise. The basic economic
policy was one of liberalism, and there were few restrictions or controls. Where the state did intervene
in the allocation of resources, it did so by offering
selective investment incentives, subsidized infrastructure and manpower training, and other institutional support services--in other words, by using a
system of passive incentives rather than by active
disincentives and controls. State enterprises have
also participated actively in the economy.

At the same time, the government won popular
support through social policies that improved the
welfare of the population and increased the productivity of workers while minimizing the necessary wage
costs of private employers. These goals were accomplished by providing mass public housing facilities at
subsidized costs to low-income earners and by investment in human capital through health and education services. Social infrastructure--public transportation
and recreational facilities--also improved.

Public expenditures were financed by an increase
in national savings, mobilized through state institutional mechanisms. This policy, together with fiscal
and monetary discipline, held down the rate of domestic
inflation. Rapid growth and employment creation, the
provision of subsidized social services, and government
political control ensured that the forced savings rate
could be progressively raised without engendering
popular dissatisfaction. In any case, the pragmatic,
thrifty, and hardworking population was used to short-
term sacrifice and long-term gain. With rapid growth
and relatively low inflation, the sacrifices were minimized and the gains quickly realized. Nor did growth
come at the expense of equity--at least from 1966 to
1976 there was a slight improvement in the distribution
of income, attributable to the rapid expansion of
labor-intensive employment opportunities for low-income
workers and the real gains in income from public social
services.

Although this blend of economic liberalism and
state intervention has been responsible for Singapore's
spectacular development and political stability in the
past quarter century, it is unlikely to continue unchanged in the immediate and long-range future.
Government plans to restructure the economy in the
direction of higher productivity activities are based
on further liberalization on the one hand, and increased privatization of many state functions on the
other. This shift may lead to greater productivity and
a more competitive economy, but at the likely expense
of some increase in inflation and inequality in the
distribution of income and benefits among the working

population. The government has warned that not all the population's expectations of continuous increases in real living standards--for example, in housing quality --can be met and that increased charges will be imposed on state services. The withering away of the state as the people's ultimate benefactor may in these circumstances undermine some of the government's popular support and tight political control.

In general, the chief lesson Singapore's development experience offers for other countries is that an efficient, honest, and forward-looking state apparatus, unencumbered by doctrinaire political or economic philosophy and always responsive to changes in market forces, can best mobilize a country's people and resources to make the most of those prevailing market forces. Popular support for the development effort is crucial and is obtained by ensuring that the basic needs of the population are met quickly, by the state if necessary, that the sacrifices required for growth are minimized, and that the benefits are realized rapidly.

Although the Singapore government may seem to have moved sharply from the left to the right of the political spectrum since self-government in 1959, its original socialist philosophy--employment creation as the primary goal of development under state direction, and state responsibility for many basic needs and social welfare--in fact laid the political, social, and economic foundation for the current shift toward a more liberalized economy.

NOTES

1.   For an account of the many conflicts between Singapore and the Malaysian federal government, see Fletcher (1969) and Milne (1966).
2.   For the story of Singapore's rise as the most important entrepôt of Southeast Asia, see Ken (1978).
3.   The 1933 Commission on Straits Settlements, in its report on Singapore's trade, noted that:

...though the interests of the local manufacturer would be best served by protection, the interference with the freedom òf the port which would be involved might be disastrous to the entrepot trade...The prosperity of Singapore has been built on its entrepot trade. Industrial development is a later growth and has not begun to approach the

entrepot trade in importance. To disturb this
merely for the sake of protecting still problem-
atical industries would be to throw away the
substance and grasp the shadow. (Commission on
Straits Settlements 1935, vol. 1, 152)

4. For a discussion of Singapore's political
system, see Chee (1976).
5. For a discussion of the evolution of Singapore's industrial relations system, see Fong (1981c).
6. Tariff rates remained low for most items
throughout the first half of the 1960s. Except for a
few industries, the effective protection rates varied
between 10 percent and 20 percent. See Tan (1978).
7. Until 1967, the Singapore dollar was pegged to
the British pound sterling. The Monetary Authority of
Singapore (MAS) used sterling as the intervention
currency to maintain an appropriate Singapore dollar
exchange rate. Other exchange rates adjusted to market
forces. Because of the weakness of the British pound,
the MAS has, since the early 1970s, used the U.S.
dollar as the intervention currency, practicing a form
of managed floating. The principle of intervention is
to prevent the Singapore dollar from appreciating too
much, for fear of hurting the competitiveness of
Singapore's manufactured exports. On the other hand,
excessive depreciation must be avoided in order to prevent inflation from arising out of Singapore's heavy
dependence on imports. In general, government intervention prevented the Singapore dollar from appreciating as much as it would otherwise have through the
1970s.
8. The monetary effects of these surpluses are
"sterilized," such that Singapore can accumulate foreign reserves, the steady accumulation of which has
contributed to the appreciation of the Singapore dollar
and its attractiveness as a currency to hold.

REFERENCES

Chee, Chan Heng. 1976. The Dynamics of One Party
    Dominance: The PAP at the Grassroots. Singa-
    pore: Singapore University Press.
Commission on Straits Settlements. 1935. Report of
    the Commission appointed by His Excellency, the
    Governor of the Straits Settlements to enquire into
    and report on the Trade of the Colony, 1933-34.
    Vol. 1.

109

Fletcher, Nancy. 1969. The Separation of Singapore from Malaysia. Ithaca, N.Y.: Cornell University Press.

Fong, Pang Eng. 1975. "Growth, Inequality, and Race in Singapore." International Labour Review 111 (January):15-28.

_____. 1981a. "Economic Development and the Labor Market in a Newly-Industrializing Country: The Experience of Singapore." The Developing Economies 19(March):3-16.

_____. 1981b. "Foreign Indirect Investment in Singapore." Paper prepared for the OECD Development Centre, Paris, February.

_____. 1981c. "Singapore." In International Handbook of Industrial Relations: Contemporary Developments and Research, edited by Albert A. Blum, 481-97. Westport, Conn.: Greenwood Press.

Fong, Pang Eng, and Han Teng Fang. 1981. "International Banking and Financial Markets in Singapore." Paper prepared for the OECD Development Centre, Paris, May.

Fong, Pang Eng, and Linda Lim. 1982. "Foreign Labor and Economic Development in Singapore." International Migration Review 16(Fall):548-76.

Fong, W. M. 1983. "The CPF as an Instrument of Macroeconomic Policy in Singapore: An Exercise in Model Manipulation." Academic exercise. Department of Economics and Statistics, National University of Singapore, Singapore.

Hewson, J. R. 1981. "Monetary Policy and the Asian Dollar Market." In Papers on Monetary Economics, 165-96, Monetary Authority of Singapore. Singapore: Singapore University Press.

Kapur, B. K. 1983. "A Short Run Analytical Model of the Singapore Economy." Journal of Development Economics 12(3):355-76.

Ken, Wong Lim. 1978. "Singapore: Its Growth as an Entrepot Port, 1819-1941." Journal of Southeast Asian Studies 10(March):50-85.

Lee, S. Y. 1981. "Recent Developments in Banking and Finance in ASEAN and Hongkong." Occasional Paper Series No. 16. Department of Business Administration, National University of Singapore, Singapore.

Milne, R. S. 1966. "Singapore's Exit from Malaysia: The Consequences of Ambiguity." Asian Survey 6:175-84.

Rao, Bhanoji, and M. K. Ramakrishnan. 1977. Economic Growth, Structural Changes, and Income Inequality, Singapore, 1966-1975. Council for Asian Manpower Studies, Discussion Paper Series No. 77-15. December. Quezon City, Philippines.

Seow, Greg. 1981. "Barriers to Traded Services in ASEAN." Economic Research Centre, National University of Singapore, Singapore. Photocopy.

110

Singapore. Department of Statistics. 1973. Report on
the Census of Population, 1970. Singapore:
Singapore National Printers.
—————. 1975. Singapore National Accounts 1960-
1973. Singapore: Singapore National Printers.
—————. 1979. Report on the Household Expenditure
Survey, 1977/78. Singapore: Singapore National
Printers.
—————. 1980. Census of Population 1957.
—————. 1981a. Census of Population, 1980. Release
no. 4. Singapore: Singapore National Printers.
—————. 1981b. Yearbook of Statistics, 1980/81.
Singapore: Singapore National Printers.
—————. 1983. Yearbook of Statistics, 1982/83.
Singapore: Singapore National Printers.
—————. 1983. Report on the Census of Industrial
Production 1982. Singapore: Singapore National
Printers.
Singapore. Economic Development Board. 1981. Annual
Report 1979-80. Singapore: Economic Development
Board.
—————. Various years. Annual Report. Singapore:
Economic Development Board.
Singapore. Ministry of Trade and Industry. 1980.
Economic Survey of Singapore 1979. Singapore:
Singapore National Printers.
—————. 1981. Economic Survey of Singapore
1980. Singapore: Singapore National Printers.
—————. 1982. Economic Survey of Singapore
1981. Singapore: Singapore National Printers.
—————. 1983. Economic Survey of Singapore
1982. Singapore: Singapore National Printers.
—————. 1984. Economic Survey of Singapore
1983. Singapore: Singapore National Printers.
Tan, Augustine. 1978. "A Study of Industrial
Protection in Singapore." Unpublished monograph.
Teh, K. P. 1983. "Discussion of S. Y. Lee's Paper."
Paper presented at the Symposium on Incomes Poli-
cies and Macroeconomic Management of the Economic
Society of Singapore and the Department of
Economics and Statistics, National University of
Singapore, Singapore, March.
Tong, Goh Ghok. 1981. "Highlights of Singapore's Eco-
nomic Development Plan for the Eighties." Budget
speech by the Minister for Trade and Industry. In
Towards Higher Achievement, vol. 1. Singapore:
Ministry of Trade and Industry, March.

6
Economic Growth and Structural Change in the Small Open Economy of Hong Kong

Dr. Yun Wing Sung

INTRODUCTION

The small colony of Hong Kong is a major manufacturing and financial center, entrepôt, and tourist resort. In 1842, the British seized this magnificent natural harbor, developing the colony as a base for trade with China. Under British rule, Hong Kong became the major entrepôt in South China, and its modern banking, trading, and transportation facilities were well-developed before World War II.

The turning point in the economic history of Hong Kong came in the early fifties. The Korean War and the subsequent UN embargo on trade with China nearly strangled the main industry of Hong Kong--entrepôt commerce. At the same time, the communist victory in China sent a million refugees into Hong Kong, including capitalists and skilled workers from Shanghai. Deprived of its traditional means of livelihood, but flushed with immigrant entrepreneurs, capital, and labor (both skilled and unskilled), Hong Kong started its metamorphosis into a manufacturing center in an environment blessed with an efficient market system and modern financial and infrastructural facilities. In 1959, the domestic exports of Hong Kong (mostly manufactures) exceeded its re-exports. The tourist industry also developed rapidly, and by 1958 the city-state was the biggest destination for tourists in the Pacific and Far East region.

Exports of manufactures expanded rapidly until the late sixties, by which time growing international protectionism by developed countries, the main markets for Hong Kong, and competition from lower cost developing countries in East Asia were threatening to end Hong Kong's economic miracle. However, the rapid development of East Asian economies implied increasing demand for the financial services and entrepôt facilities of Hong Kong. As a result, in the 1970s Hong Kong emerged as a regional financial center, while its entrepôt trade also revived. Because of the geographic and cultural proximity to China, the modernization drive in that country after 1976 strengthened the status of Hong Kong as an entrepôt and financial center.

This paper summarizes the major economic analyses and findings on the small open economy of Hong Kong. Because of the availability of data, the commodity trade in domestic exports and retained imports has been studied extensively, while the entrepôt trade has not been researched adequately. With the exception of tourist exports, researchers have barely touched the invisible trade. Similarly, the dearth of data on capital flows and the inadequacy of monetary statistics has meant that studies on the development of Hong Kong as a financial center have been confined largely to descriptive and institutional aspects.

This paper is divided into three sections. The balance of this, the first section, gives an overall picture of the Hong Kong economy, including the economic environment, the morphology and sources of economic growth, and the impact of growth on income distribution. The second looks at the determination of commodity trade and tourist exports in a factor proportions framework. The last section analyzes the main economic problems confronting policy-makers in Hong Kong in the 1980s, namely, economic diversification, control of inflation, and the rapid expansion of the relative size of the public sector.

This paper examines the visible trade in domestic exports and retained imports, and the invisible trade of tourist exports, in detail. The entrepôt trade and the emergence of Hong Kong as a financial center is discussed only briefly in the first and third sections, because these topics have not been adequately researched.

Economic Environment

Hong Kong has one of the world's freest economic systems. The government's basic economic policy has been to rely primarily on private initiative and the market process for economic development. Unlike most developing countries, the rural sector of Hong Kong is insignificant, and the market system was highly developed even before World War II. The trade and payments regime and factor markets are remarkably free of distortions. Hong Kong has complete freedom of trade and capital movements. There are no import or export duties, and excise taxes are levied only on alcoholic beverages, tobacco, vehicles, and hydrocarbon fuels. The foreign exchange market is not subject to control, and the government does not encourage or discourage banks and businesses from investing abroad or repatriating funds, but leaves such capital movements to be determined by market forces. In fact, there is no official record of capital movements.

As to the labor market, there is no mandated minimum wage for local workers, and the unions are weak and politically divided. Unlike most cities in developing countries, Hong Kong is cut off from its rural base (the Chinese mainland), and the problem of continuous, large-scale immigration from the countryside is not serious (there have been periodic waves of illegal immigrants from China, but the Hong Kong and Chinese authorities have always managed to stop them). Unemployment has been low: 3.7 percent in 1966 (census data), 4.4 percent in 1971 (census estimate) and 5 percent in 1976 (census estimate). Since 1976, the rate of unemployment declined to a record low of 2.3 percent in 1979, then rose to 4.1 percent in March 1981. The mobility of resources is judged to be high because of the absence of government intervention and the nature of Hong Kong's economic structure: most industries are light manufacturing operations with short gestation periods and low capital intensity.

Monetary and Financial System

Because of Hong Kong's position as an entrepôt in China trade, the Hong Kong dollar was linked to the Chinese silver standard before December 1935. In November 1935, China abandoned the silver standard in response to outflows of the metal triggered by an increase in world prices. Hong Kong then adopted the pound sterling as the standard for exchange. That is, the local currency was issued and redeemed for sterling at a fixed rate of exchange. Three private British commercial banks were given the right to issue bank notes backed 100 percent by sterling. Also in 1935, an Exchange Fund was established into which the banks could pay sterling to acquire, at a fixed exchange rate, certificates of indebtedness denominated in Hong Kong dollars. Bank notes could then be issued against these certificates of indebtedness. The Hong Kong currency was thus backed 100 percent by sterling. Under both the silver and the sterling exchange standards, the money supply was automatically constrained by the balance of payments, a system that suited the small open economy of Hong Kong. A deterioration in the competitiveness of Hong Kong exports because of domestically generated inflation would lead to a balance of payments deficit and a contraction of the money supply. Given the wage-price flexibility of the factor and product markets in Hong Kong, the sterling exchange standard provided a powerful automatic adjustment mechanism for the macrostability of the economy.

The international monetary crisis of the early seventies forced Hong Kong off the sterling standard, and in November 1974 the Hong Kong dollar was allowed to float. The basic nature of the monetary system was altered from a sterling exchange standard to a pure Hong Kong dollar standard: note-issuing banks were permitted to acquire certificates of indebtedness by crediting the Hong Kong dollar deposits of the Exchange Fund in commercial banks, that is, note-issuing banks pay for the certificates of indebtedness (base money) with Hong Kong dollars (deposit money). As the Exchange Fund issues certificates of indebtedness (base money) passively on demand, neither the price nor the quantity of money is controlled. The growth of the money supply is now unconstrained, and policy-makers are confronted with the problem of inflation.

Banks and Financial Companies. At the end of 1980, there were 113 licensed commercial banks and 302 deposit-taking companies (merchant banks and financial companies) in Hong Kong. Deposit-taking companies are only allowed to take deposits of not less than Hong Kong dollar (HK $) 50,000 from each depositor. They may transact all banking business except retail banking and acceptance of savings and current accounts.

The importance of Hong Kong as a financial center can be gauged from the fact that 79 commercial banks and over half the financial companies are incorporated overseas. Hong Kong has the largest number of overseas banks and financial companies after London and New York. Nonbank financial intermediaries such as insurance companies are relatively insignificant.

The Hong Kong and Shanghai Bank dominates the banking scene and controls the Mercantile and the Hang Seng Banks. It is believed that these three banks together hold around two-thirds of local deposits. As a quasicentral bank, the Hong Kong and Shanghai Bank plays a leading role in the management of the Hong Kong Association of Banks, which is a cartel largely for fixing maximum interest rates on deposits and regulating the banking business.

The development of Hong Kong as a financial center took place in the 1970s for the most part. In playing this role, Hong Kong has the advantages of complete freedom of movement of capital, low taxes, liberal regulation of financial institutions, a strategic geographic position in the Asian-Pacific region, proximity to China, and an efficient network of communications. It is no accident that Hong Kong emerged as the major syndication center in the Asian-Pacific region.

Before 1970, commercial banks dominated the financial sector, while other financial institutions were
insignificant. In 1970, a few international merchant
banks made their debut in Hong Kong, and in 10 years
the number of financial companies grew to over 300
strong. Their offshore loans at the end of 1980
totaled HK $30,232 million, exceeding their loans in
Hong Kong--HK $29,317 million--and the offshore loans
of commercial banks--HK $29,433 million. The offshore
loans of commercial banks grew rapidly, too. In Table
6.1 it can be seen that these loans went from an
insignificant HK $204 million at the end of 1969 to HK
$29,433 million at the end of 1980. The internation-
alization of Hong Kong banking can also be seen from
the increasing importance of the deposits of overseas
banks in Hong Kong: whereas local deposits increased
9.6 times in the last 11 years, the deposits of
overseas banks increased 63.8 times. At the end of
1980, deposits of overseas banks stood at HK $117,704
million, marginally exceeding local deposits (HK
$117,482 million). The huge growth in the volume of
deposits of overseas banks is partly attributable to
the activity of multinational banks in Hong Kong. The
Hong Kong subsidiaries of these banks lack a local
deposit base, and they often have to resort to loans
from their head office or the Eurodollar market. Under
the present Banking Ordinance, commercial banks can
create reserves simply by borrowing foreign funds from
overseas banks. While this system facilitates the
growth of Hong Kong as a financial center, it makes it
difficult to control the money supply.

Financial and Commodity Markets. Since the removal of the restrictions on the import and export of
gold in 1974, Hong Kong has become one of the world's
four largest gold markets, along with London, Zurich,
and New York. Commodity futures markets have not, however, developed as rapidly as expected after their establishment in May 1977. Commodities traded include
raw cotton, raw sugar, sugar beans, and new cotton.

The stock market had existed for thirty years but
only became active in the early seventies, when an
incredible boom pushed the weighted average price/
earnings ratio to 85. In March 1973, however, there
was a crash that was sharper and speedier than the Wall
Street one of 1929-1932: the Hang Seng Index declined
by 91.5 percent in twenty-two months. After that
debacle, the government established a Securities Commission and introduced the Securities Ordinance to
regulate exchange activities. Since 1977, the stock
market has recovered.

By international standards, the Hong Kong market
is quite small: market capitalization at the end of

TABLE 6.1
Consolidated balance sheet of the banking system,
1969 and 1980
(current prices, millions of HK dollars)

	End of 1969	End of 1980
Liabilities		
Deposits	12,297	117,482
Amount Owed to Banks Abroad	1,845	117,704
Other Liabilities	2,385	32,917
Total	16,527	268,103
Assets		
Cash	333	2,087
Amount Owed by Banks Abroad	5,299	90,893
Amount Owed by Deposit-Taking		
Companies	0	20,790
Loans and Advances		
Hong Kong	7,680	94,970
Abroad	204	29,433
Investments		
Hong Kong	659	7,276
Abroad	10	190
Other Assets	2,342	22,464
Total	16,527	268,103

Source: Banking Commissioner.

1978 was HK $65 billion (U.S. $13 billion), which was
only 1.5 percent of the New York market and 9.2 percent
of the Tokyo market. Only around twenty companies have
been large enough to be of interest to international
investors. For the most part, private companies have
been reluctant to use the stock market for raising
capital, although the recent sharp rise in interest
rates has increased its use as a source of funds.

Given the lack of government bonds and commercial
paper, most transactions on the Hong Kong dollar money
market are handled through the interbank market in the
form of straight deposits instead of monetary instruments. The interbank market operates like the U.S.
federal funds market, except that the maturities are
longer. Since there are no exchange controls, the offshore currency deposit market, which is largely an extension of the Eurodollar and Asian dollar markets, is
also active. Certificates of deposits (CDs) were
introduced into the local money market in the early

seventies, but their development has been hampered by
the lack of a secondary market.

Government Policy

In the free economic environment of Hong Kong, the
declared government policy is "positive noninterven-
tionism." To encourage the free play of market forces,
the government keeps regulations to a minimum, and a
simple and stable structure of low corporate and personal taxes is maintained. The tax is mildly progressive but is limited to a maximum average rate of 15
percent. The rate of the tax that is applied to profits is only 16.5 percent, with generous capital expenditure write-offs and loss carryovers. Dividends and
capital gains are not taxed. Government ownership of
goods and services is confined to law and order, postal
services, water supply, rail services and the airport. Essential services such as electricity, gas,
public transport, and communications (telephone and
telegraph) are privately owned (subject to public
supervision). However, the government does play an
important role in several areas:
    • **Land formation and disposal.** Virtually all
land in Hong Kong is Crown land owned by the government. As land is very scarce, the government has re-
claimed much of it from the sea. Land production is
the most important part of infrastructural development,
and selective land disposal is a very important form of
microeconomic intervention. Generally, leases of land
(now running for sixteen years) are auctioned to the
highest bidder, although land is available at conces-
sionary prices in the Industrial Estates to manufacturing industries that bring in modern technology and meet
the objective of industrial diversification. Firms
that do not qualify for the Industrial Estates have to
obtain land at the market price. The supply of industrial land has been quite adequate, and its price has
risen less than land for commercial and residential
purposes. In 1980, revenue from sales of land leases
exceeded that from direct taxation, and represented 35
percent of total government revenue. Despite the rapid
increase in government expenditures (they rose by 92
percent in the two years from 1979/1980-1981/1982), it
appears that the government will still be running huge
surpluses in the next few years as a result of the
large amount of projected land sales.
    • **Infrastructural development.** The government
has developed essential infrastructure such as the airport and ocean terminal. It has also developed some
large projects jointly with private enterprises, including the container terminal, the cross-harbor tun-

nel, and the subway. In the late sixties, the growth of the urban areas of Hong Kong island and Kowloon reached the limits of the surrounding mountains. Further urban growth was to involve the development of new towns in the New Territories beyond the mountains. In keeping with this policy, throughout the seventies, massive infrastructural facilities were constructed in the New Territories. Eventually, up to two million people will live in the new towns. Their construction is an important cause of the rapid expansion of government expenditure in the last few years.

• <u>Human capital formation</u>. The government heavily subsidizes general education, technical and vocational education, and medicine and health.

• <u>Technology</u>. Assistance for improving productivity and technological advancement is provided through the Hong Kong Productivity Centre.

• <u>Promotion of Exports</u>. The government promotes visible exports through the Trade Development Council, and exports of tourism services through the Hong Kong Tourist Association.

• <u>Public Housing</u>. Roughly half the population in Hong Kong lives in public housing. This program is an important channel for income redistribution and serves key social and political objectives. It is also a primary instrument in urban development: land occupied by squatters can be cleared for development, and people are more willing to move into new towns given the provision of public housing.

Government capital formation (land formation, development of infrastructure, and public housing construction) grew 183 times in current prices (or 18.3 percent a year) from 1949 to 1980, while total capital formation grew 115 times (or 16.5 percent a year), and GDP 51 times (or 13.5 percent a year). Thus, government capital formation as a percentage of GDP rose from 1.6 percent in 1949 to 6.9 percent in 1980. The share of government in total capital formation went from 15.7 percent to 24.9 percent over the same period. As a result of the development of the new towns, the growth in government capital formation was especially rapid from 1976-1980, increasing at a rate of 40 percent a year.

Government expenditures on human capital have also grown much faster than GDP. From 1949/1950 to 1980/-1981, expenditures on education grew 195 times (or 18.5 percent annually), those on medicine and health 114 times (or 16.5 percent annually). The rapid increase in government expenditures on physical and human capital has undoubtedly contributed significantly to the economic growth.

In a nutshell, the policy of the government has been to foster the sources of growth (infrastructure, human capital, and technology) on the supply side and to promote demand for exports. With few exceptions, coordination of the economy is generally left to the market. These exceptions include subsidies to agriculture and fisheries through low interest loans and technical services, and regulation of public utilities because of their monopoly power.

By and large, the government makes no attempt to carry on an active policy of macroeconomic management. (What macrointervention is carried out is discussed later.)

Morphology of Growth

Table 6.2 presents an overall view of the major economic variables and their growth rates. From 1955 to 1980, real GDP and per capita real GDP grew at the remarkable rates of 9.7 percent and 6.3 percent respectively. In 1980, per capita GDP reached HK $21,191 (U.S. $4,258), placing it behind only Japan within Asia and on a par with its sister city-state, Singapore (excluding the oil-rich Middle Eastern states). Total exports and government revenue and expenditures have grown faster than GDP. The openness of the economy is striking: the sum of total exports and imports is nearly double the amount of GDP.

The twenty-five-year period 1955-1980 is divided into five five-year periods for analysis. Average growth rates from 1960 to 1980 are also computed because the data for some variables in the late fifties are not available, while the growth rates of the early fifties are not provided because the data are not reliable. Briefly speaking, the Korean War boom reached a peak in 1951. Then, from 1951 to 1955, re-exports fell by 61 percent because of the UN embargo on trade with China, but domestic exports nearly doubled. Total exports fell by 57 percent because re-exports still represented 60 percent of total exports in 1955. In the early fifties, real GDP barely kept up with population growth, and real per capita GDP was roughly constant. The situation was reversed from 1955 to 1960 with the rapid expansion in domestic exports (21.7 percent real growth a year): domestic exports surpassed re-exports in 1959, while total exports increased briskly (real growth was 7.7 percent a year). Tourist arrivals also increased rapidly (28.5 percent a year). Despite rapid population growth (5.5 percent a year), real GDP increased so fast that real per capita GDP increased at an annual rate of 3.6 percent.

Among the developing countries, Hong Kong had the advantage of an early start in the export of labor-

TABLE 6.2
Major economic statistics of Hong Kong
(percent)

	Average Annual Growth Rates							1980 (mil.)
	1955-60	1960-65	1965-70	1970-75	1975-80	1960-80	1955-80	
Population	5.5	3.3	1.9	2.1	2.9	2.5	3.1	5.068
Employment[a]	n.a.	3.3	2.5	3.3	3.8	3.6	n.a.	2.238
GDP								
Nominal	9.8	13.4	12.6	16.1	21.3	16.3	14.3	$106,770
Real	9.4	12.5	8.1	6.9	11.5	9.7	9.7	$106,770
Real per Capita	3.6	8.9	6.0	4.7	8.5	7.0	6.3	$21,191
International Trade (Real)								
Total Exports	7.7	9.3	14.4	4.3	16.6	11.1	10.4	$98,242
Domestic Exports	21.7	10.5	15.9	3.2	14.1	10.8	12.9	$68,171
Re-exports	-8.3	5.7	8.9	9.0	23.8	11.6	7.3	$30,072
Imports	7.9	7.6	11.5	3.9	17.6	10.0	9.6	$111,789
Tourism (Real)								
Tourist Arrivals[b]	28.5	22.2	15.7	7.0	12.1	14.1	16.4	2.301
Tourist Expenditures[c]	n.a.	9.9	14.7	-1.9	5.8	6.8	n.a.	$6,060
Public Finance (Nominal)								
Revenue	13.6	13.7	13.5	15.3	35.9	19.2	18.1	$29,000
Expenditures	16.0	15.9	6.7	19.7	26.7	17.0	16.8	$19,677

Other Statistics

Area   1,052 sq km (406 sq m)

Exchange Rate (HK $ per U.S. $)
Before 11/26/74, Exchange Rate   From 11/26/74, Exchange Rate Floated
  Was Fixed as Follows: (HK $ averages)
  9/18/49 - 11/19/67   5.714   1974   5.077
 11/23/67 - 12/17/71   6.061   1975   4.940
 12/18/71 - 7/ 5/72   5.582   1976   4.904
  7/ 6/72 - 2/13/73   5.650   1977   4.662
  2/14/74 - 11/25/74   5.085   1978   4.685
                                      1979   5.003
                                      1980   4.976

Population and public finance: Hong Kong (Hong Kong Annual Report, various
issues).
Employment: Hong Kong (Economic Background, various issues); population
censuses. The 1961, 1966, and 1971 figures were obtained from the
population censuses of the respective years. The figures after 1975 were
obtained from various issues of Hong Kong (Economic Background).
GDP and trade: For the 1955-1960 figures, Chow (1966). The 1961-1980
figures were obtained from the census and the Statistics Department.
Tourism: The figures were obtained from the Hong Kong Tourist Association.

a Employment growth rates are for 1961-1966, 1966-1971, 1971-1975, and
1961-1980.
b The growth rates for tourist arrivals are for 1956-1960 and 1956-1980.
c The growth rates for tourist expenditures are for 1961-1965 and 1961-
1980.

intensive manufactures. The import substitution option adopted by many developing countries was not open to Hong Kong because of its lack of natural resources and small internal market. The modern transportation and financial facilities developed as a result of the entrepôt trade, and the injection of Chinese capital, skills, and entrepreneurship, were the key supply factors in the successful metamorphosis of Hong Kong into a manufacturing center. On the demand side, the economic expansion and resumption of free trade by developed countries, and the system of Commonwealth Preference, greatly benefited Hong Kong--particularly as there were then few competitors among the developing countries.

The United States has been the largest market for Hong Kong manufactures. The U.S. ban on imports from China in the early 1950s stimulated Hong Kong exports of Chinese-type products, and American restrictions on Japanese textiles also benefited the city-state. The U.S. share of Hong Kong domestic exports rose from 25 percent in 1959 to a peak of 42 percent in 1969, then declined to about one-third in the seventies. Great Britain had once been the second largest market--its market share was 20 percent in 1959. But the market of the Federal Republic of Germany (West Germany) expanded from an insignificant 3 percent in 1959 to 12.5 percent in 1975, surpassing the 12.2 percent share of Britain in the same year. Nevertheless, the latter market benefited Hong Kong tremendously in the early years: it is estimated that in 1967, 97 percent of Hong Kong's exports to Britain enjoyed preferences at an average margin of 19 percent.

The growth of Hong Kong greatly exceeded that of the Republic of Korea (South Korea), Singapore, and Taiwan in 1955-1960 (Chen 1979, 10), but Taiwan started its export drive in the early sixties, while Singapore and South Korea started theirs in the latter half of the sixties. However, because of world economic prosperity and two major rounds of tariff reductions (the Dillian Round in 1961 and the Kennedy Round in 1967), there was enough room for all. Still, Hong Kong had the advantage of an early start. Its export-propelled growth ended in the early seventies when the effect of the Kennedy Round ran out, and in the early seventies its economic performance was overshadowed by that of Singapore, South Korea, and Taiwan.

In the early sixties, the annual rate of growth of Hong Kong's GDP--12.5 percent--was faster than that of its domestic exports--10.5 percent, whereas domestic exports grew faster than GDP in the late sixties (15.9 percent versus 8.1 percent). This reversal was attributable to domestic demand. The early sixties were characterized by a boom in the property market, which ended in 1965 with a run on some commercial banks. Two riots occurred in 1966 and 1967--the latter a spillover of the Chinese Cultural Revolution. Investment dropped, and the annual nominal growth rate of government expenditures decelerated from 15.9 percent in the early sixties to 6.7 percent in the late sixties. Fortunately for Hong Kong, the demand for exports held up because the Vietnam War generated world prosperity and because of the Kennedy Round of tariff reductions.

The growth performance of the early seventies was the worst on record. In 1968, the domestic exports of Hong Kong had been greater than the combined total of Taiwan and South Korea. However, Taiwan and South Korea both surpassed Hong Kong's exports in 1972 and 1975, respectively. Unlike South Korea and Taiwan, Hong Kong had achieved full employment as early as 1958 and could not rely on the rural sector for a supply of cheap labor. The rapid expansion of exports in the late sixties resulted in inflation in the early seventies. The collapse of the stock market in 1973, the subsequent energy crisis, the world recession, and rising international protectionism compounded the loss in competitiveness of Hong Kong exports. Fortunately, it began to emerge as a financial center in the early seventies. Despite the slow growth of domestic exports early in that decade (3.2 percent a year), annual growth was still a respectable 6.9 percent of GDP.

The late seventies was again a period of prosperity: the annual growth rates of GDP and domestic exports were 11.5 percent and 14.1 percent respectively, while the influx of 50,000 Chinese immigrants (legal and illegal) into Hong Kong temporarily eased the labor shortage. In comparison with South Korea and Taiwan, Hong Kong appears to have been less adversely affected by rising energy costs, the reason being that both South Korea and Taiwan were trying to develop energy-intensive, heavy industries, whereas Hong Kong stuck to light manufactures because of the lack of land for heavy industries. The modernization of China revived the entrepôt trade of Hong Kong and reinforced the status of Hong Kong as a financial center. Re-exports grew at an incredible annual rate of 23.8 percent from 1975-1980, surpassing the record level of re-exports in 1951 in both nominal and real terms.

Structural Changes. Table 6.3 presents the changes in the distribution of GDP and employment among the major sectors of the economy (the primary sector includes agriculture, fisheries, and mining, the secondary sector consists of just manufacturing, and the tertiary sector includes the rest of the economy). Finance (banking, insurance, business services, and real estate) is a subsector of the tertiary sector, but is singled out for examination.

TABLE 6.3
Sectoral distribution of GDP and employment, 1961-1981
(percent)

Year	Share of GDP				Share of Employment			
	Primary	Secondary	Tertiary	Finance	Primary	Secondary	Tertiary	Finance
1961	3.7	23.6	72.7	10.8	8.0	43.0	49.0	1.4
1966	3.0	24.6	72.4	n.a.	5.5	(43.0)a	(51.5)a	n.a.
1970	2.2	30.9	66.9	14.9	n.a.	n.a.	n.a.	n.a.
1971	1.9	28.1	70.0	17.5	4.3	47.7	52.0	1.6
1974	1.6	25.8	72.6	17.6	n.a.	n.a.	n.a.	n.a.
1975	1.5	26.9	71.6	17.0	n.a.	34.8	n.a.	3.6
1976	1.5	28.3	70.2	17.9	2.7	42.6	54.7	3.6
1977	1.4	27.2	71.4	19.6	n.a.	40.5	n.a.	4.3
1978	1.4	26.7	71.9	20.7	n.a.	39.6	n.a.	4.6
1979	1.4	25.0	73.6	21.0	n.a.	41.6	n.a.	5.2
1980	1.2	26.7	72.1	22.0	n.a.	39.3	n.a.	5.6
1981	n.a.	n.a.	n.a.	n.a.	n.a.	37.6	n.a.	5.7

Sources:
GDP 1961: Chang (1969, 66).
GDP 1966: Hsia, Ho, and Lim (1975, table 7-6).
GDP 1971-1978: Hong Kong, Census and Statistics
Department (Estimates of GDP 1966-1979).
GDP 1979-1980: Hong Kong (The 1981-82 Budget, 30).
Employment: The figures for 1961, 1966, and 1971 were taken from the population censuses of the respective years. The figures for 1975-1981 were taken from Hong Kong (Economic Background, various issues).

a The industrial classification of the 1966 Census is different from that of the other censuses. It appears that the employment share of manufacturing in 1966 was approximately the same as that in 1961. The figures in parentheses are estimates.

Note: n.a. = Not available.

In the twenty years from 1961 to 1981, the share of the primary sector in GDP and employment declined on the whole, while the share of financial services in both GDP and employment rose, moving slowly in the sixties and then rapidly in the seventies. The secondary sector expanded rapidly in the sixties; its share of GDP reached a peak (30.9 percent) in 1970, while its share of employment peaked in 1971 (47.7 percent). In the early seventies, however, manufacturing suffered-- its share in employment declined markedly to 34.8 percent in 1975, its GDP share to a low of 25.8 percent in 1974. Manufacturing recovered some lost ground in the latter half of the seventies--its employment share rose to around 40 percent, its GDP share to around 27 percent. As for the tertiary sector as a whole, its GDP share was stable at around 71 percent, although its employment share rose gradually from 49.0 percent in 1961 to 54.7 percent in 1976.

From the table it can be inferred that the labor productivity of financial services was much higher than that of manufacturing, although the gap narrowed. In 1961, the value added per worker in manufacturing and financial services was, respectively, 0.55 times and 7.7 times that of the average for the economy, while the labor productivity of financial services was 14.1 times that of manufacturing. In 1980, the value added per worker in manufacturing and financial services was, respectively, 0.68 times and 3.9 times that of the average for the economy, while the labor productivity of financial services was 5.8 times that of manufacturing. (This narrowing of sectoral productivity differentials is expected as an economy matures.)

The Causes of Growth. Chen has studied the causes of growth in five Asian economies (Hong Kong, Singapore, South Korea, Japan, and Taiwan) from 1955 to 1974, and his results are summarized briefly below (Chen 1979, chaps. 4-7).

The sources of growth from 1955-1970 are presented in Table 6.4. For Hong Kong, the percentage shares of capital input, labor input, and total factor productivity were 33.5 percent, 20.0 percent, and 46.5 percent, respectively. For South Korea, Taiwan, and Singapore, the shares of total factor productivity were higher, ranging between 54 percent and 63 percent. As in Hong Kong, the contributions of capital were greater than those of labor in South Korea and Taiwan. In Hong Kong, Singapore, South Korea, and Taiwan, the contributions of factor inputs were considerably higher than the average for developed countries. The productivity gains from reallocating resources from agricultural to nonagricultural sectors were substantial for Japan, South Korea, and Taiwan, where the agricultural sectors were significant. Learning by doing was not an impor-

126

tant determinant of technical progress in Hong Kong, South Korea, and Taiwan, but learning effects were important in Japan and were of some significance in Singapore. In the cases of Hong Kong, Singapore, and Taiwan, importation of foreign technology in the form of capital equipment was the principal determinant of technical progress. In South Korea, technical progress was largely related to foreign aid directed to the manufacturing sector.

It was widely believed that the growth in Hong Kong, South Korea, Taiwan, and Singapore was export-led. Chen constructed a simultaneous-equation model that related exports to income growth through their effects on imports of capital goods. All the hypothe-sized relationships in the model were established for Hong Kong, South Korea and Singapore. The model was partly valid for Taiwan but not for Japan.

For the five Asian economies, it was found that both the savings ratio and income, and the savings ratio and capital inflow (particularly the private inflow), were positively related to each other, resulting in a virtual cycle of growth. In Hong Kong, South Korea, and Singapore, export earnings constituted the major source of domestic savings. This condition was partly true of Taiwan but not of Japan, where savings were generated by the domestic sector.

Growth and Income Distribution. According to the studies of both Chen (1979) and Hsia and Chan (1978), the rapid expansion of the labor-intensive manufactur-

TABLE 6.4
The sources of growth of real national income, 1955-1970[a]

Country	Capital Input	Labor Input	Total Factor Productivity	Growth Rate of Income
Hong Kong	3.12 (33.5)	1.86 (20.0)	4.33 (46.5)	9.31
Singapore	1.44 (22.0)	1.50 (22.9)	3.62 (55.2)	6.56
South Korea	2.12 (24.0)	1.73 (19.6)	4.99 (56.4)	8.84
Japan	2.78 (27.5)	0.98 (9.7)	6.36 (62.8)	10.12
Taiwan	2.00 (24.9)	1.72 (21.5)	4.30 (53.6)	8.02

Source: Chen (1979, 70).

[a] Percentage points with percentage distribution in parentheses.

ing sector of Hong Kong in the sixties had an equalizing effect on income distribution: the Gini coefficient decreased from 0.49 to 0.44 from 1966 to 1971.
Since the manufacturing sector had the lowest Gini
coefficient among all 1-digit ISIC industries, the
intersectoral shift of resources in favor of manufacturing had an equalizing effect. Moreover, industrial labor had the lowest inequality among occupational groups and the greatest gain in employment from
1966 to 1971. There was also a decline in intersectoral inequality: the gap in wages between manufacturing and other sectors narrowed because of the
rapid increase in the demand for labor in manufacturing. By contrast, changes in educational attainment
and household size have not affected income distribution significantly.

In 1971, the extent of equality in income distribution in Hong Kong was more or less the same as in
Singapore and more unequal than that found in South
Korea and Taiwan. The Gini coefficients of Hong Kong,
Singapore, South Korea, and Taiwan in 1971 or 1972 were
0.44, 0.44, 0.36, and 0.31, respectively (Chen 1979,
chap. 8).

There was no further equalization of income distribution in Hong Kong from 1971 to 1976, and the Gini
coefficient stayed approximately constant. The adverse
intersectoral shift of resources in favor of financial
services (a sector of high inequality) and against
manufacturing was offset by a decline in intersectoral
and intrasectoral inequality. This decline was attributable to the increase in education and training.

Accurate data for 1976-1981 are not yet available,
but most trends indicate that income inequality has
widened. The adverse intersectoral shift out of manufacturing and into financial services is continuing.
Property prices skyrocketed in the late seventies, and
massive immigration held the real wage of manufacturing
workers constant from 1979 to 1981.

According to the findings of Chen (1979, chap. 8),
rapid growth in the five Asian economies in the sixties
and early seventies led to greater income equality in
the cases of Taiwan and Singapore, but greater inequality in Japan. The result for South Korea was mixed.
The changes in inequality in Hong Kong, Japan, and
Singapore were largely the result of market forces,
whereas government policies were of some importance in
Taiwan and South Korea.

According to the study of Ho, government taxation
and expenditure had an equalizing effect on income distribution in Hong Kong (Ho 1979, chap. 5). On the side
of taxation, direct taxes (mainly on earnings and
profits) had a significant equalizing effect because
the profits tax was mainly borne by the rich, and the

earnings tax was mildly progressive. However, indirect taxes had the opposite effect on the after-tax distribution of income, with the result that the net impact of taxation as a whole in 1971 was only slightly equalizing: the Gini coefficient of after-tax income was 5 percent less than the before-tax coefficient. On the other hand, total government expenditures, especially expenditures on public housing, had a significant equalizing effect: the 1971 Gini coefficient was reduced by 15 percent. The impact of government taxation and expenditures together reduced the Gini coefficient by 20 percent.

DETERMINANTS OF COMPARATIVE ADVANTAGE: A FACTOR PROPORTIONS ANALYSIS

All studies on comparative advantage in Hong Kong's trade have confirmed the factor-proportions hypothesis of trade (Riedel 1974, chap. 2; Lin, Mok, and Ho 1980, chap. 6; Sung 1979). The most exhaustive of these is Sung's (1979). A recent study of Lin and Sung (1984) on Hong Kong tourism also analyzes tourist exports in a factor-proportions framework. In view of the rapidly rising energy prices, they quantified the energy requirements of the commodity trade and tourist exports of Hong Kong. According to conventional wisdom, rising energy prices have hurt South Korea and Taiwan relatively more severely than Hong Kong because the former two promoted heavy industries and the production of producer goods in the seventies, whereas Hong Kong stuck to light industries and consumer goods. Heavy industries are energy-intensive, while the demand for producer goods will suffer much more than the demand for consumer goods in an economic downturn. Moreover, after the energy crisis, developed countries turned to advanced energy-saving machinery instead of the less advanced machinery produced by South Korea and Taiwan.

Balance of Trade

There are no statistics on capital flows, but the balance of trade account is presented in Table 6.5. Hong Kong has always run deficits in visible trade and surpluses in invisible trade. From 1955 to 1980, commodity exports grew faster than imports (Table 6.2), and the visible trade gap (the ratio of the visible trade deficit to total imports) fell from 34.2 percent in 1961 to 4.1 percent in 1976. Further, the effective exchange rate index of the Hong Kong dollar appreciated to a record high of 114.4 at the end of 1976 (Table

TABLE 6.5
Balance of trade, 1961-1980
(current prices, HK $ millions)

	Visible Trade		Visible Trade Deficit	Invisible Trade Surplus	Visible Trade Gap %[a]	Trade Balance
	Total Exports	Total Imports				
1961	3,930	5,970	-2,042	1,450	34.2	-592
1962	4,388	6,657	-2,272	1,519	34.1	-753
1963	4,991	7,412	-2,429	1,623	32.8	-806
1964	5,784	8,550	-2,767	1,749	32.4	-1,018
1965	6,529	8,965	-2,446	1,804	27.3	-642
1966	7,563	10,111	-2,548	1,712	25.2	-836
1967	8,781	10,469	-1,688	1,941	16.2	253
1968	10,570	12,498	-1,928	2,271	15.5	343
1969	13,197	14,936	-1,739	2,792	11.7	1,053
1970	15,238	17,623	-2,385	3,427	13.5	1,042
1971	17,164	20,274	-3,110	3,367	15.3	257
1972	19,400	21,785	-2,385	3,818	10.9	1,433
1973	25,999	29,026	-3,027	4,316	10.4	1,289
1974	30,036	34,142	-4,106	4,817	12.0	711
1975	29,833	33,496	-3,664	4,619	10.9	955
1976	41,557	43,316	-1,759	6,355	4.1	4,596
1977	44,833	48,734	-3,901	6,059	8.0	2,158
1978	53,907	63,102	-9,194	7,012	14.6	-2,182
1979	75,934	85,908	-9,974	8,290	11.6	-1,684
1980	98,242	111,651	-13,409	8,850	12.0	-4,559

Source: Hong Kong (Budget Speech 1981-1982).

[a] Visible trade gap = Visible trade deficit divided by total imports.

6.6). However, because of the prosperity of the late seventies, the visible trade gap widened from 1977 on-wards. At the same time, as per capita income rose, there was a dramatic increase in outgoing tourism, and the growth of the net surplus in invisible trade slowed. The Hong Kong dollar weakened markedly--the

TABLE 6.6
Money supply, inflation, and the exchange rate

| | Growth Rate (percent) | | | | | Effective Exchange Rate Index (Dec. 18, 1971=100) |
	M1	M2	M3	Con-sumer Price Index	GDP Deflator	
1962	11.7	23.7	−	a	1.4	−
1963	15.8	22.5	−	a	2.9	−
1964	12.7	19.7	−	a	2.7	−
1965	14.6	14.0	−	2.0	0.5	−
1966	6.1	14.3	−	2.6	-1.3	−
1967	7.7	1.1	−	6.2	3.6	−
1968	7.2	20.2	−	2.5	4.3	−
1969	13.6	16.7	−	3.6	3.6	−
1970	16.1	20.8	−	7.1	11.1	−
1971	1.8	24.4	−	3.4	8.4	−
1972	44.7	28.9	−	6.1	7.8	−
1973	-6.0	6.6	−	18.2	12.9	−
1974	2.5	16.6	−	14.4	12.2	105.9
1975	22.9	16.9	−	1.2	2.3	107.4
1976	23.1	21.0	−	3.4	7.8	114.4
1977	28.7	20.7	−	5.8	4.1	106.6
1978	23.2	25.6	−	5.9	5.4	93.2
1979	3.7	13.2	29.7	11.6	14.0	92.7
1980	15.7	28.7	39.9	15.5	13.0	88.2

Source: For the figures on the money supply and consumer price index, see Hong Kong (Hong Kong Annual Report, various issues). The GDP deflator was obtained from the Census and Statistics Department. For the effective exchange rate index, see Hong Kong, Census and Statistics Department, (Hong Kong Monthly Digest of Statistics, various issues).

a Not computed.

Note: − = Not applicable.

131

effective exchange rate index depreciated to 81 in September 1981.
    Statistics on the breakdown of invisible trade, available only for 1978 and 1979, are presented in Table 6.7. The sizable surplus in "shipping and air transportation" is an indication of the growing importance of Hong Kong as an entrepôt in the late seventies. There were also considerable surpluses on the tourist account (travel).

Factor Proportions Hypothesis

    The relative capital and skill abundance of the Hong Kong manufacturing sector is much less than that of developed countries (the major trade partners of Hong Kong) and is not very different from that of developing countries (Sung 1979, 23-35). The Heckscher-Ohlin-Samuelson (HOS) model predicts that Hong Kong would save scarce factors (capital and skills) through trade, that is, the imports of Hong Kong would contain relatively more capital and skills than exports. (For the treatment of the HOS model in a three-factor framework, see Sung 1979, 7-8.)
    In the empirical work testing the HOS hypothesis, the usual practice has been to separate tradables into natural resource-based tradables (for example, agriculture and mining) and HOS tradables, since trade in natural resource-based goods is primarily determined by the endowment of natural resources instead of the endowments of capital and labor. Moreover, the supply of these goods may be limited by the availability of nat-

TABLE 6.7
Invisible trade, 1978-1979
(current prices, HK $ millions)

	1978		1979	
	Imports	Exports	Imports	Exports
Shipping and Air Transportation	2,642	7,744	3,872	10,741
Passenger Fares	1,488		1,694	
Travel	2,319	5,106	3,611	6,381
Other	1,391	2,002	1,943	2,288
Total	7,840	14,852	11,120	19,410

Source: Hong Kong (The 1981-82 Budget: Economic Background, para. 2.25).

ural resources. Another crucial distinction is between exports, here grouped as competitive and noncompetitive. Small open economies like Hong Kong can save on scarce factors (skills and capital) by complete specialization in labor-intensive goods and can import all capital-/skill-intensive goods noncompetitively. The multicountry and multigood model of Krueger predicts that, in the case of Hong Kong, the HOS noncompetitive imports would be much more capital-/skill-intensive than domestic production ones (HOS exports and competitive import replacements) (Krueger 1977). Within domestic production, HOS competitive import replacements would be slightly more capital-/skill-intensive than HOS exports, a condition that is especially true for trade with developed countries, but may not be true for trade with developing ones. If the ratio of the capital/labor intensity of HOS competitive import replacements relative to that of HOS exports is calculated, this ratio should be close to unity for trade with developing countries because the factor endowment of Hong Kong is close to that of those countries. For trade with all countries, the ratio should be greater than unity. For developed countries, it should be much greater than unity. Insofar as Hong Kong's manufactured exports to developed and developing countries differ, the capital intensity of HOS exports to the latter will be greater than to the former. The reverse is true of HOS competitive import replacements, because a lower transport cost barrier will enable developing country firms to compete with labor-intensive commodities. Last, the capital/skill intensities of Hong Kong's exports and import-competing production will increase as capital and skills accumulate in Hong Kong manufacturing.

Trade in tourist services is usually determined by natural resource endowments (scenery, culture, and location), but endowments of capital, labor, and skills may also play an important role. In any case, the capital/skill intensities of the tourist industry have important policy implications: some economists have argued for the promotion of the tourist industry on the grounds that service industries are labor-intensive, whereas others have argued against it on the grounds that the demand for skills of service industries is low, thus implying low productivity (Young 1973).

The skill requirement and energy content of trade are of particular importance in the context of economic diversification. With rising energy costs, growing international protectionism, and competition from lower cost developing countries, industrial diversification has become an issue of central concern in Hong Kong. Unlike South Korea and Taiwan, Hong Kong should develop skill-intensive, light industries instead of capital-

intensive, heavy industries, because the latter group
is likely to be energy- and land-intensive.

The Factor Content of Hong Kong Trade

The results relative to the factor content of
trade are summarized in Table 6.8 (the computational
procedure and data requirements are given in the
appendix). The depreciation/labor and depreciation/
wage ratios are measures of capital intensity. The
impact of rising oil prices on Hong Kong trade can be
gauged from the primary energy content. If the economy
is in competitive equilibrium, producers charge prices
that just cover production costs, and the increase in
the prices of output will be the same as the increase
in costs. As can be seen from Table 6.8, the energy
content of the HOS exports of Hong Kong was less than
1.5 percent in 1973, a level which implies that a
fourfold increase in the price of crude oil will
increase the cost of Hong Kong exports by no more than
6 percent. Hong Kong specializes in products that
require little energy: the energy content of its HOS
exports was only about 12-14 percent of that of HOS
noncompetitive imports. Hong Kong has weathered the
energy crisis relatively better than South Korea and
Taiwan partly because of the low energy content of its
manufacturing (Lin and Sung, forthcoming).

As can be seen from Table 6.8, the predictions of
the Krueger model are almost all fulfilled. Both in
1962 and 1973, HOS noncompetitive imports were much
more capital-intensive than (1) HOS exports, (2) HOS
competitive import replacements, and (3) tourist
exports. Within domestic production, HOS competitive
import replacements were more capital- and skill-
intensive than HOS exports in both 1962 and 1973 (the
ratios of the factor intensities of imports/exports
were all greater than one). In addition, the ratios
of capital/skill intensities for trade with developed
countries are all greater than those with developing
countries. The ratios for the latter were close to
unity, showing that the relative factor endowments of
the manufacturing sectors of Hong Kong and other
developing countries are quite similar. It may seem
surprising that the ratios of capital intensities for
trade with developing countries are above unity, the
implication being that the manufacturing sectors of
those countries were more capital-intensive than those
of Hong Kong, despite its higher level of development. However, Hong Kong manufacturing was extremely
labor-intensive because: (1) its small size and lack
of natural resources precluded a diversified industrial
structure and dictated specialization in a few
products; (2) its lack of land precluded heavy indus-

TABLE 6.8
Factor intensities of commodity trade and tourist exports, 1962 and 1973
(1973 prices)

	1962				1973			
	DW (%)	DL (HK $/ man- year)	SL (%)	PEC	DW (%)	DL (HK $/ man- year)	SL (%)	PEC
Noncompetitive Imports	n.a.	742	n.a.	0.1161	n.a.	3,227	n.a.	0.1103
Tourist Exports	0.0805	418	14.23	0.0026	0.1143	1,205	7.11	0.0731
Exports	0.0776	296	0.69	0.0136	0.1176	1,038	1.29	0.0149
Developed Country	0.0776	303	0.61	[a]	0.1129	997	1.19	[a]
Developing Country	0.797	282	0.85	[a]	0.1404	1,238	1.76	[a]
Competitive Imports	0.1021	346	1.04	0.0137	0.1509	1,336	2.29	0.0168
Developed Country	0.1046	361	1.12	[a]	0.1444	1,226	2.57	[a]
Developing Country	0.0968	317	0.89	[a]	0.1623	1,464	1.78	[a]

Ratios of Factor Intensities:
Competitive Imports to Exports

All Countries	1.3152	1.1692	1.5121			1.2834	1.2874	1.7782
Developed	1.3645	1.1898	1.8391			1.2739	1.2697	2.1578
Developing	1.2136	1.1240	1.0421			1.1562	1.1823	1.0122

Source: Computed by the author.

[a] Not computed.

Note: DW   = Depreciation/wage ratio.
SL   = Skill ratio (professional/labor).
PEC = Primary energy content per HK dollar of final demand.
DL   = Depreciation/labor ratio.
n.a. = Not available.

tries that were both capital- and land-intensive; (3) its policy of free trade encouraged specialization in labor-intensive manufactures to the full extent dictated by comparative advantage; (4) it lacked defense-related industries, which are often capital-intensive; and (5) the import-substitution policies of many developing countries resulted in inappropriately capital-intensive industries. It must be emphasized that the extreme labor intensity of Hong Kong manufacturing has brought about full employment and a more equal distribution of income.

It should be noted that the ratio of skill intensity to trade with developing countries is only marginally above unity, suggesting that the comparative disadvantage of Hong Kong in skill-intensive manufactures is less than that in capital-intensive manufactures. This finding confirms the conventional wisdom that it is easier for Hong Kong to develop skill-intensive manufactures than capital-intensive ones because of the lack of land for capital-intensive facilities.

As to the factor intensities of trade with developed and developing countries, Hong Kong's HOS exports to the latter were more capital- and skill-intensive than were its HOS exports to developed countries in both 1962 and 1973. In 1962, domestic production competing with HOS imports from developed countries was more capital- and skill-intensive than that of developing countries. These results confirm the Krueger model. However, in 1973 domestic production competing with HOS imports from developed countries was less capital-intensive than that of developing ones, although the skill intensity gives the right result. The most likely explanation of this only exception to the Krueger model is that Hong Kong's trade with developing countries was more and more dominated by the fast-growing economies of Singapore, Taiwan, and South Korea, all of whose manufacturing sectors were more capital-intensive than that of Hong Kong (Sung 1979, 23-25). Moreover, these nations have been developing capital-intensive exports such as petroleum products, basic chemicals, steel, and shipbuilding. The increasing shares of Singapore, Taiwan, and South Korea in Hong Kong trade are summarized in Table 6.9.

The capital intensity of tourism is not unlike that of domestically produced HOS tradables, although its skill intensity is much higher. However, it should be noted that its skill intensity in 1962 was grossly overstated because the important tourism hotel and restaurant sectors were lumped with the service sector in the 1962 input-output table, and the skill intensity of the service sector was much higher than that of hotels and restaurants (Lin and Sung 1984). This practice

136

The changing shares of Singapore, Taiwan, and
South Korea in Hong Kong trade
(percent of total trade with developing countries)

	1962		1973	
	Exports	Imports	Exports	Imports
Singapore	12.60	8.72	17.46	14.85
Taiwan	0.85	9.25	12.70	26.15
South Korea	0.10	1.96	3.41	9.33
Three Country Total	13.55	19.93	33.57	50.34
All Developing Countries	100.00	100.00	100.00	100.00
Value in Million HK $	1,039	1,472	3,067	6,446

Source: Hong Kong, Census and Statistics Department
(Hong Kong Trade Statistics 1962 and 1973).

Note: Developing countries exclude the planned
economies in Asia (China, Viet Nam, and Democratic
People's Republic of Korea). Imports from China
into Hong Kong are large, but most of them are
natural resource-based goods and are best
excluded.

also explains the perverse decrease in skill intensity of tourism exports from 1962 to 1973.

Between 1962 and 1973, the capital and skill intensities of domestically produced HOS tradables increased tremendously, a trend which shows that the
pattern of comparative advantage shifted toward more
capital-/skill-intensive products, again confirming the
Krueger model. Given that the energy content of HOS
exports did not change, the rise in capital/skill intensities does not signify a move to heavy industries,
but does imply a movement toward more sophisticated and
higher quality products. The results can be taken as a
tribute to the efficient market mechanism of Hong
Kong. Without overt government intervention and
promotion of selected industries, the diversification
of Hong Kong exports has proceeded in an appropriate
direction that reflects the underlying availability of
skills, capital, labor, land, and energy.

POLICY PROBLEMS IN THE 1980s

Despite past economic success, Hong Kong is confronted with thorny economic problems in the eighties. The prior strategy of exporting labor-intensive,
light manufactures has led to rapid economic growth,
full employment, and a more equitable distribution of
income, but this strategy cannot be relied on in the
1980s. Similarly, world economic malaise, international protectionism, and severe competition from South
Korea and Taiwan have made it difficult for developing
countries in general and for Hong Kong in particular to
duplicate the latter's own success in the 1950s, when
world trade expanded rapidly and Hong Kong had no
serious competitors among the developing countries.
Moreover, economic success demanded a drastic revision
of the traditional strategy: labor-intensive manufactures imply low productivity and low wages. In fact,
the earnings of the average manufacturing worker drop
with age: there are virtually no learning effects and
very little chance for promotion of labor-intensive
manufacturing industries. The traditional economic
strategy has brought about upward mobility through an
increase in the demand for labor and a rise in the
number of workers per household. Given the large size
of traditional families, a household with four or five
full-time manufacturing workers can earn enough to
invest in the education of the younger members of the
family or even to start small businesses. However,
there are limits to the increase in the rate of labor
participation, and the decrease in family size
resulting from birth control ended that channel of
upward mobility.

Given the lack of natural resources and land in
Hong Kong, the development of service industries such
as financial services, entrepôt trade, and tourism were
the logical channels for economic advancement, and
market forces indeed led the economy toward these
industries. However, the development of Hong Kong as a
financial center increased the amount of hot money moving across exchanges, thus raising the instability of
the Hong Kong economy and making it difficult to control the supply of money. Moreover, for each dollar of
value added, financial services only creates one-sixth
as much employment as manufacturing. Stagnation of
manufacturing will imply mass unemployment and a rapid
deterioration in the distribution of income. Because
the employment share of manufacturing is as high as 38
percent, industrial diversification to maintain the
viability of manufacturing is an important issue.

In the sixties, market forces automatically increased employment and equalized the distribution of
income. In the eighties, market forces automatically

increase macroinstability, unemployment, and income inequality. The government has reacted by an increase in intervention, a policy that has led to a rapid rise in the relative size of the public sector. This section elucidates the three areas of public policy mentioned above: (1) economic diversification, (2) macrostability and control of inflation and the supply of money; and (3) the rapid growth in the relative size of the public sector.

Economic Diversification

The commodity concentration of the domestic exports of Hong Kong has been very high: in the 1970s, clothing accounted for around one-third of domestic exports, while clothing together with electronics and watches accounted for over half of domestic exports. Furthermore, the degree of commodity concentration as measured by the Hirschman-Gini coefficient generally increased from 1959 to 1973 (Lin, Mok, and Ho 1980, chap. 3). Market concentration has also been high: in the 1970s, the United States generally accounted for one-third of domestic exports and, together with West Germany and Great Britain, generally accounted for over half of domestic exports. Market concentration as measured by the Gini coefficient also increased from 1959 to 1973 (Lin, Mok, and Ho 1980, chap. 3).

Given the high and increasing concentration in terms of commodities and markets, the keen competition from South Korea and Taiwan, international protectionism, and the fact that Hong Kong has in some cases been discriminated against in relation to other developing countries because of its relatively developed status, it is not surprising that there is a lot of talk about diversification. In fact, in 1977 the government appointed a committee specifically to study that approach.

It should be stressed that diversification is not a panacea. Given its natural resource scarcity and lack of land, the small economy of Hong Kong can specialize in only relatively few products. Moreover, despite considerable fluctuations in individual export industries, the overall degree of instability of Hong Kong exports from 1959 to 1973 was markedly smaller than that of the average developing country and even smaller than the average developed one (Lin, Mok and Ho 1980, 52). This situation is attributable to the fabulous flexibility of the Hong Kong economy: resources can move out of declining industries into expanding ones with incredible speed. It has also been found that, from 1964 to 1974, the rapid growth in domestic exports in Hong Kong can be attributed mostly to the "differential commodity effect," that is, Hong Kong has managed to specialize in the commodities in which expansion in world demand has been very high (Lin, Mok and Ho 1980, chap. 5). This situation is again attributable to the high speed at which Hong Kong can adjust to changing world demand. Unlike South Korea and Taiwan, increased competitiveness was insignificant in Hong Kong's export expansion.

Hong Kong's institutional framework has been characterized by minimal government interference, low taxation, freedom of trade and capital movements, and good industrial relations, characteristics that have contributed to the flexibility and resilience of the economy. Well-intentioned government intervention for the promotion of industrial diversification may damage this flexibility. In the uncertain global environment of the 1980s, the resilience and adaptability of the economy are all the more valuable. In this connection, it is comforting to note that the government's committee on economic diversification has approached the issue in the following way:

> ...the term diversification means a process whereby resources are continually re-deployed in response to shifting market conditions, to changes in the availability and relative costs of factors of production, and to technological innovations. Our main concern, therefore, has not been with how the economy should diversify but whether existing Government policies could be either modified or replaced to facilitate and stimulate this process (Hong Kong 1979, para. 10).

Thus, the committee has not proposed substituting market forces by government direction, but has instead proposed that the government facilitate and stimulate growth by (1) better coordination of policies, and (2) further development of the existing approach, namely, fostering the sources of growth and promoting demand for exports. In a nutshell, the government will facilitate the rapid growth of the financial sector by providing a better legal framework and will encourage economic diversification through the provision of technical backup services, training, and industrial land.

The diversification of manufacturing products may be expected in the 1980s, but it may be much more difficult to move into new industries. In general, capital- and skill-intensive products offer more possibilities for product differentiation. The rapidly developing industries of electronics, watches, and precision instruments are good examples of the trend toward product differentiation and improved product

design. Even the traditional labor-intensive industries of clothing and toys have been able to develop
because of the possibility of changes in styles and
design. Product diversification is a more practical
goal than industrial diversification.

The Hong Kong economy is renowned for its miracle
of rapid growth. Because of the rapid emergence of
Hong Kong as a financial center, the modernization
program of China, and the rapid economic growth of the
countries of the Far East, most economists are optimistic about its future economic growth. However, the
acid test of the eighties will be the growth of job
opportunities instead of growth in income. Mass unemployment in the midst of prosperity may lead to social
disturbances that threaten the economic well-being of
the whole community.

Control of Inflation and the Money Supply

As explained in the introductory section, the
government does not control the money supply; the automatic control imposed by the Currency Board system was
abolished when the sterling exchange standard was abandoned. Instead, the money supply automatically accom-
modates to demand, a system that aggravates the ampli-
tude of the business cycles.

The money supply as measured by M3 grew 30 percent
in 1979 and 40 percent in 1980; the rate of inflation
as measured by the consumer price index jumped from 5.9
percent in 1978 to 15.5 percent in 1980; and the
exchange rate of the Hong Kong dollar depreciated
rapidly (Table 6.6). The government has tried to
influence the supply of money in the following ways:

(1) Moral suasion and the threat of credit control if commercial banks do not behave (Bremridge 1981,
para. 39). With 113 commercial banks and a highly competitive banking industry, moral suasion cannot be very
effective. The threat of credit control does not sound
convincing because it is difficult to enforce and would
damage the reputation of Hong Kong as a financial
center.

(2) Influencing the rate of interest through the
Hong Kong Association of Banks, which is partly an
interest-fixing cartel. The government has recently
introduced legislation to strengthen the association.
Because of the dominant position of the Hong Kong and
Shanghai Bank, the government has had some success in
raising interest rates. However, raising the price of
money without controlling the quantity of reserves will
not be effective in the long run--banks can circumvent
the interest rate agreement of the association of banks
by purchasing bonds instead of extending loans. More-

over, strengthening the interest-fixing cartel impairs
the efficiency of the banking system and the interest
of the consumer.

(3) Sterilizing the government's fiscal surpluses. The effect of this move on the supply of money
does not appear to have been significant.

None of the above policies corrected the basic
flaw in the monetary system of Hong Kong: the Exchange
Fund neither controls the quantity of base money nor
guarantees its convertibility in terms of foreign currency at a specified price. Thus, the attempts by the
government to influence the money supply have not been
effective. Ho (1981) studied the causal pattern
between domestic consumer prices, import prices, and
the supply of money from 1974-1979 using the Granger
(1969) causality criteria. He found that import prices
cause domestic inflation, with the role of the money
supply nothing more than that of accommodating the
demand generated from rising import prices. Monetarists would insist that there is no imported inflation
in a floating exchange rate system, but for institutional reasons, the money supply is not an exogenous
variable in Hong Kong.

Given the passive role of the money supply and the
difficulty of using monetary policy in the Hong Kong
environment, the government should give more attention
to fiscal instruments. Before 1979, the government had
eschewed fiscal policy as an instrument of stabilization: the economy was held to be self-adjusting. In
1979, in an unprecedented move to curb inflation, the
government postponed many public construction projects. However, the government's preference for low
and stable tax rates limits the scope of fiscal
instruments.

Expansion of the Public Sector

In the thirty years from 1950 to 1980, real GDP
increased nearly 11 times, real government expenditures
24 times. The ratio of government expenditures to GDP
increased from 7.3 percent in 1950 to 21.2 percent in
1980 (Table 6.10). From 1950 to 1965, these expenditures grew faster and fluctuated less than GDP, and
the relative size of the public sector increased 2.4
times. From 1965 to 1970, Hong Kong was, as noted,
struck by a banking crisis (1965) and two riots (1966
and 1967). The growth in government expenditures
slackened, and in 1970 the relative size of the public
sector fell to 13 percent. Then, in the seventies,
public expenditures grew faster and fluctuated more
than GDP: the public sector first expanded relative to
GDP, but in the 1975 recession the government slashed

142

TABLE 6.10
Size of the public sector
(current prices, HK $ millions)

Fiscal Year	Consolidated Account Expenditures (1)	GDP (Fiscal Year)[a] (2)	Calendar Year (3)	GDP (Calendar Year)[a] (4)	Relative Size of the Public Sector (%)[b] (5)
1950/51	218	2,968			7.3
1955/56	405	3,516			11.5
1960/61	898	5,246			17.1
1965/66	1,834		1965	10,606	17.3
1970/71	2,503		1970	19,214	13.0
1974/75	6,692		1974	38,786	17.3
1975/76	6,576		1975	40,574	16.2
1976/77	7,355		1976	51,973	14.2
1977/78	9,168		1977	59,615	15.4
1978/79	12,122		1978	69,491	17.4
1979/80	15,619		1979	86,113	18.1
1980/81	22,517		1980	106,088	21.2
1981/82[c]	31,000		1981	128,780	24.1

Sources: The Consolidated Account expenditures for 1949/1950-1969/1970 and the GDP data for 1949/1950-1960/1961 were taken from Ho (1979, 24). The GDP data from 1961 to 1969 were estimated by the Census and Statistics Department. The Consolidated Account expenditures and the GDP data for 1970/1971-1980/1981 were taken from Hong Kong (The 1981-82 Budget Speech). The 1981/1982 estimates were taken from Bremridge (1981).

[a] Blank means it was not computed.
[b] Col. (5) = (1) ′ (2) for the first three lines and (1) ′ (4) for the remaining lines.
[c] Estimated.

expenditures, and the relative size of the public sector fell. However, in the late seventies, the government rapidly increased its expenditures to speed up the public projects postponed during the 1975 budget cut, and the relative size of the public sector increased from a low of 14.2 percent in 1976 to a record high of 21.2 percent in 1980. It was projected to rise even higher to 24.1 percent in 1981.

The rapid expansion of the public sector is largely attributable to capital expenditures on housing, defense, and infrastructure. The increase in expenditures on defense is the result of an imperative need to seal the border against illegal immigrants. Since the urban areas of Kowloon and Hong Kong have been fully developed, the severe shortage of land and housing has led to rocketing prices for real estate, and the building of new towns in the New Territories is inevitable. Land formation, development of infrastructure, and construction of public housing must be accorded high priority. Because of the widening inequality in income distribution, the public housing program is especially important as an instrument of income redistribution.

In general, the relative size of the public sector rises with economic development. The relative size of the public sector in Hong Kong is greater than that of the Philippines, Indonesia, and Thailand, but is appreciably less than that of the United States or Western European countries. However, the defense burden of Hong Kong is relatively small. If defense expenditures are excluded, the relative size of the public sector of Hong Kong in 1980 exceeded that of the United States in 1965 (Table 6.11). Since the real per capita income of the United States in 1965 was 2.3 times that of Hong Kong in 1980, the public sector of Hong Kong was surprisingly large for an economy famous for a philosophy of laissez-faire.

The danger of overexpansion of the government sector stemming from increases in capital expenditures is less than that from increases in recurrent expenditures. Capital expenditures can easily be postponed if the government desires to slash expenditures to fight inflation or to meet the crisis of a prolonged recession resulting in a drastic shortfall in government revenue. The rapid expansion of the relative size of the public sector from 1976 to 1980 appears to be largely justifiable.

At the same time, this rapid expansion can be dangerous if its inertia is not arrested. Government interventions that are initially justifiable may lead to an automatic and unquestioned expansion of the bureaucracy according to the famous Parkinson's Law. The growth of the public sector may hamper the flexibi-

TABLE 6.11
The relative size of the public sector:
Hong Kong and the United States
(percent)

	Including National Defense	Excluding National Defense
U.S. (1965)	27.0	19.6
H.K. (1980)	21.2	19.7
(1981) Estimated	24.1	22.7

Source: The U.S. figures are from the Economic Report of the President. The Hong Kong figures were estimated from Hong Kong (The 1981-82 Budget Speech) and Bremridge (1981).

lity and resilience of the Hong Kong economy, which is a most valuable asset in times of global economic uncertainty. Moreover, the huge fiscal reserves of the government generate pressure for increases in government expenditures from the public as well as within the government bureaucracy. These huge fiscal surpluses are not anti-inflationary because they are largely the result of the creation of credit for the purchase of land. In fact, the creation of credit for land purchases is an important factor behind the rapid increase in the money supply. In 1980/1981, the government surplus was HK $9,339 million, or 7.2 percent of GDP. This amount was slightly less than the revenue obtained from land sales (HK $10,077 million, 7.8 percent of GDP, or 35 percent of total government revenue).

The Outlook in the 1980s

Despite the world recession triggered by the second energy crisis of 1979, Hong Kong continued its double-digit growth until 1981. In 1982, however, growth slowed to 1.1 percent as a result of the prolongation of the world recession, the bust in the property market after the boom fueled by the easy credit and frenzied speculation, and last but not least, the political anxiety generated by China's declaration to resume sovereignty over Hong Kong in 1997 (92 percent of the area of Hong Kong was leased from China, and the lease expires in 1997). Then, with the world economic recovery, GDP rose by 6 percent in 1983 because of export-led growth, although investment

and the property market were still depressed by political uncertainty. China has promised to preserve
British law, the capitalist system, and the free
economic environment of Hong Kong, but investors are
still worried, and investment is likely to remain
depressed in the next few years. However, export-led
growth continued in 1984, and the economy is forecast
to grow by 7 percent.

Political anxiety led to an outflow of capital and
a chronic depreciation of the Hong Kong dollar in
1983. Since the Exchange Fund issued base money passively on demand and the supply of money was unconstrained, the government could not stop the vicious
cycle of frenzied speculation and depreciation. Therefore, in October 1983, it reverted to the Currency
Board system in essence, although the Hong Kong dollar
was linked to the U.S. dollar instead of to sterling.
Note-issuing banks now pay U.S. dollars to the Exchange
Fund to acquire certificates of indebtedness at a fixed
exchange rate, and bank notes can then be issued
against these certificates of indebtedness. As under
the old sterling exchange standard, the supply of money
is automatically constrained by the balance of payments, and the exchange rate of the Hong Kong dollar is
thus stabilized.

After the collapse of the property market, government revenue from land sales plummeted, and for three
years in a row (1982/1983-1984/1985), the budget was in
deficit, an unprecedented situation in the history of
Hong Kong. Concern over the expansion of the public
sector, which was academic in the days of the huge
fiscal surpluses, became an urgent problem.

Despite the miraculous economic success of Hong
Kong in the past thirty years, it is now confronted
with a host of new economic problems. These problems
include inflation, uncontrolled growth of the money
supply, deterioration in the distribution of income,
shortage of land, possible high unemployment, macroinstability caused by hot money attracted to a growing
financial center, a public sector that may be growing
too fast, and last but not least, a manufacturing
sector threatened by rising wages, exorbitant rents,
stiff competition from developing countries, and
protectionism in developed countries.

These problems are partly the result of economic
success and rapid growth. Nevertheless, they call for
an imaginative response from policy-makers. In the
past, the government of Hong Kong has always prag-
matically adapted its policy of positive noninter-
vention to meet the demands of the situation. The big
question now is whether the government can further
adapt its policy to meet the challenge of the eighties
without compromising the fabulous strength, flexibi-

lity, and resilience of the market mechanism in Hong Kong.

The future of Hong Kong is now also shrouded by political clouds. However, China's assurance that it will preserve Hong Kong's capitalist system and free economic environment is a flattering tribute to the principle of free enterprise on which the success of the city-state has been based. If the Chinese appreciation of free enterprise and the market system is stronger than political dogma, Hong Kong may yet sail through the recent political turbulence and flourish beyond 1997.

APPENDIX
Computation of the Factor Requirements of Trade

This appendix describes the data and computational procedures utilized in calculating the factor requirements of trade in Hong Kong. The data required for the computations included interindustry, primary input, and final demand information.

The interindustry data are summarized by two matrices, (A) and (M). (A) is a (n x n) coefficient matrix of domestically produced intermediate inputs, where the element a_{ij} of this matrix represents the requirement of domestically produced output of industry i by one unit of production of industry j.

The imported intermediate inputs are summarized by (M). Some intermediate inputs are produced by industries that do not exist in the domestic economy and therefore must be imported. Suppose there are q such industries. (M) is then of the order (n + q) x n, where m_{ij} represents the requirement of the imported output of industry i for one unit of production of industry j.

The balance equations for the domestic production of the n industries are:

$$(x) = (A)(x) + (f)$$

where (x) = A (n x 1) vector of the total outputs of the n industries

x_i = The total output of industry i

(f) = The vector of final demand for the domestic output of the economy, and

f_i = The amount of the final expenditure on the domestically produced output of industry i.

Thus

$$(x) = (I - A)^{-1}(f)$$

where (I) = The $(n \times n)$ identity matrix.

The matrix $(I - A)^{-1}$ is known as the Leontief inverse. The Leontief inverse can be used to find how much of a primary input is required (for example, capital or labor), directly or indirectly, to produce one unit of final output in one sector. In this study, since there were no data on capital stock, depreciation was used as a proxy. Labor inputs can be measured in physical terms (number of workers employed) or value terms (wages), and both methods were used in this study. The following types of primary inputs were distinguished: total labor, skilled labor, wages, and capital (depreciation). The aggregate value-added requirements were also computed. This variable is a primary input composite. The following notations were used:

(1) = A $(1 \times n)$ vector of the coefficients of labor requirements, where i_j is the direct labor requirement of the jth industry.

(s) = Direct skilled labor (professional) requirements. Skilled workers are defined to include major group 0/1 of the ISCO (professional and technical workers).

(w) = Direct wage requirements.

(d) = Direct depreciation requirements.

(v) = A $(1 \times n)$ vector of the coefficients of value added, where v_j is the direct value added of the jth industry.

The total (direct and indirect) labor requirements of the n sectors are:

$$(1') = (1) (I - A)^{-1}$$

The apostrophe is used to denote total (direct and indirect) requirements. The total labor requirement of a given vector of final demand (f) is:

$$1_f' = (1')(f) = (1)(I - A)^{-1}(f)$$

The total requirements of the other factors are similarly computed.

From the total requirements, two "capital/labor" ratios can be defined for each industry j: the depreciation wage ratio (DW_j), and the depreciation/labor ratio (DL_j).

$$DW'_j = d'_j/w'_j$$

where d'_j and w'_j = The jth elements of (d') and (w') respectively.

Similarly,

$$DL'_j = d'_j/l'_j.$$

The skill ratio (professional/labor ratio) of sector j is:

$$SL'_j = s'_j/l'_j.$$

Capital and skill intensities for a given vector of final demand (f) are defined similarly:

$$DW'_f = d'_f/w'_f$$
$$DL'_f = d'_f/l'_f$$
$$SL'_f = s'_f/l'_f.$$

There are no official input-output (I-O) tables in Hong Kong, but two have been estimated by academics. The first is the thirty-two sector table estimated by Hsia, Ho, and Lim (1975) for the year 1962; the second is the seventy sector I-O table estimated by Sung (1979) for the year 1973. The "services" industry (sector 70) of the 1973 I-O table is too aggregated for the study of tourism. With the help of recently released data, the services sector was disaggregated into three separate sectors: hotels, restaurants, and services. Data from the government's 1977 census of restaurants and hotels were used for the disaggregation. Unfortunately, there was no breakdown of material purchases in the 1977 census; thus the coefficients of material purchases from an I-O table of Japan had to be adopted. The jewelry industry was disaggregated from miscellaneous manufactures (sector 63) because it is distinguished by its high import content and low value added. For this disaggregation data were used from the 1973 Industrial Production Census (the original data used for the construction of the 1973 I-O table). The expanded I-O table thus contains seventy-three sectors.

As for primary inputs, data were needed on five vectors of inputs: wages (w), depreciation (d), skilled professionals (s), labor (l), and value added (v). All these input requirements have been estimated by Sung (1979) for both the 1962 and 1973 I-O tables. For the three new industries (jewelry, restaurants, and hotels) in the expanded 1973 table, the requirements of primary inputs were estimated from the industrial censuses of 1973 and 1977 and the population census of 1976.

Vectors of Final Demand

In this paper, the factor intensities and energy content of tourist exports, HOS exports, competitive import replacements, and noncompetitive imports of Hong Kong in 1962 and 1973 are compared. The factor intensities of HOS trade with developed and developing countries are also compared.

As a first step, define the "representative vector" of tourist expenditures (t) as an (n x 1) vector of tourist expenditures on domestic output: the t_i's are in proportion to existing tourist expenditures on domestic goods. To facilitate the comparison, total tourist expenditures on domestic and imported goods are scaled to unity (U.S. $1); for example, in 1973, since tourist expenditures on domestic goods came to 79 percent of the total tourist expenditures, the t_i's come to U.S. $.79. As such, together with the scaled expenditures on imports of U.S. $.21, total tourist expenditures would be U.S. $1.

Similarly, (e), (m), and (n) are the corresponding "representative vectors" of HOS domestic exports, competitive imports, and noncompetitive imports, respectively. The e_i's/m_i's/n_i's are in the proportion to the existing HOS exports/competitive imports/noncompetitive imports of each sector, and each group of e_i's/m_i's/n_i's also total U.S. $1.

The representative trade vectors (e), (m) and (n) are all based on trade statistics. Trade flows classified according to the 6-digit SITC were distributed to the industries in the I-O table classified according to ISIC. Natural resource-based tradables and HOS noncompetitive imports were separated from HOS domestic exports and HOS competitive imports. To separate trade flows into those with developed countries and developing countries, the 4-digit U.N. trade commodity statistics were used. The former group includes both developed market economies (as defined by the United Nations) and the Warsaw Pact countries. The latter includes developing market economies and communist nations in Asia.

The distribution of tourist expenditures on domestic output in 1962 was estimated by Hsia, Ho, and Lim (1975). However, there is no readily usable (t) vector for 1973. To compute this vector, a survey of the expenditure patterns of tourists was conducted to obtain data on the distribution of tourist expenditures in

general and on the ratio of domestically produced goods
to imported goods for each shopping item in particular.

Computation of Energy Content

To compute the energy content, it is necessary to
distinguish between primary and secondary sources of
energy. Coal, crude oil, natural gases, etc., are the
primary sources of energy for generating coal gas, refined petroleum, and electricity. A rise in the prices
of the primary sources will lead to price increases in
the secondary sources. To avoid double counting, only
the total requirement (direct and indirect) for primary
sources of energy was included. Practically all the
energy imported into Hong Kong is secondary: there are
no oil refineries, and Hong Kong imports petroleum instead of crude oil.

The production of goods and services may require
primary energy directly, or indirectly through domestic
and imported intermediate inputs. The Leontief inverse
gives the total output requirements of the n sectors.
To find the total imported petroleum required of the n
sectors, $(I - A)^{-1}$ can be premultiplied by the row
vector of input coefficients of imported petroleum (all
petroleum used in Hong Kong is imported). Then, the
primary energy requirement of refined petroleum can be
derived from the I-O table of a foreign country that
produces refined petroleum.

Domestic output also requires imported inputs,
whose primary energy content must also be included.
The energy requirements of inputs that are noncompetitive imports must be obtained from a foreign I-O table,
whereas the energy requirements of imported inputs be-
longing to sectors classified as HOS exports or competitive imports can be estimated from the domestic I-O
table. In the case of Hong Kong, noncompetitive
imports include natural resource-based goods as well as
HOS noncompetitive imports. The reason is that Hong
Kong does not have the natural resource base to produce
most kinds of natural resource-based goods.

From the matrix (M) of imported inputs, pick the
rows corresponding to HOS exports and import-competing
industries and add them to the corresponding rows of
the (A) matrix of domestic inputs, as if these imported
commodities were domestically produced. This new
matrix is (A^*). Then form a coefficient matrix of all
the inputs for noncompetitive imports (M^*), composed of
all the rows of (M) classified as natural resource-
based goods and HOS noncompetitive imports. Suppose
(M^*) is of the order (k x n), that is, there are K
noncompetitive imports. Let (h) be the (1 x k) row

vector of the coefficients of primary energy requirements for these noncompetitive commodities (estimated
from a foreign I-O table). Then the direct requirements of primary energy of the n sectors are given by:

$$(g) = (h)(M^*)$$

where (g) = A $(1 \times n)$ vector.

The total primary energy requirements of the n sectors
are:

$$(g') = (g)(I - A^*)^{-1} = (h)(M^*)(I - A^*)^{-1}.$$

The total primary energy requirement of the "representative vector" of U.S. \$1 of tourist expenditures (t)
is:

$$g_t' = (g)(i - A^*)^{-1}(t) = (h)(M^*)(I - A^*)^{-1}(t).$$

The total primary energy requirements of the other
vectors of final demand are similarly computed.

The Japanese Link I-O tables of 1960 and 1970,
with 59 and 159 sectors respectively (Japan 1975) were
used to estimate the primary energy requirements of the
noncompetitive imports of Hong Kong (Lin and Sung
1984). The factor requirements of HOS noncompeting
imports are estimated from U.S. requirements in 1947
computed by Leontief (1953) (for details see Sung 1979,
100, 155). To allow for the difference in the wage/
rental ratio between Hong Kong and the United States,
the following method is used to estimate the factor
requirements of the ith noncompeting industry:

Factor requirements of ith industry in Hong Kong	=	Factor requirements of ith industry in the United States	x	Factor requirements of Hong Kong textiles
				Factor requirement of U.S. textiles

This approach is tantamount to assuming that the textile industry and the ith industry have the same
elasticities of substitution. The textile industry was
chosen because it was the biggest and most established
industry in Hong Kong.

152

REFERENCES

Bremridge, John. 1981. "Speech to the Hong Kong Economic Association." Speech by John Bremridge, Financial Secretary, September 11, 1981. Photocopy.

Chang, E. R. 1969. Report on the National Income Survey of Hong Kong. Hong Kong: Hong Kong Government Printer.

Chen, Edward K. Y. 1979. Hyper-growth in Asian Economies. London: Macmillan.

Chow, K. R. 1966. The Hong Kong Economy, A Miracle of Growth. Hong Kong: Academic Publications.

Granger, C. W. J. 1969. "Investigating Causal Relations by Econometric Models and Cross-Spectral Methods." Econometrica 37:424-38.

Ho, Henry C. Y. 1979. The Fiscal System of Hong Kong. London: Croom Helm.

—————. 1981. "A Trivariate Stochastic Model for Examining the Cause of Inflation in a Small Open Economy--Hong Kong." Occasional Paper. Economic Research Center, The Chinese University of Hong Kong, Hong Kong, January.

Hong Kong. 1979. Report of the Advisory Committee on Diversification, 1979. Hong Kong: Government Printer.

—————. 1981a. The 1981-82 Budget. Hong Kong: Government Printer.

—————. 1981b. The 1981-82 Budget: Economic Background. Hong Kong: Government Printer.

—————. Various issues. Budget Speech. Hong Kong: Government Printer.

—————. Various issues. Economic Background. Hong Kong: Government Printer.

—————. Various issues. Hong Kong Annual Report. Hong Kong: Government Printer.

Hong Kong. Census and Statistics Department. Various issues. Estimates of Gross Domestic Product. Hong Kong: Government Printer.

—————. Various issues. Hong Kong Monthly Digest of Statistics. Hong Kong: Government Printer.

—————. Various issues. Hong Kong Trade Statistics. Hong Kong: Government Printer.

Hsia, Ronald, and Lawrence Chan. 1978. Industrialization, Employment and Income Distribution, A Case Study of Hong Kong. Geneva: International Labour Organisation.

Hsia, Ronald, Henry Ho, and Edwin Lim. 1975. The Structure and Growth of the Hong Kong Economy. Wiesbaden: Otto Harrassowitz.

153

Japan. Statistical Office. 1975. 1960-1965-1970 Link
    Input-Output Tables. Tokyo.
Krueger, Anne O. 1977. Growth, Distortions, and Pat-
    terns of Trade among Many Countries. Princeton
    Studies in International Finance No. 40. Interna-
    tional Finance Section, Department of Economics,
    Princeton University. Princeton: Princeton Uni-
    versity, February.
Leontief, W. W. 1953. "Domestic Production and Foreign
    Trade: The American Capital Position Re-
    examined." Proceedings of the American Philoso-
    phical Society 97(September).
Lin, Tzong-biau, and Yun-Wing Sung. 1984. "Tourism
    and Economic Diversification in Hong Kong."
    Annals of Tourism Research 11(2).
_____. Forthcoming. "The Impact of Rising Energy
    Costs on the Economy, Industries and Trade in Hong
    Kong--A Contrast to the Cases of Korea and
    Taiwan." Proceedings of the 13th Pacific Trade
    and Development Conference. January 14-18, 1983,
    Manila.
Lin, Tzong-biau, Victor Mok, and Yin-ping Ho. 1980.
    Manufactured Exports and Employment in Hong
    Kong. Hong Kong: The Chinese University Press.
Riedel, James. 1974. The Industrialization of Hong
    Kong. Tübingen: J.C.B. Mohr (Paul Sieback).
Sung, Yun Wing. 1979. "Factor Proportions and Com-
    parative Advantage in a Trade-Dependent Economy:
    The Case of Hong Kong." Ph.D. Thesis, University
    of Minnesota, Minneapolis.
Young, Sir George. 1973. Tourism - Blessing or Blight?
    London: Pelican.
United States. Various years. Economic Report of the
    President. Washington, D.C.: U.S. Government
    Printing Office.

ADDITIONAL SOURCE MATERIALS

Hong Kong. Report of the Advisory Committee on Diver-
    sification, 1979. Hong Kong: Government Printer,
    1979.
Hong Kong. Census and Statistics Department. Hong
    Kong B-Census 1976 (main report). Hong Kong:
    Government Printer, 1979.
_____. 1973 Census of Industrial Production.
    Hong Kong: Government Printer, 1977.

154

_____. <u>1977 Census of Wholesale, Retail and Import/Export Trades, Restaurants and Hotels.</u> Hong Kong: Government Printer, 1980.

Lin, Tzong-biau, and Yun Wing Sung. "Economic Impact of Tourism in Hong Kong." In <u>Economies of Tourism in Asia,</u> edited by Tzong-biau Lin and Elwood Pye. Ottawa: International Development Research Centre (forthcoming).

7
Opening Up and Liberalizing the Chilean Economy: The 1970s

Hernán Cortés Douglas

INTRODUCTION

The mid-1970s witnessed the beginning of a profound transformation in the Chilean economy. Its backbone was the freeing and development of several markets throughout the economy and the liberalization of trade and investment. As a result, Chile evolved from one of the most distorted countries into one of the most highly integrated into the world economy.

The program involved a complete reversal of the policies that were imposed as a consequence of the dramatic effects of the great Depression of the 1930s on Chile, policies that were intensified in the four decades following. Their common denominator was an increase in the size of the governmental sector, mostly financed by the creation of money, an approach that resulted in an environment of recurrent crises in the balance of payments, which in turn led the government to escalate the controls over prices, foreign exchange, and interest rates, as well as to augment tariff and nontariff arrangements. This trend continued except for two periods that came during the two administrations of the 1960s.

The process peaked in the early 1970s, when the fiscal deficit reached 23 percent of GDP, inflation ran 500 percent to 1,000 percent (depending on the price index), rationing was widespread, black markets flourished, the agricultural sector was paralyzed by land seizures, the urban sector was beset by strikes, the industrial sector was rendered stagnant by legal and illegal expropriations, aggregate output fell at a rate of 4 percent a year, and profound damage was done to the capital stock (particularly in agriculture). All this turmoil, a result of both policy measures and the political reaction to them, was part of the Chilean scene in 1973, when the military seized power in a coup.

One month after the military coup, the government eliminated price controls, thereby freeing the domestic markets for goods and services. In 1974, it announced a program of trade liberalization, which was completed in 1979 with a uniform 10 percent tariff. In June 1975, interest rates were freed, and the domestic financial market was liberalized. Freer access to the international financial market began in September 1977 and proceeded at a rapid pace after June 1979, when the exchange rate was fixed to the dollar. This program included a drastic tax reform in 1974 and a reduction in public sector spending and employment to create the basis for solving the fiscal deficit; it also included a series of structural reforms involving labor, social security, and other areas.

Trade policy in early 1973 had been characterized by widespread prohibitions, quotas, multiple exchange rates (the highest being fifty-two times the lowest), and an average nominal tariff of 105 percent (with a maximum of 750 percent). By June 1979, the general tariff was 10 percent, with no other restrictions on international trade and with but one temporary exception (automobiles), the latter because of international agreements.

No systematic study of the trade reform was undertaken until late 1980 (see Sjaastad and Cortés Douglas, eds. 1981, and also Cortés Douglas 1985a). This paper reports on the effects of trade liberalization in Chile. The principal focus is the impact of trade liberalization on the industrial sector's output and employment. An effort is made to disentangle trade liberalization from other policies. However, the comprehensiveness of the economic reforms of the 1970s and the different dynamics of its components render it necessary to include at least a bird's-eye view of other policies, particularly those relating to financial liberalization and the exchange rate. The latter is particularly relevant, as it constituted the main instrument of the stabilization policy.

The next section reviews the situation prior to the great Depression--a time when Chile was a very open economy--and analyzes the effects of the Depression. The ensuing economic breakdown and the extent of the damage led to a profound change in Chile's economic policies, increasing considerably its degree of market control. The effects and incidence of protectionism in the period following the Depression are the themes of the following section, which presents a summary of the empirical findings for the prereform period. The fourth section provides the background against which the impact of trade liberalization has to be viewed: the depression of 1975-1977. Unemployment jumped, never to return to the levels of employment of the

1960s. The analysis of aggregate output and employment after this depression is the theme of the fifth section. The sixth section analyzes the effects of trade reform on manufacturing production and on unemployment. The conclusion--that trade reform had no significant effect on employment or on the output of the manufacturing sector--reinforces the analysis of the third section. The seventh section briefly discusses the impact of reforms in terms of access to the international capital market, as well as the effect of financial reforms. The final section presents some concluding comments.

TRADE AND THE GREAT DEPRESSION

Until 1930, Chile's economic philosophy and policy favored free trade; there were no trade prohibitions and very few quotas, and the arguments for trade levies were of a fiscal nature for the most part (see Cortés Douglas, Butelmann, and Videla 1981). The ratio of import duty collected to the value of imports for the period 1850-1930 was 20.7 percent on average, with a minimum of 7.8 percent in 1921 and a maximum of 37.1 percent in 1881 (the latter being a war year). If anything, the trend was declining.[1]

Another indicator, the ratio of imports plus exports to gross domestic product (T/Y), fluctuated in 1908-1930 from 51.3 percent to 114.4 percent, with an average of 71.4 percent (Figure 7.1). Although estimates of national product are unavailable prior to 1908, qualitative evidence indicates a similar situation during the previous seven decades.

The Depression had, by contrast, dramatic effects on trade. In 1932, exports were but a third of their 1930 value, imports less than a quarter. This situation was to endure throughout the decade: the ratio T/Y dropped to an average of only 19.4 percent for the entire 1931-1939 period. As a consequence of the highly protectionist policies adopted during this period and intensified in later decades, the T/Y ratio remained within a range of 13.8 percent to 32.9 percent throughout 1940-1970 (the average being 24.7 percent, only a third of the 1908-1930 average) (Figure 7.1).[2]

The changes in economic philosophy during and after the Depression were not confined to commercial policy. Its severe effects on employment and output also induced a reversal of policy. Chile became protectionist in trade and interventionist in general, with an inclination toward a direct governmental role in the economy. In the late 1930s, the size of the public sector began to escalate sharply. Barriers to trade were erected not just to produce fiscal revenue

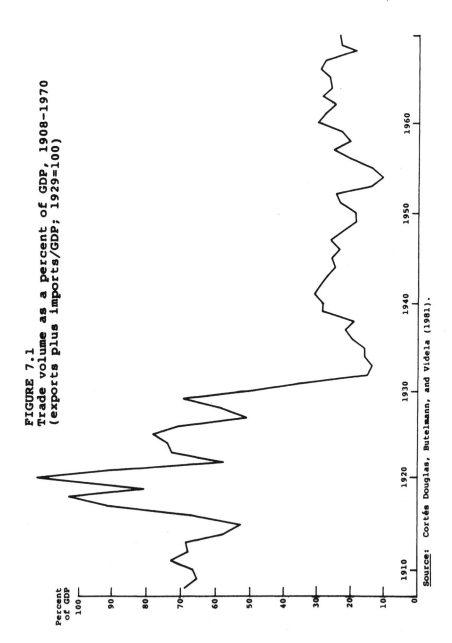

FIGURE 7.1
Trade volume as a percent of GDP, 1908-1970
(exports plus imports/GDP; 1929=100)

Source: Cortés Douglas, Butelmann, and Videla (1981).

but rather to resolve the balance of payments problems created by monetary excesses that in turn were caused by the fiscal outlays that the growing role of the state required. They proved futile, however. The government also instituted a panoply of controls, import prohibitions, quotas, prior deposits, and multiple exchange rates that were further extended over time.

Before looking at the post-Depression period and the effects of protectionist policies on the volume and composition of trade, it is useful to explore briefly the extent of the damage suffered by Chile during the Depression. Because the economy was heavily reliant on commodity exports, it was one of the most severely affected by that crisis. As mentioned above, the trade ratio, T/Y, never recovered to the pre-1930 level; indeed, during the 1940-1970 period, it was but a third of the 1908-1930 average. Further, the absolute values of imports and exports (in constant dollars) for 1928-1930 were regained only in 1955 and 1940, respectively.[3]

Once into the Depression, gross domestic product (GDP) fell dramatically. Its overall index declined from 100 in 1929 to 54.2 in 1932. Mining, the main export sector, fell particularly dramatically--from 100 in 1929 to 30.4 in 1932. The overall level of activity in 1928-1930 was not regained until 1937; that of 1929 specifically was not reached anew until 1940, while mining did not recover its 1929 level until the late 1940s. Although no data are available for the period, unemployment is known to have risen substantially. The consequences, both economic and political, of these events were to be evident for the next four decades.

To ascertain the effects of trade protectionism in the four decades between the Depression and the trade liberalization program of the 1970s, an empirical analysis of the incidence of protection is presented in the next section.

THE POST-DEPRESSION YEARS:
THE INCIDENCE OF PROTECTION

The empirical analysis here is based on the concept of a "true" tariff and export subsidies (for a complete treatment of this approach, see Sjaastad 1980). True tariffs and export subsidies are defined as the hypothetical set of nominal tariffs and subsidies that would replicate the relative price structure induced by the actual tariffs and subsidies. In the simple case of a uniform import duty at rate t, the true tariff, τ, is the resultant change in the internal price of importables relative to domestic goods. With that price as unity under free trade,

$$\tau = \Delta(p_m/p_h) = (1+t)/(1+\omega t) - 1 = (1-\omega)t/(1+\omega t) \qquad (7.1)$$

where ω = The coefficient that indicates the effect of a change in the price of importables relative to domestic goods:

$$\sigma = \Delta(p_x/p_h) = 1/(1+\omega t)-1 = -\omega t/(1+\omega t) < 0. \qquad (7.2)$$

These are the true tariff and subsidy counterparts of a tariff whose rate is t, in the sense that τ and σ generate the same relative price structure as does the actual tariff. Moreover, they make explicit that only part of a tariff is an actual subsidy to the producers of import-competing goods (and a tax on the consumers of imports), while the remainder is an implicit tax on the producers of exports (and an implicit subsidy for the consumers of those goods).

The true distortion in the tradable goods market is obviously $\tau - \sigma$. By taking the ratio of σ to $\tau - \sigma$, it can be seen that ω is the fraction of that distortion that is an implicit tax on exporters:

$$-\sigma/(\tau-\sigma) = \omega \qquad (7.3)$$

and, similarly, $(1-\omega)$ is the fraction of the distortion that constitutes true protection.

If import tariffs and export subsidies were uniform, it would be simple to estimate the incidence of trade distortion and hence the effects of trade liberalization. In the absence of that condition, it is necessary to estimate the uniform tariff equivalent, $\bar{t}$, of the existing set of tariffs and subsidies, equivalent in the sense that replacement of existing duties with $\bar{t}$ would result in the same volume (but not composition) of trade as under existing trade barriers.

For empirical purposes, assume that both imports and exports depend upon income (or production) Y, expenditure, Y^e, and relative prices, $p_1 = p_m/p_x$ and $p_2 = ph/px$. If capital letters denote the logarithms of the variables, the import demand function and the export supply functions can be specified, omitting the disturbance term for simplicity, as

$$M = \alpha + \beta P_1 + \gamma P_2 + \eta Y^e + \epsilon Y \qquad (7.4)$$

and

$$X = \alpha' + \beta' P_1 + \gamma' P_2 + \eta' Y^e + \epsilon' Y. \qquad (7.5)$$

If equation (7.4) is subtracted from equation (7.5) and rearranged, the result is the trade equation used to estimate the incidence of a tariff:

$$P_2 = \text{constant} + \omega P_1 + C_1 [M-X] + C_2 Y + C_3 BT \quad (7.6)$$

where $P_1 = \ln(P_m/P_x) = P_m - P_x$ and

$$P_2 = \ln(P_h/P_x) = P_h - P_x$$

and therefore the coefficient of P_1 is the ω as defined before, or $\omega = (\beta'-\beta)/(\gamma-\gamma')$. That coefficient will be smaller the poorer the possibility of substitution between home goods and importables is, and will be greater the poorer the relationship between home goods and exportables. BT is the trade balance in domestic currency but at _external_ prices, that is, before tariffs or subsidies.[4] Coefficients C_1, C_2, and C_3 are not specified here, but they depend on the coefficients of the structural equations.

In order to estimate the uniform tariff equivalent, substitute equation (7.6) into (7.4) and (7.5) to eliminate P_2 (the endogenous price variable), a procedure that yields the following reduced forms of the system:

$$M = \text{constant} + A_1 P_1 + A_2 Y + A_3 (BT) + A_4 (M-X) \quad (7.7)$$

$$X = \text{constant} + B_1 P_1 = B_2 Y + B_3 (BT) + B_4 (M-X). \quad (7.8)$$

At this level of aggregation, all that can be estimated is a trade function--either equation (7.7) or (7.8)--and the relative price equation--(7.6). The reason is that equations (7.7) and (7.8) are obviously not independent, as the coefficients are either identical to or are characterized by simple cross-equation constraints.

Estimates of equation (7.8) will be used to quantify the uniform tariff equivalent, $\bar{t}$. The estimate of $\bar{t}$, together with an estimate of ω from equation (7.6), allows the true tariff and subsidy equivalents-- $\tilde{\tau}$ and $\tilde{\sigma}$ -- to be estimated.

The Trade Function

The trade equation was estimated for two different periods--1930-1970 and 1944-1971--using annual data. One of the more serious difficulties with Chilean price data is that there is no good series on the _internal_ prices of tradables. As export taxes and subsidies

162

were of no great importance during the period under study, it is reasonably easy to construct a proxy for the internal price of exportables using the external price and the exchange rate; for importables, however, there is no such solution. Consequently, use was made of all data available.[5]

The results for the longer period are reported in Table 7.1. Two different relative price variables were employed. The first, PMH, is defined as $\ln(p_{m2}/p_{h2})$, where M and H refer to importables and nontradables.[6] The second relative price variable, PMX, is defined as $\ln(p_{m2}/p_{x2})$, which incorporates the import and export price indexes described above.

All of the coefficients in the regressions, estimated by both ordinary least squares and the Cochrane-Orcutt technique (reported in Table 7.1), have the expected signs and are highly significant in nearly all cases. The degree of fit is good. The coefficients of the income variable are around 0.5, while the coefficients of the PMH price variable are approximately -0.4 and are only slightly smaller in magnitude for the PMX variable.

The results for the shorter period appear in Table 7.2. In general, they are quite similar to those for the longer period, even though the price variable is of lower quality for the period 1930-1943 than subsequently.[7]

The "Omega" (ω) Function

The results for the ω equation are available from monthly observations for the period January 1959-June 1971 (reported in Sjaastad and Clements 1985). Different specifications for the weights gave a narrow range for ω--between 0.53 and 0.59--with highly stable and precise estimates. This result indicates that between 50 percent and 60 percent of the tariff is paid by exportables. The results based on annual data were relatively poor. The estimates of ω were generally very high (near or above unity) using ordinary least squares, and very low using the Cochrane-Orcutt technique. Part of the explanation may lie in the relatively high degree of time aggregation: intrayear movements in relative prices are lost when working with annual data.

The Uniform Equivalent Tariff and the True Tariff

The uniform equivalent tariff was estimated on the basis of the foregoing estimates of the trade and incidence equations. The estimate of ω used throughout was

TABLE 7.1
Regression results: Trade equation, annual data, 1930-1970

	PMH	PMX	Y	(M-X)	$(M)_{-1}$	$\bar{R}^2$	DW	a
1.	-0.41 (6.36)	-	0.53 (10.83)	0.69 (8.40)	·-	0.94	0.94	-
2.	-0.40 (5.77)	-	0.56 (6.38)	0.66 (5.81)	-	0.84	1.67	0.50
3.	-0.37 (5.64) [-0.43]	-	0.53 (7.70) [0.61]	0.48 (3.96) [0.56]	0.14 (1.69)	0.95	1.22	-
4.	-0.40 (5.59) [-0.42]	-	0.50 (4.00) [0.53]	0.65 (5.61) [0.69]	0.05 (0.60)	0.81	1.56	0.51
5.	-	-0.30 (2.35)	0.49 (5.61)	0.72 (6.45)	-	0.89	0.92	-
6.	-	-0.28 (2.03)	0.58 (4.60)	0.61 (4.08)	-	0.72	1.87	0.49
7.	-	-0.35 (3.08) [-0.50]	0.39 (3.74) [0.56]	0.32 (2.17) [0.46]	0.30 (3.09)	0.92	1.62	-
8.	-	-0.39 (2.88) [-0.43]	0.54 (3.69) [0.59]	0.46 (3.00) [0.50]	0.09 (0.77)	0.69	1.02	0.33

Source: Sjaastad and Cortes Douglas, eds. (1981).

a When a number appears in this column, the estimate was made
using the Cochrane-Orcutt technique; otherwise it is ordinary
least squares.

Note: OLS and Cochrane-Orcutt estimates: t-values are in parentheses; all estimates appearing in brackets are long-run values.
- means the variable was not included in this regression.

TABLE 7.2
Regression results: Trade equation, annual data, 1944-1971

	PMH	Y	BT	(M-X)	TT	$\bar{R}^2$	DW	a
1.	-0.43 (3.28)	1.05 (18.83)	6.17 (3.56)	-	-	0.95	1.87	-
2.	-0.42 (3.11)	1.06 (17.30)	6.64 (3.65)	-	-	0.64	1.95	0.06
3.	-0.33 (2.72)	0.84 (8.82)	8.47 (4.72)	-	0.46 (2.59)	0.96	1.87	-
4.	-0.33 (2.76)	0.83 (9.15)	9.43 (5.25)	-	0.52 (3.03)	0.74	2.13	0.01
5.	-0.22 (1.91)	0.78 (10.02)	-	0.54 (4.71)	-	0.95	1.34	-
6.	0.07 (0.54)	0.69 (6.51)	-	0.75 (7.13)	-	0.80	2.27	0.58
7.	-0.26 (2.15)	0.84 (8.94)	-	0.58 (4.87)	-0.16 (1.00)	0.95	1.51	-
8.	0.12 (0.85)	0.67 (5.29)	-	0.74 (6.71)	-0.08 (0.53)	0.80	2.29	0.61
9.	-0.30 (2.67)	0.83 (10.84)	3.45 (2.10)	0.42 (3.46)	-	0.96	1.58	-
10.	-0.11 (0.83)	0.76 (8.44)	2.77 (1.66)	0.62 (5.03)	-	0.81	2.16	0.41
11.	-0.30 (2.55)	0.80 (8.40)	4.69 (1.92)	0.35 (2.11)	0.15 (0.69)	0.96	1.57	-
12.	-0.02 (0.15)	0.71 (6.74)	3.64 (1.85)	0.56 (3.95)	0.20 (1.16)	0.82	2.27	0.5

Source: Sjaastad and Cortes Douglas, eds. (1981).

a When a number appears in this column, the estimate was made using the Cochrane-Orcutt technique; otherwise it is by ordinary least squares.

Note: OLS and Cochrane-Orcutt estimates: t-values are in parentheses.
- means the variable was not included in this regression.

0.55; the estimates of the other parameters correspond-
ed to the specific equations presented in Tables 7.1
and 7.2. On the basis of historical evidence, the
tariff level in 1930, t_{30}, was taken to be 20 percent,
that for 1980, 10 percent.

The results are presented in Table 7.3, which
identifies the periods, the equations used for the
estimation, the change in the tariff (more precisely,
the change in $\ln[1+t]$), and the implied tariff at
various times. There is considerable variance in the
estimates for any given time, but for 1945, the average
of the estimates is about 45 percent--not very different from the estimates made by others. For 1970,
the average of the estimates for the short period is 75
percent, for the long period, 90 percent. Finally, the
average estimates for 1974--after considerable cutting
of tariffs, but with no effects as yet on the composition of trade--is 95 percent. In view of other evidence such as the mean and modal tariffs of 1974 and
forward, the results seem reasonable. For the remainder of this section, then, the uniform equivalent
tariff, t, at the point at which the trade liberalization began is assumed to be 90 percent.

Referring back to the definitions of τ and σ, the
uniform equivalent true tariff for the early 1970s and
the uniform equivalent true export subsidy can be estimated as follows:

$$\tau = (1-\omega)\overline{t}/(1+\omega\overline{t}) = (.45)(.90)/(1.495) = \qquad (7.9)$$
$$0.27, \text{ or } 27 \text{ percent,}$$

and

$$\sigma = -\omega\overline{t}/(1+\omega\overline{t}) = -0.495/1.495 =$$
$$-0.33, \text{ or minus } 33 \text{ percent.} \qquad (7.10)$$

That is, the relative price structure of the early
1970s could have been replicated in broad terms by a
uniform import duty of 27 percent and a uniform export
tax of 33 percent.

The estimates show that over 50 percent of the
incidence of protection fell on exportables. This result suggests a strong development of nontraditional
exports, as was the case, and an impact on the import-
substituting industries of a significantly smaller size
than that predicted by traditional estimates of effective protection.

Before analyzing the impact of the tariff reform
on the output of industrial manufacturing and on employment, it is important to recall that trade reform
took place amidst one of the worst recessions in
Chile's history. The following section includes an
analysis of that period, to determine in particular the
length and the dimension of the disequilibrium and to

TABLE 7.3
Estimates of uniform tariff equivalent, various periods

Period	Eq. No.	$\Delta\ln(1+\bar{t})$	$\bar{t}_{45}$	$\bar{t}_{70}$	$\bar{t}_{75}$
1930-1945[a]	2, Table I	0.328	67	-	-
	4, Table I	0.032	24	-	-
	6, Table I	0.174	43	-	-
	8, Table I	0.152	40	-	-
1944-1970[b]	1, Table II	0.086	-	63	-
	2, Table II	0.112	-	68	-
	3, Table II	0.181	-	80	-
	4, Table II	0.235	-	90	-
1930-1970[a]	2, Table I	0.600	-	119	-
	4, Table I	0.270	-	57	-
	6, Table I	0.507	-	99	-
	8, Table I	0.444	-	87	-
1975-1980[c]	2, Table I	-0.704	-	-	122
	4, Table I	-0.698	-	-	121
	6, Table I	-0.486	-	-	79
	8, Table I	-0.366	-	-	59

Source: Sjaastad and Cortés Douglas, eds. (1981).

[a] Assumes t_{30} = 20 percent.
[b] Assumes t_{44} = 50 percent.
[c] Assumes t_{80} = 10 percent.

gain perspective on the behavior of the economy. In this way, the effects of the program on the manufacturing sector can be analyzed relative to the effects on the economy as a whole.

THE BACKGROUND: THE DEPRESSION OF 1975-1977

Trade reform was a fundamental pillar of the new economic policy, yet it was but one part of a radical revision of the roles of the state and the market in the economy. Moreover, it was pursued against a major breakdown of the economy caused by previous policies and the political reaction to them and was carried out during a severe recession brought on in part by the adverse external conditions of 1975. During 1974, the

price of copper--which comprised 90 percent of total
exports at the time--was at an unusually high level.
Then in 1975 it fell by nearly two-thirds. Dealing
with this problem as well as fighting inflation
required a program that involved severe fiscal
restrictions accompanied by stern monetary measures.

In the context of this paper, it is important to
emphasize two aspects of economic policy in Chile.
First, despite the critical situation in the economy in
1973 and again in 1975, a major commercial policy
reform was announced only four months after the coup
(January 1974), and its implementation did not start
until 1975, when the worst effects of the recession
were already evident. Second, the effects on the economy specific to tariff reform have to be separated from
the effects of the generally restrictive monetary and
fiscal policies that began in 1975, policies that were
to deal in the short run with the copper problem and in
the longer run with the general fiscal situation and
the degree of government intervention.

The economic program of the administration, to
cope with external imbalance, started with steep
changes in the exchange rate policy. Between December
1974 and April 1975, the exchange rate rose by 163 percent, as opposed to only 84 percent in the previous
five months. The sharp increase in the rate of inflation in early 1975 appears to have resulted from this
increase. In effect, the consumer price index rose by
136 percent between January and June 1975, whereas it
went up only 78.5 percent during the last five months
of 1974. That is, a doubling of the rate of devaluation led to a 70 percent increase in the rate of inflation with a very short lag.

On the fiscal side, an across-the-board reduction
in public sector spending of 15 percent in domestic
currency and 25 percent in foreign currency, as well as
a 10 percent increase in the income tax and other tax
reforms, reduced the fiscal deficit from 10.3 percent
of GDP in 1974 to 3.1 percent in 1975 (in spite of a
fall in real GDP of 12.9 percent in 1975), while the
local currency deficit of 5.5 percent of GDP in 1974
turned into a 1.2 percent surplus in 1975. The effect
on the balance of payments was also dramatic: the
deficit for 1975, which was estimated by the monetary
authorities at U.S. $1,200 million at the beginning of
the year, was actually only $200 million-plus at the
end of the year.

On the other hand, as a result of these measures,
public sector unemployment increased substantially in
1975. Although the effect of the measures was concentrated in a few quarters, the combination of accelerated devaluation and credit and fiscal tightening led
to a real reduction in expenditures of significant

size, creating a massive reduction in output and an
unprecedented increase in unemployment (see Table 7.4).
    The disequilibrium initiated in early 1975 did not
disappear until the end of 1977 (Sjaastad and Cortés
Douglas 1977). The current account bore the burden as
the only means of reestablishing equilibrium, which was
accomplished in three years. Two discrete revaluations
of the Chilean peso, undertaken for anti-inflationary
purposes, one during the third quarter of 1976 and a
second during the first quarter of 1977, did not help
in using the current account to restore equilibrium, as
they meant a reduction of 26 percent in the relative
prices of traded goods from January to October 1976.
    As can be seen from Table 7.4, the sharp fall in
real GDP in 1975 was followed by a recouping of 3.5
percent in 1976 and 9.9 percent in 1977. By 1978 the
real level of GDP was higher than the 1974 level, a
result compatible with the disappearance of the monetary disequilibrium by that date. Other production
data are also consistent with a restoration of the
monetary equilibrium by 1978: GDP growth rates jumped
in the 1978-1981 period in excess of 7 percent on average. Unemployment, however, peaked in 1976, reaching
in the third quarter almost 20 percent of the labor
force of Greater Santiago. Although for the most part
it declined steadily thereafter until 1981, it never
returned to the far lower levels of the 1960s (see the
third and fourth columns of Table 7.4), but stayed at
twice that rate.

UNEMPLOYMENT AFTER THE 1975-1977 DEPRESSION

    The production data and all other indicators ex-
cept unemployment suggest that the recession beginning
in 1975 lasted about three years. The figures on unemployment, on the other hand, present a puzzle. Although adjustment had been completed by 1978, the
unemployment rate in the four years of the boom period
1978-1981 averaged 12.6 percent, twice the unemployment
rate of the 1960s.
    A definitive study of the unemployment puzzle
still has to be written, a task made more difficult by
a number of data problems associated with the
unemployment surveys.[8] From a descriptive point of
view, there are several ways to classify the in-
gredients of the unemployment problem, particularly the
different responses of employment and the labor force
to the growth in output. To avoid empirical problems
with the level of the variables, a simple model with
rates of variables was estimated for the period 1967-
1979.[9]

TABLE 7.4
Growth and unemployment rates
(percent)

Year	Growth Rate of Real GDP	Unemployment Rate, National[a]	Unemployment Rate, Greater Santiago[b]	Corrected Unemployment Rate, Greater Santiago[c]
1961	4.8	8.0	6.6	n.a.
1962	4.7	7.9	5.3	n.a.
1963	6.3	7.5	5.1	n.a.
1964	2.2	7.0	5.2	n.a.
1965	0.8	6.4	5.4	18.4
1966	11.2	6.1	5.3	18.9
1967	3.2	4.7	6.1	19.9
1968	3.6	4.9	6.0	20.7
1969	3.7	5.5	6.2	20.9
1970	2.1	5.7	7.1	23.5
1971	9.0	3.8	5.5	20.6
1972	−1.2	3.1	3.7	18.8
1973	−5.6	4.8	4.6	21.7
1974	1.0	9.2	9.7	23.5
1975	−12.9	14.5	16.2	26.9
1976	3.5	14.4	16.8	26.9
1977	9.9	12.7	13.7	21.3
1978	8.2	13.6	14.0	24.1
1979	8.3	13.8	13.6	24.4
1980	7.5	12.0	11.5	24.5
1981	5.3	10.8	11.1	22.4
1982	−14.0	20.5	21.4	28.1

Source: Odeplan (various issues); Universidad de Chile (various issues); and Instituto Nacional de Estadisticas (various issues).

[a] National rate (June of each year), National Institute of Statistics.
[b] Greater Santiago (yearly averages), University of Chile.
[c] Greater Santiago (yearly averages), University of Chile, based on Wagner's (1980) definitions.

Note: n.a. = Not available.

To get an idea of the effects of the unemployment rate on the labor force, the following equation was estimated with changes in output kept constant:[10]

$$\ln (F_t/V_t) = 2.1 + 0.15 \, d_t \qquad (7.11)$$

$$r^2 = 0.83 \qquad (t = 7.23)$$

where F = The labor force
V = Real GDP
d = The unemployment rate.

The positive value of the elasticity of (F/V) with respect to d(γ = 0.15) indicates that increases in unemployment may force the secondary labor force to search for jobs to help maintain family income, a pattern that increases the labor force.

In addition, and to estimate separately the effects of cyclical changes in output on the rate of unemployment, again with the labor force kept constant, the following equation was estimated for the same period, using Cochrane-Orcutt:[11]

$$\ln d_t = 12.5 - 2.51 \, (\ln V_t) + 0.16 \, (t) \qquad (7.12)$$

$$R^2 = 0.80$$

where t = Time.

The elasticity of the rate of unemployment with respect to output, with the labor force kept constant, is -2.51. That is, the impact of cyclical fluctuations in output on the rate of unemployment indicates that in order to reduce the unemployment rate from 20 percent to 15 percent (i.e., a 25 percent fall in the rate), GDP has to grow 10 percent.

Another way to put the previous results is in terms of the effects of fluctuations in output on the labor force and unemployment. Using the definition

$$E_t \equiv F_t - d_t F_t \qquad (7.13)$$

where E = Employment,

the following elasticities are readily obtained (see note 11). The elasticity of the labor force with respect to GDP is:

$$\eta_{F,V} = 1 - \alpha\gamma \qquad (7.14)$$

and the elasticity of employment with respect to GDP is:

$$\eta_{E,V} = 1 - \alpha \ (\gamma - d_t / [1 - d_t \ ]). \qquad (7.15)$$

Using the average value for the sample period for d_t, the results are $\eta_{F,V} = 0.62$, and $\eta_{E,V} = 0.89$.

A reduction in GDP therefore has two effects. First, it increases the unemployment rate, a result that in turn induces a rise in the labor force. Second, the decline in GDP reduces the labor force directly. This latter effect dominates the first one. Thus there is, for the sample period, a strong procyclical behavior of the labor force that renders the rate of employment only weakly procyclical:

$$\eta_{E/F,V} = \alpha \ [d_t / (1 - d_t)] = 0.27. \qquad (7.16)$$

The output elasticity of the rate of employment (E/F) is only 0.27 on average for the sample period. In other words, to reduce the rate of unemployment from, say, 18 percent to 8 percent, the employment rate needs to go from 0.82 to 0.92. The value of the initial $\eta_{E/F,V}$ is $(2.51)(0.18)(0.82) = 0.55$, whereas the final value is $(2.51)(0.08)(0.92) = 0.22$. When the average of these extreme values is taken, the result is 0.385, which means that GDP must increase 38.5 percent above normal levels to lower the rate of unemployment 10 percentage points.

From this description it is clear that, if left to the growth of the economy alone, the weak procyclical behavior of that _rate_ of employment renders any sizable reduction in that rate a long-term phenomenon. In this descriptive sense, this outcome is consistent with the long amount of time it took for the rate of unemployment in 1975-1976--which was about 20 percent--to fall, despite the high rates of growth in 1978-1981. It would be interesting to go beyond this descriptive point to know why this result is so, but data limitations impede this analysis. The level of aggregation at which the survey data are elaborated has not allowed further analysis of this and other hypotheses.

In the opinion of this author, Wagner (1980) presents the most suggestive evidence in this respect. He indicates some shift in preferences that is not accounted for in the traditional definition of the rate of unemployment. He redefined the rate of unemployment to include a group called inactive persons who "desire to work" in both the numerator and denominator of the traditional definition. Wagner's presumption is that these inactive people desiring work are no different from the members of the labor force. His hypothesis is that the depression of 1975-1977 created a reduction in wealth that lowered the opportunity cost of an active job search, and that the high and fluctuating rates of inflation readily destroyed knowledge about job opportunities, a situation that lowered the productivity of a passive job search. This hypothesis is consistent with a decline in the number of inactive who desire work (passive searchers), and a corresponding increase in unemployed (active searchers), with no extraordinary changes in total (redefined) unemployment.

The figures below show a summary of the differences between the traditional definition, d, and the redefined one, d*, for a relevant aggregation of subperiods.

	Average d	Average d*
1965-1969	5.5	19.8
1975-1977	15.6	25.0
1978-1981	12.6	23.9

The period 1965-1969 is used as "normal," that is, as representative of what normal unemployment was in the decade of the sixties. The period 1975-1977 covers the depression years, commented on in the previous section. And 1978-1981 are the four post-depression years, with an average growth rate of 7.3 percent.

When the traditional definition of the rate of unemployment is used, the rate for 1978-1981 was 2.3 times the rate for 1965-1969. These figures are the unemployment puzzle: why is there a 130 percent increase in unemployment when the growth rate exceeds 7 percent a year? When the redefined rate of unemployment is used, however, the ratio is only 1.2. That is, the redefined unemployment rate was only 20 percent higher in 1978-1981 than in 1965-1969. If Wagner's hypothesis is true and the presumptions correct, most of the recorded increase in unemployment, as well as the elasticities in the description of the unemployment process above, are explained by large numbers of people shifting from being passive job searchers to active job searchers, and then only 20 percent of the redefined unemployment in 1978-1981 exceeded the normal unemployment of the 1960s.

Further work along these lines has also been hampered by the level of aggregation of the data; nevertheless, the data are highly suggestive, and the effort is worth pursuing.

TRADE REFORM, MANUFACTURING PRODUCTION,
AND EMPLOYMENT

The issue of unemployment remains open in Chile
and requires more research; it is included because it
relates to the problems that confront any attempt to
analyze the effects of trade reform on employment.
Both tariff and nontariff restrictions were present at the end of 1973 at levels that highly constrained Chile's international trade. The average nominal tariff at the end of 1973 was 105 percent, the
modal tariff, 90 percent. Half the items had duties in
excess of 80 percent. Only 4 percent of the items had
tariffs lower than 25 percent, whereas 8 percent had
tariffs ranging between 220 and 750 percent (with an
average of 320 percent).[12] In addition to tariffs,
187 items were prohibited and 2,872 items required
previous deposits of 10 percent at the Central Bank
during 90 days. This requirement made importation
prohibitive. Discretionary approval was a prerequisite
for 2,278 items (a study concluded that the latter
approval was used to prohibit the importation of 159
items). In summary, through these mechanisms more than
60 percent of imports were directly or indirectly
prohibited. The scope of the reforms from 1974 to 1979
can be seen in Table 7.5.
The manufacturing sector produces most import substitutes in Chile, and hence it would potentially be
affected by reform of the commercial policy. To begin
with and to allow for the economic depression of the
period, it is helpful to look at the value of manufacturing production relative to total production as
reported in the national accounts. This proportion
decreased from an average of 26.8 percent for 1960-1969
to 24.8 percent during 1970-1974, and to a stable 22.0
percent during 1975-1980. The downward trend clearly
began before the tariff reform; in addition, the stability of the ratio at 22.0 percent since 1975 indicates that growth in manufacturing in the latter period
was equal to that of the overall economy (which grew at
more than 7 percent a year).
The figures on unemployment in manufacturing show
a similar picture. The ratio of the unemployed whose
last job was in manufacturing to total unemployment
(excluding those seeking a job for the first time) was
33.1 percent for 1960-1969, and fell to 32.6 percent
during the recession (1975-1977). During 1978-1980, it
rose to 33.6 percent, 1.5 percent higher than the level
during the 1960s. (The 1970-1974 average was 33.6 percent.)
Thus there is little evidence that the tariff reform had a strong impact on the manufacturing sector.

TABLE 7.5
Trade reform: Number of tariff items subject to each tariff level

Tariff Rates(%)	January 1974	January 1975	February 1976	August 1977	July 1979
220-750	416	0	0	0	0
125-215	911	0	0	0	0
60-120	2,493	1,923	394	0	0
35-55	959	2,394	2,968	78[a]	0
25-30	223	585	696	1,469	0
15-20	142	167	366	1,817	0
10	42	20	24	600	4,273
0-5	39	36	42	12	0
Average Nominal Tariff	105	57	44	15	10
Modal Tariff	90	55	50	13	10

Source: Sjaastad and Cortés Douglas, eds. (1981, 230-31).

[a] It corresponds to 35 percent (the maximum tariff).

This impression is supported by further analysis of industrial employment. The Association of Manufacturing Development (SOFOFA) collects monthly data on both output and employment for a detailed classification of firms. The sample has a fixed number of firms, and no new firms have been added. As bankrupt firms remain in the sample, with their levels of employment and output equal to that reported just before they went bankrupt, there is a downward bias; on the other hand, new export-oriented firms will not appear in the sample.

The statistical analysis was carried out using dummy variables to capture time, industrial classification, and trade orientation (the latter referring to the degree to which firms compete with imports and the fraction of output that is exported).[13] The results for firms classified by degree of import competition reveal a sharp decline in employment during 1976-1977 of about 8 percent relative to the change during 1974-1975 (the reference period). The dummies that capture the degree of competition with imports

have positive but only marginally significant coefficients and indicate that firms which did not
compete with imports increased their employment by
about 4 percent more a year than did those facing competition. The evidence, however, is not strong. On
the other hand, the dummies for export intensity have
nonsignificant coefficients, a result that indicates no
stimulus to employment from that source. As noted
above, the sample is strongly biased against encoun-
tering such a relation, as no new firms have been added
since 1968. Finally, the dummies for industrial classification had insignificant coefficients.

Given the limitations of the data, it can be
reported that there is no strong evidence to support
the hypothesis that the tariff reform adversely affected employment in the manufacturing sector. There
is some indication of an adverse effect among firms
that compete heavily with imports, but no evidence of a
strong sectoral bias.

In short, whatever the explanation for the persistence of the rate of unemployment in Chile, one fact
is clear: the sharp increases in that rate occurred in
1975 and 1976--before the effects of the trade reform
could be felt. Furthermore, the major changes in the
composition of trade started to take place in the
second semester of 1977, a sequence that is consistent
with unemployment in the 1975-1977 period being mainly
a result of the monetary contraction.

There is a final caveat that must be noted regarding the results which were obtained here. As was
explained above, a major effort was made to separate
out the effects that variables other than commercial
policy had, so that the "net" effects of the latter on
manufacturing output and employment could be ascer-
tained. There is, however, one important variable that
has not been dealt with and that can result in a strong
bias if the results reported here are applied in a
different context. That variable is the boom in the
financial sector, which resulted in firms engaging
heavily in debt financing, particularly those firms
that did not believe in the continuity of tariff
policy. If the availability of credit had been less
enormous than it was, the results of the commercial
reform could have been significantly different.

ACCESS TO THE INTERNATIONAL CAPITAL MARKET
AND FINANCIAL REFORM

The opening of the Chilean economy to the international financial markets started later and followed a
less clear path as compared to trade liberalization.
Throughout the period, the Central Bank was concerned

about the effects of opening the economy to foreign borrowing totally or abruptly. As of this date, there is no study of the effects of the process of financial reform comparable to the one on trade reform already discussed. The analysis in this section is therefore essentially descriptive and selective, highlighting what are probably the most important problems in this area.

The prohibition on Chilean banks to take risks and to arbitrage by using external borrowing in dollars to lend in domestic currency was not eliminated until July 1982. In addition, the minimum average maturity on external borrowing was two years until May 1982, when this restriction was eliminated. All other quantitative restrictions were eliminated in 1979 and 1980, as is described succinctly below.[14]

As of September 1977, the restrictions on capital movements were greater than in the years of the previous administration. On that date, banks, which were essentially conducting trade financing, were guaranteed access to foreign exchange for the servicing of their external borrowing (under the so-called article 14 of the Foreign Exchange Law). Several quotas were imposed on external borrowing by banks, namely, on the flow per month (5 percent of capital and reserves as of September 1977); on borrowing through article 14 (25 percent of capital and reserves as of January 1978); and on total borrowing (150 percent of capital and reserves as of June 1976). These limits were increased by stages in the period 1977-1979, with particular emphasis on borrowing at more than three years (Rosende 1981; Gutiérrez 1982). In April 1979, the government introduced reserve requirements on external borrowing at the same time that it increased the limits. Moreover, the reserve requirements were higher the lower the maturity of the debt (25 percent for loans between two and three years and decreasing until zero requirements were in effect for loans of more than five-and-a-half years).

In June 1979, the global limits on external borrowing were eliminated, and in April 1980, the limits on article 14 borrowing were ended. The only restrictions in effect as of April 1980 were: (1) the reserve requirements; (2) the prohibition on arbitrage; and (3) the minimum period of two years. The latter reforms signified a substantial opening up of the capital account, as can be seen from Table 7.6.

In spite of huge capital flows, interest rates in Chile were substantially higher than the international rates in the period following the liberalization of interest rates in 1975. In fact, their real levels since the decontrol of interest rates in 1975 have been staggering. In the first few years after the free-

TABLE 7.6
Net capital inflows
(million U.S. dollars)

Year	Total	Article 14
1975	240	58
1976	199	238
1977	572	240
1978	1,946	679
1979	2,247	922
1980	3,165	1.809
1981	4,769	2.918

Source: Chile, Ministerio de Hacienda
(1982); and Central Bank of Chile.

ing the insulation of the domestic capital market from
the international capital market and the uncertainty
about the exchange rates made the interest rate a
domestic phenomenon in Chile (Sjaastad 1981).[15]

After the exchange rate was fixed in 1979 and the
capital account was opened gradually, interest rates in
pesos were still more than twice the level for the dollar throughout the three years of the fixed exchange
rate regime. Curiously enough, the spread between the
peso deposit rates and LIBOR was quite stable on average; indeed, the annual averages were between 1.0 and
1.6 a month in 1979-1982 (although the monthly figures
fluctuated between a low of 0.89 and a high of 2.67 a
month).

The massive expansion of both peso credit (at
more than 50 percent a year in real terms) and dollar
credit (at more than 25 percent a year in real terms)
that took place in 1979, 1980, and 1981 are an
indication that a phenomenal demand for credit arose
since 1979.

The very high, persistent level of interest rates
in pesos in Chile is one of the main characteristics of
the period under analysis, as discussed later in this
section. Short-term bank deposit rates in real terms
averaged 20 percent a year in 1977 and 26 percent in
1978, and then dropped to 5 percent in 1979 and 1980;
they resumed their previous high levels at 29 percent a
year in 1981 and exceeded 30 percent a year in the
first semester of 1982.[16]

In other words, real interest rates in peso
deposits were always between 20 and 30 percent a year,

except for 1979 and 1980, when they were only 5 percent
a year. As has been seen, before 1979 the exchange
controls were tight, and the capital account flows were
controlled by the Central Bank. The fixing of the
exchange rate in mid-1979 and the lifting of many of
the controls on the capital account both reduced
uncertainty about the exchange rate and started to open
up the capital account.

The nominal level of peso deposit rates in 1979
and 1980 averaged 35 percent a year and was equivalent
to international interest rates plus the relatively
stable and high spread. Together with domestic inflation of 30 percent a year, the result was real rates of
only 5 percent a year.

The final stage began with the revaluation of the
dollar against other major currencies in late 1980.
This revaluation caused the dollar prices of many
Chilean imports to fall, reversing the previous situation in which Chilean tradables were increasing in
price at a higher rate than the U.S. price index was.
It also brought domestic inflation down in 1981 to -4
percent according to the WPI, and 9 percent according
to the CPI. This abrupt decline in the rate of inflation increased real interest rates in Chile from 5
percent in 1980 to almost 30 percent in 1981, in turn
the first symptom and cause of the current depression.

If the peso deposit rates have been high, peso
loan rates have been even higher by a very large internal spread: 0.9 percent a month in 1979, 0.6 percent
in 1980 and 1981, and almost 1.0 percent a month in the
first semester of 1982. Thus an average of 10 percentage points a year was added to the reported deposit
rates. The large amount of unrecoverable loans, which
became evident in late 1981 and 1982, is proof, however, that these loan rates were ex-ante.

The problems, omissions, and inconsistencies in
banking regulation and control set up a time bomb that
culminated in the critical condition of the Chilean
banking industry today. The financial conglomerates
used an important part of the cheaper foreign resources
in dollars for loans for their own enterprises. In
this sense, the bigger private banks were not clearcut
financial intermediaries, but, rather, were fund-
raisers for the conglomerates' enterprises. This behavior was an outstanding characteristic of the financial sector in this period.

This behavior was aided and this belief fostered
by a general perception of a permanent boom in the
economy. This belief led, among other things, to an
overvaluation of capital goods, land, stocks, etc. In
the banking sector, it also led to an overvaluation of
investment projects and loan guarantees, and a strong
increase in the demand for credit. The expectations of

a permanent boom, together with the extraordinary increase in capital inflows since 1979, and the evidence that when things go well, banks earn profits, but if they go sour, the monetary authority pays the bill, and a legal system that allowed the "protection" of personal wealth through "paper" firms and property transfers to wives and others, generated a financial bubble that rendered the financial sector fundamentally insolvent.

The failures in bank regulation and the persistence of the high interest rates were undoubtedly the primary domestic factor responsible for the extremely severe impact of the international recession on the Chilean economy (for further analysis see Cortés Douglas 1985b, 1985c).

The important appreciation of the U.S. dollar against other major currencies that started with President Reagan's election in late 1980 led to a decline in the dollar prices of traded Chilean goods. On the one hand, the dollar prices of Chile's imported goods declined sharply, a trend that led to a rapid decline in the rate of inflation in 1981. Together with the increase in international interest rates (in dollars), the drop in inflation brought domestic interest rates (in Chilean pesos) to around 30 percent in real terms. This increase brought the construction sector, which had boomed in 1979 and 1980 because of the low interest rates (23.9 percent and 25.7 percent real growth, respectively), to a complete halt and caused a severe depression in the economy. In addition, because of the appreciation of the dollar, important export prices fell, particularly those for copper and agricultural and forestry products, which represented a large proportion of the total value of exports.

The resurgence of extraordinarily high real interest rates, coupled with the deterioration in the terms of trade, had a rapid and profound depressionary impact, especially because of the weakness of the banking system and the high level of indebtness of most business firms in both pesos and dollars.[17]

To this scenario must be added the automatic wage escalator clauses for past inflation: the new Labor Plan kept them as is. That is, in August 1981, when inflation was practically zero, a wage increase of 14 percent was enacted.

Thus business enterprises were caught by a 500 percent increase in real interest rates in 1981 and an increase in real wages of about 20 percent (from July 1979, when the exchange rate was fixed, to December 1980), at the same time that their prices were mostly falling (the WPI index showed a drop of -4 percent in 1981), with export prices dropping even more given the dollar's appreciation.

And all this occurred <u>before</u> the abrupt reduction
in the capital inflow at the end of the third quarter
of 1981. Just as the enormous capital inflow in 1980
and 1981, in excess of $500 million a quarter, with a
peak of $830 million and $1,000 million in the second
and third quarters of 1981, financed the price rise for
Chilean tradables in 1980 and the increase in
expenditures relative to income, the decrease in the
capital inflow at the end of 1981 needed a
corresponding reduction in the relative prices of
nontraded goods and a reduction in expenditures. But
the economy was already squeezed by the dollar appreciation that had started almost a year earlier.

CONCLUDING COMMENTS

The opening and liberalization of the Chilean
economy represented a radical transformation of both
the country's real and financial situation. Through
the trade reforms especially, the economy became, in a
brief span of time, one of the most open to international trade. On the other hand, and not without
reason, the Central Bank feared the effects of external
borrowing. The analysis presented here has shown that
the inconsistencies of bank regulation created a feeble
domestic financial sector that, together with high
interest rates, made the economy extremely vulnerable
to external shocks.

From the analysis of the trade reform and the incidence of protection, it is clear that 50 percent to
60 percent of the protection was effectively a burden
on the export industries, and that the uniform
equivalent tariff at the time of trade reform can be
estimated at 90 percent.

Data limitations hampered efforts to measure the
effect of trade liberalization on the manufacturing
sector in Chile. The data do reveal, however, only
mild negative effects on employment, an outcome that is
surprising in view of the pace and scope of the
reform. The effects of the financial boom cannot be
separated out, however, a limitation that leaves the
results open to this important qualification.

The dramatic reduction in protection in Chile
since 1974 does not appear to explain the high rates of
unemployment experienced during the period of the commercial policy reform.[18] The unemployment problem in
Chile was an outgrowth of the contractionary policies
of 1975. While certain dislocations were inevitable,
there is no evidence that trade liberalization in Chile
by itself had a serious adverse effect on production.

The absence of a study of comparable depth for the
policies in the financial sector leaves several ques-

tions unanswered. It is clear, however, that access to the international capital markets was slowly liberalized until the reforms of 1979-1980, and that the resulting capital inflows did not have a sound counterpart in the domestic financial sector. The overall result was an intensification of the impact of the international recession.

The Chilean experience indicates the necessity of global consistency in all liberalization efforts, particularly in the financial sector, where the role of confidence and the externalities associated with risk-taking can make the difference between success and failure.

NOTES

1. The average values for the periods 1850-1880, 1881-1907, and 1908-1930 are 29.6, 27.2, and 14.7 percent, respectively.
2. In 1980, one year after the liberalization was completed, the T/Y ratio was 40 percent.
3. Trade was exceptional in 1930, the last pre-Depression year. Only in 1960 and 1964 were the levels of 1930 regained for imports and exports, respectively.
4. Although not readily apparent, (M-X) and BT are quite different. By definition, $(M-X) = \ln(m/x) = \ln[1+(m-x)/x] = (m-x)/x$, whereas $BT = (m'-x')/y$. Thus there are important differences between (M-X) and BT. The variable (M-X) is a version of the trade balance measured as a quantum index, whereas BT is measured in value terms; second, BT is deflated by income and (M-X) by a quantum of exports. Variations in either the terms of trade (from year to year) and/or the ratio of exports to income will permit BT and (M-X) to behave quite differently.
5. For a description of these difficulties and for the results in full, see Sjaastad and Cortés Douglas, eds. (1981) and in particular Sjaastad (1981a). No data were used after 1971 because of the problems with the price indicators in the 1971-1974 period. In the four years between 1971 and 1975, the consumer price index decreased 974 times, whereas the wholesale price index increased only 76 times. If account is taken of black markets and rationing during 1972 and 1973, it is very difficult to trust any of these indicators as they stand.
6. Time series on nominal wages and salaries were used as a proxy for the price of domestic goods for the

longer period. The price of exportables was represented by the price of copper (external price times the exchange rate), and the price of importables was the ECLA (CEPAL) unit-value series, again multiplied by the exchange rate. A quantum index of imports was used as the dependent variable. For the shorter period, the price of home goods was based on the consumer price index, after eliminating food items. For that period, the exportables price index was represented by the mining products category of the wholesale price index, and the imported goods price index (discussed above) of the wholesale price index was used as the price of importables.

7. A number of additional experiments carried out for the short time series strengthened the credibility of these results.

8. See Cortés Douglas and Sjaastad (1981). The longer, more complete series are derived from the University of Chile unemployment surveys for Greater Santiago, but they are full of pitfalls. Meller, Cortázar, and Marshall (1979) have argued convincingly that the Greater Santiago estimates are quite unreliable because of inaccurate figures for population and migration that render any extrapolation extremely suspicious. Despite substantial revisions, the population estimates still leave serious doubt. Even the sample information, which reflects the rates of unemployment rather than the number of unemployed, raises questions. For example, there are wide variations over time in ratios that are expected to be highly stable, such as the ratio of persons 14 years of age and over to total population. Further, an examination of the results of the sample for "government and financial sector employees" against actual data from the Budget Office on the number of public employees reveals wide discrepancies that indicate errors in the unemployment survey. According to the Budget Office, government employment increased from 200,000 people in 1970 to 300,000 in the three Allende years, after which a decline began that accelerated in 1980. This reduction is one of the major factors accounting for the enormous increase in unemployment in 1975 and 1976. However, the unemployment survey shows a drop of 100,000 employees during 1974, a figure that is completely out of the question, even after allowing for the fact that the survey data do not separate the government from the financial sectors. The survey also indicates that the number of public employees began to increase after 1974, similarly unbelievable, since the fiscal contraction and the contraction of public sector employment were especially acute in 1975 and 1976 (and the growth in the financial sector prior to 1978 was total-

ly insufficient to offset the decline in government employment).

9. The model is developed in Cortés Douglas and Sjaastad (1981).

10. This equation comes from making the labor force, F, a function of real GDP, V, and the rate of unemployment, d, as follows,

$$F_t = K(V_t)^\beta (d_t)^\gamma$$

and assuming

$$\eta_{F,V} = 1$$

i.e., $\beta = 1$.

11. Unemployment, D, is defined with a permanent component, which rate is d, and a cyclical component, such that

$$D_t = dF_t \, e^{-\alpha \nu_t}$$

where ν_t depends on the discrepancy between actual and expected V.

$$\nu_t = f \, (V_t / V_t^*); \quad f(1) = 0; \quad f' > 0.$$

If $V_t^* = a \, e^{bt}$, and defining $\nu_t \equiv \ln V_t - \ln V_t^*$, then

$$\ln d_t = \text{constant} - \alpha \ln V_t + b\alpha t \, .$$

12. Cauas and de la Cuadra (1981) classify the process of tariff reform into three stages: one ending in January 1975, in which the maximum tariff was 120 percent; a second ending in August 1977, in which the maximum tariff was 35 percent; and the last, ending in July 1979, in which a uniform tariff of 10 percent was reached. In August 1976, during the second stage, both the required deposits and the direct prohibitions were eliminated. Table 7.5 presents the main dates of the reform and their value; 1976 is included as an intermediate step in the second stage of the reform.

13. Thanks go to SOFOFA for its help in preparing this classification for this study and for providing access to its data. The results are presented in full in Sjaastad and Cortés Douglas, eds. (1981).

14. The timing of these measures appears in full in Rosende (1981) and Gutiérrez (1982).

15. See Sjaastad and Cortés Douglas (1977).
16. In addition, there was the very high spread between deposit rates and loan rates discussed later.
17. There is no doubt that the assets of the Chilean banking system were less sound than they appeared. As of December 1982, the unpaid loans of the banking system were estimated at three times the banks' capital.
18. This result is quite consistent with Carlos Rodríguez's analysis, which indicates that a tariff reduction can easily result in a rise, rather than a fall, in the real wage and that that rise will have to come about through an increase in the demand for labor (Rodríguez 1981).

REFERENCES

Cauas, Jorge, and Sergio de la Cuadra. 1981. "La política económica de la apertura al exterior en Chile" [The Economic Policy of the External Opening up of Chile]. In "La economía política de la reforma comercial en Chile" [The Political Economy of Commercial Reform in Chile], Cuadernos de Economía (54-55), edited by L. A. Sjaastad and H. Cortés Douglas.

Chile. Instituto Nacional de Estadísticas. Various issues. Encuestas de Desempleo [Unemployment Surveys]. Santiago.

_____. Ministerio de Hacienda. 1982. Estado de la Hacienda Pública [Report on Public Finances]. Santiago, October.

Cortés Douglas, H. 1985a forthcoming. "The Chilean Experience in Trade Reform: A Progress Report on Consequences and Implications." In The Free Trade Endeavour in Latin America, by L. A. Sjaastad (ed.). London: Macmillan.

_____. 1985b. "Crisis financiera internacional y de la economía mundial; el caso de Chile" [International Financial and World Economic Crises: The Case of Chile]. In Pensamiento Iberoamericano [Iberoamerican Thought].

_____. 1985c forthcoming. "Stabilization Policies in Chile: Inflation, Unemployment and Depression 1975-1982." In The National Economic Policies of Chile, edited by G. Walton. JAI Business and Economics Series. Greenwich, Conn.: JAI Press.

Cortés Douglas, H., and L. A. Sjaastad. 1981. "Protección y empleo" [Protection and Employment]. In

185

"La economía política de la reforma comercial en
Chile" [The Political Economy of Commercial Reform
in Chile], Cuadernos de Economía (54-55), edited
by L. A. Sjaastad and H. Cortés Douglas.
Cortés Douglas, H., Andrea Butelmann, and Pedro
Videla. 1981. "Proteccionismo en Chile: Una
visión retrospectiva" [Protectionism in Chile: A
Retrospective Look]. In "La economía política de
la reforma comercial en Chile" [The Political Econ-
omy of Commercial Reform in Chile], Cuadernos de
Economía (54-55), edited by L. A. Sjaastad and H.
Cortés Douglas.
Gutiérrez, M. 1982. "Reflexiones sobre apertura finan-
ciera: El caso chileno" [Reflections on the Finan-
cial Opening Up: The Chilean Case]. Research
Report (Central Bank of Chile) (14)(May).
Meller, P., R. Cortázar, and J. Marshall. 1979. "La
evolución del empleo en Chile: 1974-1978" [The
Evolution of Employment in Chile: 1974-1978]. Es-
tudios Cieplan (2).
Odeplan. Various issues. Cuentas Nacionales [National
Accounts]. Santiago.
Rodríguez, Carlos. 1981. "Política comercial y
salarios reales" [Commercial Policy and Real
Wages]. In "La economía política de la reforma
comercial en Chile" [The Political Economy of
Commercial Reform in Chile], Cuadernos de Economía
(54-55), edited by L. A. Sjaastad and H. Cortés
Douglas.
Rosende, F. 1981. "Algunas reflexiones acerca del
proceso de apertura financiera en Chile" [Some
Reflections on the Process of the Financial Opening
up in Chile]. Research Report (Central Bank of
Chile) (3)(July).
Sjaastad, L. A. 1980. "Commercial Policy, 'True' Tar-
iffs, and Relative Prices." In Issues in Commer-
cial Policy and Diplomacy, edited by John Black and
Brian Hindley. London: Macmillan for the Trade
Policy Research Center.
——————. 1981a. "La protección y el volumen de
comercio en Chile: la evidencia." [Protection and
Trade in Chile: The Evidence]. In "La economía
política de la reforma comercial en Chile" [The
Political Economy of Commercial Reform in Chile],
Cuadernos de Economía (54-55), edited by L. A.
Sjaastad and H. Cortés Douglas.
——————. 1981b. "Stabilization and the Exchange
Rate: The Conflicting Experiences of Argentina and
Chile." Working Paper (Centro de Estudios
Públicos) (1)(October).
Sjaastad, Larry A., and Kenneth W. Clements. 1985.
"The Incidence of Protection: Theory and Mea-
surement." In The Free Trade Endeavour in Latin

186

America, by L. A. Sjaastad (ed.). London: Macmillan.

Sjaastad, L. A., and H. Cortés Douglas. 1977. "The Monetary Approach to the Balance of Payments and Real Interest Rates in Chile." Photocopy. Also published in Spanish in Estudios de Economía [Studies of Economics] (11)(I semester 1978).

_____, eds. 1981. "La economía política de la reforma comercial en Chile" [The Political Economy of Commercial Reform in Chile]. In Cuadernos de Economía (54-55).

Universidad de Chile. Various issues. Encuestas de Desempleo [Unemployment Surveys]. Santiago.

Wagner, G. 1980. "Empleo y desempleo: una interpretación" [Employment and Unemployment: An Interpretation]. Catholic University of Chile, Santiago. Photocopy.

8
The Experience and Lessons of Asia's Super Exporters

Anne O. Krueger

Asia's super exporters--Hong Kong, the Republic of Korea (South Korea), Singapore, and Taiwan--have experienced remarkable transformations in their economies in the past two decades. With annual average rates of growth of real per capita income of 6.5, 6.9, 7.4, and 6.6 percent, respectively, over the period 1960 to 1978, the four were exceeded only by Japan, Iran, Romania, and Saudi Arabia (World Bank, 1980). Since these last three were all oil exporters, the growth performance of the "gang of four" is clearly all the more remarkable, as they maintained that growth in the 1970s despite sharply adverse movements in their terms of trade.[1]

Interesting and important questions arise with respect to: (1) the causes of the success of these four countries; (2) the similarities and differences among them; (3) the extent to which their geographic proximity to each other and to the other super exporter, Japan, contributed to their performance; and (4) the extent to which special factors accounted for their success, a point that has a bearing on the degree to which the lessons may be generalizable.

This paper explores these questions, with the focus on comparative analysis and the degree to which lessons may be drawn for other countries. The first section provides a brief comparative summary of the structure and growth of the four countries and contrasts them with the norm for all middle-income countries as defined by the World Bank. The second section examines the experience of each country individually, with emphasis on the factors commonly thought to be divergent among the four. The third section assesses the contribution that their export orientation made to growth. The final section examines the lessons for other countries.

STRUCTURE AND GROWTH OF THE SUPER EXPORTERS

Table 8.1 provides some basic data on the four Asian exporters, along with a weighted average for all middle-income countries.[2] Singapore and Hong Kong have substantially higher per capita income than do South Korea and Taiwan. This difference reflects largely the absence of any sizable rural sector in the two city-states: when urban income is contrasted, the differences are far smaller. The rapid growth rates are reflected not only in the data in rows 3a, but also in the sharp rise in per capita income between 1960 and 1978. Whereas both South Korea and Taiwan had per capita income substantially below the average for middle-income countries in 1960, by 1978 Taiwan's per capita income exceeded the group mean, while South Korea had almost attained it (after moving from a substantially lower base in earlier years).

The biggest difference among the four is between Hong Kong and Singapore, on the one hand, and South Korea and Taiwan, on the other. The former are small city-states, with virtually no agricultural sector (see rows 3a), while Taiwan and South Korea have much larger populations and a rural sector that, although it is declining in relative importance, is still sizable.[3]

The data in the rows under item 3 reflect some aspects of the structural shifts that accompanied the growth in each of the countries. Even though agricultural output was negligible in both Singapore and Hong Kong in 1960, its relative share declined still further during the subsequent eighteen years. For South Korea and Taiwan, agricultural output as a share of GDP dropped sharply. South Korea's decline was even more precipitous than that of Taiwan, largely because Taiwan initiated its economic reforms and rapid growth in the mid-1950s, while South Korea did not commence its until 1960. It should be noted, however, that agriculture itself still grew rapidly: at 4.2 percent annually in South Korea and 5.5 percent annually in Taiwan over the 1960-1978 period.

The obverse of the coin is the rapid increase in the proportionate and absolute size of the manufacturing sector in all countries except Hong Kong (where rapid growth began in the 1950s and where the share remained constant). The relatively small size of the manufacturing sector in Singapore in 1960 reflects largely the fact that the split between Singapore and Malaysia had not yet occurred; Singapore did not become independent until 1963.

The statistics in rows 3c indicate the share of investment in GNP in each of the super exporters. As is apparent, in 1960 all four had investment/GNP ratios below the average for middle-income countries. By 1978,

TABLE 8.1
Comparative structure and growth

	Hong Kong	South Korea	Singapore	Taiwan	All Middle-Income Countries
1. Per Capita Income (1969 prices)					
1960	1,042	373	978	472	674
1978	3,040	1,160	3,290	1,400	1,250
2. Population 1978 (mil.)	4.6	36.6	2.3	17.1	872.8
3. Percent of GDP in					
a. Agriculture					
1960	4	40	4	28	22
1978	2	24	2	10	16
b. Manufacturing					
1960	25	12	12	22	22
1978	25	24	26	38	25
c. Investment					
1960	19	11	11	20	21
1978	26	32	36	26	22
4. Average Annual Growth Rate, percent					
a. Per Capita Real GDP					
1960–1978	6.5	6.9	7.4	6.6	3.7
b. Real GDP					
1960–1970	10.0	8.5	8.8	9.2	6.0
1970–1978	8.2	9.7	8.5	8.0	5.7
c. Real Manufacturing Output					
1960–1970	n.a.	17.2	13.0	17.3	7.6
1970–1978	5.6	18.3	9.2	9.2	6.8
d. Exports					
1960–1970	12.7	35.2	4.2	23.7	5.5
1970–1978	4.8	28.8	9.8	9.3	5.2
e. Imports					
1960–1970	9.2	20.1	5.9	17.9	6.8
1970–1978	3.2	13.5	8.1	9.1	5.8
5. Structure of Trade					
a. Percentage Manufactured Exports					
1960	80	14	26	n.a.	14
1977	96	85	44	49	37
b. Exports of Goods and Services as Percent of GNP					
1960	79	3	163	11	15
1977	98	34	164	59	21

Source: World Bank (1980, various tables).

n.a. = Not available.

all of them had sharply increased their investment as a fraction of GNP (as well as absolutely), reaching ratios considerably above the mean for all middle-income countries. Singapore and South Korea show the strongest increases, reflecting the relatively low base from which they started in 1960, and both also had a rising savings ratio and encouraged foreign capital inflows (foreign direct investment in the case of Singapore and borrowing in the case of South Korea).

The data under row 4 give rates of growth for variables of particular interest. Rows 4b show the growth rates experienced by each country for the sub-periods 1960-1970 and 1970-1978. Growth decelerated in all countries except South Korea (and even there a slowdown would be discerned if the cutoff point were 1973),[4] but still remained well above the average for all middle-income countries and, for that matter, most other countries in the world. One of the remarkable features of the gang of four is their comparatively greater ability to withstand the oil price increases of the 1970s, despite their relatively larger participation in the international economy and the very adverse movements in their terms of trade.

The data in rows 4d and 4e when compared with row 4b indicate what is perhaps the most important feature the four have in common: in all cases except Hong Kong during the 1970s and Singapore in the 1960s (again, a reflection of the latter's dependent status in the early 1960s), the share of both exports and imports in GNP rose, as export and import growth exceeded the rate of growth of GNP. Exports were, at least statistically, a leading growth sector. All four countries had adopted policies conducive to export growth as part of their overall growth and industrialization strategy, and by 1977, all four super exporters had shares of exports in GNP that substantially exceeded the average for developing countries. The level for South Korea was the lowest among the four--34 percent--and yet was still more than 10 times what it had been in 1960, when exports constituted only 3 percent of GNP.

Finally, rows 5a give the percentage of manufactured goods in exports. As can be seen, that percentage rose sharply.[5] The very high shares for Hong Kong and South Korea reflect the fact that both countries have a strong comparative disadvantage in natural resources. For Singapore, the failure of the share of manufactures to be higher reflects the high level of re-exports of petroleum products and the practice of recording some Indonesian exports in the Singaporean trade statistics.

These, then, are the salient characteristics of the impressive growth performances of the four super exporters. All have grown at extremely rapid rates and have been able to sustain that growth remarkably well despite the increase in oil prices and the slowdown in the rate of growth in world trade in the 1970s. In all four, export growth spearheaded GNP growth and was an important factor in their success. Before analyzing the reasons for their success, and the lessons that may be gleaned applicable to other developing countries, it is necessary to examine the individual economies in somewhat more detail, in order to ascertain the sorts of governmental policies and features that were important in particular cases.

THE EXPERIENCE OF INDIVIDUAL COUNTRIES

The data in Table 8.1 above fail to do justice to the impressive performance of the super exporters, in part because the dates at which they began their rapid growth differ and in part because aggregates conceal many aspects of their transformation. This section looks at the particular situations of the individual economies at the time they began their rapid growth, the policies that were implemented accompanying that growth, and other features of importance in understanding the experience of the super exporters.

South Korea[6]

South Korea has one of the worst resource endowments per capita in the world. In the late 1950s it was one of the poorest countries in Asia and was viewed as a very dismal prospect for development. Indeed, during the 1950s, the South Korean economy received inflows of aid equal to approximately 10 percent of GNP, while domestic savings were equal to only 2-3 percent of GNP. U.S. aid policy was based largely on the assumption that sustained growth by the South Korean economy was not feasible and that assistance would be allocated simply to support existing standards of living.

As of the late 1950s, South Korea had a highly overvalued exchange rate and rapid inflation (the latter had been in excess of 100 percent during the Korean War and was about 25 percent annually in the mid-1950s). Growth had been only moderate despite the opportunities for recovery after the Korean War and the sizable volume of American aid. The balance-of-payments position was extremely difficult, as exports were less than one-fifth of imports. Foreign aid financed the import bill.

The inflows of aid peaked in 1957, at which time the American government announced it would gradually reduce its assistance. It became obvious to all that South Korea's economic prospects were dim unless a means of increasing export earnings was found. It is noteworthy that, at the time, 88 percent of South Korea's exports were raw materials.

In 1960, the government devalued the exchange rate significantly. In addition, exporters were given credits at low rates of interest, exemptions from import duties on both raw materials and capital goods, tax reductions, and export bonuses. Thereafter, export incentives were increased whenever exports began lagging or whenever South Korean inflation outstripped that in the rest of the world. These incentives served largely to offset the protection that domestic producers were receiving in their home market. Over time, the role of the exchange rate increased in importance, while other export incentives diminished or were phased out.

From a very small base, South Korean exports began expanding rapidly, from 3 percent of GNP in 1960-1962 to 28 percent of GNP in 1973-1975, for an average annual rate of growth of over 40 percent. Given the low initial real wage in South Korea, it is hardly surprising that the initial export bundle was highly labor-intensive: textiles, clothing, footwear, wigs, and plywood (produced from logs imported from Indonesia) were among the export industries that boomed in the early and mid-1960s. By the late 1960s, the labor force had acquired greater skill, and a high rate of capital formation meant that there was more capital available per worker. Electronics began emerging as another export industry, and, in the early 1970s, some components of machinery and transport equipment entered the export list.[7] There was thus in the 1970s some tendency to shift toward slightly less labor-intensive activities, as South Korea's labor force was fully utilized and the real wage was rising.[8]

By 1966, it became clear that South Korea's economic growth potential was greater than could be sustained if only domestic savings were employed to finance new investment. It therefore began to borrow from abroad and to permit private foreign investment. Thus, while aid was diminishing sharply and finally ceased, foreign lending increased in importance, financing about two-fifths of gross investment in the late 1960s and over a third in the early 1970s (Frank, Kim, and Westphal 1975, 106ff). Until the 1970s, equity investment was relatively small.

Foreign borrowing could not have been undertaken on the scale it was had it not been for the rapid rate of increase in export earnings. Export growth made South Korea creditworthy, thus providing ready access to the private international capital market.

South Korean imports rose rapidly along with exports. Although, as seen in Table 8.1, the rate of growth of imports did not match that of exports,[9] the increase in absolute terms was nonetheless spectacular: imports rose from U.S. $344 million in 1960 to U.S. $1,982 million in 1970 and U.S. $14,972 million in 1979. Imports equaled 12.6 percent of GNP in 1960 and 36.4 percent in 1978. Thus, the growth was not simply an export-based boom: the economy underwent a structural transformation, as all segments of economic activity were opened to the international economy.

The South Korean government had a significant role in the opening up. Investment was made in infrastructure of all kinds--electricity, transport facilities including roads, railroads, and ports, and communications--all had to be expanded in step with production and exports. The government played a major role in estimating the feasible rate of growth of industrial production and the infrastructural support needed to sustain it, and then generated the infrastructure to insure that industrial capacity could be utilized. The government also served as an indicator for the private sector of approximately what rate of expansion could be expected. While it did not to any significant degree intervene with quantitative or other direct controls, incentives were altered in ways designed to assure that the social objectives were met.[10] When signs of increased inflationary pressure appeared, targets were cut back. When slack appeared to be developing in the economy, they were increased. Thus, macroeconomic policy was geared to achieving the appropriate rate of economic growth.

The South Korean authorities followed an exchange rate policy that maintained the purchasing power parity of the won at a realistic level in the late 1960s. During some periods, this balance was accomplished by an announced "sliding peg" policy of small, frequent adjustments in the exchange rate. During other periods, export incentives were altered to keep the real proceeds to exporters per dollar of exports fairly constant. In practice, this goal was met because the government reacted quickly to restore incentives whenever exports started to lag. By the early 1970s, South Korea was well-established in the world markets, and there was some scope for real appreciation of the won.

Several other aspects of the South Korean experience deserve note. There were monetary reforms (in 1964-1965) that markedly increased the real cost of borrowing. Although the interest rate reforms were largely reversed by the more rapid inflation that occurred after the oil price increase of 1973, they nonetheless reduced the degree to which the capital and credit markets were distorted during a crucial period. They thus permitted a smoother flow of resources into profitable (generally export) activities than would otherwise have been possible.

South Korea's growth appears to have been accompanied by a fairly even income distribution that (at least until the late 1970s) appears to have become no worse, and perhaps even to have become more equal, during the rapid growth period.[11]

Finally, the agricultural sector was not neglected during the rapid shift toward an industrial base. Agricultural output grew at an average annual rate of 4.5 percent during the decade of the 1970s, and at a rate of 4.0 percent from 1970 to 1978. This increase took place despite a fairly rapid outmigration from the rural areas, as manufacturing employment expanded at an average annual rate of 10.9 percent.

Taiwan

There are some strong similarities between Taiwan and South Korea. Both experienced dislocation in the 1945-1955 period, Taiwan because most of her population consisted of refugees from the mainland, and South Korea because of the partition and the Korean War. Both were major recipients of American foreign aid during the early 1950s, and both experienced rapid inflation, multiple exchange rates, and severe balance-of-payments difficulties. Taiwan, like South Korea, had a period of import substitution in the early 1950s, and again like South Korea, it reversed this policy starting about 1955. The major difference is that Taiwan had a relatively abundant endowment of arable land, so that its resource base was considerably better than South Korea's.

Taiwan's policy shift actually began before South Korea's. The Taiwanese government introduced a series of reforms in the late 1950s, including a significant devaluation of the currency, unification of the multiple exchange rate system in 1958, and removal of many quantitative restrictions on imports. In addition, the monetary policy was altered so that the rate of inflation during the 1960s was less that 2 percent annually, compared with a rate of 15 percent in the 1950s. These reforms were followed by an export boom and a sharp increase in the rate of economic growth. Exports, which constituted 12.2 percent of national income in 1958 (with imports equaling 20 percent of national income and foreign aid covering much of the difference) rose to 19.6 percent of national income by 1965. By 1969, exports were almost equal to imports, as the rapid growth of exports continued. During the decade of the 1960s, the volume of exports rose fivefold, while imports rose fourfold: exports grew sufficiently to substitute for foreign aid and to permit large increases in imports. The latter was necessary if the economy was to open up significantly.

Taiwan's initial rapidly growing exports included a number of processed foodstuffs, including canned pineapples, canned mushrooms, and similar products. Very quickly, however, the list of exports expanded to include textiles, clothing, electrical machinery, and other manufactures.[12] As in South Korea, the boom in exports and real income was accompanied by rapidly rising employment and real wages. Most observers credit Taiwan, as with South Korea, for a fairly even distribution of income, a situation that remained substantially unaltered during the growth process (Fei, Ranis, and Kuo 1979).

Taiwan's policies appear to have been generally similar to South Korea's, in that government policy was aimed at export promotion in general, rather than at particular commodities. Incentives were fairly uniform across different types of economic activity, and there may have been somewhat less bias toward exporting in Taiwan than in South Korea. In contrast to South Korea's relatively late decision to encourage private foreign investment, Taiwan attempted at a very early stage to provide an environment that would be attractive to foreign investors. Thus foreign investment was regarded as a more important source of growth in Taiwan than it was in South Korea.

Hong Kong and Singapore

As Table 8.1 shows, both Hong Kong and Singapore have grown rapidly, with export orientation a key ingredient. Singapore has welcomed foreign capital, and much of Singapore's industrial development has been in relatively capital-intensive industries (such as petroleum refining) financed with private foreign investment. Singapore has had a relatively tight labor supply and has therefore permitted some immigration of workers from South and Southeast Asia to supplement the domestic labor force. By the early 1970s, the Singaporean government was discouraging expansion of labor-intensive industries.

In contrast, Hong Kong's relatively abundant labor supply from mainland China has led to much greater reliance on labor-intensive industries in the development process, and private foreign capital has played a much smaller role. This pattern evolved not through any conscious policy of the government's (as in the case of Singapore), but rather through the workings of the market. Hong Kong has been aptly characterized as "the world's last bastion of nineteenth-century free-trading laissez-faire" (Lin and Ho 1980; see also Rabushka 1979), although land use in both Hong Kong and Singapore is carefully regulated by the government, and investment in infrastructure has been important in permitting rapid growth.

In both cases, as is necessary for an export orientation, there have been few quantitative restrictions on international transactions, and the currency has generally been readily convertible. Both Hong Kong and Singapore have developed their financial markets and played roles as Asian centers for Eurodollar transactions. From the beginning of their export-oriented efforts, both have relied almost exclusively on a realistic exchange rate, and a lack of protection on imports, to encourage exports. They did not have a high wall of tariff protection to offset and thus did not have to dismantle the complex machinery of an earlier, protective regime of exchange control.

A question of some importance is the extent to which lessons can be learned from the experience of these two city-states. They are small in size, have no rural sector to speak of, and can thus control immigration (at least to some extent, although in practice Hong Kong has not, in response to economic considerations, restricted immigration from mainland China). On the one hand, it has been argued that the very absence of a rural sector has permitted rapid growth because food availability has not been a limit on growth. On the other hand, it has been argued that the small size of the two has meant that their growth experience was more akin to that of particular cities in other developing countries than to entire, larger economies.

Several counterarguments can be made. Hong Kong and Singapore each had exports in the late 1970s equal to two-and-a-half times India's exports. Since India has several cities approximately the size of Hong Kong or Singapore, the argument, to be completely convincing, would have to be that increasing size leads to fewer exports, not simply proportionately smaller exports, when considered in relation to GNP. Moreover, Hong Kong's population of over 4 million is larger than that of many small developing countries, including Jamaica, Panama, Uruguay, and Paraguay. Whether the fact that the population is concentrated in a smaller geographic region is an advantage or disadvantage for development is at least arguable. Finally, the absence of an agricultural sector matters only if urban development is somehow linked to the rate of growth in food supplies: if there is access to the international economy, the presence of a rural sector should not diminish the rate of urban growth. In the South Korean case, for example, the shift to an outward-oriented strategy permitted the authorities to import additional food grains in years of poor harvest, which in turn permitted urban growth to proceed unaffected by the vagaries of the weather. Why the urban sector of any country should be constrained by the rural sector in the presence of an outward-oriented trade strategy is a question that at least deserves consideration.

THE ROLE OF EXPORT PROMOTION

The Importance of Exports

What seems clear, both from an analysis of the experience of the four areas and from comparison with countries continuing to adhere to more restrictive, import substitution, trade, and industrialization strategies is that export growth has played a key role in their excellent performance. In addition, the policies that had to be implemented in order to mount an export-oriented industrialization strategy also helped.

There is, by now, fairly general agreement that the export-oriented strategy and export growth were integrally associated with the achievement of high overall rates of growth. Likewise, the reasons the export-oriented growth has been so successful have been identified. What is not agreed upon is the relative importance of each factor, which may have differed from country to country as well as at different times within the same country. This section explores the various reasons an export-oriented strategy seems to have been so vastly superior to the alternatives, without assessing the relative importance of each factor.[13] As an empirical proposition, those countries that have not followed an export promotion policy have followed import substitution. Thus the question is why growth under export promotion has so considerably exceeded that under import substitution.[14]

A successful export-oriented development strategy does three things. First, it permits countries to take better advantage of the technological opportunities available to them. It also prevents them from making some of the costly mistakes often associated with inner-oriented, restrictive, trade and development industrialization strategies. Third, it forces policies upon governments that generally lead to better economic performance by the private sector.

Turning first to technology, there are several reasons why an export-oriented strategy has generated such vastly superior performance. Poor countries, even those such as Brazil with relatively large populations, generally have relatively small domestic markets for

most manufactured goods. When protection makes profitability dependent on selling in the domestic market,
production runs and capacity are often of such small
size as to be uneconomic. By orienting production
toward exports, producers in developing countries are
able to construct manufacturing facilities of efficient
size and to produce in economic-size batches, thereby
taking advantage of economies of scale and overcoming
the indivisibilities in the production process.

In addition to considerations of the minimum efficient size, a second technological factor may be
important. That is, poor developing countries have, by
definition, abundant supplies of relatively unskilled
labor and relatively little capital (and skills). An
export-oriented strategy permits countries to use the
international market to exchange their own, relatively
labor-intensive, commodities for capital-intensive
goods. They are thus able to take advantage of the
division of labor and of specialization. This ability
contrasts sharply with import-substitution policies
under which labor-abundant developing countries produce
the entire spectrum of manufacturing goods and experience high and rising capital/labor ratios. Given
their small stock of capital, it proves impossible to
employ the labor force productively, and the growth
rate slackens.

The second apparent reason for the success of
export-oriented strategies lies in their need to rely
on incentives to guide economic activity and to avoid
direct controls. Under import substitution, there
appears to be an almost irresistible pressure on
policy-makers to regulate domestic markets using price
controls, physical allocations, investment licensing,
and other interventions in all aspects of economic
life. These interventions often fight the market in
that policy-makers are attempting to induce individuals
to undertake unprofitable actions or to refrain from
taking profitable ones. Regulations and controls become increasingly detailed and complex over time. Usually, it becomes impossible to ascertain the degree to
which relative prices and costs are distorted. Consequently, import substitution regimes often end up with
a highly variable, erratic, and complex incentive
structure that mixes quantitative controls and pricing
incentives. The fact that there are large differences
in the degree of protection accorded the different industries (and firms), that many controls entail dead-
weight losses in resource allocation, and that the
system becomes increasingly cumbersome over time all
combine to reduce the rate of growth of output and
productivity.

By contrast, under an export orientation, policy-
makers cannot intervene quantitatively to the same

extent. Incentives, whether they are embodied in a realistic exchange rate or in favorable treatment of exporters, are relatively uniform among exporting firms, as the measure of success is export earnings rather than physical units of individual export commodities. Both because the exchange rate must be kept fairly realistic and because detailed quantitative interventions are not feasible in the export market, the wide variation in incentives and effective rates of protection often encountered in import-substitution regimes is usually absent in export-oriented ones.[15]

In addition to these features of policy, another factor seems to contribute to better growth performance under an export promotion strategy. That is, the stop-go aspects of macroeconomic policy associated with periodic foreign exchange crises under import substitution are avoided. In almost all developing countries with import-substitution policies, there has been a chronic tendency for the rate of growth of demand for foreign exchange to exceed the rate of increase in the availability of foreign exchange. Policy-makers have periodically had to adopt restrictive monetary and fiscal policies, as mounting levels of foreign indebtedness have led to debt rescheduling and stabilization policies. These stop-go cycles are largely avoided under export promotion, as export earnings grow rapidly enough to finance the increased demand for imports and to increase the share of both exports and imports in GNP.

The third factor, economic behavior, is closely related to the second. Under export-oriented policies, individual enterprises must compete in the international market. Competition itself tends to make firms more efficient. In addition, at any given time some firms are more efficient than others. Under a competitive system, those firms are more profitable and expand relatively rapidly, while the least efficient firms are subject to the opposite pressures. Growth takes place not only through across-the-board expansion in output and cost reductions, but also through a shift in resources toward the more efficient producers. Under import substitution, generally the industrial structure comprises just a few firms producing a particular item. This reason is in large part the small size of the domestic market, referred to earlier. In addition, the mechanisms for allocating scarce foreign exchange tend to protect market shares and reduce whatever competitive forces there may be. The absence of competition and the fixity of market shares under import substitution are undoubtedly important in explaining the much slower growth of factor productivity and higher capital/output ratios in countries under import-substitution than under export promotion.

As the above discussion implies, an export-oriented strategy is not a government decree that exports are desirable: that is true in all countries. Rather, it is an entire set of policies oriented toward encouraging the production of goods and services efficiently.[16] For that reason, a significant question is the extent to which it is the fact of exporting itself, or the other policies that have accompanied export efforts, that have led to the superior growth performance. While there is no definitive answer, it seems evident that some accompanying policies—improvement of the functioning of credit markets, financial reforms, and rationalization of incentives—enhance the benefits that accrue from export-oriented strategies, while others, such as liberalization of the import regime and adoption of a realistic exchange rate, are necessary for the success of the export-promotion strategy. Likewise, some of the growth-enhancing features of an export orientation mentioned above originate in the utilization of the international market, while others are byproducts of more rational economic policies.

What seems clear is that all four successful exporters have had governments that were committed to economic growth and to growth through exporting. In all cases, not only did domestic producers receive adequate incentives for exporting, but they could be reasonably confident that the incentives could continue to be adequate. This relatively assured stability in policy has undoubtedly been a factor of some significance in fostering economic growth, and it is doubtful whether, in the presence of a shaky government, the same incentives would have called forth the same response.

Likewise, the fact that the governments were committed to economic growth led them to evaluate policy alternatives largely on the basis of their presumed impact on that growth. This orientation in itself may be a central distinguishing feature of the gang of four, although a number of countries have adopted restrictive trade regimes despite political rhetoric indicating that growth was a primary objective.

Finally, there is the consideration that success breeds success. The four were, in hindsight, successful. As their governments embarked upon the export promotion and related policies, it was by no means clear that high growth would be achieved. Indeed, in many other countries, efforts to alter the trade and payments regime and related policies have been undertaken, only to meet with political opposition when they were not initially overwhelmingly successful. Once the four met with initial successes, the desirability of the export-oriented policies was evident to large segments of their societies, and support for continuation of the effort arose out of the success.

In other countries where initial efforts have not been so successful, opposition to continuing them has mounted. It is at least arguable that those countries, too, might have been among the rapid growth group if their policies had initially met with greater success. One of the major lessons of the experience of developing countries over the past two decades is that once in a highly restrictive, inner-oriented trade regime, it is extremely difficult to undertake major liberalization (Krueger, 1978). South Korea and Taiwan did so, but with a factor of luck, all four embarked upon their growth and export effort against a background of rapid expansion in international trade. Their success would have been less probable had the international economic environment been less favorable.

Factor Markets in the Super Exporters

It was mentioned earlier that all four super exporters began their export drive by developing manufactured exports of labor-intensive products. With success and capital accumulation, new, more capital-intensive industries have developed and new exports have evolved, while simultaneously rising real wages (at full employment) have resulted in a loss of competitive position in some of the labor-intensive industries.

Two features of this growth pattern are noteworthy. First and foremost, there seems to be an appropriate sequence in which different industries are ripe for development. Had some of the more capital-intensive industries begun development at an earlier stage (when investible resources were fewer and rural immigrants had not yet been productively absorbed into the urban labor force), it is arguable that the consequent failure of employment to grow might have resulted in lower wages, higher capital costs, and an inability of the capital-intensive industries to compete in the world markets. That the South Korean cement industry became a major export industry in the late 1960s, for example, does not prove that it would have been appropriate to develop it in the early stages of the rapid growth period.

Second, a feature shared by all the super exporters is that there was little, if any, intervention in the labor market. In all four countries, governmental intervention (and the ability of unions to use monopoly power) was extremely limited: there is every evidence that labor markets functioned in response to market forces (for South Korea, see Hong 1981; for Taiwan, Fei, Ranis, and Kuo 1979).

The absence of intervention in the labor market was probably a necessary condition for the emergence of the very labor-intensive commodities that constituted the early successful exports in all four countries. Tables 8.2-8.5 give the particulars on the composition and growth of manufactured exports during the periods of rapid growth.

Turning to the individual country tables first, Hong Kong's initial concentration on textiles and clothing is apparent. Between 1959 and 1962, 54 percent of its growth in total exports involved increases in exports of clothing and textiles. By the late 1960s, textiles and clothing were still growing rapidly, but new exports--particularly electrical machinery and instruments--were emerging. By the mid-1970s, exports of textiles were declining in relative importance (although still increasing absolutely) as these newer export commodities increased in relative importance.

In contrast with Hong Kong, Singapore has not had the relatively abundant labor necessary for comparative advantage in textiles, clothing, and footwear. Its export industries have continually shifted toward relatively less labor-intensive goods, with exports of machinery and equipment, especially electrical machinery, growing rapidly. In Singapore's case, refined petroleum is a sufficiently important export that the apparent concentration reflected in Hong Kong's export statistics fails to show up for Singapore, as the items listed account for only 40 percent of Singapore's exports, compared with almost 90 percent for Hong Kong. As is well-known, petroleum refining is not labor-intensive: Singapore's comparative advantage, alone among the four super exporters, apparently never lay in labor-intensive industries.

Table 8.4 presents comparable data for South Korea. As can be seen, its exports of manufactured goods in 1957 were negligible and were scattered across many commodity groups: less than 20 percent of all exports were manufactured items, and even those that were relied in large part on the availability of domestic raw materials for their comparative advantage.

The emergence of labor-intensive exports, including plywood (under wood products) and textiles, is apparent in the data for 1962. By 1967, plywood, textiles, and clothing had grown rapidly, together accounting for 37 percent of total South Korean exports. By 1972, plywood and textiles were already diminishing in relative importance (although still growing absolutely), as iron and steel products, electrical machinery, and footwear emerged as important commodities.

TABLE 8.2
Composition of Hong Kong's exports
(U.S. $ millions and percentage)

SITC No.	1957		1962		1967		1972		1977	
6 Basic Manufactures	195.51	(37.0)	185.5	(24.1)	346.3	(22.7)	709.2	(20.3)	1,507.9	(15.7)
64 Paper Products	nsl		3.7	(0.5)	5.3	(0.3)	8.0	(0.2)	33.4	(0.4)
65 Textiles	131.8	(24.9)	120.9	(15.7)	221.4	(14.5)	383.7	(11.0)	824.9	(8.6)
66 Nonmet. Min.	7.0	(1.3)	22.5	(2.9)	62.6	(4.1)	205.9	(5.9)	318.6	(3.3)
67 Iron and Steel	17.3	(3.3)	6.0	(0.8)	10.6	(0.7)	6.3	(0.2)	nsl	
68 Nonferrous Metals	1.3	(0.2)	6.9	(0.9)	7.9	(0.5)	9.3	(0.3)	38.8	(0.4)
69 Metal Manuf. n.e.c.	21.5	(4.1)	22.1	(2.9)	34.3	(2.2)	83.1	(2.4)	246.6	(2.6)
7 Machinery and Transport Equipment	18.8	(3.5)	39.5	(5.1)	141.8	(9.3)	461.7	(13.2)	1,557.7	(16.1)
71 Nonelec. Mach.	6.0	(1.1)	7.5	(1.0)	20.0	(1.3)	51.8	(1.5)	225.7	(2.3)
72 Elec. Mach.	6.5	(1.2)	27.8	(3.6)	109.1	(7.1)	390.6	(11.2)	1,275.1	(13.2)
73 Trans. Equip.	6.4	(1.2)	4.1	(0.5)	12.8	(0.8)	19.2	(0.6)	57.0	(0.6)
8 Miscellaneous Manufacturing	149.8	(28.3)	395.9	(51.5)	798.4	(52.2)	1,947.1	(56.0)	5,546.2	(57.6)
84 Clothing	76.8	(14.5)	218.0	(28.4)	404.3	(26.5)	1,078.4	(31.0)	2,985.8	(31.0)
85 Footwear	12.9	(2.4)	23.3	(3.0)	40.0	(2.6)	338.7	(9.7)	84.6	(0.9)
86 Instruments, etc.	12.8	(2.4)	9.8	(1.3)	33.1	(2.2)	116.1	(3.3)	702.7	(7.3)
Total Exports	528.4		768.1		1,526.9		3,477.5		9,624.1	

Source: United Nations (Yearbook of Commodity Trade Statistics, various issues).

Note: Where necessary, the values were converted to U.S. dollars at the rate given in
International Monetary Fund (International Financial Statistics, various issues) for the
end of the year.
nsl = Item was too small to be listed separately.
The figures in parentheses indicate the percentage of total exports constituted by the item.

TABLE 8.3
Composition of Singapore's exports
(U.S. $ millions and percentage)

SITC No.	1958		1962		1967		1972		1977	
6 Basic Manufactures	119.0	(11.6)	126.2	(11.1)	117.1	(10.3)	211.3	(9.7)	657.2	(8.0)
62 Rubber Products	nsl		5.7	(0.5)	4.5	(0.4)	7.8	(0.4)	nsl	nsl
63 Wood Products	nsl		nsl		6.8	(0.6)	42.0	(1.9)	122.1	(1.5)
64 Paper Products	nsl		6.8	(0.6)	6.8	(0.6)	10.9	(0.5)	28.4	(0.3)
65 Textiles	57.5	(5.6)	51.2	(4.5)	42.1	(3.7)	86.5	(4.0)	191.7	(2.3)
66 Nonmet. Min.	8.2	(0.8)	18.2	(1.6)	13.6	(1.2)	11.4	(0.5)	43.9	(0.5)
67 Iron and Steel	nsl		17.8	(1.3)	18.2	(1.6)	19.6	(0.9)	108.0	(1.3)
68 Nonferrous Metals	24.6	(2.4)	7.9	(0.7)	5.7	(0.5)	5.5	(0.2)	47.0	(0.6)
69 Metal Manuf. n.e.c.	13.3	(1.3)	19.3	(1.7)	20.5	(1.8)	26.4	(1.2)	93.8	(1.1)
7 Machinery and Transport Equipment	54.4	(5.3)	111.4	(9.8)	87.5	(7.7)	432.9	(19.8)	2,017.1	(24.5)
71 Nonelec. Mach.	18.5	(1.8)	34.1	(3.3)	37.5	(3.3)	175.0	(8.0)	477.4	(5.7)
72 Elec. Mach.	11.3	(1.1)	20.5	(1.8)	18.2	(1.6)	164.9	(7.5)	1,176.5	(14.2)
73 Trans. Equip.	24.6	(2.4)	52.3	(4.6)	33.0	(2.9)	93.0	(4.3)	363.1	(4.4)
8 Miscellaneous Manufacturing	31.8	(3.1)	38.6	(3.4)	52.3	(4.6)	175.9	(8.1)	575.2	(7.0)
84 Clothing	8.2	(0.8)	9.1	(0.8)	15.9	(1.4)	79.1	(3.6)	210.9	(2.6)
85 Footwear	nsl		nsl		nsl		7.2	(0.3)	nsl	nsl
86 Instruments, etc.	nsl		6.3	(0.6)	7.9	(0.7)	33.6	(1.5)	154.9	(1.8)
Total Exports	1,026.2		1,116.6		1,137.0		2,181.0		8,241.5	

Source: United Nations (Yearbook of Commodity Trade Statistics, various issues).

Notes: Where necessary, the values were converted to U.S. dollars at the rate given in International Monetary Fund (International Financial Statistics, various issues) for the end of the year.
nsl = Item was too small to be listed separately.
The figures in parentheses indicate the percentage of total exports constituted by the item.

TABLE 8.4
Composition of South Korea's exports
(U.S. $ millions and percentage)

SITC No.	1957		1962		1967		1972		1977	
6 Basic Manufactures	2.4	(14.5)	6.2	(11.3)	101.3	(31.6)	514.2	(31.7)	3,032.4	(30.3)
62 Rubber Products	nsl		nsl		2.0	(0.6)	11.3	(0.7)	160.0	(1.6)
63 Wood Products	nsl		2.3	(4.2)	36.5	(11.4)	170.4	(10.5)	393.1	(3.9)
64 Paper Products	nsl		nsl		1.8	(0.5)	6.4	(0.4)	72.2	(0.7)
65 Textiles	0.9	(5.5)	1.8	(3.3)	49.0	(15.3)	176.6	(10.9)	1,093.5	(10.9)
66 Nonmet. Min.	nsl		nsl		1.0	(0.3)	24.3	(1.5)	268.4	(2.7)
67 Iron and Steel	nsl		0.5	(0.1)	1.9	(0.6)	92.8	(5.7)	39.2	(3.9)
68 Nonferrous Metals	nsl		nsl		1.8	(0.6)	5.9	(0.4)	nsl	
69 Metal Manuf. n.e.c.	nsl		nsl		7.0	(2.2)	22.1	(1.4)	581.3	(5.8)
7 Machinery and Transport Equipment	nsl		1.4	(2.6)	9.6	(3.0)	171.6	(10.6)	1,853.3	(18.5)
71 Nonelec. Mach.	nsl		nsl		3.6	(1.1)	32.2	(2.0)	26.3	(0.3)
72 Elec. Mach.	nsl		nsl		5.1	(1.6)	125.1	(7.7)	35.8	(0.4)
73 Trans. Equip.	nsl		nsl		0.8	(0.2)	14.3	(0.9)	nsl	
8 Miscellaneous Manufacturing	0.1	(0.6)	2.0	(3.6)	59.2	(18.4)	642.7	(39.6)	3,426.1	(34.2)
84 Clothing	nsl		nsl		33.4	(10.4)	442.2	(27.2)	2,069.4	(20.7)
85 Footwear	nsl		nsl		5.6	(1.7)	55.4	(3.4)	487.6	(4.9)
86 Instruments, etc.	nsl		nsl		nsl		8.3	(0.5)	nsl	
Total Exports	16.5		54.8		320.2		1,624.1		10,016.3	

Source: United Nations (Yearbook of Commodity Trade Statistics, various issues).

Note: Where necessary, the values were converted to U.S. dollars at the rate given
in International Monetary Fund (International Financial Statistics, various issues)
for the end of the year.
nsl = Item was too small to be listed separately.
The figures in parentheses indicate the percentage of total exports of the item.

TABLE 8.5
Composition of Taiwan's exports
(U.S. $ millions and percentage)

SITC Code	1957		1962		1967	
6 Basic Manufactures	ns1		66.9	(30.6)	192.2	(30.0)
63 Wood Products	0.9	(0.6)	10.7	(4.9)	42.9	(6.7)
64 Paper Products	ns1	ns1	2.6	(1.2)	5.1	(0.8)
65 Textiles	4.0	(2.7)	37.5	(17.2)	83.3	(13.0)
66 Nonmetallic Minerals	ns1	ns1	7.0	(3.2)	25.6	(4.0)
67 Iron and Steel	ns1	ns1	0.9	(0.4)	17.9	(2.8)
68 Nonferrous Metals	ns1	ns1	2.2	(1.0)	3.8	(0.6)
69 Metal Manuf. n.e.c.	ns1	ns1	ns1	ns1	9.0	(1.4)
7 Machinery and Transport Equipment	ns1	ns1	3.7	(1.7)	58.3	(9.1)
71 Nonelectrical Machinery	ns1	ns1	ns1	ns1	14.7	(2.3)
72 Electrical Machinery	ns1	ns1	1.1	(0.5)	38.4	(6.0)
73 Transport Equipment	ns1	ns1	ns1	ns1	4.5	(0.7)
8 Miscellaneous Manufacturing	ns1		14.6	(6.7)	95.5	(14.9)
84 Clothing	ns1	ns1	11.1	(5.1)	46.8	(7.3)
85 Footwear	ns1	ns1	ns1	ns1	7.7	(1.2)
Total Exports	148.3		218.3		640.7	

Source: United Nations (Yearbook of Commodity Trade Statistics, various issues).

Notes: Where necessary, the values were converted to U.S. dollars at the rate given in International Monetary Fund (International Financial Statistics, various issues) for the end of the year.
ns1 = Item was too small to be listed separately.
The figures in parentheses indicate the percentage of total exports constituted by the item.

The Taiwanese experience was similar
Korea's.[17]   Almost all exports consisted oᵢ
commodities in 1957.   By 1962, wood products (ᵢ
textiles, and clothing had emerged as signifᵢ
rapidly growing export industries.   Already ᴜy ⅼყ₆⁷,
other products were emerging in the export list.

The important point here is the significance of
the relatively free labor markets in the initial period
of the drive for exports in the experience of all four
super exporters, but especially the three labor-
abundant ones.   Had minimum wages or union contracts
been in existence during the early stages of that
drive, it is difficult to imagine the exporters being
able to establish themselves in those markets in which
their comparative advantage lay.   While well-function-
ing labor markets are not a sufficient condition for
successful export-oriented growth, they may be a necessary one.[18]

PREREQUISITES FOR AN OPEN, OUTWARD-ORIENTED ECONOMY

Because there are always so many unique features
surrounding the experience of individual countries,
generalizations emerge only after considerable time and
research.   In the case of the four successful Asian
super exporters, many questions remain for analysis and
research, and many cannot be satisfactorily resolved.
Judgments will inevitably differ, at least somewhat.

Nevertheless, there are some lessons that seem to
be fairly clearcut.   They pertain more to the minimum
set of prerequisites that must be present if an
outward-oriented growth strategy is to stand a chance
of success.   Admittedly, not all the prerequisites need
be in place from the initiation of the strategy, and
there are always departures in implementation of fully
optimal policies because markets never function entirely perfectly, and even the most laissez-faire governments intervene on occasion.   Nonetheless, several
broad generalizations do stand out from the experience
of the four that are worth stressing by way of
conclusion.

There are eight prerequisites for a successful
outward-oriented strategy.   While many other factors
will assist the strategy, and particulars vary from
country to country and time to time, the prerequisites
are:

(1)   The government's policy cannot be half-
      oriented toward import substitution and half-
      oriented toward export promotion.   Either the
      economy is outward-oriented, and the rewards
      and incentives are for performance in the

international market, or the economy is inward-oriented, and firms are sheltered and find the domestic market rewarding. The bias on average must not be toward the internal market.

(2) There must be a clearcut commitment on the part of the government that it is undertaking an export-oriented strategy, will continue to do so, and will make exporting profitable.

(3) At least in the longer run, prerequisites 1 and 2 imply that a realistic exchange rate is essential for the continued pursuit of an outward-oriented trade strategy. This requirement implies both that the level of the exchange rate must be appropriate and that exporters must feel assured that the exchange rate will be adjusted in accordance with differentials in inflation rates between the exporting country and its major trading partners.

(4) An outward-oriented strategy is possible only if the quantitative restrictions on trade are removed. In general, an outward-oriented strategy is not consistent with detailed government quantitative intervention in any aspect of trade.[19]

(5) Exporters must have ready access to the international market for whatever purchases they may require, including raw materials, spare parts, technical services, marketing skills, freight, insurance, and transport. It should be noted in particular that a duty drawback system is probably too cumbersome administratively and otherwise to provide the required access.

(6) Related to item 5, it is probably not feasible to generate a successful outward-oriented trade strategy unless the communications and transport infrastructure make possible both rapid communications with the rest of the world and relatively quick receipt and delivery of goods.

(7) It is unlikely that an outward-oriented trade strategy can generate rapid growth unless the labor market functions in response to market forces.

(8) It is impossible for a government to identify ex ante the industries that are likely to become successful exporters. Policies assisting those attempting to export have a high probability of success; policies determining what commodities shall be exported are probably destined to failure.

When these prerequisites are met, the evidence is that rapid growth, usually with a pronounced increase in economic efficiency, can be achieved. The evidence also suggests that it is politically extremely difficult to set the prerequisites in place and to weather the initial economic readjustments that are required as resources are reallocated from import-competing to exportable sectors at the margin. If the readjustment period can be successfully passed through, with decision-makers convinced that the outward-oriented commitment will continue, it would appear that outward-oriented growth becomes relatively easier to sustain.

NOTES

1. The oil price increase of 1973-1974 represented a decrease in gross national product (GNP) attributable to a shift in the terms of trade of -8.3 percent for South Korea, -18.1 percent for Singapore, and -10.4 percent for Taiwan.

2. Middle-income developing country is defined by the World Bank as having a 1978 per capita income in excess of U.S. $360 and as not being capital-surplus oil-exporting.

3. The question of the extent to which the experience of a city-state may be useful for other countries is considered later.

4. South Korea experienced a pronounced recession in 1979-1981, attributable in part to political uncertainties and in part to the adverse consequences of currency overvaluation and a decision in 1976 to promote investment in heavy industry. Following the adjustment of the exchange rate and successful implementation of a stabilization program, growth resumed in 1983.

5. The percentage of manufacturing value added in exports is naturally somewhat lower.

6. For additional information on South Korea, see Frank, Kim, and Westphal (1975); Krueger (1979a); and Kim and Roemer (1979).

7. Some have questioned the extent to which South Korea's successful drive for exports was made possible by its special relationship with Japan and/or the United States. The evidence does not suggest that either was of prime importance: Japan's share of South Korea's exports fell during the growth period of the 1960s, and there is no evidence that Korean exports received treatment different from that which exports

from other countries might have received. See Frank, Kim, and Westphal (1975, 81ff). See Table 8.4 for details on the composition of manufactured exports.

8. In the middle 1970s, the government began a push to develop highly capital-intensive industries. These large-scale investments have not, to date, proven economic and appear to have led to some structural difficulties in the economy. Resolution of these problems is not yet in sight.

9. This discrepancy occurred because some export earnings went to reducing the proportionate size of the trade balance deficit and to offsetting the declining volume of aid.

10. The incentive policies even carried over into family planning. As a result, the crude birth rate fell sharply, from 41 to 21 per thousand, over the period 1960 to 1978. The rate of population growth thus fell from 2.8 to 1.3 percent.

11. There is some evidence that the real wage declined during the first several years of the export drive, although it rose rapidly thereafter. Whether this decline resulted in an improvement or a worsening of the income distribution is difficult to say: employment in industry rose extremely rapidly, so that low-income persons from rural areas experienced an improvement in their lot, at the same time that persons already in the industrial labor force were, at least temporarily, worse off. After 1964, the real wage began increasing rapidly, and the economy was generally at full employment. From 1964 to 1977, the manufacturing real wage was estimated to have risen at an average annual rate of 7.4 percent. See Hong (1981).

12. See Table 8.5 for more details on the composition of Taiwanese manufactured exports.

13. This section draws on Krueger (1979b).

14. By export promotion is meant a set of policies that leaves relative domestic rewards for exporting (compared to importing) at least equal to, and possibly greater than, the rewards that would exist under free trade.

15. The feedback on policy mistakes also seems to be quicker under an export-oriented strategy. If the exchange rate starts becoming overvalued, for example, flagging exports quickly bring the situation to the attention of policy-makers. If export subsidies are used to compensate, the cost of these subsidies creates pressure to alter the exchange rate. If policy-makers decide to encourage exports from the wrong industry, they experience the cost of that decision in the size of the export inducements they must pay or in poor export performance.

16. Many import-substitution countries, notably India and Turkey, have special policies to promote ex-

ports and provide export subsidies for individual manufacturing commodities if they are exported. Those policies really serve only to offset the very strong incentives to produce for the domestic market, and they
can lead to the same chaotic set of high rates of
implicit subsidy and protection for the exporters as
exists for import-substitution firms. Careful analysis
of those trade regimes suggests that the export incentives are really for import-substitution industries to
export some part of their output.

17. The data for Taiwan are presented only
through 1967 because they are not reported by the
United Nations for the 1970s.

18. There is evidence that the capital markets of
the four, while functioning significantly better under
export-oriented growth than they had earlier, were not
functioning quite so smoothly, at least in South Korea
and Taiwan. There were significant elements of credit
rationing in both those countries.

19. In South Korea, certain luxury consumer goods
that were not produced domestically were subject to
quantitative restrictions. Exporters were awarded the
import licenses. This exception was possible because
the goods in question were not inputs into any exports
and because the quantitative restrictions did not protect domestic industry.

REFERENCES

Fei, John, Gustav Ranis, and Shirley Kuo. 1979. Growth
with Equity: The Taiwan Case. London: Oxford
University Press.
Frank, Charles R., Jr., Kwang Suk Kim, and Larry E.
Westphal. 1975. Foreign Trade Regimes and
Economic Development: South Korea. New York:
Columbia University Press.
Hong, Wontack. 1981. "Export Promotion and Employment
Growth in South Korea." In Trade and Employment
in Developing Countries: Individual Studies,
edited by Anne O. Krueger, et al. Chicago: Uni-
versity of Chicago Press.
International Monetary Fund. Various issues. Interna-
tional Financial Statistics. Washington, D.C.:
International Monetary Fund.
Kim, Kwang Suk, and Mel Roemer. 1979. Growth and Struc-
tural Transformation. Cambridge: Harvard University Press.

212

Krueger, Anne O. 1978. Foreign Trade Regimes and Economic Development: Liberalization Attempts and Consequences. Cambridge, Mass: Ballinger Publishing for the National Bureau of Economic Research.
_____. 1979a. The Developmental Role of the Foreign Sector and Aid. Cambridge: Harvard University Press.
_____. 1979b. "Trade as an Input to Development." American Economic Review (May).
Lin, Tzong-Blau, and Yin-Ping Ho. 1980. "Export-Oriented Growth and Industrial Diversification in Hong Kong." Paper presented at the Eleventh Pacific Trade and Development Conference, Korea Development Institute, Seoul, September.
Rabushka, Alvin. 1979. Hong Kong: A Study in Economic Freedom. Chicago: University of Chicago Press.
United Nations. Various issues. Yearbook of Commodity Trade Statistics. New York.
World Bank. 1980. World Development Report. Washington, D.C.: The World Bank.

9
Sources of Growth and Structural Change in the Republic of Korea and Taiwan: Some Comparisons

Jaime de Melo

INTRODUCTION

The phenomenal economic growth of the Republic of Korea (South Korea) and Taiwan has been amply documented. Perceptive interpretive essays on the causes of their success, which range from a common cultural background to export-led development strategies, are also available (for example, Galenson 1979; Krueger 1979). This paper takes a narrower focus and compares the "accounting" sources of growth in the two countries. From the supply side, the sources of growth are measured by the accumulation of both physical and human capital, along with technological progress; from the demand side, changes in the structure of production are decomposed into changes in intermediate and final demand, with changes in final demand further broken down into changes in domestic demand and trade.

In this paper, the sources of growth and structural change are looked at in a comparative framework, with the comparison taking place at two levels. At the more aggregate level, the sources of growth in South Korea and Taiwan are compared with the sources of growth in other countries, developing and developed. At the more detailed sectoral level, mostly the manufacturing sector where growth has been so remarkable, the comparison is restricted to the two countries.

The paper is organized into three sections. The first contains the comparison of the sources of growth in the two countries with those in other countries. The same methodology is applied to all countries throughout so as to eliminate the possibility of differences in results attributable to alternative approaches. The second section compares the experience of the two countries directly during a period starting in the mid-fifties and going to 1973. The third section looks in detail at the pattern of labor use in manufacturing. The reason is that developing countries with surplus labor are likely to derive large benefits from a development strategy that is associated with a high rate of labor absorption. In line with the quantitative focus of this comparison, the emphasis throughout is on differences in the magnitude of the identified sources of growth and on the more easily quantifiable causes of these differences.

COMPARISON WITH OTHER COUNTRIES

A useful way to begin a comparison between South Korea and Taiwan is to see how similar they are as compared with other countries. Doing so has the advantage of introducing the data and methodology on which the paper is based. The comparison is carried out along two lines: on the supply side, the patterns of growth in the factors of production and in productivity are compared with other developing as well as developed countries. On the demand side, the contributions of various components of intermediate and final demand are contrasted for a sample of nine countries.

Sources of Growth: Supply Side

Most international comparisons of the sources of growth have been carried out under two broad approaches. One, developed by Denison and Solow, takes the factor shares in national income as weights in combining individual factor inputs and denotes that part of output growth that cannot be explained by increases in factor inputs as total factor productivity (TFP), or technical progress. The other, developed by Christensen and Jorgenson, uses translog index numbers to connect the theory of production with data on prices and quantities. Growth in real factor input accounts for a much larger proportion of growth in real product under the Christensen-Jorgenson methodology than under the Denison methodology.[2]

Table 9.1 contrasts the sources of growth in South Korea and Taiwan with that in other countries as measured by these two methodologies. Chen derived the figures in his study using Denison's approach, while Elias obtained his figures for Latin America using the Christensen-Jorgenson methodology. For all countries, the rates of growth of capital are higher than the rates of growth of labor and are quite close to the rates of growth of real product.

The results from Chen's study for five Asian countries show a strikingly similar pattern for the sources of growth, results that resemble closely those obtained from studies of growth in Western Europe. Thus, for the

TABLE 9.1
Comparison of total factor productivity growth
in South Korea and Taiwan with other countries[a]
(average yearly growth rates)

Country	Labor	Capital	Output	TFP[b]	TFP[b] ÷ Output
Study 1[c]					
South Korea	2.9	5.3	8.8	5.0	0.57
Taiwan	2.9	5.0	8.0	4.3	0.54
Hong Kong	3.1	7.8	9.3	4.3	0.46
Singapore	2.5	3.5	6.5	3.6	0.64
Japan	1.4	9.3	10.1	5.6	0.55
Study 2[d]					
South Korea	5.0	6.6	9.7	4.1	0.42
United States	2.2	4.0	4.3	1.3	0.30
Canada	2.0	4.9	5.1	1.8	0.35
Japan	2.7	11.5	10.9	4.5	0.41
France	0.4	6.3	5.9	3.0	0.51
Germany,F.R.	0.0	7.0	5.1	2.8	0.55
Study 3[c]					
Argentina	3.7	3.4	4.1	0.5	0.12
Brazil	3.6	4.1	6.2	2.1	0.34
Chile	2.1	4.0	4.5	1.2	0.27
Colombia	3.0	3.4	4.8	1.4	0.29
Peru	2.7	4.6	4.9	0.8	0.16

Sources: Study 1--Chen (1977); Study 2--
Christensen, Cummings, and Jorgenson (1980);
and Study 3--Elias (1978).

[a] All figures are economywide.
[b] Total factor productivity.
[c] 1955-1970.
[d] 1960-1973.

Asian group (and for Western Europe), the contribution
of total factor productivity accounts for around 50
percent of income growth. These results stand in
striking contrast to the estimates for other developing
countries when the same methodology is used. In those
countries, the contribution of factor inputs to growth
was much more important than that of total factor
productivity[3]. For instance, Correa's (1970) study of
nine Latin American countries during the period 1950-

1962 finds that an average of only 34 percent of the growth in output was explained by total factor productivity.[4]

These results are confirmed by estimates based on the alternative methodology. Christensen, Cummings, and Jorgenson show that for the period 1960-1973, the contribution of total factor productivity to growth in South Korea was quite similar to that for Japan, France, and the Federal Republic of Germany. It is also higher than in the group of Latin American countries examined by Elias, reported in the bottom part of Table 9.1.

It can therefore be concluded that for the group of Asian exporters, total factor productivity growth was an important source of real growth in output during the postwar period and that its percentage contribution to growth was similar to that found for Japan and the industrialized Western European countries. This finding contrasts with that for Latin American countries, where the growth in factor inputs has been the dominant influence on the rate of growth of real output. Thus, it appears, at this stage of the comparison, that South Korea and Taiwan are similar to each other and different from non-Asian developing countries.

Sources of Growth and Structural Change: Demand Side[5]

Among other factors, the process of industrialization involves a shift of the bulk of economic activity out of agriculture and into industry and services. On the supply side, this transformation is reflected in different rates of growth in factor inputs across sectors and different rates of growth in TFP. In turn, the resulting differences in the growth rates of output can be decomposed on the demand side in terms of the relative contribution of each component of final and intermediate demand. Changes in the composition of demand are useful in providing an understanding of sectoral growth and structural change. First, there is excess capacity in the manufacturing sector in developing countries; and second, primary factors such as unskilled labor are often in highly elastic supply. Under these circumstances, adjustments to disequilibrium will take place more frequently by changes in quantity than by changes in price.

Before comparing these sources of output expansion for the manufacturing sector in both countries, their experience is contrasted with a group of countries ranging from large industrialized ones like Japan to small semi-industrialized ones like Israel.

Methodology. The input-output methodology used to decompose the sources of growth and structural change applied here is that of Chenery, Shishido, and Watanabe (1962). The presentation below follows the extension by Syrquin (1976). Because imported and domestically produced goods of the same sector classification are not perfect substitutes in all uses, imports are separated from domestic production by defining ratios for imports ($m_i = M_i/[W_i + D_i]$) and domestic demand ($u_i = [X_i - E_i]/[W_i + D_i]$). In matrix notation, the material balance equations above become:

$$X = \hat{u}(W + D) + E^d \qquad (9.1)$$

and

$$M = \hat{m}(W + D) \qquad (9.2)$$

where W = Ax, the sum of domestic and $\qquad$ (9.3)
    imported intermediate inputs,
  D_d = Domestical final demand, and
  E^d = Export demand.

The symbol ^ indicates a diagonal matrix, and the flows describing the material balances are deflated in real terms so that they are comparable over time and across countries.[6]

Denoting the change that occurs in a variable by the symbol Δ (for example, ΔX = X [t + 1] - X [t]), the change in total domestic demand can be written (after some algebraic manipulation) as:

$$\Delta X = R_1 \hat{u}_1 (\Delta D) \qquad \text{Expansion in domestic demand}$$

$$+ R_1 (\Delta E^d) \qquad \text{Expansion in exports}$$

$$+ R_1 (\Delta \hat{u}) (D_2 + W_2) \qquad \text{Import substitution}$$

$$+ R_1 \hat{u}_1 (\Delta A) X_2 \qquad \text{Change in input-output (9.4)} \\ \text{coefficients}$$

where $R_1 = (I - \hat{u}_1 A_1)^{-1}$ and subscripts 1 and 2 refer to time periods. Since each term is multiplied by elements of the Leontief domestic inverse, this equation captures both the direct and indirect impact of each factor on gross output.

When analyzing changes in the composition of output, it is often useful to examine deviations from pro-

portional growth (see Table 9.2). Defining the deviation from proportional growth of output of sector i as

$$\delta X_i^2 = X_i^2 - \lambda X_i^1 \tag{9.5}$$

where λ is the ratio of total GNP in period 2 to GNP in
period 1, the material balance equation can be defined
in deviation form, and the nonproportional growth in
output can be decomposed in analogous fashion with the
same four contributing factors. Likewise, the basic
decomposition equation can be further applied to
analyze the sources of growth in imports. When, as in
the case of South Korea and Taiwan, imports can be
separated into final and intermediate use, and an
import matrix is available, the sources of growth in
imports can be analyzed along the same lines, with, in
addition, import substitution being broken down in
terms of intermediate and final demand.

Comparison with Other Countries. Table 9.2
contrasts the pattern of growth and structural change
in South Korea and Taiwan with the pattern of growth in
seven other countries: Japan, Turkey, Mexico, Colombia, Israel, Norway, and Yugoslavia. This group of
countries varies widely in size, income, and foreign
trade. Their diversity reflects a wide range of initial conditions relating to factor endowment, natural
resources, internal market size, and policy-making.
Two questions are whether there are any commonalities
or "mainstreams"[7] within this diversity, and how
distinct South Korea and Taiwan are from the rest of
the group.

The sources of differential output growth in the
primary, manufacturing, and services sectors reported
in Table 9.2 reveal two interesting patterns. First,
there is a similarity across all countries, including
South Korea and Taiwan, with respect to the relative
decline in primary production. Second, there is a
great deal of diversity within the manufacturing sector. The decline in primary production is the result
of the compositional shift in domestic demand caused by
the low income elasticity of demand for primary products and the high elasticity of demand for most manufactured products. Changes in input-output coefficients also reduce the demand for primary products in
almost all countries and increase the demand for manufactured goods. The effects of changes in the input-
output coefficients are thus important, and together
with the changes in the composition of demand, they
account for over 75 percent of the relative decline in
primary production in all countries except Norway and
Mexico, where the figure is about 50 percent.

Whereas there is great uniformity in the sources
of output growth for the primary sector, there is much

TABLE 9.2
Sources of output deviation from balanced growth
(percent change in aggregate gross output)

	Average Output Growth Rate	Output Deviation	Sources of Output Deviation			
			Domestic Demand Expansion	Export Expansion	Import Substitution	Changes in Input-Output Coefficients
South Korea (1955–1973)						
Primary	5.7	-11.3	-7.7	1.8	-2.3	-3.1
Manufacturing	15.8	27.5	4.7	21.1	1.4	0.2
Services	10.3	4.6	0.9	4.3	0.2	-0.7
Taiwan (1956–1971)						
Primary	7.1	-7.6	-4.2	1.5	-2.7	-2.2
Manufacturing	16.2	28.2	0.7	20.1	3.0	4.4
Services	9.7	-2.0	-4.5	3.5	0.1	-1.2
Japan (1914–1935)						
Primary	1.9	-10.8	-9.9	1.1	-3.2	1.2
Manufacturing	5.5	23.6	13.6	10.6	2.5	-3.1
Services	4.2	13.1	6.2	6.4	-0.5	0.9
Japan (1955–1970)						
Primary	2.2	-7.6	-3.2	-0.2	-1.9	-2.4
Manufacturing	13.3	12.6	5.0	2.8	-1.2	5.9
Services	11.4	1.0	-1.0	1.2	-1.0	1.7
Turkey (1953–1973)						
Primary	2.5	-17.9	-11.4	-1.3	0.2	-5.4
Manufacturing	8.0	16.4	5.6	2.1	2.4	6.3
Services	6.7	9.1	3.8	1.8	0.2	3.3
Mexico (1950–1975)						
Primary	4.8	-6.2	-2.1	-2.7	-0.2	-1.2
Manufacturing	7.7	9.8	4.6	-0.3	3.5	1.9
Services	6.4	0.4	0.3	-0.5	0.5	0.04

(Continued)

TABLE 9.2 (Cont.)

	Average Output Growth Rate	Output Deviation	Sources of Output Deviation			
			Domestic Demand Expansion	Export Expansion	Import Substitution	Changes in Input-Output Coefficients
Colombia (1953-1970)						
Primary	4.5	-3.7	-7.9	3.8	0.3	0.1
Manufacturing	8.1	16.1	1.4	1.4	7.8	5.6
Services	5.5	1.9	-0.8	1.2	0.4	1.0
Israel (1958-1972)						
Primary	6.4	-3.5	-4.2	1.6	-0.4	-0.5
Manufacturing	12.5	13.4	6.9	11.9	-10.1	4.8
Services	8.9	-4.4	-9.3	7.6	-1.9	-0.8
Norway (1953-1969)						
Primary	2.5	-4.7	-3.1	0.1	-2.0	0.3
Manufacturing	3.2	7.7	-1.6	12.4	-9.2	6.0
Services	4.8	6.2	-0.8	9.3	-3.1	0.8
Yugoslavia (1962-1972)						
Primary	2.6	-17.7	-10.3	1.8	-3.9	-5.4
Manufacturing	12.1	21.1	13.6	10.9	-10.1	6.8
Services	8.8	4.6	4.5	1.4	-1.5	0.3

Source: Data generated under research project, "A Comparative Study of the Sources of Industrial Growth and Structural Change," RPO 671-32, World Bank, Washington, D.C.

Note: Column 1 shows the average annual growth rates of sectoral gross output. Sectoral output deviations and the contributions of the sources of growth are expressed as percentages of the change in aggregate gross output over all sectors during the specified period in each country. For each subperiod, columns 3-6 add up to column 2.

greater variation among the nine countries for the manufacturing sector. In South Korea and Taiwan, the significant deviation of manufacturing output from balanced growth is largely attributable to the rapid expansion of exports, a trend that accounts for over 70 percent of the deviation, with all other factors playing a minor role. Thus, the rapid structural change experienced in these two countries is attributable to their export-led, outward-looking industrial development strategies, adopted in the early 1960s. Japan also adopted various export promotion schemes in the postwar period, with fairly restrictive import controls. The fact that the effect on export expansion was not as pronounced as in South Korea and Taiwan is because of the much larger size of Japan's domestic market relative to exports, a factor that also accounts for the importance of the expansion in domestic demand in its industrial growth. In the period before the war, the role of export expansion was greater, as Japan had a smaller domestic market. In many respects, Yugoslavia's pattern of structural change resembles that of Japan in the earlier period for both the primary and manufacturing sectors.

In contrast, the expansion of manufacturing in Colombia, Mexico, and Turkey has depended only slightly on the expansion of exports. Instead, import substitution has played the most important role (about 45 percent) in the overall expansion of manufacturing production, a pattern that has been reinforced by the effect of changes in the input-output coefficients. Thus, the development experience in these countries reflects their import substitution-oriented development strategies. Turkey, where the effects of import substitution and changes in the input-output coefficients account for half the deviation in manufacturing output, may also be classified in this group, although import substitution played a more limited role than in the other two countries. It is not surprising to observe a sizable effect from changes in the input-output coefficients in these countries, as import substitution often requires the introduction of new technologies, although this pattern is not specific to the countries that adopted an import-substitution strategy.

Finally, Norway and Israel, the two smallest and most developed countries in the sample at the outset, show a different pattern of growth in manufacturing. On the one hand, both countries had achieved a major structural transformation prior to the period under study. On the other hand, with relatively small domestic markets, both countries pursued more open development strategies. For both, expansion of exports and changes in the input-output coefficients more than offset the small growth in domestic demand, and the

increased dependence on imports is reflected in negative import substitution (or import liberalization).
In Norway, in particular, rapid export expansion has
been associated with a significant increase in import
dependence, reflecting increased specialization and
openness resulting from a liberal trade policy. In
turn, as Norway's main exports have been manufactured
products, the significant effect of changes in the
input-output coefficients for the manufacturing sector
can be viewed as reflecting technological changes
required to meet international competition.

In spite of their higher per capita income, Israel
and Norway are the two countries that most resemble
South Korea and Taiwan, insofar as they both have
pursued outward-looking growth strategies and have
limited domestic markets.[8] Considering the manufacturing sector alone, for the entire period, export
expansion accounted for 44.5 percent of the total
change in output in South Korea and 51.7 percent in
Taiwan, whereas in Norway and Israel it contributed 36
percent of the growth in manufacturing. Although the
differences are still significant, and the performance
of South Korea and Taiwan remains remarkable, the differences are not as striking as they seem at first
sight. One reason is that most small countries are
aware of the existence of economies of scale in key
manufacturing sectors. For this reason, countries with
small internal domestic markets should engage in relatively more international trade than larger countries
in order to expand their effective market size.

Not all countries follow that path. In Colombia,
which initially had the same internal market size for
manufactured products as Israel, expansion of exports
contributed very little (6 percent) to the growth in
manufacturing. Of course, export expansion did contribute 40 percent to growth in the primary sector, as
is expected for a natural resource-rich country. Yet
because of the primary sector's more limited potential
for growth, with respect to the economy as a whole export expansion contributed only 14 percent in Colombia.

A final comparison across all countries involves
the trade strategies in the manufacturing sector. The
analysis of contributions to manufacturing growth by
time period expressed in first difference form leads
both to a typology with countries clustered into group-
ings (according to the role of export expansion and of
import substitution) and to alternative sequences for
the contributions of trade to growth according to
whether export expansion either preceded or succeeded
import substitution.

Figure 9.1 plots the percentage contribution of
import substitution and export expansion to manufactur-

ing growth for each subperiod, as determined by the years for which input-output data were available. It is apparent that in only South Korea, Taiwan, and Colombia did import substitution contribute substantially to growth in the initial period. The reason in part is the choice of benchmark years, however. For example, Colombia and Mexico had about the same level of income per capita as South Korea and Taiwan did during the 1930s, at which time they underwent an intensive phase of import substitution in the wake of the great Depression. A clustering in Figure 9.1 (it is not shown) would also bring out clearly that South Korea and Taiwan are the countries that stand out in terms of the contribution of export expansion to growth in the manufacturing sector. Furthermore, South Korea and Taiwan are also the only countries that underwent a period in which import substitution contributed approximately a third of manufacturing growth. These countries are thus at both extremes of a spectrum that ranges from import substitution to export expansion.

Finally, there are three periods (for Israel and Norway) that could be considered to have involved significant trade liberalization or foreign exchange constraint relaxation in the sense that export expansion was coupled with negative import substitution. It is also apparent that import substitution has preceded export expansion in all countries in the sample in which the expansion of domestic demand alone was not the main contributing factor to growth in manufacturing. These patterns partly reflect the change in attitude toward the appropriate role of trade policies relative to industrialization that evolved during the sixties. With the more detailed calculations presented in Table 9.3 below, these patterns support the view that the experience gained from sales in the domestic market is a prerequisite for successful exports of manufactures.

This sequencing from import substitution to export-led growth in manufacturing leads to a classification of countries into three groups: one includes South Korea, Taiwan, and Israel and involves a period of import substitution followed by a period of export-led growth; the second includes Yugoslavia, Norway, and Japan and involves either continued import liberalization (Yugoslavia and Norway) or no significant import substitution (Japan), combined with an increasing role for export expansion in later periods; and the third includes Turkey, Mexico, and Colombia and involves export expansion as a minor source of growth, with import substitution generally playing a role in later periods, perhaps because it had already reached its limit at the end of the first period.

224

FIGURE 9.1
Trade sequences

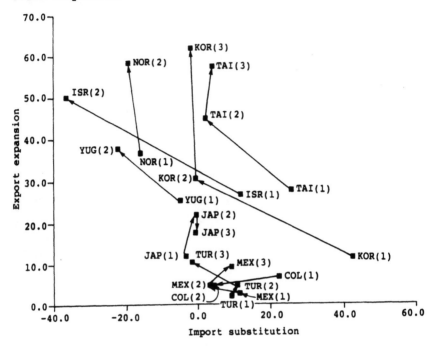

S. Korea	(1) 1955-1963	Mexico	(1) 1950-1960
	(2) 1963-1970		(2) 1960-1970
	(3) 1970-1973		(3) 1970-1975
Taiwan	(1) 1956-1961	Colombia	(1) 1953-1966
	(2) 1961-1966		(2) 1966-1970
	(3) 1966-1971		
		Israel	(1) 1958-1965
Japan	(1) 1955-1960		(2) 1965-1972
	(2) 1960-1965		
	(3) 1965-1970	Norway	(1) 1953-1961
			(2) 1961-1969
Turkey	(1) 1953-1963		
	(2) 1963-1970	Yugoslavia	(1) 1962-1966
	(3) 1970-1973		(2) 1966-1972

TABLE 9.3
Sources of growth in real national income

Country	Capital Input		Labor Input		Total Factor Productivity		Of Which Resource Reallocation Gain [b]	Income Growth Rate(%)
				Contributions to Growth[a]				

Economywide

Country	Capital Input		Labor Input		Total Factor Productivity		Of Which Resource Reallocation Gain	Income Growth Rate(%)
S. Korea								
1955–60	0.87	(20.6)	1.35	(32.0)	2.00	(47.4)	[40.5]	4.22
1960–66	0.67	(9.7)	2.14	(31.0)	4.10	(59.3)	[18.5]	6.91
1966–70	3.67	(36.3)	1.38	(13.6)	5.06	(50.1)	[14.1]	10.11
1955–70	2.12	(24.0)	1.73	(19.6)	4.99	(56.4)		8.84
Taiwan								
1955–60	1.07	(20.4)	1.05	(20.0)	3.12	(59.5)	[16.4]	5.24
1960–66	1.79	(19.3)	1.45	(15.6)	6.04	(65.1)	[14.9]	9.28
1966–70	3.07	(38.0)	3.18	(39.4)	1.82	(22.6)	[12.6]	8.07
1955–70	2.00	(24.9)	1.72	(21.5)	4.30	(53.6)		8.02

Agricultural Sector

Country	Capital Input		Labor Input		Total Factor Productivity			Income Growth Rate(%)
S. Korea								
1960–70	1.31	(27.6)	0.10	(2.1)	3.34	(70.3)		4.75
Taiwan								
1955–70	1.84	(49.1)	0.71	(18.9)	1.20	(32.0)		3.75

Manufacturing Sector

Country	Capital Input		Labor Input		Total Factor Productivity			Income Growth Rate(%)
S. Korea								
1960–66	2.28	(18.3)	7.54	(60.6)	2.62	(21.1)		12.44
1966–70	4.80	(32.7)	5.12	(34.8)	4.77	(32.5)		14.69
1960–70	3.59	(26.0)	7.14	(51.7)	3.08	(22.3)		13.81
Taiwan								
1955–60	2.42	(21.0)	3.73	(32.3)	5.39	(46.7)		11.54
1960–66	4.25	(43.0)	1.84	(18.6)	3.80	(38.4)		9.89
1966–70	5.45	(38.7)	5.35	(38.0)	3.28	(28.3)		14.08
1955–70	4.16	(36.1)	2.78	(24.1)	4.58	(39.8)		11.52

Services Sector

Country	Capital Input		Labor Input		Total Factor Productivity			Income Growth Rate(%)
S. Korea								
1960–70	1.36	(14.5)	3.43	(36.5)	4.62	(49.1)		9.41
Taiwan								
1955–70	1.37	(14.1)	2.98	(30.6)	5.38	(55.3)		9.73

Source: Chen (1977, Tables 1, 3, 4, 5).

[a] Percentage points, with percentage distribution in parentheses.
[b] Percentage of the contribution of TFP to growth attributable to the reallocation of labor out of agriculture.

Comparisons with other countries indicate that South Korea and Taiwan had virtuous circles of growth: high rates of growth in total factor productivity coupled with export-led growth. The high rates of export growth undoubtedly helped overcome balance of payments problems and in addition had favorable effects on investment and productivity. Those effects were assuredly helped by an elastic supply of well-trained and educated workers. What is difficult to ascertain and remains to be investigated are the causal links in this virtuous circle.

To sum up, South Korea and Taiwan appear to be very similar to each other and often quite different from other countries. With respect to the role of technical progress in growth, both closely resemble the developed rather than developing countries. On the demand side, their pattern of growth also stands in contrast to that of other countries, particularly with respect to the role of export expansion in the manufacturing sector. However, the contrast is probably less pronounced when the size of the domestic market is controlled for and comparisons are made with countries of similar size. It was also found that the pattern of the contributions of demand to growth in the agricultural and services sectors in South Korea and Taiwan is quite similar to that in other countries. Thus the contrast is greatest in the manufacturing sector. Accordingly, the following comparisons are directed mostly to the manufacturing sector in both countries.

DIRECT COMPARISONS

Growth Estimates of Total Factor Productivity

The comparisons of the relative contributions of factor inputs and technical progress reported here are taken from Chen's study mentioned earlier. Although his estimates are fairly crude, they are available for both countries and for agriculture, manufacturing, and services. They are also broken down into subperiods that correspond quite closely to the periods underlying the sources of growth on the demand side.

The approach for the comparison starts from a neoclassical CRS production function and assumes that factors are paid the value of their respective marginal products so that factor shares may be used to yield an equation similar to the following:[9]

$$\hat{A} = \hat{Y} - \hat{\beta}_K K - \hat{\beta}_L L \qquad (9.6)$$

where ^ = Growth rates

β_K = Factor share of 0.4 (a constant)

β_L = Factor share of 0.6 (a constant)

$\hat{A}$ = Rate of technical progress, TFP.

This residual includes a host of factors, the most important of which are likely to be, for countries such as South Korea and Taiwan: changes in the quality of inputs (education, new techniques embodied in new capital goods); advances in knowledge; economies of scale associated with the rapid growth of markets; and resource reallocation from the agricultural sector to the rest of the economy.[10] Unfortunately, Chen's estimates are available for only the resource reallocation effect.

The direct comparison of the contributions to growth between the two countries, reported in Table 9.3, indicates a remarkable similarity in both. At the economywide level for the period 1955-1970, there is hardly any significant difference. Both countries grew at about 8 percent over the period, with the growth in capital stock contributing about 2 percentage points, growth in employment another 1.7 percentage points, and, finally, TFP another 4.5 to 5.0 percentage points. Looking at the subperiods, a clear pattern emerges in Taiwan, with the growth in factor inputs increasing its contribution at the expense of total factor productivity. In South Korea, too, the contribution of total factor productivity declines in the last period (as does the growth in employment) in the face of an increasing contribution by capital growth. The contribution of capital growth during the period 1966-1970 is the same in both countries. Thus, at the aggregate level, the main difference appears to be the role of growth in employment: its contribution rises in Taiwan, both in percentage points and in absolute terms over time, whereas in South Korea it declines in both percentage and absolute terms. As will be seen below, this difference has much to do with the fact that an important source of the increased growth is exports of food products, which receive inputs from agriculture, where employment growth was important compared with South Korea.

According to Chen's calculations, one of the main reasons for the high contribution of TFP is the high rate of structural change in these countries, which is accompanied by a reallocation of the labor force from the agricultural sector to the rest of the economy. In measuring this gain, Denison found that it proved to be one of the major factors in the differences in growth rates among industrialized countries. As indicated in the bracketed figures in Table 9.3, the gain from reallocating labor from agriculture, where wages are low, to the rest of the economy, where wages are high, is an important element in accounting for the role of TFP. As expected, the importance of the effect declines with time in both countries. It is much higher during the 1955-1960 period in South Korea, where the agricultural sector was initially much larger in relation to the rest of the economy, than in Taiwan. Since this resource reallocation effect ties in with the sources of growth from the demand side, it is worth emphasizing that the reallocation of labor away from agriculture may have contributed as much as 0.5 percentage point of income growth in South Korea and 1.0 percentage point of income growth in Taiwan.[11]

At the sectoral level, the most interesting results pertain to the manufacturing sector.[12] Although its effect declines over time, total factor productivity contributes more to output growth in Taiwan than it does in South Korea. However, if the focus is in the period 1966-1970, the differences in the sources of growth are again minimal.

What can be concluded from these figures? Even when taking the turning points (1960 for Taiwan, 1966 for South Korea) as rough indicators of change in development strategy and relating them to the results in Table 9.3, no firm conclusions emerge. The contribution of total factor productivity rose in Taiwan after the reforms at the economywide level, but fell in the period 1966-1970. Surprisingly, the contribution of total factor productivity fell in manufacturing. Likewise, it cannot be said that the reforms produced a significant change in total factor productivity in the case of South Korea. However, the fact that the overall growth rate picked up significantly after the reforms in both countries, thus allowing the absolute contribution of TFP to growth to increase as well, is important.

Contributions of Final Demand to Manufacturing Growth

The contributions to growth in the group of nine countries can be addressed through more disaggregated sectoral computations. In the case of South Korea and Taiwan, comparable results are available at the twenty-two sector level for the period 1955-1973 for South Korea and 1956-1971 for Taiwan. Although the benchmark years that determine the periods for which the calculations are made do not correspond exactly to the years in which significant policy changes were carried out, it is fortunate that the first period for each country corresponds roughly to the pre-reform or pre-turning point period. However, in South Korea that period covers the years 1955-1963, in Taiwan, the years 1956-1961.

Table 9.4 contrasts, sector by sector, the contributions to growth in the manufacturing sector of both countries. To bring out the main differences and similarities, manufacturing is split into four sectors: food processing; light industry, which corresponds to consumer goods (excluding food processing); heavy industry, which corresponds to basic intermediates; and machinery, which includes transport equipment. For each sector, the contributions are measured as the percentage change in that sector's output over the period. Finally, the average structure of output provides a measure of the share, economy-wide, originating from that sector.

The first observation is that the pattern revealed in Figure 9.1 in which manufacturing growth with import substitution precedes export expansion for manufacturing as a whole is observed in both countries for virtually every sector. With the exception of the machinery sector in Taiwan, where the contribution of import substitution to that sector's growth is greatest in the second period, the role of import substitution is greatest in the first one. The negative values for import substitution in the latter two periods for most sectors indicate rising ratios of imports to domestic supply, implying periods of import liberalization. As will be examined further below, a characteristic feature of their export-led growth is a high level of imported inputs in exports. Thus, import liberalization as defined here was a key ingredient in the development strategies of both countries.

Another observation relates to the greater variation in the contribution of export expansion to sectoral growth. For instance, exports of food products played a leading role in Taiwan. Not only was that sector among the largest throughout both periods, but, in addition, export expansion contributed between 36 percent and 28 percent of that sector's output growth. By contrast, in South Korea, exports of processed foods did not make an important contribution to that sector's growth. At this level of aggregation, there was no leading export sector in South Korea in the early period. Nevertheless, for both countries the contribution of export expansion to sectoral growth increased significantly in almost every sector in the second and third periods. That increase, which is associated with the overall acceleration in sectoral growth rates,[13] is most pronounced in the consumer

TABLE 9.4
Sources of manufacturing growth

Country	Period	Average Output Growth	Average Output Structure[a]	Domestic Demand[b]	Export Expansion[b]	Import Substitution[b]	Changes in I-O Coefficients[b]
				Food			
S. Korea	1955-63	8.68	8.67	62.84	7.07	17.72	12.38
	1963-70	15.80	9.42	91.70	9.66	-2.93	1.57
	1970-73	18.75	9.85	79.23	17.45	1.92	1.40
Taiwan	1956-61	4.34	19.19	54.93	35.77	-0.67	9.98
	1961-66	9.99	16.28	60.14	29.65	-7.51	17.71
	1966-71	6.50	12.28	65.18	28.04	2.13	4.65
				Light Industry			
S. Korea	1955-63	7.56	15.20	73.67	17.62	56.57	-47.86
	1963-70	18.27	17.94	61.07	49.23	-6.53	-3.76
	1970-73	20.97	20.16	34.06	80.50	-5.77	-8.79
Taiwan	1956-61	30.99	7.55	33.15	26.50	25.63	14.73
	1961-66	15.43	10.75	47.23	72.63	1.01	-20.87
	1966-71	29.92	17.52	27.67	63.68	0.72	7.93
				Heavy Industry			
S. Korea	1955-63	20.05	5.92	37.58	9.91	44.51	8.00
	1963-70	22.19	10.57	61.81	20.07	13.60	4.51
	1970-73	25.56	13.42	32.82	57.57	-3.56	13.18
Taiwan	1956-61	13.13	5.98	6.07	24.24	57.24	12.45
	1961-66	24.78	9.19	44.23	42.37	-0.86	14.27
	1966-71	20.24	12.52	42.22	53.40	7.47	-3.09

Machinery

S. Korea	1955-63	17.70	2.30	47.33	5.26	40.69	6.72
	1963-70	21.93	3.93	87.66	22.00	-10.85	1.19
	1970-73	39.34	6.18	23.34	69.19	1.98	5.49
Taiwan	1956-61	21.83	1.18	67.47	15.69	16.36	0.49
	1961-66	41.97	3.43	44.25	29.10	21.99	4.66
	1966-71	33.93	8.00	29.83	58.62	6.57	4.98

Source: Data generated under research project, "A Comparative
Study of the Sources of Industrial Growth and Structural Change,"
RPO 671-32, World Bank, Washington, D.C.

a Economywide share.
b Percentage of the changes in average sectoral output growth
during the period. Except for rounding, the last four columns
add up to 100 percent.

goods sector, where export expansion contributed over 80 percent of the output expansion in South Korea in the period 1970-1973, and 64 percent in Taiwan during the period 1966-1971. Perhaps the most remarkable achievement is in machinery, typically a sector that develops late in a country's industrialization. By the last period, the yearly growth rates exceeded 30 percent in both countries, while export expansion contributed around 60 percent of that sector's growth. Moreover, because of the high growth rates in machinery, that sector contributed an important share to each economy's total product.

As noted above, the numbers in Table 9.4 confirm the sequence from import substitution to export expansion-led growth observed in Figure 9.1. Moreover, in five out of the eight observations, a further sequence is observed in which the contribution of the expansion in domestic demand is highest in the middle period, while the contribution of import substitution is highest in the first period and export expansion is highest in the last period. Export-led growth is thus preceded not only by the replacement of imports, but also by the growth in sales to the domestic market. This sequence lends further support to the theories that emphasize the role of demand conditions and internal markets as determinants of the pattern of trade prior to exporting.

The changes in the input-output coefficients reported in the last column of Table 9.4 represent a widening and deepening of interindustry relationships over time brought about by the changing mix of required intermediate inputs. These changes are caused by changes in production technology as well as by substitution among inputs. With a few exceptions, the changes in input coefficients usually contributed positively to growth, indicating increases in intermediate use. In fact, other calculations not reported here indicate that the 10-year rate of growth of the ratio of intermediate demand to total gross output was 7.5 percent for South Korea and 10 percent for Taiwan.[14] These high rates of increase in the share of intermediate demand in relation to gross output associated with a rapidly growing manufacturing sector allowed South Korea and Taiwan to achieve approximately the same rates of intermediate goods in total output as did Japan, Norway, and Yugoslavia. Thus the high contribution to growth of changes in input-output coefficients is a reflection of the catching up achieved by these two countries.

Contrasting the contributions of demand to growth in sectoral output provides an indication of the relative importance of each component of final demand in the sectoral changes in output. It was seen that for both countries, exports increasingly led the growth in manufacturing throughout the period in question. To examine further whether the increasing role of export expansion followed a different path in each country, it is useful to trace each sector's contribution to the total expansion in manufactured exports across periods. The changing shares of export growth thus indicate which sectors were leading the expansion in exports.

Figure 9.2 indicates, for each period and for each manufacturing sector in both countries, its share in the total expansion of manufactured exports. Again, the similarities between the two countries are striking. Consumer goods as a group are plotted on the top section of Figure 9.2. It is apparent that with the exception of paper products, for which high transport costs have been a major natural impediment to trade (especially for countries such as South Korea and Taiwan that are far away from their major trading partners), consumer goods as a whole accounted for the bulk of manufactured exports in both countries. It is also clear that with the exception of textiles, which maintained a leading role across all episodes, the contribution of consumer goods to export growth declined with time. In particular, the contribution of food processing declined dramatically for both South Korea and Taiwan in the second and third periods. Although less pronounced, light industry followed the same pattern.

The similarities in consumer goods carry over for intermediates and machinery and transport equipment. Thus, for both countries, the contribution of exports of commodities with relatively low degrees of processing, such as metal products, declined, while the share of exports of machinery and transport equipment with higher degrees of processing rose. Thus, for both South Korea and Taiwan, the share of machinery and transport equipment in the expansion of manufactured exports rose from approximately 5 percent to over 20 percent. This remarkable achievement, noted earlier, shows how dramatically the pattern of manufactured exports changed over a decade.

By restricting the comparison to the manufacturing sector, where the role of products based on natural resources and of exogenous factors in a country's natural resource endowment is more limited, it is possible to infer the changing pattern of comparative advantage that is governed mostly by choice of policy. It is clear that with the accumulation of physical and human capital, which is itself influenced by trade policy, South Korea and Taiwan shifted their pattern of comparative advantage.[15] For both countries there was a shift away from consumer goods toward other manufac-

FIGURE 9.2
Changing pattern of manufacturing exports

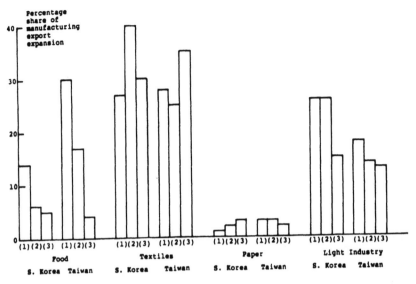

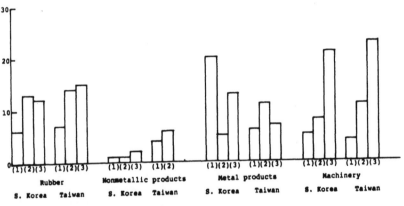

S. Korea (1) 1955-1963   Taiwan (1) 1956-1961
         (2) 1963-1970   (2) 1961-1966
         (3) 1970-1973   (3) 1966-1971

Source: Data generated under research project, "A Comparative Study of the Sources of Industrial Growth and Structural Change," RPO 671-32, World Bank, Washington, D.C.

tured goods more intensive in physical and human capital. This shift resulted in a pattern of manufactured exports that involved a higher degree of processing.

Because both countries had a poor natural resource endowment, they were obliged to import the bulk of the raw materials used in manufacturing production. Therefore it is not surprising that the import content of exports in both countries is high. This assumption is confirmed by the figures in Table 9.5, which indicate the import content of exports and domestic demand for each benchmark year. It is significant that Japan, South Korea, and Taiwan were the only countries in the group of nine for which the import content of exports was higher than that of domestic demand.

These figures confirm that a country need not have a strong natural resource base to become an important exporter of manufactured goods, provided that it is ready to allocate foreign exchange for imports to be used by export industries. As has been documented for both countries elsewhere, the pursuit of trade policies by both countries that did not lead to a bias against export activities made this pattern possible.[16] By providing producers of exports with free access to imported raw materials and intermediate goods, and by discouraging the use of imported intermediates in domestic production, both countries increasingly diverted

TABLE 9.5
Total import content of exports and final demand, direct plus indirect
(percent)

Country	Year	Domestic Demand	Exports
South Korea	1963	11.2	15.8
	1970	14.8	18.7
	1973	17.9	25.5
Taiwan	1956	9.7	13.6
	1961	9.8	12.9
	1966	14.3	19.7
	1971	17.9	25.5

Source: Data generated under research project, "A Comparative Study of the Sources of Industrial Growth and Structural Change," RPO 671-32, World Bank, Washington, D.C.

imported intermediates toward export activities. Indeed, in both South Korea and Taiwan, the import content of exports rose steadily.

Further scrutiny of the contribution to growth of
various components of final demand reveals a remarkable
similarity in the growth strategies of both countries. In particular, the contribution of import substitution and export growth followed the same path in
both. Furthermore, although there are some differences
as to which export sectors led in the early period,
they are quite small. For both countries, there is
also a strong correlation between sectoral growth rates
and the share of exports in gross output across periods. Toward the end of the sixties and early seventies, both countries embarked on an export drive led by
consumer goods, and the lead in the drive for exports
shifted toward machinery (mostly electrical and appli-
ances). In turn, this evolving comparative advantage
resulted in an increasing import content of exports.

THE PATTERN OF EMPLOYMENT ABSORPTION
IN MANUFACTURING

For countries such as South Korea and Taiwan,
where in the 1950s the marginal productivity of labor
in agriculture was relatively low, there were many benefits to be derived from a highly labor-intensive development strategy, since the real cost to the economy
of supplying labor was low. A virtue of the South
Korean and Taiwanese development strategies that is
often pointed out is that they emphasized labor-
intensive activities, thereby achieving unusually high
rates of growth in labor absorption (see, for instance,
Westphal 1978; Little 1980, 497-98). This section
looks into the factors that, from an accounting point
of view, have contributed to the high rate of labor
absorption in each country's manufacturing sector.

Labor Productivity, Capital Accumulation, and
Structural Change

The first measure to be used is a simple shift-
share identity that allows the delineation of the
effects on the rate of industrial employment expansion
of: (1) changes in labor productivity; (2) capital
accumulation; and (3) changes in the composition of
manufacturing output. In turn, changes in the structure of manufacturing output may be decomposed into the
various components of final demand according to the
methodology for decomposing sources of growth presented
above. As with the other accounting identities used in

this paper, it is assumed that the components contributing to actual employment are treated as independent of one another. However, it is to be expected
in any economy, and a fortiori in economies undergoing
rapid growth and structural change, that there are significant causal relationships between the growth of
labor productivity, the growth of exports, and changes
in domestic demand and import competition. Unfortunately, these effects cannot be captured on the basis
of accounting identities alone. Behavioral relations
must be added to capture such interrelationships, a
subject beyond the scope of this paper.

The shift-share identity to be used is:[17]

$$L^1 - L^0 \equiv \Sigma \ell_i^1 x_i^1 - \Sigma \ell_i^0 x_i^0$$

$$\equiv \underbrace{\Sigma x_i^0 (\ell_i^1 - \ell_i^0)}_{(1)} + \underbrace{\Sigma \ell_i^0 (\bar{x}_i^1 - x_i^0)}_{(2)}$$

$$+ \underbrace{\Sigma \ell_i^0 (x_i^1 - \bar{x}_i^1)}_{(3)} + \underbrace{\Sigma (\ell_i - \ell_i^0)(x_i^1 - x_i^0)}_{(4)} \qquad (9.6)$$

where

L^j = Total industrial employment in year j; for Taiwan,
j = 1961, 1966, 1971, and
for South Korea, j = 1963,
1970, 1973

x_i^j = Output of ith sector in year
j, valued in constant prices

$\ell_i^j = L_i^j = L_i^j / X_i^j$ = Labor output ratio in the
i^{th} sector in year j

$\bar{x}_i^1 = \Sigma_i x_i^1 \cdot \dfrac{x_i^0}{\Sigma x_i^0}$ = Output of ith sector in
year 1, assuming the struc-
ture of production remains
the same as in year o.

The first term (1) on the right-hand side of
identity (9.6) expresses the effect of productivity
changes on employment with output held constant. It
expresses the combination of technological change and
capital deepening. The second term (2) gives the pure
growth effect when productivities and the output
structure are held constant. The third term (3)
expresses the effect of a change in the structure of
production, with sectoral productivities and overall
growth held constant. The fourth term (4) describes
the cross-effect, which is the combination of all

factors working simultaneously. The cross-effect is expected to be large for the two countries because of the high rates of growth and structural change.[18]

Table 9.6 summarizes the results from applying this identity to South Korea and Taiwan for the manufacturing sector. For both countries, data were available only starting in the early sixties, so that the analysis is confined mostly to the outward-looking period. Comparing the two countries indicates an acceleration in the rate of employment growth in Taiwan from an average of 3.5 percent a year over the period 1961-1966 to an average of 11.2 percent during the period 1966-1971. South Korea, on the other hand, experienced a slowdown, from 10.3 percent during 1963-1970 to 4.8 percent during 1970-1973.

The pure growth effect is by far the dominant one in both countries. The figures indicate that if there had been no increase in labor productivity and no structural change, employment in the manufacturing sector would still have grown an average of more than

Table 9.6
Decomposition of the expansion in
manufacturing employment

Country		Employ-ment Expansion	Because of			
			Product-ivity Change	Pure Growth	Struc-tural Change	Cross-Effect
Taiwan 1966-1961	A	104.8	-243.0	624.1	241.4	-517.7
	B	20.9	-48.6	124.8	48.2	-103.5
	C	3.5	-8.2	21.1	8.1	-17.5
Taiwan 1971-1966	A	502.7	-232.2	1,030.0	291.3	-586.3
	B	100.5	-46.4	206.0	58.2	117.2
	C	11.2	-5.2	23.0	6.5	-13.1
S. Korea 1963-1970	A	677	-217	1411	88	-6.5
	B	97	-31	2.2	13	-86
	C	10.3	-3.3	21.5	1.3	-9.2
S. Korea 1973-1970	A	198	-496	1141	51	-498
	B	66	-165	380	17	-166
	C	4.8	-12.1	27.7	1.3	-12.1

Note: A = Total employment change (1,000 man-years).
B = Average annual employment change, percent.
C = B as percent of average annual employment.

20 percent a year. There is little doubt, however, that the phenomenal rates of growth in employment observed here, which were directly linked to the boom in exports experienced in both countries, were also aided by the high rates of growth in labor productivity, even though this effect in an accounting framework shows up as a negative effect on employment growth. Without the high rates of growth in labor productivity, it is unlikely that either country could have achieved such high rates of export growth. The slowdown in the growth in employment in South Korea can be ascribed to the extremely high rate of growth in labor productivity during the period 1970-1973. On the contrary, the slowdown in the rate of labor productivity in Taiwan accounted for the acceleration in the rate of employment growth.

In both countries, the cross-effect is important and indicates that changes in employment, productivity growth, and industrial structure were occurring simultaneously.[19] It is also interesting to contrast the role of structural change in both countries. Clearly, in Taiwan the pattern of structural change in manufacturing was directed toward the labor-intensive sectors. This effect alone would have allowed labor to grow between 6.5 percent and 8.1 percent annually. These figures are certainly suggestive of the important role that policy can have on employment by providing incentives toward labor-intensive activities. By contrast, in South Korea this effect is consistently small, accounting for only for 1.3 percent employment growth. Thus, although both countries pursued a development strategy favorable to labor-intensive activities, Taiwan achieved a much greater rate of labor absorption in manufacturing through structural change than did South Korea.

Factor Intensity of Trade[20]

To demonstrate fully that the export-led growth strategies pursued by South Korea and Taiwan resulted in higher growth than might otherwise have been achieved under alternative strategies cannot be done solely on the basis of ex-post calculations of the kind undertaken here. However, even though the determinants of comparative advantage include many elements other than resource endowments, indirect evidence that supports an efficient allocation of resources can be obtained by examining the factor intensity of trade in both countries.

Table 9.7 gives the trends in labor/capital ratios for manufacturing and all goods and services. The figures for manufacturing are more reliable, given the

TABLE 9.7
Factor intensity of trade
(capital/labor ratios)

	South Korea			Taiwan		
	1963	1970	1973	1961	1966	1971
Direct Factor **Requirements**						
Manufactured Products						
Domestic Final Demand	3.63	2.58	1.73	27.13	20.46	14.41
Exports	3.34	2.96	2.04	21.69	19.24	16.11
Imports	2.99	1.74	1.17	27.32	19.34	14.42
Exports/Imports	1.12	1.70	1.74	0.79	0.99	1.12
All Goods and Services						
Domestic Final Demand	2.03	1.87	1.40	17.24	15.66	13.76
Exports	2.24	1.70	1.29	9.68	9.87	10.25
Imports	5.03	3.42	2.07	23.52	19.60	17.67
Exports/Imports	0.45	0.49	0.62	0.41	0.50	0.58
Total Factor **Requirements**						
Manufactured Products						
Domestic Final Demand	3.01	2.19	1.53	22.49	19.03	14.28
Exports	2.56	2.05	1.37	20.64	17.75	13.42
Imports	2.29	1.59	1.02	16.07	13.45	10.89
Exports/Imports	1.12	1.29	1.34	1.28	1.32	1.23
All Goods and Services						
Domestic Final Demand	2.19	1.84	1.36	16.84	15.53	12.93
Exports	2.26	1.73	1.22	14.95	13.15	11.42
Imports	3.13	2.17	1.35	16.56	14.59	12.92
Exports/Imports	0.72	0.79	0.90	0.90	0.90	0.88

Source: Data generated under research project, "A Comparative Study of the Source of Industrial Growth and Structural Change," RPO 671-32, World Bank, Washington, D.C.

difficulty of estimating capital stock (and employment) in the agricultural and services sectors. With attention to the manufacturing sector, the estimates indicate that the direct capital/labor requirement of exports exceeds that for the replacements of imports for all time periods in South Korea, whereas the opposite was the case in Taiwan. For both countries, however, a rising trend in the labor/capital ratio for exports as compared with import-competing production can be observed. The difference between the two countries is attributable to the fact that food processing, which accounts for the bulk of manufactured exports in Taiwan, is more directly capital-intensive than the average bundle of exports.

With respect to total factor intensities, which include both direct and indirect requirements, it can be seen, however, that both countries have about the same difference in factor intensity of export industries as compared with import-competing ones.[21] Here the similarity in resource allocation within the manufacturing sector suggested by these ratios is quite striking. They indicate that both countries allocated capital and labor between export- and import-competing activities in roughly the same manner. These results are consistent with the observation made about both South Korea and Taiwan regarding factor pricing. In particular, wages were market-determined in the export sector and only rose when an increase would not undermine competitiveness (Fields 1982).[22] Whether because of periodic devaluations, as in the South Korean case, where inflation was higher, or because of a fixed exchange rate with low inflation as in Taiwan, factor prices were relatively close to opportunity costs in both countries. This condition held true during the period under study, since most of the time the two economies provided both positive real rates for borrowers and wages close to the opportunity cost of labor. Combined with similar factor endowments and similar incentives to production, fairly close patterns of factor intensities in the manufacturing sector of each country might be expected when comparing exports with import-competing industries. The figures in Table 9.7 indicate just that. The only difference between the two countries appears to be a rising trend in the labor/capital ratio in South Korea, which is not the case in Taiwan.[23]

The role of the labor-intensive development strategy pursued by both countries can be further examined by measuring the contribution of exports to employment. Table 9.8 gives the percent in total employment (economywide) attributable to exports for the same years. Not surprisingly, both countries show a rising contribution of employment over time generated by exports. However, because Taiwan is a more open economy than South Korea (in the sense that its ratio of exports to total output is higher), it is not surprising that the employment contribution from exports is higher there than in South Korea. It is also interesting to compare the direct employment contribution of exports with the total contribution when linkages with other sectors are taken into account. In Taiwan in particular, the linkage effect is especially strong in the manufacturing sector, since the employment contribution of exports is 4.4 times greater in 1961 and 2.5 times in 1971. Of course, as the direct employment contribution rises, the indirect contribution falls. While this outcome is surely to be

Table 9.8
Percent of employment resulting from exports

	South Korea			Taiwan		
	1963	1970	1973	1961	1966	1971
Manufacturing Sectors						
Direct Employment in Production for Exports	3.6	7.6	6.2	3.7	4.4	9.8
Total Employment from All Exports	11.9	16.8	12.0	16.1	14.7	24.1
All Sectors						
Direct Employment in Production for Exports	2.8	6.6	11.8	5.4	10.4	14.3
Total Employment from All Exports	4.6	11.3	19.0	15.2	22.6	27.4
Export/Output Ratios						
Manufacturing	3.6	8.9	17.0	9.5	14.4	20.6

Source: Data generated under research project, "A Comparative Study of the Sources of Industrial Growth and Structural Change," RPO 671-32, World Bank, Washington, D.C.

expected at the economywide level, it need not be the case for the manufacturing sector alone. The declining importance of indirect effects for manufacturing in both countries is probably mostly the result of the observed shift in comparative advantage in the last period away from exports such as foodstuffs, which purchase labor-intensive products from the agriculture sector.

This investigation leads to an inquiry about the relationship between growth in total factor productivity and the composition of the growth in demand. Unfortunately, the sources of productivity growth are not available at a disaggregated level for the manufacturing sector. The figures presented here, however, support the view that trade liberalization generates economies of scale by extending the domestic market. It is also likely that trade liberalization further reduces the costs of production by increasing competitiveness and reducing interfirm differences in efficiency, as well as by raising the rate of growth of TFP. Furthermore, a cumulative effect is also likely to take place across industries as a result of rising interindustry linkages, found by comparing the input-output tables in both countries. At the same time, the figures showing a period of strong import substitution in the early postwar period would also be consistent with a different conjecture: sufficient expansion of the home market allowed for economies of scale, with resulting declines in the average costs of production that allowed both countries to expand their sales in foreign markets. In any case, an important characteristic of import substitution in both countries is that it was not pursued for an extended period, as in many other countries.

CONCLUSIONS

The quantitative comparisons in this paper confirm the widely held view that the unusually high rates of growth and structural change achieved by South Korea and Taiwan followed the same pattern. Both countries experienced an unusually high rate of growth in total factor productivity for their level of per capita income. Furthermore, the relative contribution of total factor productivity was unusually high in comparison with other countries, especially developing ones. Associated with this like pattern of high growth rates for inputs and total factor productivity was a pattern of final demand in which import substitution played an important role in the late fifties and early sixties, prior to the phenomenal increase in export growth. Although this performance was undoubtedly influenced by noneconomic factors and exogenous or quasiexogenous economic factors--such as the synergistic effects of the high rates of growth of trading partners--it still stands in sharp contrast with the contributions to growth in developing countries in other parts of the world, notably Latin America.

Three further observations that emerged from the comparisons may be applicable elsewhere. First, both countries early on established their comparative advantage in the manufacturing sector. Whether or not a poor resource endowment was an important cause for this development, it certainly provided some impetus. The result was a more rapid shift of resources away from low productivity activities toward higher ones, a pattern that gave rise to higher growth than would otherwise have been the case. Second, the high labor intensity of exports allowed a higher rate of labor employment absorption than would have been the case had resources been channeled toward domestic activities. The figures indicate that the differences in factor intensity were sufficiently pronounced to make a substantial difference. Third, the export drive was associated with a rising content of imports in exports. With comparative advantage changing rapidly in both economies toward goods requiring more processing, it was probably necessary that liberal policies toward imports be followed along with promoting exports. To what extent import liberalization promoted further competition domestically and higher rates of factor productivity growth indirectly is an issue that remains to be investigated.

NOTES

1. An earlier version of this paper was presented at the Conference on Lessons and Experiences from Small Open Economies, held in Santiago, Chile, November 11-13, 1982. This paper is based on ongoing research at the World Bank entitled "A Comparative Study of the Sources of Industrial Growth and Structural Change" (RPO 671-32). It draws particularly on the work of Kuo (1979) and Kim (1978) in that project. I would like to thank the codirectors of the project, Hollis Chenery, Sherman Robinson, and Moshe Syrquin, for their guidance and for allowing me to draw on the findings of that project. I also thank Juan Eduardo Coeymans, Yuji Kubo, Shujiro Urata, S. C. Tsiang, and Jeffrey Williamson for their comments and

Maria Kutcher and Narayana Poduval for their research assistance. The views expressed in this paper are those of the author and do not necessarily represent those of the World Bank or its affiliates.

2.   For further discussion and explanation of this divergence, see Christensen, Cummings, and Jorgenson (1980, 599-601).

3.   After reviewing the evidence on the contribution of total factor productivity to growth in developing countries, Nadiri (1972, 151) concludes that the "Contribution of factor productivity is small in developing countries compared to its critical importance in industrialized countries."

4.   Bruton's (1969) study of the period 1940-1964 finds an even lower percentage (28) and attributes it to underutilization of installed capacity.

5.   The results described here are based on the ongoing project (RPO 671-32) at the World Bank, "A Comparative Study of the Sources of Industrial Growth and Structural Change."

6.   For the deflation procedures used and further discussion of the methodology, see Chenery, Robinson, and Syrquin (1986 forthcoming, chap. 5).

7.   The expression "mainstream" comes from Kornai (1972).

8.   An approximation of their market size is provided by the value of manufacturing value added in each country in the initial year. The figures are (in U.S. $ million 1970):   South Korea (364), Taiwan (448), Israel (678), and Norway (1,393) (conversion to dollars at market exchange rates).

9.   This equation is used by Chen (1977). For an alternative approach allowing for disequilibrium in the factor markets, see Bruno (1967).

10.   Denison divides the residual into eleven items. See Denison and Chung (1976) for a study along these lines for Japan for the period 1953-1971. If, as is often conjectured, South Korea and Taiwan have experienced a growth pattern that is similar to Japan's, it is probable that, like Japan, the contribution to growth of each element will be higher than in almost all developing countries. Japan consistently scored higher on all counts than did the ten other industrialized countries.   See Denison and Chung (1976, Table 2.13).

11.   It should be noted that major assumptions must be made for this kind of calculation, in particular, that the reduction in agricultural employment has a relatively small effect on agricultural output. For details, see Chen (1977, appendix B).

12.   Chen's sectoral results should be interpreted cautiously, since it appears that he used the same values for the factor shares mentioned above at the

sectoral level. He reports that his results are not significantly altered for values of $0.3 < \beta_K < 0.5$ and $0.5 < \beta_L < 0.7$. Chen's results are challenged by Kuo, whose calculations are also based on a CRS production function. Her results for the manufacturing sector are as follows (the percentage contribution of technical change to the growth rate is in brackets): 1952–1961 (6.5 [42]); 1961–1971 (6.4 [20]); and 1971–1980 (1.1 [7]). Kuo attributes this decline in the rate of technical progress to an increase in the capital/labor ratio. See Kuo (1983).

13. However, at a more disaggregated level, when the sectoral growth rates are regressed on the contribution of export expansion to growth, the results are inconclusive.

14. In no other country among the nine did this rate exceed 4.5 percent.

15. Balassa (1979) refers to this evolution as a "stages" approach to comparative advantage.

16. See, for instance, Little (1979), Westphal (1978), and Lee and Liang (1982). Bias is defined in the sense of providing different effective exchange rates for import substituting and exporting activities within and across sectors.

17. For an application of this identity to India and Taiwan, see Banerji and Riedel (1980).

18. For an elaboration of the well-known problems associated with the use of expressions like (9.6), see Martin and Evans (1979).

19. The cross-effect would disappear if the decomposition were carried out by integration in continuous time.

20. The figures were kindly provided by Shujiro Urata, an economist with the World Bank.

21. In computing total factor requirements, the domestic input-output matrix A^d was used for exports, the total matrix A for import-competing industries. The results are essentially the same when the A matrix is used for exports as well.

22. Fields reports that real wages in manufacturing rose by 300 percent in Taiwan from 1954 to 1979 and by 190 percent in South Korea from 1966 to 1980. He argues that a major cause of success in both countries was that wages were pulled up by supply and demand rather than being pushed above market-cleaning levels by a variety of institutional forces.

23. The figures in Hong (1976) indicate a rising capital/labor ratio in exports of manufactured products between 1968 and 1973. The results are not strictly comparable, since the estimation methods and data were different. For instance, Hong uses 1973 input/output coefficients for every year.

REFERENCES

Balassa, B. 1979. "A Stages' Approach to Comparative Advantage." In Economic Growth and Resources, edited by I. Adelman, 121-56. London: Macmillan.

Banerji, R., and J. Riedel. 1980. "Industrial Employment Expansion under Alternative Trade Strategies: Case of India and Taiwan 1950-70." Journal of Development Economics 7:567-78.

Bruno, M. 1967. "Estimation of Factor Contribution to Growth Under Structural Disequilibrium." International Economic Review 49-62.

Bruton, H. J. 1969. "Productivity Growth in Latin America." American Economic Review 62:1099-1116.

Chen, E. K. 1977. "Factor Inputs, Total Factor Productivity, and Economic Growth: The Asian Case." The Developing Economies 15:121-43.

Chenery, H., S. Robinson, and M. Syrquin, eds. 1986 forthcoming. Industrialization and Growth: A Comparative Study. Oxford: Oxford University Press.

Chenery, H., S. Shishido, and T. Watanabe. 1962. "The Pattern of Japanese Growth: 1914-54." Econometrica 30:98-139.

Christensen, L., D. Cummings, and D. Jorgenson. 1980. "Economic Growth, 1947-53: An International Comparison." In New Developments in Productivity Measurement and Analysis, edited by J. Kendrick and B. Vaccara. Chicago: University of Chicago Press for the National Bureau of Economic Research.

Correa, H. 1970. "Sources of Economic Growth in Latin America." Southern Economic Journal 37:17-31.

Denison, E. F., and W. K. Chung. 1976. "Economic Growth and Its Sources." In Asia's New Giant: How The Japanese Economy Works, edited by H. Patrick and H. Rosovsky. Washington, D.C.: The Brookings Institution.

Elias, V. 1978. "Sources of Economic Growth in Latin American Countries." Review of Economics and Statistics 60:363-70.

Fields, G. 1982. "Industrialization and Employment in Hong Kong, Korea, Singapore and Taiwan." Cornell University, Ithaca, N.Y. Photocopy.

Galenson, W., ed. 1979. Economic Growth and Structural Change in Taiwan: The Postwar Experience of the Republic of China. Ithaca, N.Y.: Cornell University Press.

Hong, W. 1976. Factor Supply and Factor Intensity of Trade in Korea. Seoul: Korea Development Institute.

Kim, K. S. 1978. "Industrialization and Structural Change in Korea." Korea Development Institute, Seoul. Photocopy.

Kornai, J. 1972. Rush Versus Harmonic Growth. Amsterdam: North-Holland Publishing Company.

Krueger, A. 1979. Studies in the Modernization of the Republic of Korea: 1945-75: The Developmental Role of the Foreign Sector and Aid. Cambridge: Harvard University Press.

Kuo, S. W. 1979. "Economic Growth and Structural Change in the Republic of China." Taipei. Photocopy.

_____. 1983. The Taiwan Economy in Transition. Boulder, Col.: Westview Press.

Lee, T. H., and K. S. Liang. 1982. "Taiwan." In Development Strategies in Semi-Industrial Countries, by Bela Balassa and associates. Baltimore: Johns Hopkins University Press.

Little, I. 1979. "An Economic Reconnaissance." In Economic Growth and Structural Change in Taiwan: The Postwar Experience of the Republic of China, edited by W. Galenson. Ithaca: Cornell University Press.

Martin, J. and J. Evans. 1979. "Notes on Measuring the Employment Displacement Effects of Trade by the Accounting Procedure." Oxford Economic Papers. 155-64.

Nadiri, M. 1972. "International Studies of Factor Inputs and Total Factor Productivity: A Brief Survey." Review of Income and Wealth 18:129-54.

Syrquin, M. 1976. "Sources of Industrial Growth and Change: An Alternative Measure." Paper presented at the European Meetings of the Econometric Society, Helsinki, August.

Westphal, L. E. 1978. "The Republic of Korea's Experience with Export-Led Industrial Development." World Development 6:347-82.

10
Employment, Income Distribution, and Growth in the East Asian Context: A Comparative Analysis

Gustav Ranis

INTRODUCTION

Certain outstanding features dominate the post-World War II landscape of development. One is that the overall growth of developing countries, in spite of the oil shocks and stagflation in the developed countries, has been surprisingly strong. Over the past three decades, growth has generally been in excess of postwar targets. A second feature is that this record hides very substantial differences between the upper tier--the so-called newly industrialized countries of East Asia and Latin America--and the really poor developing countries concentrated in South Asia and Africa. Third, with respect to performance in terms of employment and income distribution, a further distinction must be made between the East Asian newly industrialized countries, where the record has generally been good, and the Latin American newly industrialized countries, where it has been less satisfactory.

This paper analyzes the achievements of the major East Asian representatives in this general context. It also suggests some of the reasons for the observed differences in performance between East Asia and Latin America over this period. The second section is devoted to a historical analysis of the East Asian newly industrialized countries, while the third section provides some comparisons with the typical situation in Latin America and draws conclusions about the likely range of options for future development strategy.

EMPLOYMENT, INCOME DISTRIBUTION, AND GROWTH

A comparative study of the past thirty years of transitional growth in the four East Asian mixed economies--Hong Kong, South Korea, Singapore, and Taiwan--presumes that an underlying generalizable, typological

250

approach can be used. As such, there must be a family
affinity among these countries, that is, as a group
they must exhibit sufficiently similar initial conditions and behavior patterns over time. At the same
time, it is recognized that even within any one sub-
family of developing countries there are always important and instructive differences. Nevertheless, any
approach aimed at learning something from the experience of East Asian developing countries assumes, at
least implicitly, an underlying family affinity.

Where appropriate, empirical information is presented on all four East Asian newly industrialized
countries. However, the analytical and statistical
focus is on Taiwan and South Korea specifically. The
reason is that Hong Kong and Singapore, while members
of the same family in most respects, are really city-
states whose small size and relative absence of an
agricultural sector render them extremely "special" and
thus less instructive in terms of their development
experience and its possible applicability to other
parts of the developing world.

Taiwan and South Korea, at the time they began
their transition growth in the early 1950s, typified
the case of the relatively small- to medium-size,
heavily labor-surplus economy, relatively poor in natural and relatively rich in human resources. In both
cases their colonial Japanese masters paid heavy attention to infrastructural and organizational investments
in the rural sector and to the production of food
crops. In addition, the initial conditions included a
fairly equal distribution of assets, especially of
land, thanks both to reforms in the earlier, that is,
Japanese, period, and to later, that is, early postwar,
legislation. The Gini coefficient for land ownership
was in the neighborhood of 0.6 for Taiwan in 1950, and
fell to 0.46 in 1960, in strong contrast to the Gini
coefficient for land ownership of around 0.8 typical of
much of the developing world, including Latin America.

The very notion of transition growth used in this
paper presumes an evolutionary view of economic development: a country passes through a sequence of subphases in the course of transition to Kuznetsian modern
growth. Each subphase is characterized by a distinct
mode of operations around which this analysis of postwar performance focuses. This description does not
mean that there was an inevitable movement along a
fixed historical pattern in the four East Asian countries, only that there seems to have been a sequence of
evolutionary phenomena the four followed--a sequence
that, incidentally, also characterized Japan earlier.

The family affinity among the four East Asian
countries can be summarized in terms of their cultural
and geographic proximity. All four are in a region of

East Asia of dense population and poor natural resources. They share the same demographic and cultural
tradition: a surplus labor force endowed with unusually favorable levels of literacy and general education. Each country is, moreover, relatively small.
Given their initial endowment of plentiful, high-
quality labor and scarce natural resources, the importance of the international dimensions of development,
especially trade and capital flows, was quite great.

The intrafamily differences within the group of
four are both economic-geographic and historical in
origin. During the pretransition colonial period, the
East Asian countries routinely consumed imported manufactured products of the nondurable consumer goods
variety and exported traditional agricultural products,
for example, rice and sugar in the case of Taiwan.
While Taiwan possessed somewhat more favorable natural
geographic features in terms of climate, soil, and the
potential for changing to multiple cropping and agricultural technology, both South Korea and Taiwan
benefited from the Japanese emphasis on such infrastructural investment as irrigation and such institutional investment as farmers' organizations.

The basic structural form in Taiwan's pretransition phase, S_1, is shown in Figure 10.1. The agricultural sector, A, produces the domestic food supply,
F, as well as traditional exports, E_a,[1] which help
finance the import of manufactured nondurable consumer
goods, M_t, such as textiles, which are consumed by the
household sector, H. South Korea differs slightly, as
it had some nonagricultural exports, E_1, early on,
while, because of its less favored agricultural sector,
some net food imports, M_f, were already in evidence, in
addition to the manufactured nondurables, M_t.

Given this colonial heritage, Taiwan and South
Korea initiated their modern transition growth, S_2,
with the customary pattern of primary import substitution (Figure 10.1). A part of the traditional export
earnings, mainly E_a, is now diverted from the import
of nondurable consumer goods, M_t, to the import of
producer goods, M_p. This shift permits the emergence
of new import-substituting industries, I_n, which now
produce the domestic nondurable consumer goods, D_t,
that gradually substitute for the previously imported
M_t in the domestic market. This type of growth, fueled
by traditional exports, entails two observable substitution phenomena, that is, substitution in the sense
of the allocation of foreign exchange, that is,

$$M_p/(M_p + M_t),$$

and substitution in the sense of the domestic market,
that is,

252

FIGURE 10.1 Phases of economic development

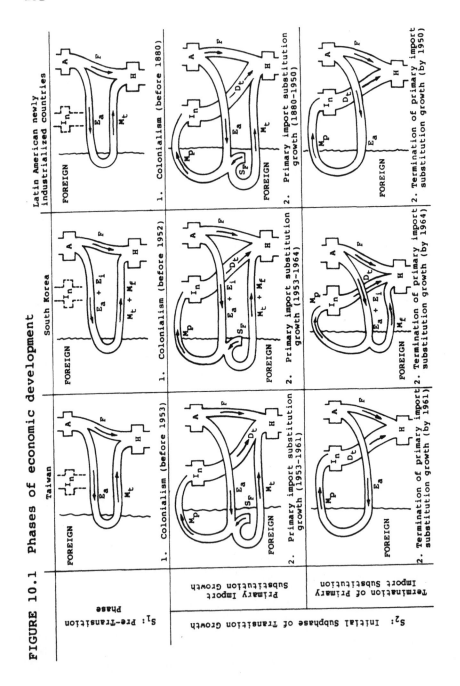

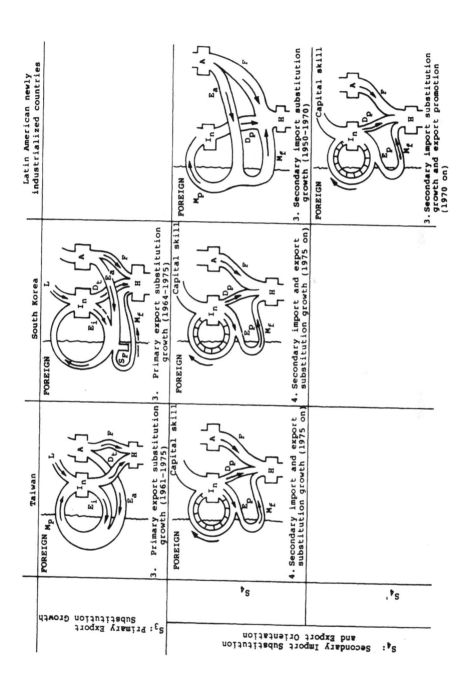

$$D_t/(M + D_t),$$

both of which rise markedly over this period.

Moreover, foreign trade as a percentage of national income can be expected to decline during this primary import substitution subphase, given that the policy syndrome that accompanies it strongly favors the domestic market and offers protection in support of the new industrial class.[2]   Given a long-run relative shortage of natural resources, an abundance of unskilled labor, and a good educational base, the development of human resources, entrepreneurial and managerial, appropriate for industrial production becomes an essential ingredient in the growth process.   It clearly takes time for entrepreneurial experience and maturation to develop before an economy's underlying comparative advantage can be realized in foreign trade.   In other words, in this early subphase, S_2, modern factory production for domestic markets is seriously initiated for the first time, often with the help of foreign capital, S_F.   Traditional populations are converted into modern factory workers; land-based or commercial entrepreneurs gradually become industrial entrepreneurs capable of absorbing modern science and technology; and law- and order-oriented civil servants try to become agents of developmental change.   Once these necessary factors are in place, countries with a strong comparative advantage in unskilled labor can presumably become viable partners in international production and trade.

It is common knowledge that during the S_2 subphase, all the policies of government are directed toward supporting the new industrial class. Because of the government's support, industrial profits have a windfall character that is not necessarily connected with productive efficiency.   As such, in this phase there is a tendency for inefficient mixes of capital-intensive technology and output, a neglect of rural industry, and an even more serious neglect of the food-producing agricultural sector.

What is noteworthy here is that the East Asian countries chose a relatively milder version of the usual import substitution syndrome: they paid relatively more attention to their agricultural sectors and maintained lower levels of effective protection for their industries than has typically been the case. Thus, while the well-known package of tariffs, import licensing, overvalued exchange rates, artificially low interest rates, and so on all conformed to the usual strategy, its execution in the East Asian countries was milder and more flexible.

This growth through primary import substitution lasted about ten to fifteen years in the East Asian newly industrialized countries, inevitably coming to an end. That result is in fact inevitable: once domestic output, D_t, has substituted for all the imports of nondurable manufactured goods, M_t, any further industrialization must slow to the pace of population change and per capita income. The picture of the resource flow for the two East Asian countries that emerges at this point, roughly in the early 1960s (Figure 10.1).

Difficult societal decisions now have to be made, that is, whether to maintain the import substitution strategy--but shifting it to domestic production of previously imported producer and durable consumer goods--or to move toward the export of the same nondurable consumer goods being produced for the domestic market. The East Asian countries, after some hesitation, chose the latter, that is, they entered the S_2 subphase pictured in Figure 10.1. This phase is termed "primary export substitution" because the basis for the comparative advantage in trade now shifts gradually from land to unskilled labor. During this subphase, exports, E_n, became increasingly important relative to E_a and E_m. Their relative roles became virtually reversed during the decade of the 1960s, that is, the countries went from 90 percent agriculture-based to 80 percent industry-based (Table 10.1), while the overall trade orientation, E/GNP, reversed itself, increasing markedly (Tables 10.2 and 10.3).

Moreover, the rate of labor reallocation, that is, the shift in the labor force from agricultural to nonagricultural pursuits over time, accelerated substantially during this S_3 subphase because of the rapid rate of growth in labor-intensive industrial output now destined for a relatively unlimited international market. Once the entrepreneurial maturation during S_2 had borne fruit, labor-intensive export industries offered an opportunity for the first time to absorb the system's surplus labor on a massive scale. This labor-based "vent for surplus" led to a pronounced increase in the rate of intersectoral labor reallocation. That increase culminated not only in a relative but also in an absolute decrease in the agricultural labor force and, in the course of little more than a decade, in the exhaustion of the labor surplus, as indicated by the hitherto nearly constant level of unskilled wages giving way to rapidly rising wages in both countries. The export substitution mode implies, of course, a much more substantial integration of the East Asian economies into the world economy, not only in terms of the spectacular expansion of trade, but also in relation to private capital inflows. These inflows more than replaced the earlier infusion of concessional foreign capital--in spite of the considerable political and strategic uncertainties, especially in Taiwan.

TABLE 10.1
Breakdown of exports

Newly Indus. Countries	1950	1960	1965	1970	1975	1977

A. Share of Agricultural Exports in Total Exports, Ea/E

East Asia

Taiwan	n.a.	51.7[a]	57.9	22.5	17.5	13.4
South Korea	82.3[b]	51.4	25.3	16.7	15.1	12.8

Latin America

Mexico	53.5	64.1	64.7	48.8	38.1	42.1[c]
Colombia	83.1[d]	78.9	75.3	81.2	71.7	76.9
Chile	n.a.	n.a.	7.6[e]	7.5	17.3	n.a.
Brazil	96.8[f]	88.8	80.8	75.2	57.9	63.9

B. Share of Mineral Exports in Total Exports, Em/E

East Asia

Taiwan	n.a.	2.1[a]	0.4	0.7	1.1	1.6
South Korea	11.2[b]	8.3	22.7	8.3	7.9	6.2

Latin America

Mexico	38.6	24.0	22.3	21.2	32.4	n.a.
Colombia	16.3[d]	18.9	18.0	10.8	7.7	4.1
Chile	n.a.	n.a.	88.1[e]	88.3	77.1	n.a.
Brazil	2.1[f]	7.9	11.7	14.3	16.7	12.3

C. Share of Manufactured Exports in Total Exports, Ei/E

East Asia

Taiwan	n.a.	46.2[a]	41.7	76.8	81.4	84.9
South Korea	6.4[b]	40.3	52.0	74.9	76.8	80.9

Latin America

Mexico	7.9	11.9	13.0	30.0	29.5	n.a.
Colombia	0.5[d]	1.4	6.7	8.0	20.6	18.6
Chile	n.a.	n.a.	4.2[e]	4.0	5.3	n.a.
Brazil	0.8	3.3	7.5	9.7	23.3	23.0

Sources: (1) 1970-77 statistics are from UNCTAD (Yearbook
of Trade and Development Statistics 1979); (2) 1950-65
data are calculated from United Nations (Yearbook of
International Trade Statistics, various years).
Agricultural exports are defined as SITC 0+1+2-27-28+4;
mineral exports are defined as SITC 27+28+3+67+68; and
manufactured exports are defined as SITC 5+6-67-68+7+8.
(3) For Taiwan, data are from China, Directorate-General of
Budget, Accounting, and Statistics (Statistical Yearbook of the
Republic of China, 1978). Agricultural exports are defined as
SITC 0+1+2+4; mineral exports are defined as SITC 3; and
manufactured exports are defined as SITC 5+6+7+8+9.

[a] 1962. [b] 1952. [c] 1976. [d] 1951. [e] 1966. [f] 1954.

Note: n.a. = Not available.

TABLE 10.2
Export orientation ratio (exports, E, as a percent of GDP)

Newly Indus. Countries	1950	1955	1960	1965	1970	1975	1977
East Asia							
Taiwan	10.5	7.6	11.7	18.3	27.0/ 29.6[a]	41.2	53.8
South Korea	2.3	1.9	3.4	8.6	14.3	27.6	34.8
Hong Kong	n.a.	n.a.	84.0	76.9	99.7	94.3	95.1
Latin America							
Mexico	18.7	16.7	10.3	9.3	8.2	7.7	10.5
Colombia	14.8[b]	13.6	15.6	11.4	14.2	15.1	17.4
Chile	10.2	9.3	13.8	14.0	16.0	19.8	17.3
Brazil	6.7	8.8	6.1	7.4	6.6	7.4	7.8

Source: United Nations (Yearbook of International
Trade Statistics and Yearbook of National Accounts
Statistics, various years).

[a] 1969. [b] 1953.
Note: n.a. = Not available.

TABLE 10.3
Annual growth rate of total exports, E (percent)

Newly Indus. Countries	1950– 1955	1955– 1960	1960– 1965	1965– 1970	1970– 1975	1975– 1977
East Asia						
Taiwan	8.2	4.8	15.4	21.1	15.3	24.1
South Korea	n.a.	n.a.	32.1[a]	28.1	28.2	15.1
Hong Kong	n.a.	n.a.	n.a.	12.8[b]	3.5	14.0
Singapore	n.a.	n.a.	n.a.	n.a.	7.0[c]	15.4
Latin America						
Mexico	n.a.	n.a.	n.a.	0.9[d]	3.7	7.9
Colombia	4.7	0.3	0.5	2.4	2.1	n.a.
Chile	3.2	0.4	5.2	0.6[e]	n.a.	n.a.
Brazil	-0.7	3.3	3.3	7.6	11.2	1.0

Source: United Nations (Yearbook of International
Trade Statistics, various years); for Taiwan, China,
Directorate-General of Budget, Accounting, and
Statistics (Statistical Yearbook of Republic of China,
various years); and for South Korea, Bank of Korea
(Economic Statistical Yearbook, various years).

[a] 1963–1965 [c] 1972–1975. [e] 1965–1969.
[b] 1968–1970. [d] 1966–1970.
Note: n.a. = Not available.

A shift to export substitution must be facilitated by a shift in public policies. Any enhanced orientation toward international markets on a competitive basis requires a reduction in protection, the maintenance of more realistic exchange rates, interest rates closer to their shadow levels, and the improvement of the usually depressed terms of trade of domestic agriculture. The export of labor-intensive manufactured goods may also be facilitated, as they were in South Korea and Taiwan, by such direct government actions as the establishment of export processing zones and rebates of import duties on raw materials destined for exports, as well as other devices to ease the transition between subphases S_2 and S_3.

The primary export substitution or S_3 subphase also has a limit: once the unskilled labor surplus has been exhausted, as it was by the early 1970s in both Taiwan and South Korea, real wages begin to rise on a sustained basis. Industrial output and competitive exports tend to become more oriented toward skilled labor, technology, and capital intensity, that is, the subphase of secondary import and export substitution, S_4, is reached. Since the mid-1970s, as their skill, entrepreneurial, and technological capacities increased, Taiwan and South Korea moved into production for the domestic market and, almost simultaneously, for the foreign markets for capital goods, consumer durables, and processed raw materials. The simultaneity is related to the greater prevalence of economies of scale in the context of relatively small domestic markets. At the same time, the slack in the system's agricultural sector, in the form of sustained increases in productivity, was substantially mopped up: as that sector became less of a leading sector and more of an appendage to the rest of the economy, the need for food imports grew. As indicated in Figure 10.1, both Taiwan and South Korea now increasingly supply the domestic market, D_p, and export markets, E_p, with producer goods, while importing an increased volume of food, M_f.

The growth rates in South Korea and Taiwan during their more than quarter century of transition have been remarkably high (Table 10.4). At least as interesting is their performance relative to employment, labor share, and income distribution. Their performance has also been outstanding by developing country standards. Equity improved during S_4, a not surprising occurrence. Once the labor surplus was absorbed, wages rose and industrial output shifted according to the product cycle in continuing response to changes in endowments and in policy. This trend is in accordance with both the cross-sectional evidence and the crude theorizing surrounding the inverse U-shaped or Kuznets

TABLE 10.4
Annual real per capita GNP growth rates
(percent a year)

Newly Indus. Countries	1950	→	1955	→	1960	→	1965	→	1970	→	1975	→	1977
East Asia			PIS				PES				SIS & SES		
Taiwan			5.7a		2.8		5.1		6.2		5.7		8.3
South Korea			4.5b		1.5		3.2		7.5		7.1		9.5
Hong Kong			n.a.		n.a.		9.5c		5.8		3.8		12.0
Singapore			n.a.		n.a.		2.4		7.1		18.6		5.8
Latin America			PIS				SIS				EP		
Mexico			3.1		2.7		3.4		3.4		2.1		-1.0d
Colombia			3.0		1.7		1.4		3.0		3.3		n.a.
Chile			3.3		1.6		2.5		2.0		-2.4		8.6
Brazil			2.8		6.2		1.6		4.5		7.4		3.8

Source: Calculated from indices in United Nations (Statistical Yearbook, various years); for Taiwan, calculated from International Monetary Fund (IMF Yearbook, various years).

a 1951-1955. b 1953-1955. c 1963-1965. d 1975-1976.

Note: n.a. = Not available.
PIS = Primary import substitution
PES = Primary export substitution
SIS = Secondary import substitution
SES = Secondary export substitution
EP = Export promotion.

curve hypothesis (Bacha 1979). What is of special interest, however, is that the distribution of income does not seem to have worsened; rather, it even seems to have improved (Table 10.5) during the subphases of most rapid early transition growth, S_2 and S_3. That trend runs counter to the overall experience of developing countries and counter to the inverse U-shaped hypothesis.

A methodology for decomposing the Gini coefficient permits the establishment of a link between the way output is generated and the level of equity in income distribution that results (Fei, Ranis, and Kuo 1978). Briefly put, among the more important determinants of the size distribution of income is the functional distribution, which is in turn closely related to the employment-generating capacity of the system under labor surplus. Other determinants include the changing distributional equity of particular factor incomes, such as that from wages, property, and (merged) agricultural income, in turn closely related to the distribution of human and physical assets across families, plus the rate at which the reallocation of families between more equally and less equally distributed sectors takes place. In a society that has a substantial agricultural sector, as do South Korea and Taiwan, it is also helpful to differentiate between rural and urban households. The reason is the differences in the organizational and spatial dimensions of economic activity, which physically affect the way output decisions are made and income is distributed. For example, while urban families are engaged almost entirely in industrial and service activities, in East Asia rural families are also substantially engaged in nonagricultural activities that generate wage and property income. In other words, rural family income can be separated between agricultural and nonagricultural activities; the latter can be further subdivided into wage and property income, with each component weighted by the equity of its own distribution and its own relative importance in the families' total income.

The inequality in employment and income that results over time from the growth in a society's output can be analyzed as the weighted sum of the changes in the distribution of various family income factor components and their respective weights. These in turn can be directly related to the way output is generated and to the way both process and product choices are made in the course of development. For example, an increase in the share of labor income, which is usually more equally distributed than total income, and a decrease in the share of property income, which is usually less equally distributed, customarily favors overall

TABLE 10.5
Income distribution

Newly Ind. Countries	1955	1960	1965	1970	1975	1978

A. Gini Coefficients

East Asia

	1955	1960	1965	1970	1975	1978
Taiwan	0.58[a]	0.46[b]	0.33[c]	0.28[d]	0.29	n.a.
S. Korea	n.a.	n.a.	0.30[e]	0.34[f]	0.41	n.a.
Hong Kong	n.a.	n.a.	n.a.	0.43[g]	n.a.	n.a.
Singapore	n.a.	n.a.	0.50[h]	n.a.	.45	n.a.

Latin America

	1955	1960	1965	1970	1975	1978
Mexico	n.a.	0.55[i]	0.57[j]	0.58[k]	n.a.	n.a.
Colombia	n.a.	0.50[l]	0.61[c]	0.56	n.a.	n.a.
Chile	n.a.	n.a.	n.a.	0.51[m]	n.a.	n.a.
Brazil	n.a.	0.59	n.a.	0.59	n.a.	n.a.

B. Income Share of the Bottom 20 Percent of Households

East Asia

	1955	1960	1965	1970	1975	1978
Taiwan	n.a.	2.9[a]	5.0[b]	7.8[c]	8.8[d]	n.a.
S. Korea	n.a.	n.a.	n.a.	8.2[e]	7.5[f]	n.a.
Hong Kong	n.a.	n.a.	n.a.	n.a.	5.6[f]	n.a.

Latin America

	1955	1960	1965	1970	1975	1978
Mexico	n.a.	n.a.	3.9[i]	3.7[j]	4.2	n.a.
Colombia	n.a.	n.a.	5.0[l]	3.0[c]	3.2	n.a.
Chile	n.a.	n.a.	n.a.	n.a.	4.8[m]	n.a.
Brazil	n.a.	n.a.	3.0	n.a.	2.7	n.a.

Source: Jain (1975); for Singapore, Rao and Ramakrishnan (1978); for South Korea for 1975, Choo (1978); for Taiwan for 1975, Chen (1978); and World Bank (World Development Report, various years).

[a] 1953.
[b] 1959-1961.
[c] 1964.
[d] 1972.
[e] 1966-1968
[f] 1969-1971.
[g] 1971.
[h] 1966.
[i] 1963.
[j] 1967-1968.
[k] 1969.
[l] 1962.
[m] 1968.

Note: n.a. = Not available.

distributional equity as measured by the overall Gini coefficient.

Taiwan and South Korea provide striking cases of remarkably strong growth during their S_3 phase in the 1960s, combined with low and falling levels of income inequality. The reason is largely the initially high relative share of labor and the rapid absorption of unskilled labor in new rural and urban activities over the decade. The distribution of the merged "agricultural incomes" of rural families also showed an improvement during the 1950s and 1960s, not only because of the initially favorable effects of land reform, but also because technologies were developed and promoted that rendered small farm holdings more productive over time. This situation was a function both of the more intensive use of land via double-cropping and of the shift to such new, more labor-intensive crops as mushrooms and asparagus, in contrast to the more land-intensive rice and sugar. Such shifts in the cropping pattern were of particular benefit to poorer farmers, who were able to participate more than proportionately.

In the East Asian cases, this same potential poverty group of poor and/or landless families benefited from the unusually decentralized nature of the industrialization process. In Taiwan, a large number of small-scale rural industries and services provided 30 percent of total rural family income at the beginning and in excess of 50 percent at the end of S_3, with higher percentages for the smaller (poorer) farmers throughout. Given the even more equitable distribution of rural nonagricultural than rural agricultural income, this shift was vitally important to the overall improvement in the distribution of rural family income. It was further abetted by the fact that these rural non-agricultural activities were increasingly labor-absorbing, as witnessed by the high and rising wage share (ϕ_w) shown in Table 10.6. Especially as the administered controls over such scarce inputs as foreign exchange, credits, fertilizers, etc. were lessened over time, as South Korea and Taiwan moved from import to export substitution, it became much easier to avoid the normal discrimination in developing countries against rural and small-scale enterprises.

The prior existence of a substantial rural infrastructure, generally maintained and expanded by the independent post-colonial governments, especially in Taiwan, permitted vigorous rural growth, with a balance between fast-growing agricultural and nonagricultural activities. This feature was essential even if not spectacular to the success story of the East Asian newly industrialized countries. With rural industries

TABLE 10.6
Labor's share
(percentage)

	Taiwan			Colombia		
	1953	1960	1975	1950	1960	1975
ϕ_w^r	n.a.	62.7[a]	79.8[b]	37.9	31.8	24.1[c]
ϕ_w^u	51.1	53.2	58.7	34.8	39.2	40.5[c]

Source: Fei, Ranis, and Kuo (1979); and Ranis (1971).

[a] 1964.
[b] 1972.
[c] 1974.

Note: n.a. = Not available.

providing more sideline employment opportunities and higher income, the rural orientation of much nonagricultural growth reduced transport and urbanization costs. The result was an effective compromise, with economies of scale favoring somewhat larger market areas. In addition, but harder to prove, the proximity of a modern nonagricultural sector in the rural areas contributed to the modernization of agriculture in terms of both incentives and input-output interactions.

With respect to the urban sector, where virtually all family income is generated within industry and services, the remarkably high relative share of labor income in total value added should be noted--it was in the neighborhood of 0.5 and was moving up to 0.6 over time, as opposed to the 0.4 in the more typical case (see Table 10.6). This evidence suggests that even in the urban, relatively more capital-intensive, sectors, the East Asian newly industrialized countries managed greater mixes of labor-intensive products and processes than did most contemporary developing countries. The reason is a growth strategy that entailed a greater sensitivity to factor endowment, especially during the S_3 primary export substitution subphase. This pattern of relatively high and rising labor shares before the end of the labor surplus was reached runs counter to the expectations of both Arthur Lewis and Simon Kuznets and contributed powerfully to the low levels and steady trend of the overall Gini coefficient for total population, especially in the case of Taiwan.

The tendency of dispersed decision-makers in both rural and urban areas of East Asia to choose more appropriate output mixes and technologies relates not only to the lesser distortion of relative factor prices, as changes in government policy at the end of S_2 reduced the veil between endowments and relative factor prices. It also relates to the generally more competitive nature of the overall industrial setting. The impact of windfall profits on growth in the industrial sector and on the level of pressure to choose better output mixes and technologies is often underestimated. Import licensing systems, overvalued exchange rates, official low interest rates for favored borrowers, and all the rest of the import substitution policy paraphernalia create an environment that induces satisfying rather than maximizing behavior throughout the system. If it is true, as believed here, that there is a wide range of options both in terms of the international shelf of technology and, more importantly, the capacity to create indigenous adaptive technologies and output specifications, economic actors have to feel some pressure to engage in the necessary searches and R&D. Often the range of options is artificially restricted by a simple lack of information or by such institutional barriers as "tying" by aid donors or multinational salesmen. Patents and licensing systems may be used to block market access rather than to widen the range of options and opportunities. In the East Asian case, such barriers were kept in check by the reforms of the early 1960s, which led governments to play a more catalytic rather than directly interventionist role. This trend materially improved the interest of dispersed producers in searching for and the opportunity of their finding the proverbial "better mousetrap." This environment has made a large difference in terms of both the employment-generating capacity of the path of balanced rural growth, based on import replacement rather than import imitation, and in terms of finding the appropriate niche in the markets of both mature and other developing countries.

COMPARISON WITH LATIN AMERICA AND POLICY OPTIONS

Most observers wince at the very notion of a Latin American type. Indeed, there is very substantial heterogeneity among the developing countries in the Western hemisphere. Even among the so-called newly industrialized countries that are the focus here, it is hard to establish the same strong family affinity that exists in East Asia or sub-Saharan Africa.

Nevertheless, there are typological differences between South Korea and Taiwan, on the one hand, and countries such as Chile, Colombia, and Mexico, on the other. These differences are significant and are part of the essential backdrop for any discussion of the relevance or irrelevance of the East Asian experience. Among Latin America's significant distinguishing characteristics are, inter alia, their earlier start along the path of transition growth, their more favorable person/land ratios and natural resource endowments, the more concentrated structure of their assets, their larger size, and possibly their somewhat weaker human resource endowments, as reflected in literacy rates, entrepreneurial capacity, and the like. Nevertheless, as is indicated in Figure 10.1, the initial pattern of the flow of colonial resources during S_1 in the Latin American case in general bears a substantial resemblance to the East Asian case, that is, mainly land-based raw materials (mostly minerals and tropical cash crops), E_a, were exported in exchange for mainly industrial consumer goods, M_t. An essentially similar pattern holds true for S_2, the first subphase of the transition, variously dated as starting in the late 19th century or in the Depression of the 1930s. Again, the focus was on reallocating the proceeds from the traditional natural resource-based exports to the financing of new nondurable consumer good types of import-substituting industries.

It should be noted (see Table 10.4) that growth rates during this primary import substitution period were generally as high in Latin America as they were in East Asia. Undoubtedly, the reason for this phenomenon was the higher levels of initial endowments and per capita income. On the other hand, the import substitution policy package may be judged to have been more severe, perhaps in part because of its substantially longer duration. One important consequence was a relatively much greater neglect of the food-producing agricultural subsector, reinforcing the colonial policy that had concentrated on lucrative mining activities. In short, both typologies shared an infant industry rationale that called for the creation of a new industrial class out of a landlord or commercial elite, with the help of reasonable levels of protection and transfers of profits. The difference between them resides in the precise tools employed, their severity, and their longevity.

This latter point is best illustrated by the contrasting choice made by the Latin American newly industrialized countries at the end of S_2, the subphase of transition involving primary import substitution. Faced, as in the East Asian case, with a decline in the rate of industrial growth and the threat of price wars in the protected domestic markets for consumer nondurable goods, as early as the 1930s, and certainly by

the end of the 1950s, the Latin American newly industrialized countries decided to continue with import
substitution, although with a shift in focus to the
manufacture of producer and durable consumer goods--
first for the domestic market (Figure 10.1) and, after
1970, on exports as well (Figure 10.1). This development is reminiscent, at first blush, of the secondary
import and export substitution subphase previously
encountered in the East Asian cases. However, the
difference is that the Latin American system moved
directly from primary import substitution into the
production of the more skilled labor-, capital-, and
technology-intensive products. Generally those areas
require more than the mere maintenance of the prior
policy structure oriented toward protection and
control--they need a further deepening and strengthening of this system. Thus, at the end of primary import
substitution phase, whereas the rate of effective
protection had declined in East Asia, it had risen in
Latin America.[3] Interest rates generally remained at
low, if not negative real levels, the terms of trade in
agriculture continued to be depressed, and even tradi-
tionally food self-sufficient or exporting countries
began to be net importers.

More recently, given the still narrow domestic
markets for these products, the Latin American newly
industrialized countries have experienced sizable
increases in their nontraditional, industrial exports
(Table 10.1C). While some of this expansion has
admittedly been in the area of consumer nondurable
goods, particularly shoes, gloves, and textiles, much
of it has involved such higher technology, highly
capital-intensive areas as cars, aircraft, and electrical machinery. In many cases, it has been related
less to the march of dynamic comparative advantage or
the product cycle and more to the government's willingness to subsidize the industrial exports that are now
generally recognized as the hallmark of successful
development, even by Prébisch and his followers. Moreover, as Table 10.7 indicates, a much smaller percentage of Latin American (as compared to East Asian)
manufactured exports has been going to advanced country
markets where the former's comparative advantage is
presumably greatest. Note also that during the 1960s
the East Asian newly industrialized countries seemed to
be increasing their overall industrial export orientation substantially toward developed countries, while in
the Latin American newly industrialized countries, that
market was declining.

The Latin American industrial exports phenomenon
thus differs from the primary export substitution to
secondary import and export substitution sequence encountered in East Asia. It entailed, instead, the pro-

TABLE 10.7

Exports of manufactured goods, total and consumer nondurables, by destination [a]
(percentage)

NICs	Total 1962 DCs	1962 LDCs	1970 DCs	1970 LDCs	1977 DCs	1977 LDCs	Consumer Nondurables 1962 DCs	1962 LDCs	1970 DCs	1970 LDCs	1977 DCs	1977 LDCs
Latin America												
Brazil	63.2	36.6	54.7	43.4	55.7	43.1	75.7	20.6	78.3	16.4	74.7	19.2
Colombia	50.5	49.4	42.4	57.0	42.9	56.6	47.9	51.8	60.2	38.1	70.7	28.4
Mexico	78.3	21.6	76.0	23.5	73.8	25.6	68.8	31.0	72.0	28.0	87.4	10.1
Chile	41.7	57.4	33.4	66.8	24.5	71.3	n.a.	99.9	1.1	97.9	n.a.	99.6
East Asia												
Hong Kong	83.3	15.6	84.0	15.9	82.2	17.0	75.8	24.0	84.3	15.4	84.4	14.1
Singapore	3.4	96.5	27.4	72.1	50.3	48.6	2.2	97.6	27.4	71.3	49.6	47.7
South Korea	83.3	15.6	87.3	12.7	73.3	26.6	98.4	n.a.	85.5	14.4	78.9	20.8
Taiwan	42.0	58.0	68.7	31.3	n.a.	n.a.	42.8	56.7	68.1	31.9	n.a.	n.a.

Source: United Nations (Commodity Trade Statistics, various issues); and China,
Directorate-General of Budget, Accounting, and Statistics (Monthly Trade Statistics,
various years).

[a] Nonmarket economies are not included.

Note: DC = Developed countries.
       LDC = Developing countries.
       n.a. = Not available.

motion of exports on top of a secondary regime of import substitution. It is distinguished both by a difference in the composition of industrial output and by the fact that it was not preceded by a similar overall change in the total policy package. Instead, particular industries or firms were selected for direct encouragement via public sector tax rebates, differential interest rates, and export subsidies, or via enforced private sector cross-subsidization, that is, by assuring companies of continued high windfall profits in protected domestic markets in exchange for their meeting rising export targets.

The prolongation of import substitution in this fashion, with export promotion added eventually, is likely to be socially costly even if privately profitable (for obvious reasons). But it can be paid for by a favorable natural resource base, as exports and the proceeds from taxes can continue to pay the piper and help maintain very respectable growth rates (Table 10.4). This scenario has generally been the one followed by the Latin American newly industrialized countries. What is less clear, however, is whether the consequences of skipping the S_3 export substitution subphase and moving, instead, directly from S_2 into S_4 and a modified S_4' are acceptable from the perspective of employment and income distribution. It is interesting to contrast briefly some of the relevant indicators in the Latin American newly industrialized countries with those presented earlier for the East Asian ones.

First, while the breakdown of exports between traditional and nontraditional is not all that different in Latin America, the overall export orientation presents a startling contrast. Latin America has been much more oriented toward the domestic market (Table 10.2). Second, the relative neglect of food-producing agriculture, already noted during S_2, was exacerbated during S_4 and S_4' as protectionism deepened. As a consequence, with more and more traditional granaries empty, more of the proceeds from the exports of cash crops, supplemented by foreign capital, have had to go for food imports.

With respect to employment and income distribution, the different transition paths have yielded very different outcomes. Among the Latin American newly industrialized countries, in the rural agricultural sector the combination of a worsening distribution of land with the relative shift toward, rather than away from, traditional primary export cash crops, has tended to make for a lower labor intensity and a higher (less favorable) agricultural income Gini coefficient. As to rural nonagricultural income, which is more equally distributed than agricultural income, it constituted (for example, in Colombia) only 15 percent of farm family income initially and declined to 10 percent over time, in contrast to the 30 percent to 50 percent-plus figures in Taiwan. Moreover, the range of Latin American rural industry and services, given the maintenance of the import substitution regimes, has been much more capital-intensive and has contributed less to favorable employment and distributional outcomes (Table 10.5A and 10.5B). As Table 10.6 indicates, urban labor's share has been markedly lower and has been falling in the typical Latin American case as compared with the East Asian countries. That situation held true over virtually the entire period under discussion here.

Even in the more difficult post-1973 era, the East Asian newly industrialized countries have been able to maintain a fairly healthy growth in exports, and from an already high base, despite the combination of increases in energy prices, global stagflation, and some increase in protectionism in developed countries. That combination of factors has made continued growth difficult for nonoil developing countries generally. Overall growth rates have been maintained at high levels, as was seen; high foreign indebtedness resulting from too much reliance on foreign capital has been avoided, more so in Taiwan than in South Korea; and both have demonstrated a lot of resilience in response to increasing quotas, nontariff barriers, and other evidence of a creeping new protectionism in the developed world.

Contrary to a widely held view, the typical East Asian newly industrialized country enjoyed no special access for its industrial exports in U.S. and other Western markets during this period. In fact, there is ample evidence that any sectoral success in terms of the rapid penetration into the markets for "sick industries" in advanced countries has almost invariably led to the rather swift imposition of voluntary quota arrangements in East Asia, while less successful or laggard countries such as Indonesia remained exempt.

It is only fair to conclude that once a country has moved into a path of growth in primary export substitution, with all that trend connotes for the improvement of employment, income distribution, and growth performance, it has also achieved greater entrepreneurial and policy flexibility. That flexibility permits it to work around obstacles and to overcome the admittedly noxious defensive measures advanced countries may resort to.

Given its generally higher levels of income and lower levels of labor surplus, it might be expected that the scope and duration of any primary export substitution pattern embarked on in Latin America would be less. The analysis indicates that, to the contrary, the typical Latin American newly industrialized country tried to skip the labor-intensive primary export substitution phase and as a consequence was unable effectively to mobilize its still existent pockets of unskilled labor en route to economic maturity. Moreover, it was essentially the relative abundance of land-based raw materials, augmented by foreign capital, that has always favored the Mexicos of this world. They permitted Mexico and others not only to move directly into the production and export of more technology- and capital-intensive industrial products, but also to afford the relative luxury of neglecting domestic agriculture and, instead, to import food in order to keep wages and the prices of goods from rising too much.

In theory, in buffering the difficult problems of policy adjustment, a system should be better, not worse, off if it has access either to a natural resource bonanza or to additional foreign capital. But it is not difficult to see why those bonanzas are often used to put off, or even avoid entirely, difficult decisions--in the Latin American case, to skip the labor-intensive export substitution phase, coupled with the mobilization of an always stubborn agricultural sector. In most developing countries, including the Latin American newly industrialized prototype discussed here, many decades of growth in import substitution have led to deeply entrenched habits, with strongly vested interest groups, especially in the protected industrial sector. These groups have been able to resist reform or even less radical, marginal policy changes. A good natural resource base may not only render the system's underlying exchange rate too strong, thus effectively discouraging labor-intensive exports, it may also provide a psychological cushion or opiate that makes it possible for the system to afford continued protectionism in support of import substitution, as it moves into ever more expensive and capital-intensive areas of production and export.

The essential point is that growth along with improvement in employment and income distribution is a feasible development strategy. In Latin America, that strategy will probably require in the years ahead a somewhat heavier emphasis on the blade of balanced domestic growth relative to its complementary blade, labor-intensive export-oriented industrialized. This policy is needed in part because of the relatively larger size of the Latin American newly industrialized countries, but also because growth in the developed world is likely to be less buoyant in the years ahead than it was during 1950-1973. Consequently, a fuller mobilization of the rural sector, so often the object of decades of neglect, is required even more. A balanced domestic growth strategy, alongside the shift to

primary export substitution, would tend to diminish dependence on trade without using costly autarkic measures. Even though the East Asian newly industrialized
countries are smaller and have a much higher export or
trade orientation, their ability to integrate their
export enclave into the workings of a vigorous domestic
economy in balanced triangular fashion has been crucial
to their ability to adjust flexibly to sudden adver-
sity, whether foreign or domestic in origin.

The availability of additional natural resources
and/or easy access to foreign capital can help ease the
transition from one policy regime to another. Unfortunately, human affairs being what they are, that resource can also be, and often has been, used to avoid
what some interest groups see as unpleasant policy
changes. For example, it is not always easy to shift
industrialists away from windfall profits in protected
low volume/high margin domestic markets to earned profits in high volume/low margin export markets and/or to
balanced domestic growth.

In a very real sense, natural resource-poor Japan
and the East Asian newly industrialized countries did
not have the same easy alternatives and thus were
forced to stay more in step with their changing long-
run comparative advantage. Given the normal resistance
of industrialists and other interest groups to major
policy reforms, it is never politically easy for a
country to reverse itself. Technically, however, selective export promotion can be moved gradually in the
direction of generalized export substitution to absorb
the remaining pockets of unskilled surplus labor. The
"Kuwait Effect" that natural resource bonanzas can have
on the exchange rate can be controlled by running a
surplus to try to sterilize the inflows. Minimum wage
legislation plus union power can be made to lag until
the labor surplus has been exhausted at its base. Most
important, the rural sector can be given more attention
in terms of infrastructure, R&D, and the adjustment of
those paternalistic spectacles through which local
governments and rural actors are generally viewed.

In the real world, economies move in ambiguous,
uncertain, and nonmonotonic paths, lurching forward in
one direction, then sideways, then partially retracing
their steps. Moreover, they are too complicated as
economic systems to be neatly packaged into well-
defined typologies or transition phases as was done
here (mainly for reasons of expositional emphasis).
But this array of subtle, real-world shades of grey
should be viewed as a source of flexibility and
strength for any given system at any time. There are
no inevitable sequences or unbreakable straitjackets--a
point well-illustrated by noting that some representatives of the East Asian family, for example, South

Korea, have quite a lot in common with some representatives of the Latin American family, for example,
Brazil. South Korea shows evidence of more than a
sprinkling of export promotion along with its dominant
export substitution pattern, especially since the early
1970s, when physical export targets were set, combined
with a substantial amount of arm-twisting and government threats to individual firms.

South Korea as noted, relatively early neglected
agriculture, a policy that was reversed only recently. As such, it had to rely on foreign capital much
more heavily--almost ten times as much as Taiwan did--
both to support the rapid industrial expansion as well
as to finance food imports. In the same vein, Brazil's
performance, especially in the 1963-1973 period, contained substantial elements of primary export substitution, along with the dominant secondary import
substitution/export promotion. This mix yielded occasional bursts of labor-intensive exports of shoes and
textiles. There are strong indications that Brazil may
now be turning seriously toward balanced domestic
growth via more attention to food production relative
to exportable cash crops.

There clearly exists a very wide variety of individual situations among the newly industrialized
countries, not to mention developing countries generally. In fact, the number of typologies required even to
begin to capture the important differences halfway
intelligently is uncomfortably large. Consequently,
all that can be claimed here is that an examination of
the East Asian experience may yield some useful in-
sights of comparative value. Not every developing
country, regardless of resource endowment, income
level, and wage structure, must pass through a phase of
exporting light manufactured goods on its way to a
diversified regime of mature growth. But past performance among initially labor surplus newly industrialized countries has demonstrated rather convincingly
that more growth can be achieved via--rather than in
spite of--a more equitable, employment-intensive growth
path. The achievement of that pattern requires the
recognition that a successful development strategy has
two blades, with their relative weights dependent on
such factors as country size, population density, geog-
raphy, and transport costs.

NOTES

1. These may actually include agricultural cash
crops, E_a, as well as minerals, E_m, as seen later.

2. As already pointed out, the differences
between the two newly industrialized East Asian
countries are also instructive. For example, South
Korea's relatively less favorable initial conditions
and subsequent actions with respect to its agricultural
sector can be observed as initially lower levels and
lower rates of increase in its levels of agricultural
labor productivity, and as an initially higher and
faster growing need for food imports.
3. In the mid-1960s, for example, South Korea had
a negative rate of effective protection on nondurable
consumer goods, while Brazil's rates were 50-60
percent.

REFERENCES

Bacha, Edmar. 1979. "The Kuznets Curve and Beyond:
Growth and Changes in Inequalities." In Economic
Growth and Resources. Vol. 1. The Major Issues,
edited by E. Malinvaud. Proceedings of the 5th
World Congress of the International Economic Asso-
ciation, Tokyo, August 29-September 4, 1977.
London: Macmillan.
Bank of Korea. Various years. Economic Statistical
Yearbook. Seoul: Bank of Korea.
Chen, C. 1978. "Over Time Changes of Personal Income
Distribution in Taiwan (1964-1974)." In Income Dis-
tribution by Sectors and over Time in East and
Southeast Asian Countries, edited by Harry T.
Oshima and T. Mizoguchi. Selected papers presented
for the CAMS-Hitotsubashi Seminar, Narita, Septem-
ber 5-7, 1977. Tokyo: Hitosubashi University.
China. Directorate-General of Budget, Accounting, and
Statistics. Various years. Statistical Yearbook
of Republic of China. Taipei: Directorate-General
of Budget, Accounting, and Statistics.
──────────. Various issues. Monthly Trade Statis-
tics. Taipei: Directorate-General of Budget, Ac-
counting, and Statistics.
Choo, H. 1978. "Probable Size Distribution of Income
in Korea: Over Time and by Sectors." In Income
Distribution by Sectors and over Time in East and
Southeast Asian Countries, edited by Harry T.
Oshima and T. Mizoguchi. Selected papers presented
for the CAMS-Hitotsubashi Seminar, Narita, September 5-7, 1977. Tokyo: Hitosubashi University.
Fei, J., G. Ranis, and S. Kuo. 1978. "Growth and the
Family Distribution of Income by Factor Components." Quarterly Journal of Economics 92(Feb-
ruary):17-53.

274

_____. 1979. Growth with Equity: The Taiwan Case. New York: Oxford University Press.

International Monetary Fund. Various years. IMF Year-book. Washington, D.C.: International Monetary Fund.

Jain, Shail. 1975. "Size Distribution of Income: A Compilation of Data." Washington, D.C.: World Bank. Photocopy.

Ranis, G. 1971. "Algunos Comentarios sobre el Plan de Desarrollo Colombiano" [Comments on the Colombian Development Plan]. Controversía sobre el Plan de Desarrollo [Controversy on the Development Plan]. CORP. Bogotá.

Rao, V. V. B., and M. K. Ramakrishnan. 1978. "Struc-tural Changes and Change in Income Distribution, Singapore 1966-75." In Income Distribution by Sectors and over Time in East and Southeast Asian Countries, edited by Harry T. Oshima and T. Mizoguchi. Selected papers presented for the CAMS-Hitotsubashi Seminar, Narita, September 5-7, 1977. Tokyo: Hitotsubashi University.

United Nations. 1978 and other years. Statistical Year-book. No. E/F/XVII.1. New York: United Nations.

_____. Various issues. Commodity Trade Sta-tistics. Statistical Paper Series D. New York: United Nations.

_____. Various years. Yearbook of International Trade Statistics. New York: United Nations.

_____. Various issues. Yearbook of National Accounts Statistics. New York: United Nations.

UNCTAD. Various years. Yearbook of Trade and Development Statistics. New York: United Nations.

World Bank. Various years. World Development Report. Washington, D.C.: World Bank.

11
Financial Structure, Monetary Policy, and Economic Growth in Hong Kong, Singapore, Taiwan, and South Korea, 1960-1983

Maxwell J. Fry

INTRODUCTION

The economies of Hong Kong, Singapore, Taiwan, and the Republic of Korea (South Korea), known collectively as Asia's super exporters, or the gang of four, exhibit three common characteristics: rapid economic growth, spectacular expansion of exports, and substantial increases in the rates of saving and investment over the past two decades (Table 11.1). In all four countries, strong and stable governments set fast economic growth as a high priority (Little 1979, 466; Rabushka 1979, 56). In every case the objective was attained through the promotion of exports (Krueger, Chapter 8 of this book; Kuo 1983, 175-78; Kuo, Ranis, and Fei 1981, 73). However, implementation of this outward-looking growth strategy took a different form in each country. Hong Kong's relatively laissez-faire approach, for example, contrasts sharply with the degree of government involvement and intervention in Taiwan and South Korea, while Singapore lies somewhere in between.

This diversity shows up particularly strongly in a comparison of the financial structures and monetary policies of the four countries. Nevertheless, two common characteristics emerge: the complementarity between monetary and exchange rate policies, and the absence of pressure for monetary expansion to finance government deficits. Unlike the majority of developing countries, the gang of four has not allowed its currencies to appreciate in real terms solely as a result of accelerated monetary expansion and domestic inflation. Similarly, none of the Asian super exporters has had virtually any recourse to deficit financing. In other respects, however, the differences in their financial structures and monetary policies are more prominent than the similarities. For example, bank ownership is private in Hong Kong and Singapore, but predominantly public in Taiwan and South Korea.

TABLE 11.1
Growth, exports, saving, and investment, 1960–1983

| Country | Average Annual Percentage Change | | | | Percentage of Gross National Product | | | | | |
| | Gross National Product | | Exports | | Exports | | Saving | | Investment | |
	1960–70	1970–83	1960–70	1970–83	1960	1983	1960	1983	1960	1983
Hong Kong	10.1	8.5	12.5	8.8	82	83	10	25	21	27
Singapore	9.2	8.6	6.4	12.2	160	187	8	41	13	46
Taiwan	9.6	8.6	21.6	14.2	11	55	13	32	20	23
South Korea	8.4	7.8	28.5	18.4	3	42	5	24	13	27
Middle Income Oil-Importing Economies (GDP)	5.8	5.1[a]	6.7	4.0[a]	15	22[b]	19	19[b]	20	23[b]

Source: World Bank (1984, 220, 26, 234); China, Directorate–General of Budget, Accounting, and Statistics (1982b); and Asian Development Bank (1984b, 118–19).

[a] 1970–82.
[b] 1982.

Apart from the consistency in monetary and exchange rate policies, it is difficult to draw lessons for financial development strategies and monetary policies from the experience of Asia's super exporters as a group. Although Taiwan and South Korea are frequently noted for their financial reforms, neither country has nearly such efficient financial systems as Hong Kong or Singapore. In fact, South Korea's 1964-1965 reforms were somewhat short-lived, with substantial reversals occurring after 1972. And in neither Taiwan nor South Korea has much attention been paid to efficient resource allocation as opposed to resource mobilization.

The monetary policies pursued in Hong Kong and South Korea have been procyclical and hence destabilizing. In general, however, the monetary policies implemented by the gang of four have neither reduced economic growth nor deterred export expansion. On the other hand, financial policies such as the setting of interest rates and the selective allocation of credit have retarded economic growth. Sustained rapid growth was achieved despite rather than because of these policies.

These general conclusions are drawn from the material presented in this paper. The next section gives a bird's-eye view of the financial systems and developments in the gang of four over the period 1960-1983. Interest rate policies are analyzed in the third section, followed by a review of selective credit policies in the fourth section. The gang of four exemplifies the costs of inappropriate rather than the benefits of appropriate interest rate and selective credit policies. The fifth section describes the exchange rate policies of Asia's super exporters both before and after the collapse of the Bretton Woods system in 1973.

The final section examines the monetary policies pursued by Asia's super exporters since 1960. From time to time the supply of money got out of control in all four countries, more seriously so in Hong Kong and South Korea than in Singapore and Taiwan. However, in almost every instance, each government took remedial action relatively speedily to bring the money supply under control again. Even South Korea has kept monetary growth and inflation moderately stable, albeit at fairly high rates. Many other developing countries have taken much longer and found it considerably more difficult to tame their runaway monetary expansion.

The stabilization measures introduced by the gang of four have been relatively painless in terms of foregone output. In part, the reason was the credibility of the government in carrying out its monetary policy. Many other developing countries have found not only that monetary control is harder to achieve, but also that stabilization is more expensive than was the case with the gang of four. And the key determinant of credibility may well be the degree of fiscal disequilibrium (Tanzi 1982).

FINANCIAL STRUCTURE, DEVELOPMENT, AND REFORM

The Economist (1982b) noted, in a recent survey of finance in the Far East,

> ...governments in the fastest-growing developing countries since 1945 have placed themselves at the centre of the economic stage by controlling the financial system. Savings are allocated to those industries earmarked for growth according to coordinated investment plans. (P. 6)

Even in Hong Kong, interest rates are set by a bank cartel with which the government maintains close contact. This section presents a brief sketch of the financial structures of Asia's super exporters, with particular emphasis on the areas of government intervention.

Hong Kong

Hong Kong's financial sector produces a relatively large fraction of the gross domestic product (GDP) (over 20 percent for financial, real estate, and business services combined), the result of Hong Kong's role as an international financial center. The majority of the financial intermediation is done on behalf of nonresidents.

At the end of 1982, the financial system consisted of the Exchange Fund, 131 commercial banks, 343 registered deposit-taking companies (DTCs) (or finance companies), and 115 representative offices of foreign banks, as well as insurance companies, money brokers, and commodity, gold, and stock exchanges (Hong Kong Government 1983, 46-47). There is no central bank, and banknotes are issued by two of the commercial banks.

Commercial banks dominate Hong Kong's financial system. The Hongkong and Shanghai Banking Corporation performs several central banking functions: issuance of currency, banking for the government, and leadership of the Hong Kong Association of Banks, the organization that sets the rates for deposits. As of December 1982, there were thirty-five locally incorporated banks, only a minority of which were independent of foreign participation and control (Lee and Jao 1982, 14). Four of the locally incorporated banks are associated with the People's Republic of China (PRC), while a further nine PRC banks operating in Hong Kong are incorporated in China. The 13 PRC banks, which have over 200 branches, 12 deposit-taking companies and joint participation in 2 more deposit-taking companies, constitute the second largest banking group in Hong Kong, next to the Hong Kong Bank group, which consists of the Hongkong and Shanghai Banking Corporation, Hang Seng Bank, Mercantile Bank, and Wayfoong Finance Co. (Jao 1983, 7).

Many of the domestic banks are multipurpose or universal (Fry 1981d; Khatkhate and Riechel 1980). Since Hong Kong's banking regulations are relatively unrestrictive, there is little enforced segmentation and specialization within the financial sector. McCarthy (1982) concludes,

...because of close links of some of the banks with the great trading companies and the willingness and ability of the banks to take equity stakes, even controlling interests, in industry and commerce, their influence upon the real economy is substantial. (P. 99)

Lee and Jao (1982, 23) also suggest that Hong Kong's rapid economic growth is attributable, in part, to a banking system "untrammelled by artificial government restrictions."

There are over seventy foreign banks in Hong Kong, including the Chartered Bank (the first to start business in Hong Kong--in 1859--and possessing a number of characteristics similar to those of the domestic banks), Malaysian and Bengali state banks, and the large international banks. Foreign banks licensed after 1978 have in general ignored the retail end of the banking business and have concentrated instead on foreign trade and offshore financing. The reason is that they are only permitted to open one office each. The major international banks have competed aggressively for funds through the sale of certificates of deposit (McCarthy 1982, 103).

The absence of exchange controls, the regular inflow of deposits from the Chinese living in Southeast Asia, and Hong Kong's traditional position as an entrepôt center, as well as the more recent development of offshore business, have all contributed to the outward-looking orientation of Hong Kong's commercial banks, both domestic and foreign (Youngson 1982, 30). The lack of exchange controls has also blurred the distinction between the offshore and onshore financial markets. Until recently, for example, no differentiation was made between deposits denominated in domestic currency and those denominated in foreign currencies, even for statistical purposes.

Until 1978, taxes were levied on profits from offshore business, and there was a 15 percent withholding tax on interest earned on both domestic and foreign currency deposits. Since Singapore did not tax interest on offshore deposits, although it did levy a profits tax, it was possible to book the transactions in Singapore, record the profits in Hong Kong, and avoid taxation altogether. Since 1978, however, a net profits tax of 17 percent has been levied on the offshore activities of financial institutions based in Hong Kong that arise through or from business in which there has been no substantial involvement of a branch elsewhere. In March 1982, Hong Kong abolished the interest withholding tax on foreign currency deposits (The Economist, 1982b, 25).

In the wake of the banking crises in the first half of the 1960s, a moratorium was imposed on the issue of new bank licenses in 1965. That moratorium was lifted briefly in 1978 but was reimposed in August 1979. In May 1981, it was lifted in the case of major international banks and well-established deposit-taking companies (Hong Kong Government 1982, 49).

During the moratorium, foreign banks wanting a base in Hong Kong were obliged to establish or buy finance companies (now classified as deposit-taking companies). The number of finance companies expanded rapidly from 1965 until the moratorium was lifted in 1978. The Deposit-Taking Companies Ordinance now sets minimums on the size and maturity of the deposits these institutions may accept (McCarthy 1982, 107). Since July 1981, deposit-taking companies have been divided into two categories. Registered ones may not accept any short-term deposits except from a bank or other deposit-taking company, but may take time deposits (of three months or more and over Hong Kong dollars (HK $) $50,000). Licensed companies may accept large (over HK $500,000) short-term deposits, that is, deposits with maturities of less than three months, as well as large time deposits (Jao 1983, 3). Between October 1981 and December 1983, twenty-two deposit-taking companies obtained licenses (Hong Kong Government 1983, 47), and one converted into a commercial bank. All these companies are subject to supervision and monthly reporting, as are the banks. The deposit-taking companies are not, however, subject to the Association of Banks' agreement on deposit rates (McCarthy 1982, 107-08). Hence, even after the moratorium on new bank licenses was lifted, deposit-taking companies have maintained a high rate of growth.

Singapore

Singapore's financial sector, like Hong Kong's, produces a sizable proportion of GDP (16 percent for financial and business services combined) because of its role as an international financial center. The financial system consists of a Currency Board, the Monetary Authority of Singapore, the Central Provident Fund, the Post Office Savings Bank, the Development Bank of Singapore, 100 commercial banks, 48 representative offices of foreign banks, 37 merchant banks, 34 finance companies, 7 international money brokers, 4 discount houses, and 120 Asian Currency Units (ACUs) (Ishihara and Kim 1982, 913; Lee and Jao 1982, 243). The commercial banks consist of thirteen local and twenty-four foreign full-license banks, thirteen international banks with restricted licenses according to which they may establish one branch in which they may not accept savings deposits or any other deposit under Singapore dollars (S$) 250,000, and fifty offshore banks, which may not accept deposits from or extend loans to residents of Singapore in excess of S $30 million per bank (Ishihara and Kim 1982, 921). Unlike Hong Kong, Singapore has until very recently attempted to insulate the onshore from offshore financial markets. Commercial banks engaged in domestic business are subject to requirements as to the ratios for both reserves and liquid assets, as well as to detailed regulations concerning the types of loans they may extend. While Singapore commercial banks are not multipurpose or universal as are the commercial banks in Hong Kong, they have a similar outward orientation:

> The driving forces behind the rapid development of commercial banking in Singapore have been foreign trade, foreign investments, and economic development. (Ishihara and Kim 1982, 919)

The rapid financial development over the past fifteen years has not been accidental. The Monetary Authority of Singapore (1981) explains the development strategy mapped out in the late 1960s:

> The financial sector was to be developed as a major growth industry in its own right, rather than fulfil a subsidiary role to meet the needs of the other sectors of the economy. The policy was to expand the role of the financial sector beyond its traditional functions. The aim was to develop it into a modern sophisticated financial centre to serve the financial needs not only of Singapore and the surrounding region but also beyond. The

main potential benefits of this policy were
perceived to be the increase in the flow of trade
and investment and the economic growth and
development of Singapore and the region. (P. viii)

With these objectives in view, banks were permitted in 1968 to establish separate Asian Currency
Units to accept nonresident deposits, which were not
subject to interest withholding taxes, and to make
offshore loans. Other fiscal incentives followed, for
example, a reduction in the tax rate for corporate
profits from offshore lending from 40 percent to 10
percent in 1973 (Hodjera 1978, 223-24). In 1970, the
first license in six years was granted to a foreign
bank. The Monetary Authority of Singapore was
established in 1971. The bank cartel that fixed
interest rates was disbanded in 1975. To develop an
efficient money market, the government switched from a
tap to a tender issue of treasury bills, promoted the
establishment of four discount houses (1972-1974), and
supported the issue of negotiable certificates of
deposit denominated in Singapore dollars (1975). To
develop the capital market, securities legislation was
passed in 1973, the rules and bylaws of the stock
exchange were amended, and the Asian Bond Market was
set up (Lee and Jao 1982, 81-82).

Taiwan

Taiwan's financial system consists of the Central
Bank of China (established in 1961), 15 domestic
commercial banks with 550 branches (as of October
1982), 24 branches of foreign banks (one branch each),
8 medium-sized business banks with 182 branches, the
Postal Savings System with 1,019 post offices and 505
postal agencies, and a variety of other financial
institutions, such as 7 investment and trust companies,
9 life and 14 fire and marine insurance companies, and
359 credit cooperatives and credit departments of
farmer and fishery associations (Central Bank of China,
Financial Statistics Monthly, November 1982, 118).
There is also an extensive noninstitutional money
market.

Taiwan's financial system, which is dominated by
government-owned banks, has behaved almost like a
department of the Ministry of Finance:

Newspapers in Taiwan report regularly on the
arrest and punishment of bank officials who make
bad loans. All but three banks are owned by the
government, and bankers are forbidden to do any-

thing as immoral as to take risks. (The Economist, 1982a, 10)

Because of the constraints on bank lending, including
stringent requirements for collateral, along with past
government policies, the banking system has not been a
significant direct source of long-term investment
financing (Economist Intelligence Unit 1982b, 15).
Large businesses obtain investment funds from the
medium-sized business banks and the government-owned
Bank of Communications, which became Taiwan's national
development bank in 1979. Large businesses, including
large government-owned ones, have also borrowed
extensively abroad, while small businesses have had
very limited access to institutional credit.

There has been rapid growth in the number of foreign bank branches since 1980. In that year, nine new
foreign banks were granted licenses, with two more
licenses issued since then (Far Eastern Economic Review
1981, 72). There are now twice the number of foreign
banks (half of them American) in Taiwan as there were
in 1979. However, foreign banks cannot compete freely
with the domestic banks:

> Foreign bankers too have been kept on a short
> leash in Taiwan. The bargain between the author-
> ities and the bankers is familiar: foreign banks
> are allowed to do those pockets of business which
> the locals cannot do well, in return for lending
> plenty of money to the country's big international
> borrowers. (The Economist 1982a, 10)

Specifically, foreign banks may not accept time
deposits of over six months' maturity, nor may they
open more than one branch in Taiwan.

The government has made some effort to develop a
capital market, but the value of the securities outstanding still remains well under 20 percent of the
broadly defined money stock, M2. The difficulty in
developing a capital market can be explained in part by
the long-standing tradition of ensuring that the
public's holdings of government bonds would always be
redeemed at par (Khatkhate 1977, 93-96). The stock
market is still small and is used to a considerable
extent for speculation rather than investment. The
corporate bond market is virtually nonexistent.

South Korea

South Korea's financial system consists of its
central bank (Bank of Korea), six national city banks,

ten small local banks, forty-four branches of foreign banks, seven special banks (for example, the Korea Exchange Bank and Korea Housing Bank), three development institutions (such as the Korea Development Bank), various nonbank financial institutions such as mutual savings companies, credit unions, investment and finance companies, and the like, and the Korea Stock Exchange (Bank of Korea 1983, Chart 1). As in Taiwan, there is also a substantial noninstitutional money market.

Until the early 1980s, the government held a controlling interest in all the national banks and owned all the special banks and development institutions:

> Because they are quasi-public enterprises, the nationwide city banks are subject to comprehensive government controls ranging from the appointment of senior officers to receiving detailed instructions on bank business operations. (Bank of Korea 1978, 21)

In 1981, however, the national banks were given autonomy over the allocation of their annual budgets (Far Eastern Economic Review 1981, 82). Furthermore, the government has recently begun selling the state-owned banks to the private sector (Bank of Korea 1983, 24; The Economist, 1982b, 12). One bank was denationalized in 1981, another in 1982, and a third in 1983. Furthermore, two new private banks were authorized in 1982 and 1983 (Bank of Korea 1983, 24-25). But,

> Until now [the commercial banks] have had virtually no discretion over interest rates, lending policies, customer services or other major area of their organisation or operations. (Far Eastern Economic Review 1981, 82)

In 1972, investment and finance companies were permitted to start business. This innovation was followed in 1975 by the establishment of five merchant banks. These financial institutions have grown considerably more rapidly than the national banks because they have been able to offer and charge higher rates of interest (Economist Intelligence Unit, 1982a).

The capital market, like commercial banking, has been characterized by pervasive government control, with the terms and conditions for the securities underwriting set by an underwriters' cartel. However, recently, the government has showed renewed interest in developing a capital market. In 1980, it lifted the ceiling on bond issues, raised the maximum interest rate payable on debentures from 25 percent to 30 percent, simplified the repurchase legislation, and introduced bonds with yields linked to the twelve-month deposit rate of interest. Merchant banking corporations expanded their activities in 1980 as a result of the liberalization of the Merchant Banking Corporation Act, which permitted an increase in the issuance of trust bonds, debentures, and notes. These recent developments serve to highlight the restrictiveness of regulations on the financial system over most of the past two decades.

INTEREST RATES

There is perhaps no set of prices over which governments throughout the world have exerted more direct or indirect control than institutional interest rates. In general, real institutional interest rates in the gang of four were held below their competitive, free market equilibrium levels during the period 1960-1982. One direct consequence of the resulting disequilibrium has been excess demand for institutional credit. In contrast to the exchange rate policies (discussed in a later section), the interest rate policies of the gang of four failed to insulate real institutional interest rates from the changes in inflation rates. Typically, accelerated inflation was accompanied by a decline in the real deposit rates of interest (Table 11.2). Higher inflation therefore led to greater disequilibrium between the demand for and supply of institutional credit.

In 1964, Hong Kong's Exchange Banks' Association formed an interest-rate fixing committee with government approval to prevent a recurrence of the cutthroat competition of the early 1960s that was held partially responsible for the banking crises of that period (Lee and Jao 1982, 30; McCarthy 1982, 101; Youngson 1982, 32). In January 1981, the Hong Kong Association of Banks replaced the Exchange Banks' Association. Membership in the new association is compulsory, and its rules, including maximum deposit rates, are binding on all commercial banks (McCarthy 1982, 101). Previously, the smaller nonmember banks were able to offer higher rates than members of the Exchange Banks' Association could. At present, the smaller banks are allowed to offer deposit rates half of 1 percent higher than the larger banks. Deposit-taking companies are still free to set their own rates for deposits and loans.

The spread between the twelve-month deposit rate of the commercial banks and the best lending rate increased over the past decade from 1 to 3 percentage points. Part of the explanation lay in the fact that the tilt in the deposit rate maturity structure became

TABLE 11.2
Inflation and real deposit rates of interest, 1960–1983

Date	Hong Kong				Singapore				Taiwan				South Korea			
	D	π	π^e	$d-\pi^e$	D	π	π^e	$d-\pi^e$	D	π	π^e	$d-\pi^e$	D	π	π^e	$d-\pi^e$
1960	4.00	-4.06	-0.23	4.2	3.88	-2.23	-2.26	6.1	18.44	12.77	12.77	4.2	10.00	10.95	10.83	-1.3
1961	4.00	-4.18	-4.14	8.1	4.42	-0.09	-0.80	5.1	16.90	4.72	4.72	10.9	12.29	12.90	8.74	2.9
1962	4.00	3.16	0.71	3.2	4.38	0.86	0.54	3.7	14.88	2.10	2.10	11.8	15.00	16.74	9.32	4.7
1963	4.00	3.94	3.68	0.2	4.00	0.95	0.92	3.0	13.42	3.37	3.37	9.2	15.00	25.97	14.96	-1.0
1964	4.00	2.69	3.10	0.8	4.08	0.73	0.81	3.2	11.57	4.13	4.13	6.8	15.00	26.23	19.54	-5.6
1965	4.67	-0.04	0.87	3.7	5.00	1.35	1.15	3.7	11.35	-0.69	-0.69	11.4	17.85	6.11	17.50	-1.1
1966	5.00	-0.72	-0.50	5.4	5.00	1.33	1.34	3.5	10.66	2.72	2.72	7.4	26.40	13.28	17.06	6.4
1967	5.50	4.08	2.48	2.9	5.08	0.61	0.85	4.1	10.30	4.42	4.42	5.4	26.40	14.71	16.46	7.0
1968	6.00	3.59	3.76	2.1	6.00	1.11	0.94	4.9	10.16	6.57	6.57	3.1	26.10	14.80	14.70	8.5
1969	6.00	3.62	3.61	2.2	6.00	2.27	1.89	3.9	10.16	6.22	6.22	3.5	23.80	13.63	12.88	8.5
1970	6.00	10.56	8.24	-2.4	6.00	1.65	1.86	4.0	9.45	3.40	3.40	6.3	22.80	14.58	14.23	6.3
1971	5.17	8.08	8.90	-3.9	5.87	4.42	3.50	2.3	9.00	3.01	3.01	6.0	21.60	11.50	13.69	5.9
1972	4.88	7.47	7.68	-2.9		5.96	5.45	0.3	9.31	5.68	5.68	2.9	14.95	14.49	13.74	0.2
1973	6.46	12.14	10.58	-4.3	6.50	12.23	10.14	-3.8		13.87	13.87	-5.0	12.00	12.36	13.25	-1.9
1974	8.84	11.50	11.71	-3.2	8.67	14.20	13.55	-5.2	14.35	27.95	27.95	-14.5	14.75	25.93	16.30	-2.5
1975	5.79	2.29	5.36	0.3	6.53	2.17	6.18	0.1	12.34	2.30	2.30	9.3	15.00	22.05	18.00	-4.0
1976	5.29	7.51	5.77	-0.6	5.55	1.36	1.63	3.8	11.85	5.40	5.40	5.8	15.50	16.31	18.53	-4.1
1977	4.00	4.02	5.19	-1.3	5.42	0.65	0.89	4.4	9.92	5.98	5.98	3.5	15.75	15.11	18.26	-3.6
1978	4.68	5.61	5.08	-0.5	5.77	1.72	1.36	4.2	9.50	4.62	4.62	4.5	16.68	18.75	19.15	-3.7
1979	9.88	13.17	10.65	-1.2	6.69	2.72	2.38	4.1	10.94	10.71	10.71	-0.3	18.60	17.63	17.82	-0.8
1980	11.10	12.28	12.57	-2.0	8.91	5.38	4.49	4.0	12.50	14.90	14.90	-3.1	22.90	23.01	18.52	2.1
1981	13.93	9.18	10.21	2.8	10.92	4.94	5.08	5.3	13.58	11.30	11.30	1.4	19.25	14.96	17.98	-0.4
1982	15.00	11.19	10.52	3.5	8.03	-1.00	0.98	6.7	11.20	3.69	3.69	6.9	10.95	7.42	15.78	-5.4
1983	9.40	5.82	7.15	1.8	6.77	2.48	4.28	2.3	7.50	1.67	1.67	5.6	8.00	2.96	13.04	-5.3

Source: Hong Kong – Asian Development Bank (1983); Hong Kong, Census and Statistics Department (1969 and various issues); and World Bank (1981). Singapore – Asian Development Bank (1983); Monetary Authority of Singapore (various issues); Bank Negara Malaysia (various issues); and World Bank (1981). Taiwan – Asian Development Bank (1983); Central Bank of China (Financial Statistics Monthly, various issues); and China, Directorate-General of Budget, Accounting, and Statistics, (1982a, 1982b). South Korea – Asian Development Bank (1983); Bank of Korea (Monthly Economic Statistics, various issues, and Annual Report, various years); and World Bank (1981).

Note: D – Simple nominal rate of interest on twelve-month deposits. The lack of data necessitated some estimation. For Hong Kong, 1960–1970, D is estimated at 2 percentage points below the banks' agreed best lending rate. For Singapore, 1960–70, D, is taken from Bank Negara Malaysia publications.
π – The continuously compounded rate of change in the GNP deflator.
π^e – Expected inflation is estimated as a polynomial distributed lag of current and past changes in the rate of inflation in a function explaining the rate of change in per capita real money holdings. The weights are:

Country	t	t-1	t-2	t-3	t-4
Hong Kong	0.6667	0.3333			
Singapore	0.6667	0.3333			
Taiwan	1.0000				
South Korea	0.2452	0.2226	0.2000	0.1774	0.1548

d – Continuously compounded nominal rate of interest on twelve-month deposits.
d-π – Continuously compounded real deposit rate of interest.

less pronounced. In 1976, for example, the twelve-month deposit rate was almost twice the three-month deposit rate. By 1980, a twelve-month deposit yielded only 24 percent more than a three-month deposit.

From 1970 to 1980, the real rates of return on twelve-month deposits in Hong Kong commercial banks were almost continuously negative (Table 11.2). The government held the cartel's sluggish response to the speculative demand for credit starting in 1977 responsible for both the rapid expansion of money and credit and the depreciation of the Hong Kong dollar. Since the late 1970s, the government has, with some success, exerted pressure on the Association of Banks to raise interest rates in order to check excessive monetary expansion (Far Eastern Economic Review 1981, 71; Lee and Jao 1982, 39).

The ceilings on interest rates have led to non-price credit rationing. From November 1978 to October 1979, for example, U.S. short-term interest rates exceeded Hong Kong short-term rates by an average of 4.5 percentage points. At the same time, however, the U.S. dollar commanded a premium of half a percentage point in the forward market (Lee and Jao 1982, 44). With transaction costs of under half of 1 percent, arbitrageurs would have exploited the spread until it was eroded had there been no credit rationing in Hong Kong. More recently, however, interest rates on large deposits have been freed, and large borrowers have been able to obtain funds at rates one-quarter to one-half of 1 percent above the competitively determined inter-bank rate. Hence, at present the main effect of the cartel's fixing of interest rates is to discriminate against small depositors.

In 1975, Singapore's interest-rate fixing bank cartel was abolished, and since then interest rates have been determined competitively. Apart from 1973-1975, however, when real deposit rates were negative, the deposit rate ceilings have never been very far below their equilibrium levels (Table 11.2); since 1975, the real twelve-month deposit rate has been in the same range as it was in the 1960s. As in Hong Kong, the spread between the twelve-month deposit rate and the prime lending rate has increased from 1.5 percentage points in the 1970s to over 2.5 percentage points in the 1980s as nominal rates rose.

When U.S. interest rates increased sharply in February and March 1980 and then fell in April and May, the Monetary Authority of Singapore maintained relatively stable rates through its activities in the treasury bill market, that is, through open market operations and through choosing the volume of bills to tender (Ishihara and Kim 1982, 925). It requested that the banks not lend Singapore dollars to nonresidents and not provide forward cover to arbitrageurs. Despite this policy, the Singapore dollar depreciated substantially as U.S. interest rates rose, and appreciated again when U.S. rates subsequently fell (Hewson 1981, 190). Hence, the attempt to insulate Singapore from the effect of volatile U.S. interest rates was completely ineffective. Interest rates were stabilized only at the expense of fluctuations in the exchange rate. The requests to the banks appear to have been ineffectual. Blejer and Khan (1980, 284-85) find that throughout the period March 1976 to July 1980, covered interest parity held. Furthermore, the efficiency of Singapore's foreign exchange market was unimpaired by the Monetary Authority's requests (Blejer and Khan 1983).

In Taiwan, the government set all institutional interest rates in the period 1960-1981. Only within the last couple of years have commercial banks been allowed to vary their interest rates, and then only within a range set by the government. The banks now fix interest rates through a bankers' cartel (The Economist 1982b, 12). Real deposit rates of interest have been kept positive, except briefly in 1973-1974 and 1979-1980, and indeed were relatively high in the 1960s (Table 11.2).

The spread between the twelve-month deposit rate and the banks' discount rate has been small. This measure of spread is, however, misleading as an indicator of efficiency. Short-term loans carry higher rates than long-term loans, and loans to priority sectors, for example, exports, are subsidized (Little 1979, 481; Tsiang 1980, 342). Furthermore, the term structure of rates of interest on deposits rises relatively steeply, with increments at one, three, six, nine, and twelve months.

The structure of institutional interest rates in Taiwan is fairly typical of that imposed by the governments in several other Asian developing countries. Deposit rates are finely graduated by the maturity of the deposits; long-term loan rates are lower than short-term loan rates and have sometimes been held below comparable deposit rates; and heavily subsidized loans have been offered to exporters. Until recently, banks were not allowed to make loans exceeding a maturity of five years (Little 1979, 481). The maximum loan maturity in 1985 has been seven years.

Even the rates for regular bank loans have been kept below their free market equilibrium levels by wide margins. Firms with well-established reputations have invariably been prepared to offer 10 percentage points more than the bank loan rates for deposits (Tsiang 1980, 342). Moreover, a thriving noninstitutional market, in which interest rates have also been substan-

tially higher than bank rates, existed throughout the
period 1960-1981 (Lundberg 1979, 292). In particular,
the implicit yield on postdated checks has exceeded the
rates on bank loans by about 15 percentage points
(Tsiang 1980, 342).

In South Korea, the government set all institutional interest rates until 1979. Since then, the
Korean Bankers' Association has fixed the rates on
deposits and loans within ranges set by the Monetary
Board. After the doubling of nominal deposit rates as
part of the 1965 financial reform, the real twelve-
month rate of interest on deposits remained relatively
high for the following six years. However, real deposit rates have been negative for virtually all of the
post-1973 period, particularly 1974-1978 (Table 11.2).

The twelve-month deposit rate was increased from
15 percent to 30 percent in 1965, whereas the general
loan rate was set at 26 percent. The negative spread
was covered by subsidies to the commercial banks from
the Bank of Korea (Park 1976, 129). By 1972, the
deposit rate had been reduced to 12.6 percent, and the
normal loan rate to 15.5 percent. Loans for exports
have consistently carried rates below the deposit
rate. This subsidy has been financed almost entirely
through low interest rediscounts from the Bank of Korea
(Bank of Korea 1978, 14-15).

The spread between the rates for deposits and
loans is as difficult to measure in South Korea as it
is in Taiwan. For one, South Korean banks typically
collect the interest in advance and require compensat-
ing balances. The Bank of Korea has used the technique
of paying interest on banks' required reserves at
whatever rate banks need to cover costs and report
reasonable profits. Que (1979) notes:

> According to the Bank of Korea the rate structures
> and operating costs of the banks require a 6.02
> percent spread to guarantee coverage of all ex-
> penses and dividend payments of 15 percent on par
> to shareholders other than government. (P. 399)

Intermediation costs seem to be considerably higher in
both Taiwan and South Korea than they are in Hong Kong
and Singapore.

The term structure of deposit rates is even steep-
er in South Korea than in any of the other three countries. In November 1980, for example, deposit rates
exhibited the following term structure:

Notice deposits	10.5
Savings deposits	12.3
Three-month time deposits	14.8
Six-month time deposits	16.9

Twelve-month time deposits	19.5
Two-year workmen's wealth accumulation deposits	28.4
Three-year workmen's wealth accumulation deposits	30.9
Four-year workmen's wealth accumulation deposits	33.6

This maturity structure can be viewed in terms of differential inflation taxes on components of the stock of money (Fry 1981a, 1981c). A greater inflation tax is levied on demand and short-term time deposits for which there are no close substitutes, while a smaller tax is extracted from deposits for which closer substitutes do exist. Monopolistic product differentiation is designed to tap the consumer surplus, in this case from money-holders. The tax is used in South Korea and Taiwan, as well as most other Asian developing countries, as one source of financing for credit subsidies for priority sectors. It is also absorbed by the high administrative costs of these uncompetitive financial systems.

Monopolistic product differentiation of deposits in South Korea is also exhibited by the wide variety of deposit categories:

Demand Deposits	Time Deposits
Ordinary checking	Ordinary
Personal checking	Special household
Passbook	Multiple maturity
Temporary	Negotiable certificates
Money in trust	Savings
Installment savings	
Notice	
Mutual installment	
Housing installment	
Workmen's wealth accumulation	
Children's savings stamps	

In addition to this differentiation, a variety of types of deposits is subject to a variety of fiscal incentives--exemptions, deductions, credits, and lower tax rates on interest income. A special fiscal subsidy is provided for saving by lower income workers. This incentive produces an effective net return of 38 percent on long-term workmen's wealth accumulation deposits. Similarly, household, farmer, fisherman, and student deposits receive up to 4 percentage points more interest than the standard rate. Holders of housing installment deposits get priority for buying government-built apartments and houses.

Institutional interest rates in South Korea, as in Taiwan, were invariably below their free market equilibrium levels throughout the period 1960-1983. The noninstitutional money market that had flourished prior to the financial reforms of 1965 was expected to contract in response to the newly liberalized institutional markets. In fact, however, by the late 1960s most business firms were heavily indebted in the noninstitutional money market, where rates on loans did not fall below 4 percent a month until 1971, the reason being the nonavailability of institutional credit for working capital. By 1974, the maximum rate on bank loans was 15.5 percent, while the annualized noninstitutional money market rate averaged 49 percent (Min 1976, 32). In August 1972, institutional interest rates were cut dramatically, and a ceiling of 16.2 percent was placed on noninstitutional money market loan rates in an attempt to stabilize the precarious financial position of many businesses in South Korea. The 1972 measures effectively ended South Korea's program of financial liberalization (Min 1976, 35).

Because of the extreme nature of South Korea's experiment with interest rates, the effects of changes in interest rates are easier to detect there than elsewhere. Between 1966 and 1971, the real deposit rate of interest averaged about 7.5 percent. Most loan rates were substantially positive over the same period. Of particular note is that not only did money demand, saving, and investment all grow dramatically, but so did the average rate of capacity utilization in manufacturing, which went up considerably between 1962 and 1971 (Westphal and Kim 1982, 264). This effect has also been substantiated in an econometric study of investment and growth in South Korea: Sundararajan and Thakur (1980, 852) conclude that the cost of capital exerted "a strong positive efficiency effect on capital."

Shaw (1973) maintains that greater financial intermediation between savers and investors, which results from financial liberalization, that is, an increase in real institutional interest rates toward their competitive, free market equilibrium levels, increases the incentive to save and invest, and also raises the average efficiency of investment. Financial intermediaries can raise real net returns to savers and at the same time lower real gross costs to investors by accommodating liquidity preferences, reducing risk through diversification, reaping economies of scale, and lowering information costs to both savers and investors. The amount of financial intermediation is suboptimal when institutional interest rates are fixed below their competitive, free market equilibrium levels. When interest rates are employed to a greater extent as rationing devices, that is, are allowed to rise toward their competitive, free market equilibrium levels, financial intermediaries can increase the efficiency of resource allocation (Fry 1982).

Raising real loan rates deters potential investors with relatively low-yielding investment projects from borrowing. Hence, it can raise the average efficiency of investment. Since real institutional deposit and loan rates generally move in close parallel when nominal rates are fixed by administrative decision or cartel agreement, the former can be used as a proxy for the latter. The incremental output/capital ratio, v (adjusted for year-to-year fluctuations in agricultural production) is taken as a proxy for investment efficiency (Fry 1980b, 539). The ordinary least squares (OLS) pooled time series estimate of v on the real deposit rate of interest, $d-\pi^e$, for the gang of four over the period 1961 to 1981 (eighty-four observations) is:

$$v = 1.058(d-\pi^e) \qquad \qquad (11.1)$$
$$\quad (2.560)$$

$$\bar{R}^2 = 0.09.$$

(The figure in parentheses is the "t" statistic.)

The real deposit rate of interest was also found to have a small but significant effect on national saving ratios in pooled time series estimates for a sample of fourteen Asian developing countries that includes the gang of four (Asian Development Bank 1984a; Fry 1978, 468, 1981b, 76, 1984b, 1985; Fry and Mason 1982, 434-35). However, the real deposit rate coefficient is not significantly different from zero in the saving rate functions for the gang of four by itself.

The real rate of economic growth, g, can be expressed as the product of the ratio of investment to GNP, I/Y, and v. If national saving, Sn, is a determinant of I under disequilibrium interest rate systems, then $d-\pi^e$ may affect g indirectly through both Sn and v. For a thirteen country sample of developing countries examined in Fry (1978, 1979, 1980a, 1981b), the cost of disequilibrium interest rate systems appears to have averaged about a half of 1 percentage point in foregone economic growth for every 1 percentage point by which $d-\pi^e$ is held below its competitive, free market equilibrium level. For the gang of four, the direct relationship between g and $d-\pi^e$ is:

$$g = 0.126(d-\pi^e) + 0.952g^+ \qquad (11.2)$$
$$\quad (1.428) \qquad \qquad (19.710)$$

$$\bar{R}^2 = 0.12$$

where g^+ = The trend in growth adjusted for fluctuations in agricultural output.

SELECTIVE CREDIT POLICIES

Only in Hong Kong is there no government involvement and/or intervention in the allocation of credit. Despite free market determination of interest rates in Singapore, the government there wields considerable influence over the allocation of investible funds. It offers only one direct subsidy for interest rates--a priority rediscount rate for exports (Lee and Jao 1982, 88-89). Until 1975 Singapore did, however, pursue a selective credit policy with credit floors and ceilings and priority loan rates, and it still exerts moral suasion to affect bank lending (Aghevli, et al. 1979, 805).

The Singapore government's main means of influencing the allocation of credit is through its ownership and control of the Central Provident Fund, to which virtually all employees must contribute 23 percent of their income, with almost matching contributions from employers; through the Post Office Savings Bank; through the Development Bank of Singapore; and through the Small Industries Finance Scheme, the Capital Assistance Scheme, and the Product Development Assistance Scheme (Lee and Jao 1982, 89; Tan and Hock 1982, 307). The Central Provident Fund and the Post Office Savings Bank channel private saving to the government and its agencies listed above at below market rates of interest. Another mechanism for allocating credit is through the use of fiscal incentives (The Economist 1982b, 15). Until 1975, however, Singapore implemented its selective credit policy by imposing credit floors, that is, by setting minimum percentages of total loans to go to the priority sectors, and by allowing banks to earn a reduced reserve ratio by lending more to priority sectors (Lee and Jao 1982, 87).

To implement its selective credit policy, Taiwan uses subsidized rates for loans to priority sectors in conjunction with preferential rediscount rates for those loans. Selective credit controls and differential loan rates have been used in the main to encourage exports, although some import-substituting industries as well as agriculture have also been favored (Little 1979, 481; Lundberg 1979, 293). Recently, Tsiang (1980) wrote with respect to Taiwan,

Although the function of interest rate on deposits as a necessary inducement to attract savings into the banking system appears to be well understood and to have frequently been put to good use, the function of the interest rate as a necessary criterion for efficient allocation of scarce investable funds seems not yet to have been recognized. (P. 341)

Taiwan's financial sector appears to have been relatively successful in allocating credit. Here, the financial institutions have undoubtedly been assisted by the fact that "even the most favored businesses have had to pay positive real rates." (Little 1979, 481) This policy has deterred potential investors with inefficient projects from borrowing, as pointed out previously. Nevertheless, there now seems to be some recognition that the allocation of credit could be improved: "As in South Korea the Taiwanese authorities are cautiously trying to allocate savings more efficiently." (The Economist 1982b, 12) So far, however, civil service-type bankers have resisted measures designed to reduce intermediation costs and increase competition. In addition, long-term financing has been scarce in Taiwan, in large part because of government regulations on bank lending.

In sharp contrast to Taiwan, long-term relative to short-term credit has been abundant in South Korea. The latter country has made more extensive use of selective credit policies than have the other three. About 60 percent of bank lending is for government-designated purposes, such as support for exports. Subsidized loans for priority sectors are usually automatically eligible for special rediscount rates at the Bank of Korea. The generous use of the rediscount facility to support the selective credit policy has frequently conflicted with its use for monetary control.

Rediscounts have been differentiated in South Korea with respect to both the percentage of the loan eligible for refinancing and the rediscount rate. Loans for exports have always been favored the most, but special rates are also provided for loans used to import essential raw materials, for agriculture and fishing, and for priority industries (Bank of Korea 1978, 10). Government guarantees have also been provided for foreign borrowing by almost any firm showing a capacity to export (Jones and Sakong 1980, xxx). Since July 1982, however, the rates for bank loans have been unified at 10 percent, irrespective of their purpose, except for general loans on bills and overdrafts, which are charged 11 percent (Bank of Korea 1983, 34; Economist Intelligence Unit, QER: Korea, 3rd Quarter, 1982).

In addition to the rediscount facility, the South Korean government has pursued its selective credit policy by setting credit floors, for example, 35 percent of the increase in each commercial bank's total loans and 55 percent of the increase in each local bank's loans must go to small- and medium-sized firms. There are also credit ceilings. And the government uses specialized financial institutions (Bank of Korea 1983, 16). Their lending is financed by a requirement that the commercial banks buy National Investment Fund bonds and hold relatively large required reserves. To an increasing extent, general lending guidelines issued by the Monetary Board have been replaced by specific directives about credit allocation to priority sectors, subsectors, and even individual projects:

> ...the government has had to provide more and more distorted incentives through the low interest rates and credit rationing to the preferred sectors and has intensified its direct interference in the allocation of financial resources; financial liberalization has been terminated and replaced by repression. (Park 1976, 84)

Since March 1982, however, the government has relaxed the guidelines for bank lending to some extent (Bank of Korea 1983, 16).

South Korea's selective credit policy has produced a considerable amount of financial layering that has increased the costs of financial intermediation. Instead of raising funds from a common pool of loanable funds, each group of financial institutions has its own special source of funds earmarked for special uses (McKinnon 1980, 106-10). A four-tier structure of financial layering exists in the case of agricultural credit. Primary cooperatives obtain funds from the country cooperatives. The county cooperatives borrow from the National Agricultural Cooperative Federation, which in turn borrows from the government and the Bank of Korea. The cooperatives cannot raise funds from deposits because their loan rates are set too low for them to offer competitive deposit rates. Hence, the government and the Bank of Korea provide subsidies. In turn, the Bank of Korea raises funds from the commercial banks through the low-interest reserve requirements. Similar financial layering occurs in the case of fisheries cooperatives (Bank of Korea 1978, 34-36). A three-tier structure of financial layering applies to all the other specialized financial institutions, which are obliged, because of their low loan rates, to obtain most of their resources directly from the Bank of Korea and indirectly from the deposit money banks. Clearly, financial layering of this kind makes each institution's costs additive to the total cost of intermediation between the saver and the ultimate borrower.

The South Korean government has also influenced the allocation of credit through public sector investment, which has averaged about 25 percent of the total fixed investment since 1960. Sundararajan and Thakur (1980) suggest that public sector investment in South Korea has been relatively efficient:

> ...the motivation was primarily pragmatic, in that the public sector entered areas where private investment was not forthcoming or entered strategic areas where excessive concentration of private power was feared. (P. 818)

They also concluded from their econometric work that public sector investment had been complementary to private investment.

Selective credit policies use interest-rate ceilings and subsidies to direct investible funds through a nonprice rationing system to priority investment projects that the planning authorities believe might not be undertaken at higher interest rates. If deposit-taking financial institutions are to remain solvent, however, a concomitant of high reserve requirements, binding ceilings on ordinary loans, and/or floors for low-interest priority sector loans is a lower average rate of interest on deposits. Lower deposit rates reduce the real demand for money. The decline in the real value of the banking system's deposit liabilities must be matched by a similar fall in the real value of the banking system's assets (or by a corresponding increase in bank capital). The primary asset of most banking systems is domestic credit. Hence, a fall in the real demand for money causes a decline in the real supply of credit. To some extent, a reduction in real money demand also appears to reduce net foreign assets, as anticipated by the monetary approach to the balance of payments.

The traditional link between credit and output is through demand--the increase in credit created by mone- tary expansion is accompanied by an increase in demand that stimulates real output. Within the past decade, Kapur (1976), Keller (1980), Mathieson (1980), McKinnon (1973), and Shaw (1973) have analyzed the link between credit and real output through the supply side. This Wicksellian view holds that the availability of working capital determines, ceteris paribus, the volume of production that can be financed. In particular, as Keller (1980, 455) argues, "production expansion may depend, entirely or in part, on credit availability and/or the cost of credit." Evidently, this supply link between credit availability and real economic growth springs from the ratio of credit to output, or from the real rather than the nominal volume of credit.

Faster expansion of money and nominal credit raises the inflation rate. If the nominal deposit rate is fixed, the ensuing increase in expected inflation reduces the real rate of interest on deposits--and this drop in turn reduces the real demand for money or decreases the ratio of money to nominal GNP. The ratio of domestic credit, DC, to nominal GNP, PY, also falls. In this way, an acceleration in nominal domestic credit and in the supply of money reduces the availability of credit in real terms, that is, DC/PY declines.

As inflation accelerates and as real deposit rates, real money demand, and the real credit supply decline, the government may find that the gap between conventional tax receipts and public expenditures widens. This gap has to be financed by heavier reliance on seigniorage and the inflation tax. The government extracts greater seigniorage by increasing the proportion of domestic credit allocated to the public sector and thus reduces the ratio of private sector credit, DCp, to total domestic credit, DC. The government levies an inflation tax by creating more money than the public wishes to hold at the current level of prices. This situation creates a double squeeze on the credit available for private sector working capital, that is, DCp/PY falls because of the decline in both DC/PY and DCp/DC.

This credit availability mechanism is apparent in the following OLS pooled time series estimates for the gang of four over the period 1961-1981:

$$DC/PY = 0.277(d-\pi^e) + 1.034(DC/PY)_{t-1} \qquad (11.3)$$
$$\quad\quad (3.35) \qquad\qquad (92.918)$$

$$\bar{R}^2 = 0.95$$

$$\Delta\ln(DC/PY) = 0.944(d-\pi^e) \qquad\qquad (11.4)$$
$$\quad\quad\quad (2.947)$$

$$\bar{R}^2 = 0.11$$

$$\Delta\ln(DCp/PY) = 1.211(d-\pi^e) \qquad\qquad (11.5)$$
$$\quad\quad\quad (4.314)$$

$$\bar{R}^2 = 0.17$$

$$\frac{\Delta(DCp/P)}{Y} = 0.171(d-\pi^e). \qquad\qquad (11.6)$$
$$\quad\quad\quad (2.028)$$

$$\bar{R}^2 = 0.14$$

EXCHANGE RATE POLICIES

Government control over the price of foreign exchange, that is, the exchange rate, is as ubiquitous as
government control over interest rates in Third World
countries. The material presented in this section
shows that the gang of four avoided overvaluation of
their domestic currencies. Their real exchange rates
did not appreciate solely because of domestic inflation. In fact, real exchange rates in Singapore and
South Korea depreciated substantially over the period
1960-1979 as a result of the liberalization in trade
and payments.

Under Bretton Woods

From 1960 to 1973-1974, the governments of Asia's
super exporters, like most other governments, fixed the
exchange rate of their currencies. The Hong Kong
dollar was tied to sterling until 1972, although it was
devalued by less than sterling in 1967. Then in July
1972, it was pegged to the U.S. dollar at HK $5.65 to
U.S. $1 and stayed tied to the U.S. dollar (albeit with
a revaluation to HK $5.085 in February 1973) until
November 1974 (McCarthy 1982, 98). Until June 1973,
the Singapore dollar maintained its gold parity at S $1
to 0.290299 grams of gold, despite the devaluation in
sterling in 1967 and the devaluation of the U.S. dollar
in 1971 (Lee and Jao 1982, 90). Singapore's real
effective exchange rate depreciated by 24 percent from
1960-1973 (Table 11.3). Over the period 1960-1973, the
New Taiwan (NT $) dollar was pegged at NT $40 to U.S.
$1. Taiwan's real effective exchange rate depreciated
by 15 percent over the same period (Table 11.3). In
contrast, the South Korean won (W) was devalued in a
series of discrete steps from W 65 to U.S. $1 in 1960
to W 484 to U.S. $1 in December 1974. The real
effective exchange rate peaked prior to the devaluations in 1960, 1963, 1970, and 1974. Nevertheless,
there was a significant downward trend in the real rate
throughout this period (Table 11.3).

Hong Kong and Singapore followed gold standard
rules during the fixed exchange rate period, with
changes in high-powered money being determined almost
exclusively by the overall balance of payments. This
approach was, of course, an automatic outcome of the
currency board systems in these two countries. In
both, domestic currency has had a foreign asset cover
of at least 100 percent. In all but a couple of years
since 1960, the government budgets of these two
countries have been in surplus. Hence, neither
government has been a net borrower from the banking

system. There has, therefore, been no pressure for monetary expansion to finance budget deficits. Over the decade 1960-1970, inflation averaged 2.4 percent annually in Hong Kong and 1.1 percent in Singapore.

Taiwan chose to pursue gold standard rules in conjunction with discretionary monetary policy measures such as changes in reserve requirements. Between 1960 and 1970, Taiwan's real exchange rate remained virtually constant, except for a small depreciation in 1962-1966 (Table 11.3) (Lee and Liang 1982, 314). It was in these years that the government budget ran substantial surpluses. After appropriating about 45 percent of domestic credit until 1962, the government sector's net borrowing from the banking system declined continuously until 1970, when net domestic credit to the public sector represented 9 percent of total domestic credit. Taiwan's inflation rate averaged 3.4 percent annually over the period 1960-1970. Its real exchange rate also declined in 1972-1973, when tariffs were reduced (Table 11.3).

Inflation in South Korea averaged 17.4 percent annually over the period 1960-1970. Hence, there was a sharp divergence between the movements in South Korea's nominal and real exchange rates (Table 11.3). Relatively high inflation did produce an overvaluation of the won from time to time. However, this rise in value was offset consistently by variations in export incentives (Little 1979, 483). The net real exchange rate for exports was kept reasonably steady between 1961 and 1972. After a 15 percent appreciation in 1973, the net real exchange rate for exports was brought back to its 1972 level in 1974 (Westphal and Kim 1982, 218). Net domestic credit to the public sector as a percentage of total domestic credit also fell, from 36 percent in 1960 to 3 percent in 1971. It was not the direct needs of the government that produced South Korea's relatively high rate of monetary expansion, but rather the government's selective credit policy. Loans for export activities have been heavily subsidized through an automatic rediscount mechanism. A rapid increase in exports and, hence, export credit has caused a rapid expansion in high-powered money in the form of increased export rediscounts.

After Bretton Woods

Hong Kong's exchange controls were abolished in 1973, Singapore's in 1978. Between 1974 and October 1983, the Hong Kong dollar floated relatively freely, with the Exchange Fund intervening to stabilize the exchange rate to only a very limited extent. From HK $5.085 in 1974, the Hong Kong dollar appreciated to HK

TABLE 11.3
Nominal and real effective exchange rate indices, 1960-1982

Date	Hong Kong Nominal	Singapore Nominal	Singapore Real	Taiwan Nominal	Taiwan Real	South Korea Nominal	South Korea Real
1960		1.000	1.000	1.000	1.000	1.000	1.000
1961		0.996	0.998	1.007	1.057	0.502	0.527
1962		0.997	0.983	1.016	1.057	0.493	0.531
1963		0.995	0.993	1.016	1.038	0.493	0.608
1964		9.994	1.081	1.018	1.009	0.333	0.517
1965		0.994	1.136	1.022	0.974	0.242	0.410
1966		0.782	0.965	1.023	0.958	0.238	0.433
1967		0.630	0.864	1.024	0.958	0.239	0.466
1968		0.633	0.843	1.028	0.995	0.233	0.483
1969		0.632	0.831	1.025	0.995	0.224	0.497
1970		0.631	0.843	1.026	0.972	0.208	0.503
1971		0.623	0.828	1.011	0.934	0.183	0.477
1972	0.985	0.581	0.797	0.953	0.869	0.150	0.420
1973	1.002	0.522	0.760	0.936	0.846	0.138	0.365
1974	1.041	0.506	0.809	0.965	1.107	0.143	0.398
1975	1.060	0.495	0.753	0.972	1.061	0.119	0.374
1976	1.100	0.478	0.668	0.987	1.027	0.121	0.405
1977	1.123	0.477	0.667	0.953	0.988	0.115	0.396
1978	1.000	0.463	0.612	0.884	0.914	0.102	0.378
1979	0.920	0.460	0.645	0.910	0.958	0.103	0.423
1980	0.916	0.475	0.650	0.920	1.027	0.083	0.409
1981	0.870	0.500	0.684		1.026	0.075	0.422
1982	0.860	0.522	0.707			0.075	0.426

Source: Data supplied by the International Monetary Fund.

Note: The nominal effective exchange rate index is measured against a trade-weighted currency basket. An increase signifies appreciation in the domestic currency vis-a-vis the basket. The real effective exchange rate index adjusts the nominal index for relative changes in wholesale prices. An increase in the index implies an appreciation or overvaluation of the domestic currency vis-a-vis a purchasing power parity rate.

$4.66 to U.S. $1 in 1977. Thereafter, as domestic inflation accelerated, it depreciated to HK $9.60 on September 24, 1983. Inflation averaged 12.9 percent annually over the period 1970-1981. During the 1974-1983 floating episode, Hong Kong's money supply mechanism was unstable. On October 15, 1983, therefore, the Hong Kong government announced that it was pegging the exchange rate at HK $7.80 to U.S. $1 to stop further speculation. Forward rates for periods up to six months vis-à-vis sterling and the U.S. dollar are now quoted daily (Lee and Jao 1982, 20).

The Singapore dollar floated from 1973 to 1975. Since 1975, the Monetary Authority of Singapore has pegged it to a trade-weighted basket of currencies (Blejer and Khan 1983). Forward rates for periods up to one year vis-à-vis the U.S. dollar are quoted daily (Ishihara and Kim 1982, 925-26). From S $3 in 1970, the Singapore dollar appreciated fairly steadily to S $2 to U.S. $1 in 1981. In contrast, Singapore's real exchange rate depreciated substantially until 1978 (Table 11.3). Since the beginning of 1981, however, the real effective exchange rate has appreciated rapidly. Inflation in Singapore averaged 7.1 percent annually over the period 1970-1981. For virtually the entire period 1960-1981, growth in the money supply and the inflation rate has been determined by Singapore's nominal exchange rate policy. Singapore has chosen to appreciate its currency in order to maintain domestic price stability.

Taiwan recorded a huge balance of payments surplus in 1972 that produced a dramatic acceleration in its monetary growth. Despite a revaluation from NT $40 to NT $38, another balance of payments surplus and concomitant monetary expansion occurred in 1973. In 1974, inflation shot up to 47.5 percent (Fry 1984a, Table 3, 88-89). However, by lifting the restrictions on luxury imports, Taiwan produced a trade deficit, and monetary expansion decelerated rapidly in that year (Kuo 1983, 212-18; Tsiang 1980, 335). The NT $38 exchange rate was maintained until 1978, when another revaluation to NT $36 followed by the introduction of a managed float took place. In February 1979, a foreign exchange market in which the exchange rate was allowed to float within preset daily limits was established. However, a bout of high inflation over the period 1979-1981 resulted in a devaluation to NT $38 in August 1981.

Taiwan's real effective exchange rate has been remarkably stable since 1974 (Table 11.3). Net domestic credit to the public sector as a percentage of total domestic credit remained virtually constant at under 10 percent from 1970 to 1980. However, the government ran deficits in 1981 and 1982 to offset the decline in export earnings. Despite the high rate of inflation in 1973-1974 and 1979-1981, the average annual rate for the period 1970-1981 was only 10.4 percent, compared to 13.2 percent for all middle-income developing countries.

South Korea continued to peg the won to the U.S. dollar at W 484 to U.S. $1 from December 1974 to January 1980. The won was devalued by 16.6 percent in January 1980, and at the end of February it was pegged to a currency basket and depreciated further. The won is now classified officially as being on a managed float. At the end of October 1982, it had depreciated to W 745 to U.S. $1. Although inflation averaged 16.9 percent annually over the period 1970-1981, both consumer and wholesale prices barely rose at all in 1982, despite the continued depreciation of the exchange rate. Like the Taiwanese government, the South Korean government also ran deficits in 1981 and 1982. Even though South Korea posted the highest inflation rate among the gang of four, the exchange rate policy combined with appropriate variations in export incentives enabled it to achieve the fastest rate of export growth within the group by a comfortable margin (Table 11.1). The real effective exchange rate peaked in 1974 and 1979 prior to nominal devaluations. On average, however, the real effective exchange rate has been substantially below its pre-1973 level in the post-1973 period (Table 11.3).

MONETARY POLICY AND MONEY SUPPLY

The framework used in this section to examine monetary policy and the money supply process in the gang of four is the consolidated balance sheet of the banking system, or the monetary survey:

$$DCp + NDCg + NFA \equiv M2 + NOI \tag{11.7}$$

where
DCp = Domestic credit to the private sector,
NDCg = Net domestic credit to the government or public sector,
NFA = Net foreign assets,
M2 = The broad definition of money (currency in circulation plus demand, savings, and time deposits), and
NOI = Net other items, for example, net worth

The variables on the left-hand side of equation (11.7) are the banking system's assets, those on the right-hand side the liabilities plus net worth.

Equation (11.7) can be rearranged:

$$M2 \equiv DCp + NDCg + NFA - NOI. \qquad (11.8)$$

Ceteris paribus, an increase in any asset item raises the supply of money, while an increase in net other items lowers it. Since net other items are invariably small relative to other items in the balance sheet, they are ignored hereafter. Attention is focused on the effects of changes in the three asset items in the monetary survey on the supplies of money in the gang of four.

Hong Kong

Apart from a very small fiduciary issue backed by British and Hong Kong government securities, banknotes issued by the two note-issuing banks in Hong Kong are backed by noninterest bearing Exchange Fund certificates of indebtedness. The Exchange Fund meets the cost of maintaining the nonfiduciary component of the note issue (Hong Kong Government 1982, 54).

The value to the banknotes issued may be increased only after an equal value of Exchange Fund certificates has been bought. This purchase is effected simply by crediting the fund's account with the note-issuing bank. The Exchange Fund then draws down its balances in these accounts to buy domestic or foreign interest-earning assets. In practice, certificates of indebtedness and hence the note issues are backed almost entirely by foreign assets. Since October 1983, the Exchange Fund has bought and sold foreign currency at the fixed exchange rate to stabilize the value of the Hong Kong dollar, as it did until 1974. Under the fixed exchange rate system, certificates of indebtedness are issued and redeemed automatically with the fund's purchases and sales of foreign exchange (Greenwood 1984).

Lee and Jao (1982, 38) suggest that "the belief in automacity persisted after the advent of the floating rate regime" in 1974. The Exchange Fund does not appear to have set monetary targets. Furthermore, it intervened in the foreign exchange market to only a limited extent between 1974 and 1983. Hence, the quantity of banknotes in circulation was determined not so much by any Exchange Fund policy over the issue of certificates of indebtedness, but rather by the demand of the note-issuing banks for certificates.

Since seigniorage from note issue accrues to the Exchange Fund instead of the note-issuing banks, the value of outstanding banknotes is also determined on the demand side. Given the stock of money, it is the public's desired currency/deposit ratio and the banks' desired ratio of vault cash to deposits that determine the demand for banknotes. In effect, therefore, banknotes are supplied by the note-issuing banks simply as a service to their clients when the demand arises.

Under a floating exchange rate, this monetary process is unstable (Fry 1984a, 103-04; Greenwood 1983; Jao 1983, 22-25). The speculative property boom that started in 1977 illustrates the problem. It generated a substantial increase in the demand for credit. In part, the increased demand was met through capital inflows that put upward pressure on the Hong Kong dollar. However, the expansion of credit produced a concomitant increase in the stock of money, and the demand for banknotes rose. Domestic prices started to rise, and the Hong Kong dollar began to depreciate, despite continued inflows of capital.

Eventually, the government intervened--in March 1979--by imposing direct controls on the expansion of domestic credit and pressure on the Association of Banks to raise interest rates (Lee and Jao 1982, 39). The Hong Kong dollar's nominal effective exchange rate peaked at 112 in 1977 (1971 = 100) and then fell sharply to 92 in 1979 (Table 11.3). It subsequently declined more gradually to 80.1 in December 1982 (Hong Kong, Census and Statistics Department, Hong Kong Monthly Digest of Statistics, March 1983, Table 9.10, 61). The nominal effective exchange rate plunged dramatically between July and September 1983 before the government pegged the exchange rate in October 1983.

Jao (1980, 180-81) notes that the depreciation of the Hong Kong dollar since 1977 coincided with the lifting of the moratorium on new bank licenses and suggests that these two events were not coincidental. The newly established international banks could more easily satisfy their required 25 percent liquid asset ratio through deposit swaps with their head offices. However, banks have not been subject to any cash reserve requirement, and the requirement relating to liquid assets was introduced for prudential reasons in 1964. It serves no monetary control function, since liquid assets can be created readily by accepting a deposit from a bank abroad (for example, the home office in the case of foreign banks) and redepositing the funds back in the same bank. The Hong Kong branch's deposit counts as a liquid asset, while the deposit from abroad is not subject to any liquidity requirement at all (Lee and Jao 1982, 42).

The excessive monetary expansion starting in 1977 cannot be blamed on the multinational banks. The M1 money multiplier fell from 2.71 in 1976 to 2.05 in 1981, while the M2 money multiplier rose slightly from 9.35 in 1976 to 9.49 in 1981 (based on end-of-year

306

figures) (Hong Kong Census and Statistics Department,
Hong Kong Monthly Digest of Statistics, various
issues). Evidently, the issue of banknotes was increased somewhat more rapidly than M1 and almost in
step with M2. Had the newly established multinational
banks been circumventing a restrictive monetary policy,
the M2 money multiplier would have risen substantially. The increase in banknotes suggests that the
Exchange Fund pursued, in essence, the real bills
doctrine and accommodated passively the increased
demand for certificates. Monetary stability in Hong
Kong necessitated that the Exchange Fund adopt either a
monetary or an exchange rate target. Given the scope
for financial innovation, including currency substitution (Jao 1983, 35) in Hong Kong, an exchange rate
target might have been expected to work better than a
monetary growth target (Greenwood 1983). The government therefore adopted a fixed exchange rate system in
October 1983.

The present fixed exchange rate system makes the
Exchange Fund redundant. The note-issuing banks could
themselves be obliged to hold foreign exchange reserves
to maintain convertibility between Hong Kong and U.S.
dollars at HK $7.80. Given the political uncertainty
over Hong Kong's future and, hence, the possibility of
violent fluctuations in the relative prices of tradable
and nontradable goods, price stability might well require a more flexible exchange rate policy in the
future. In such a case, the Exchange Fund could then
play an active role.

Despite a deliberate policy of keeping taxes low,
the Hong Kong government has run budget deficits in
only four years since 1947--in 1959/1960, 1965/1966,
1974/1975, and 1982/1983. There is now no marketable
public debt (Chen 1980, 37; Rabushka 1979, 51-56). The
last government bond issue was repaid fully in 1980
(Jao 1983, 39). However, the ratio of government
expenditures to GDP has risen from about 7 percent in
1950 to over 20 percent in the 1980s. In recent years,
more than one-third of government expenditure has been
financed from sales of government land leases.

Singapore

The Currency Act of 1967 established a Board of
Commissioners of Currency to issue currency in Singapore. The board is required to maintain a cover of at
least 100 percent foreign assets against its issue of
Singapore dollars. Until 1973, when the Singapore dollar was floated, the Currency Board's activities were
automatic. It simply bought and sold unlimited quantities of domestic currency at the fixed exchange rate.

Since 1973, however, Singapore has pursued an independent monetary policy. It established the Monetary Authority of Singapore on January 1, 1971, to assume all central banking functions, except the issuance of notes. Until 1981, the authority set monetary targets, but they were always subordinate to the primary aim of maintaining a strong and stable Singapore dollar. The Monetary Authority also attempted to smooth out fluctuations in domestic interest rates (Hewson 1981, 171). Clearly, these objectives were not always compatible with one another, as discussed earlier.

Since 1981, the Monetary Authority has shifted from monetary targets toward exchange rate targets designed to keep inflation down through a steadily appreciating Singapore dollar. However, the exchange rate policy is pursued flexibly, with appropriate rate changes as events dictate. The authority uses a trade-weighted currency basket for its exchange rate targets and has employed Singapore dollar/U.S. dollar swaps as its main monetary policy instrument to achieve its new goals. Over the period July 1981 to July 1982, inflation was reduced to 2 percent (Economist Intelligence Unit, QER, Singapore, 3rd Quarter, 1982), and prices actually declined in 1982 as a whole (Table 11.2).

During the 1970s, the Monetary Authority of Singapore made use of reserve requirements as an instrument of monetary policy. Commercial banks were required to maintain a minimum cash balance with the authority equal to 6 percent of their total liabilities and to hold a minimum liquid assets ratio of 20 percent, of which half had to be in the form of primary liquid assets (deposits with the Monetary Authority, call money with the discount houses, treasury bills, and other short-term government securities). The required reserve ratio was changed five times for monetary policy purposes during the 1970s. Together with the rediscount rate, reserve requirements constituted the main instrument of monetary policy in Singapore over the period 1971-1981 (Aghevli et al. 1979, 807).

The required reserves earn zero interest; since they reduce the average return on bank assets, they amount to an implicit tax on depositors. This tax rises with the rate of inflation (Fry 1981d, 15-16). In Singapore's case, the reserve requirement tax encouraged currency substitution into U.S. dollar Asian Currency Unit (ACU) accounts, which have not been subject to any reserve requirement since the exchange controls were abolished in 1978. When the Monetary Authority discovered what was going on, it exerted moral suasion on the banks to stop that substitution (Hewson 1981, 183-185). The authority is now considering lowering the reserve requirements for longer term

TABLE 11.4
Percentages of net domestic public sector credit
to total domestic credit (NDCg/DC) and net foreign
assets to money (NFA/M2), 1960-1983 (end of the year)

Year	Singapore		Taiwan		South Korea	
	$\frac{NDCg}{DC}$	$\frac{NFA}{M2}$	$\frac{NDCg}{DC}$	$\frac{NFA}{M2}$	$\frac{NDCg}{DC}$	$\frac{NFA}{M2}$
1960			45.6	48.1	36.4	26.9
1961			48.0	29.5	28.0	45.2
1962			45.1	23.1	35.2	23.5
1963	-370.6	101.1	38.2	35.8	34.9	7.1
1964	-228.5	91.4	33.8	37.8	27.8	18.8
1965	-125.1	84.4	25.6	33.2	27.7	19.4
1966	-105.6	82.6	19.8	33.6	22.9	33.1
1967	-115.9	84.1	19.8	32.9	14.9	31.5
1968	-99.6	82.2	13.5	27.3	7.9	19.7
1969	-119.4	83.1	9.4	25.9	6.0	15.3
1970	-129.1	84.1	8.9	30.3	4.5	12.6
1971	-185.3	91.1	10.3	28.3	3.1	3.9
1972	-154.9	81.5	6.1	36.6	8.6	7.6
1973	-138.2	75.0	-3.7	38.6	8.4	15.6
1974	-161.2	82.4	5.5	22.5	9.5	-4.5
1975	-152.3	84.5	7.2	15.5	15.4	-5.4
1976	-104.5	79.6	8.3	21.5	13.5	7.3
1977	-105.1	79.9	9.5	24.4	12.2	16.6
1978	-101.9	88.4	6.0	28.1	11.0	9.1
1979	-96.4	86.7	5.6	25.7	8.7	2.4
1980	-67.3	74.1	12.1	20.3	9.3	-4.5
1981	-13.2	64.5	16.8	21.5	12.6	-14.3
1982	-34.9	63.3	18.8	25.0	12.5	-21.7
1983	-13.2	52.7	14.9	31.1	11.3	-21.8

Source: International Monetary Fund (1982, 1985); and
Central Bank of China (Financial Statistics, various
issues).

TABLE 11.5
Reserve requirements in Taiwan, 1959-1975
(percent)

Guarantee Reserve Requirements	Commercial Banks		Industrial Banks		Savings Banks	
	Demand Deposits	Time Deposits	Demand Deposits	Time Deposits	Passbook Deposits	Time Deposits
Feb. 1 1959	15	10	12	8	a	5
Jan. 1 1966	12	8	10	6	a	5
May 6 1967	15	10	12	8	a	5
Sept. 30 1968	15	10	12	8	10	5
May 10 1969	12	8	10	6	10	5
July 21 1971	15	10	12	8	10	5
July 11 1973	15	10	12	8	10	10
Nov. 15 1974	15	7	12	7	10	7
Legal Minimum	10	5	8	5	10	5
Legal Maximum	15	10	12	8	15	10
Payment Reserve Requirement	15	7	12	6	10	5

Source: Central Bank of China (Financial Statistics Monthly 1982, 97).

Note: For the purpose of reserve requirements, the Bank of Taiwan, the Bank of Communications, the Farmers Bank of China, the Central Trust of China, Land Bank of Taiwan, the Co-operative Bank of Taiwan, City Bank of Taipei, and the International Commercial Bank of China were classified as industrial banks.

a None.

liabilities, where currency substitution is most likely to take place, to reduce the incentive for switching.

Ishihara and Kim (1982) summarize the use of monetary policy instruments in Singapore as follows:

> Since 1973, with the emergence of inflation and recession, monetary policy has assumed an active role through the use of moral suasion, changes in requirements on minimum cash balances and on liquidity ratio, special deposit requirements, overall as well as selective credit control, and money market operations. (P. 914)

The Monetary Authority appears to have followed a pragmatic approach in using monetary policy instruments. In response to inflationary pressures in 1973, it imposed temporary credit ceilings on bank lending. On various occasions, it has also exerted moral suasion to deter banks from lending for specific purposes (Ishihara and Kim 1982, 804-05). In contrast to monetary policy in Hong Kong, Singapore's policy has been active: there has been little reliance on any automatic adjustment mechanisms.

Net domestic credit to the Singapore government has been negative continuously since 1963 (Table 11.4). However, the government was a net borrower from the banking system from 1963 to 1966, in 1976, and heavily in 1981. Between 1980 and 1981, net domestic credit to the government rose from -67.3 percent of total domestic credit to -13.2 percent. Despite this huge volume of government borrowing, net foreign assets continued to rise steadily.

Taiwan

The basis of monetary control in Taiwan has been gold standard rules under a fixed exchange rate system. Even more than in the case of Singapore, however, Taiwan has pursued an active monetary policy both to sterilize the effects of the large overall balance of payments surpluses on the supply of money and to counteract monetary disruptions generated domestically. Nevertheless, rapid increases in net foreign assets jeopardized monetary control in 1971-1973 and 1977-1980 (Kuo 1983, 203).

As noted in the previous section, the excessive monetary growth and inflation resulting from large balance of payments surpluses in 1971-1973 were countered speedily by relaxing import restrictions as well as by revaluation of the exchange rate. At the same time, the Central Bank of China raised reserve requirements in 1971 (Table 11.5). The required reserves consist of deposits with the central bank and vault cash. In fact, the reserve requirements have been changed consistently as part of a package of monetary policy measures. When used by themselves (until 1975), they had proven rather ineffective because banks held ample excess reserves on the one hand and the ranges between legal minima and maxima were small on the other hand. Consequently, in 1975 the reserve requirement system was modified (Table 11.6). Banks are also subject to a required liquid assets ratio, for which treasury bills, commercial paper, bank acceptances, and trade bills must be held. The liquid assets ratio was increased from 5 percent to 7 percent of total deposits in July 1978.

Growth in money and credit accelerated again in 1977 and 1978. Once more, a major contributing factor was the rise in net foreign assets held by the banking system. The measures taken to reduce this source of monetary expansion included further liberalization of imports and tariff reduction, a lowering by 2 percentage points of the rates of interest on loans for imports of industrial raw materials, another revaluation of the New Taiwan dollar, provision of special foreign currency loans for imports of oil and high-technology equipment, and the temporary suspension of short-term foreign currency loans for conversion into domestic currency. In addition, the reserve requirements against checking and passbook demand deposits were raised by 5 percentage points, while the liquidity ratio against all deposits was increased from 5 percent to 7 percent.

Other domestic instruments of monetary policy that have typically been included in monetary policy packages in Taiwan since 1961 include rationing of rediscounts and of advances to the banks and changes in interest rates. For example, the central bank's rediscount rate was raised from 9.5 percent to 14 percent between July 1973 and January 1974, while rediscounts were tightly rationed in 1974 (Lundberg 1979, 287). At the same time, deposit rates of interest were raised as a deliberate anti-inflationary measure (Kuo 1983, 212-18). As in most other developing countries, open market operations have been impossible because there has been no functioning bond market (Lundberg 1979, 279).

The Taiwanese monetary authorities have recognized that raising the demand for money is as effective in reducing inflationary pressure as is reducing the supply of money. Indeed, the fact that the Taiwanese economy has not suffered major cyclical fluctuations, despite prompt and sizable monetary policy measures when inflationary pressure was building up, can be attributed in large part to interest rate policy. Although reducing the supply of money has the same impact

312

Table 11.6
Reserve requirements in Taiwan, 1975-1982

	Checking Accounts	Passbook Deposits	Savings Deposits		Time Deposits
			Passbook	Time	
July 21 1975	25	23	17	11	13
Nov. 21 1978	30	28	17	11	13
May 16 1979	25	23	17	11	13
Aug. 21 1979	25	23	15	9	11
June 29 1982	23	21	14	8	10
Legal Minimum	15	10	5	5	7
Legal Maximum	40	35	20	20	25

Source: Central Bank of China (Financial
Statistics Monthly 1982, 97).

on inflation as increasing the demand for money, it has
a very different effect on the level of economic activity. Reducing the supply of money or decelerating
monetary growth produces a growth-inhibiting credit
squeeze, as discussed at some length in an earlier section. Under a disequilibrium interest rate system,
however, raising the demand for money by increasing the
deposit rates of interest increases the availability of
credit in real terms by reducing inflation, as shown by
the econometric estimates at the end of this section.
In this case, inflation can be reduced without a
growth-reducing credit squeeze (Fry 1981b, 1981e).
This is perhaps the key lesson to be learned from the
post-1960 history of monetary policy in Taiwan.
    Net domestic credit to the public sector in Taiwan
fell rapidly from 48.0 percent of total domestic credit
in 1961 to -3.7 percent in 1973. It rose considerably
in 1974-1975 and in 1980-1981 to counteract the recessionary pressures in these years (Table 11.4). Between
1975 and 1979, net domestic credit to the public sector
averaged just over 7 percent of total domestic credit. This percentage had increased to 16.6 percent by
the end of 1982.

South Korea

Between 1962 and 1971, net domestic credit to the public sector in South Korea fell from 35.2 percent to 3.1 percent of total domestic credit (Table 11.4). This percentage then rose to 15.4 in 1975, fell to 8.7 in 1979, and then increased to 12.1 in 1982.

Until September 1965, credit ceilings constituted the main instrument of monetary policy in South Korea. Overall credit ceilings were set quarterly and then divided into subceilings by bank and by loan use. Priorities were set within each subceiling. South Korea's rediscount system followed a similar format, with each bank allocated a given rediscount ceiling. If a bank exceeded its credit ceiling, the Bank of Korea provided no additional funds through its rediscount facility.

In 1965, when South Korea initiated a series of standby agreements with the International Monetary Fund, direct credit ceilings on individual banks were abolished. Since 1965, much more emphasis has been placed on reserve requirements as an instrument of monetary policy. The reserve requirements imposed on the deposit money banks have been changed frequently since then (Table 11.7). Somewhat lower reserve requirements apply to deposits held in agricultural and fisheries cooperatives. The Bank of Korea is also authorized to impose marginal reserve requirements (up to 100 percent) on the growth of deposits (Bank of Korea 1978, 12), and it did impose them in the second half of the 1960s and again in 1976 (Cole and Park 1983, 228-35).

The 1965 financial reform changed the emphasis from monetary control through credit ceilings to monetary control through reserve requirements and rediscount rationing. Although the ordinary loan rate was increased from 16 percent to 26 percent in September 1965, institutional interest rates remained below their competitive, free market equilibrium levels. Hence, rationing of bank credit and rediscounts still occurred. The substantial increases in real deposit rates of interest exerted a strong anti-inflationary effect by raising the demand for money. However, in 1966 and 1967, monetary control was jeopardized again, this time by huge inflows of foreign capital (Table 11.4) (McKinnon 1973, 161-66).

Periodically, South Korea has lost monetary control because of the dual purpose of the rediscount mechanism. When priority loans for financing exports expand, rediscounts are automatically made available at subsidized rates. Hence, rapid export growth has produced excessive expansion of high-powered money in the form of increased export rediscounts. To counter-

Table 11.7
Reserve requirements in South Korea, 1960-1981

Date			Demand Deposits	Time and Savings Deposits
Before	July	1965	12	10
July	16	1965	16	10
Dec.	1	1965	20	10-12
Feb.	1	1966	35	15-20
Nov.	16	1967	35	18-25
Jan.	1	1968	32	18
Jan.	1	1971	26	16
Nov.	1	1971	18	12
Dec.	16	1972	19	14
May	16	1973	22	18
Aug.	1	1974	19	15
Jan.	1	1975	21	17
Mar.	1	1975	23	19
July	1	1975	24	17
Feb.	23	1978	25	18
Mar.	23	1978	26	19
Apr.	23	1978	27	20
Jan.	8	1980	20	11
Sept.	23	1980	14	10

Source: Bank of Korea (Monthly Economic Statistics, various issues).

act this tendency, the Bank of Korea raised the required reserve ratios in stages from 1974 to 1978. In 1980, however, the required reserve ratios against demand and time deposits were reduced from 27 and 20 to 14 and 10 percent, respectively. This action was taken in order to raise bank profits. However, the funds released were sterilized by the requirement that they had to be used first to repay any outstanding loans from the Bank of Korea and then to buy interest-earning stabilization bonds issued by the Bank of Korea. In fact, the Bank of Korea pays interest on required reserves, special accounts, and monetary stabilization accounts for the express purpose of ensuring the profitability of deposit money banks.

Despite the 1965 financial reform, open market operations have not been an important instrument for monetary policy because the government has preferred to borrow from the Bank of Korea rather than sell bonds in an open market (Bank of Korea 1978, 11). Even during the period of "high" interest rates, 1965-1972, institutional rates were set continuously below their free market equilibrium levels. Hence, the government could borrow at a lower cost from the financial institutions than it could from an open market.

After 1972, real institutional interest rates were reduced, and more reliance was again placed on overall credit ceilings as an instrument of monetary policy, particularly in 1979-1980, when another stabilization program was undertaken. This effort also involved substantial increases in interest rates (6 percentage points) in January 1980. With much lower inflation in 1982, interest rates were reduced by 4 percentage points in June 1982. The ordinary loan rate was brought down to the export credit rate of 10 percent, and an almost uniform loan rate structure was adopted by not reducing the export loan rate pari passu with the reduction in other interest rates.

Automatic rediscounts for export credit, inflexible Annual Financial Stabilization Programs, and government ownership of the large commercial banks have combined to undermine the efficacy of monetary policy in South Korea. After a detailed examination, Cole and Park (1983) conclude:

> The relation of phases in monetary policy and business cycles for the past twenty years...shows that, except for a few phases, monetary policy has been procyclical rather than anticylical as it should have been. Perhaps one could go so far as to say that monetary policy has accentuated rather than moderated cyclical movements. (P. 252)

Money and Inflation

The effect of a change in the real deposit rate on inflation in the gang of four can be estimated using a simple monetary model. Provided that the money market clears, demand equals supply:

$$M^S = M^d \qquad (11.9)$$

or

$$M^S = P \cdot N \cdot m^d \qquad (11.10)$$

where M^S = The nominal supply of money, broadly defined to include savings and time deposits as well as currency in circulation and demand deposits, that is, M2,

N = Population,

P = The price level (GNP deflator), and

m^d = Per capita demand for real money balances $(M^d/P)/N$.

Equation (11.10) can also be expressed in first difference logarithmic form:

$$\Delta \ln(M^S) = \Delta \ln(P) + \Delta \ln(N) + \Delta \ln(m^d), \qquad (11.11)$$

which can in turn be rearranged as

$$\pi = \frac{\overset{\bullet}{M}^S}{N} - \overset{\bullet}{m}^d \qquad (11.12)$$

where $\bullet = \Delta \ln$ and
π = The continuously compounded rate of change in the GNP deflator.

The real demand for money is determined by the real deposit rate of interest $(d-\pi^e)$. The long-run money demand function used here takes the form:

$$\ln(m^*) = \alpha_0 + \alpha_1(d-\pi^e) \qquad (11.13)$$

where m^* = The long-run or the desired level of per capita real money balances.

The actual level of real money balances may be adjusted with a lag to changes in the determinants of money demand. To allow for this possibility, short-run or actual money demand is specified as:

$$\ln(m^d) = \ln(m_{t-1}) + \lambda[\ln(m^*) - \ln(m_{t-1})]. \qquad (11.14)$$

Here, some fraction λ of the gap between desired money balances and money balances held in the previous time period is eliminated in the current time period.
Equations (11.13) and (11.14) can be combined as follows:

$$\ln(m^d) = \lambda\alpha_0 + \lambda\alpha_1(d-\pi^e) + (1-\lambda)\ln(m_{t-1}). \qquad (11.15)$$

Taking first differences, equation (11.15) becomes:

$$\overset{\bullet}{m}^d = \lambda\alpha_1 \Delta(d-\pi^e) + (1-\lambda)\overset{\bullet}{m}_{t-1}. \qquad (11.16)$$

Finally, equation (11.16) is substituted into equation (11.12):

$$\pi = \frac{\overset{\bullet}{M}^S}{N} - \lambda\alpha_1 \Delta(d-\pi^e) - (1-\lambda)\overset{\bullet}{m}_{t-1}. \qquad (11.17)$$

The OLS estimate of equation (11.17) in which the coefficient of $\overset{\bullet}{M}^S/N$ is no longer constrained to one for the gang of four over the period 1961-1981 is:

$$\pi = 0.510(\overset{\bullet}{M}/N) - 0.866\Delta(d-\pi^e) - 0.122(\overset{\bullet}{m}_{t-1}) \quad (11.18)$$
$$(10.524) \qquad (-4.922) \qquad (-2.737)$$
$$\bar{R}^2 = 0.31.$$

CONCLUSION

A summing up of the diverse financial structures and monetary policies of Asia's super exporters over the period 1960-1981 is a perilous task. At the risk of gross oversimplification, the following is a list of some of the most striking findings presented above.

(1) Possibly the most important conclusion is that government finance was well-managed in all four countries. In none of the countries was there any pressure for monetary expansion to finance large and continuous government deficits. The importance of good fiscal policies is that they are prerequisites for good monetary and financial policies in almost all developing countries.

(2) The governments of Taiwan and South Korea set bank deposit and loan rates below their free market equilibrium levels, as did the cartel of banks in Hong Kong. Singapore has kept the rates on loans for the priority sectors below that of the free market. The empirical evidence presented in this paper is consistent with the hypotheses that below equilibrium loan rates discourage efficient use of the existing capital stock and reduce the average efficiency of new investment. Hence, the high growth rates of the gang of four were the result of considerably higher than average investment rates rather than greater average investment efficiency. Indeed, when investment efficiency was calculated using incremental output/capital ratios as a proxy, the average for Singapore, Taiwan, and South Korea was no better than that for the middle-income developing countries in general. Hong Kong's investment efficiency, however, has been above average.

(3) Selective credit policies have been pursued to a greater extent in Taiwan and South Korea than in Singapore, and not at all in Hong Kong. The main effects of selective credit policies are financial layering, which raises the costs of financial intermediation, and reduced availability of domestic credit, since selective credit policies necessitate the imposition of below equilibrium interest rates. Again, there is no evidence that administrative allocation of investible funds through selective credit policies accelerated the rate of economic growth by raising the average efficiency of investment. Quite the contrary, the empirical evidence suggests that these policies

318

lowered economic growth by reducing both the availability of credit and the efficiency of investment.
However, the negative effects of financial repression
in the gang of four have been much less pronounced than
they have been in developing countries, such as Turkey,
that have suffered rampant inflation (Fry 1980b).

(4) All four countries followed consistent monetary and exchange rate policies, and they thereby
ensured that the net real effective exchange rate never
appreciated solely as a result of inflationary monetary
expansion.

(5) The predominant source of monetary instability, particularly in Taiwan, was favorable movements in
the terms of trade leading to unanticipated surpluses
in the overall balance of payments.

(6) The monetary authorities in Singapore,
Taiwan, and South Korea reacted both speedily and
forcefully to counteract exogenous monetary disturbances. Hong Kong, however, lost control of its supply
of money over the period 1977-1979 and again in 1982-
1983 by pursuing an accommodative real bills approach
to the increased demand for high-powered money.

NOTES

1. My thanks to Kathy Alberti, Hang-Sheng Cheng,
Sebastian Edwards, Yan-Ki Ho, Y. C. Jao, Basant Kapur,
Mohsin Khan, Deena Khatkhate, Cheryl Larsson, Fai Nan
Perng, Edward Shaw, V. Sundararajan, and Vito Tanzi.

REFERENCES

Aghevli, Bijan B., Mohsin S. Khan, P. R. Narvekar, and
    Brock K. Short. 1979. "Monetary Policy in Select-
    ed Asian Countries." International Monetary Fund
    Staff Papers 26(December):775-824.
Asian Development Bank. 1983. Key Indicators of
    Developing Member Countries of ADB XIV (April).
    Manila: Asian Development Bank, Economics Office.
——————. 1984a. Domestic Resource Mobilization
    through Financial Development. Manila: Asian De-
    velopment Bank, Economics Office, February.

319

——————. 1984b. Key Indicators of Developing Member Countries of ADB 15(April). Manila: Asian Development Bank, Economics Office.

Bank of Korea. 1978. Financial System in Korea. Seoul: Bank of Korea, December.

——————. 1983. Financial System in Korea. Seoul: Bank of Korea, March.

——————. Various years. Annual Report. Seoul: Bank of Korea.

——————. Various issues. Monthly Economic Statistics. Seoul: Bank of Korea.

Bank Negara Malaysia. Various issues. Quarterly Economic Bulletin. Kuala Lumpur: Bank Negara Malaysia.

Blejer, Mario I., and Mohsin S. Khan. 1980. "Foreign Exchange Market Regularities in a Developing Economy." Economics Letters 6(3):279-86.

——————. 1983. "The Foreign Exchange Market in a Highly-Open Developing Economy: The Case of Singapore." Journal of Development Economics 12 (February/April):237-49.

Central Bank of China. Various issues. Financial Statistics. Taipei: Central Bank of China.

——————. Various issues. Financial Statistics Monthly. Taipei: Central Bank of China.

Chen, Edward K. Y. 1980. "The Economic Setting." In The Business Environment in Hong Kong, edited by David G. Lethbridge, 1-50. Hong Kong: Oxford University Press.

China. Directorate-General of Budget, Accounting, and Statistics. 1982a. Monthly Bulletin of Statistics 8(August). Taipei: Directorate-General of Budget, Accounting, and Statistics.

——————. 1982b. Quarterly National Economic Trends: Taiwan Area, Republic of China . (18) (August). Taipei: Directorate-General of Budget, Accounting, and Statistics.

Cole, David C., and Yung Chul Park. 1983. Financial Development in Korea, 1945-1978. Cambridge: Council on East Asian Studies, Harvard University, and distributed by Harvard University Press.

The Economist. 1982a. "Taiwan: A Survey." The Economist, July 31.

——————. 1982b. "Now for the Next Miracle...Finance in the Far East: A Survey." The Economist, November 13.

Economist Intelligence Unit. Various issues. QER [Quarterly Review]: Hong Kong, Macao. London: Economist Intelligence Unit.

——————. Various issues. QER [Quarterly Review]: Korea. London: Economist Intelligence Unit.

——————. Various issues. QER [Quarterly Review]: Singapore. London: Economist Intelligence Unit.

320

_____. 1982a. QER: South Korea, Annual Supplement. London: Economist Intelligence Unit.
_____. 1982b. QER Taiwan, Annual Supplement. London: Economist Intelligence Unit.
Fry, Maxwell J. 1978. "Money and Capital or Financial Deepening in Economic Development?" Journal of Money, Credit and Banking 10(November):464-75.
_____. 1979. "The Cost of Financial Repression in Turkey." Savings and Development 3(2):127-35.
_____. 1980a. "Saving, Investment, Growth and the Cost of Financial Repression." World Development 8(April):317-27.
_____. 1980b. "Money, Interest, Inflation and Growth in Turkey." Journal of Monetary Economics 6(October):535-45.
_____. 1981a. "Monopoly Finance and Portugal's Government Deficit." Economia 5(May):315-23.
_____. 1981b. "Interest Rates in Asia: An Examination of Interest Rate Policies in Burma, India, Indonesia, Korea, Malaysia, Nepal, Pakistan, the Philippines, Singapore, Sri Lanka, Taiwan and Thailand." Paper prepared for the Asian Department of the International Monetary Fund, Department of Economics, University of Hawaii, Honolulu, June. Photocopy.
_____. 1981c. "Government Revenue from Monopoly Supply of Currency and Deposits." Journal of Monetary Economics 8(September):261-70.
_____. 1981d. Financial Intermediation in Small Island Developing Economies. Commonwealth Economic Papers No. 16. London: Commonwealth Secretariat, September.
_____. 1981e. "Inflation and Economic Growth in Pacific Basin Developing Economies." Federal Reserve Bank of San Francisco Economic Review (Fall):8-18.
_____. 1982. "Analysing Disequilibrium Interest-Rate Systems in Developing Countries." World Development 10(December):1049-57.
_____. 1984a. "Inflation and Monetary Policy in Hong Kong, Indonesia, Korea, Malaysia, Philippines, Singapore, Taiwan and Thailand, 1960-1982." In Inflation in East Asian Countries 83-137. Conference Series No. 2. Taipei: Chung-Hua Institution for Economic Research.
_____. 1984b. "Econometric Analysis of National Saving Rates." In Domestic Resource Mobilization through Financial Development, Volume II: Appendixes, 21-53. Manila: Economics Office, Asian Development Bank, February.
_____. 1985 forthcoming. "Terms of Trade Dynamics in Asia: An Analysis of National Saving and Domestic Investment Responses to Terms-of-Trade

Changes in 14 Asian LDCs." Journal of Inter-
national Money and Finance 4(December).
Fry, Maxwell J., and Andrew Mason. 1982. "The Va-
riable Rate-of-Growth Effect in the Life-Cycle
Saving Model: Children, Capital Inflows, Interest
and Growth in a New Specification of the Life-Cycle
Model Applied to Seven Asian Developing
Countries." Economic Inquiry 20(July):426-42.
Greenwood, John G. 1983. "How to Rescue the HK$:
Three Practical Proposals." Asian Monetary Mon-
itor 7(September-October):11-40.
————————. 1984. "The Operation of the New Exchange
Rate Mechanism." Asian Monetary Monitor 8(January-
February):2-12.
Hewson, John R. 1981. "Monetary Policy and the Asian
Dollar Market." In Papers on Monetary Economics,
edited by the Economics Department, Monetary Autho-
rity of Singapore, 165-95. Singapore: Singapore
University Press for the Monetary Authority of
Singapore.
Hodjera, Zoran. 1978. "The Asian Currency Market:
Singapore as a Regional Center." International
Monetary Fund Staff Papers 25(June):221-53.
Hong Kong. Census and Statistics Department. 1969.
Hong Kong Statistics, 1947-1967. Hong Kong: Census
and Statistics Department.
————————. Various issues. Hong Kong Monthly Digest
of Statistics. Hong Kong: Census and Statistics
Department.
Hong Kong Government. 1982. Hong Kong 1982: A Review
of 1981. Hong Kong: Hong Kong Government.
————————. 1983. Hong Kong 1983: A Review of 1982.
Hong Kong: Hong Kong Government.
International Monetary Fund. 1982. International
Financial Statistics: 1982 Annual Supplement.
Washington, D.C.: International Monetary Fund.
————————. 1985 and various issues. International
Financial Statistics (38)(June). Washington,
D.C.: International Monetary Fund.
Ishihara, Michio, and Hyong Chun Kim. 1982. "Finan-
cial System of Singapore." In Emerging Financial
Centers: Legal and Institutional Framework, edited
by Robert C. Effros, 913-32. Washington, D.C.:
International Monetary Fund.
Jao, Y. C. 1980. "Hong Kong as a Regional Financial
Centre: Evolution and Prospects." In Hong Kong:
Dilemmas of Growth, edited by Leung Chi-keung, J.
W. Cushman, and Wang Gungwu, 161-94. Canberra:
Research School of Pacific Studies, Australian
National University.
————————. 1983. "The Financial Structure." In The
Business Environment in Hong Kong, 2d ed., edited
by David G. Lethbridge. Hong Kong: Oxford Univer-

322

sity Press. (The page numbers cited in this chapter refer to the manuscript version.)

Jones, Leroy P., and Il Sakong. 1980. Government, Business, and Entrepreneurship in Economic Development: The Korean Case. Cambridge: Harvard University Press.

Kapur, Basant K. 1976. "Alternative Stabilization Policies for Less-Developed Economies." Journal of Political Economy 84(August):777-95.

Keller, Peter M. 1980. "Implications of Credit Policies for Output and the Balance of Payments." International Monetary Fund Staff Papers 27(September):451-77.

Khatkhate, Deena R. 1977. "Evolving Open Market Operations in a Developing Economy: The Taiwan Experience." Journal of Development Studies 13 (January):92-101.

Khatkhate, Deena R., and Klaus-Walter Riechel. 1980. "Multipurpose Banking: Its Nature, Scope, and Relevance for Less Developed Countries." International Monetary Fund Staff Papers 27 (September):478-516.

Kuo, Shirley W. Y. 1983. The Taiwan Economy in Transition. Boulder, Col.: Westview Press.

Kuo, Shirley W. Y., Gustav Ranis, and John C. H. Fei. 1981. The Taiwan Success Story: Rapid Growth with Improved Distribution in the Republic of China, 1952-1979. Boulder, Col.: Westview Press.

Lee, Sheng-Yi, and Y. C. Jao. 1982. Financial Structures and Monetary Policies in Southeast Asia. New York: St. Martin's Press.

Lee, Teng-Hui, and Kuo-Shu Liang. 1982. "Taiwan." In Development Strategies in Semi-Industrial Economies, by Bela Balassa and associates, 310-50. Baltimore: Johns Hopkins University Press for the World Bank.

Little, Ian M. D. 1979. "An Economic Reconnaissance." In Economic Growth and Structural Change in Taiwan: The Postwar Experience of the Republic of China, edited by Walter Galenson, 448-507. Ithaca, N.Y.: Cornell University Press.

Lundberg, Erik. 1979. "Fiscal and Monetary Policies." In Economic Growth and Structural Change in Taiwan: The Postwar Experience of the Republic of China, edited by Walter Galenson, 263-307. Ithaca, N.Y.: Cornell University Press.

Mathieson, D. J. 1980. "Financial Reform and Stabilization Policy in a Developing Economy." Journal of Development Economics 7(September): 359-95.

McCarthy, Ian S. 1982. "Financial System of Hong Kong." In Emerging Financial Centers: Legal and Institutional Framework, edited by Robert C. Effros

95-114. Washington, D.C.: International Monetary Fund.

McKinnon, Ronald I. 1973. Money and Capital in Economic Development. Washington, D.C.: Brookings Institution.

──────. 1980. "Financial Policies." In Policies for Industrial Progress in Developing Countries, edited by John Cody, Helen Hughes, and David Wall, 93-120. London: Oxford University Press for the World Bank.

Min, Byoung Kyun. 1976. "Financial Restriction in Korea, 1965-1974." Ph.D. diss., Department of Economics, University of Hawaii, Honolulu, December.

Monetary Authority of Singapore, ed. 1981. Papers on Monetary Economics. Singapore: Singapore University Press for the Monetary Authority of Singapore.

──────. Various issues. Quarterly Bulletin. Singapore: Monetary Authority of Singapore.

Park, Yung Chul. 1976. The Unorganized Financial Sector in Korea, 1945-75. Studies in Domestic Finance No. 28. Washington, D.C.: World Bank, November.

Que, Agustin V. 1979. "Financial System." In Korea: Policy Issues for Long-Term Development, edited by Parvez Hasan and D. C. Rao, 365-403. Baltimore: Johns Hopkins University Press for the World Bank.

Rabushka, Alvin. 1979. Hong Kong: A Study in Economic Freedom. Chicago: University of Chicago, Graduate School of Business.

Shaw, Edward S. 1973. Financial Deepening in Economic Development. New York: Oxford University Press.

Sundararajan, V., and Subhash Thakur. 1980. "Public Investment, Crowding Out, and Growth: A Dynamic Model Applied to India and Korea." International Monetary Fund Staff Papers 27(December): 814-55.

Tan, Augustine H. H., and Ow Chin Hock. 1982. "Singapore." In Development Strategies in Semi-Industrial Economies, by Bela Balassa and associates, 280-309. Baltimore: Johns Hopkins University Press for the World Bank.

Tanzi, Vito. 1982. "Fiscal Disequilibrium in Developing Countries." World Development 10(December): 1069-82.

Tsiang, Sho-Chieh. 1980. "Exchange Rate, Interest Rate and Economic Development." In Quantitative Economics and Development: Essays in Memory of Ta-Chung Liu, edited by Lawrence R. Klein, Marc Nerlove, and Sho-Chieh Tsiang, 309-46. New York: Academic Press.

Westphal, Larry E., and Kwang Suk Kim. 1982. "Korea." In Development Strategies in Semi-Industrial Econo-

mies, by Bela Balassa and associates, 212-79.
Baltimore: Johns Hopkins University Press for the
World Bank.
Youngson, Alexander J. 1982. Hong Kong: Economic
Growth and Policy. Hong Kong: Oxford University
Press.
World Bank. 1981. World Tables computer tape. Wash-
ington, D.C.
_____. 1984. World Development Report 1984.
Washington, D.C.: World Bank.

Index